MODERN HUMANITIES RESEARCH ASSOCIATION
LIBRARY OF MEDIEVAL WELSH LITERATURE

GENERAL EDITORS
ERICH POPPE
SIMON RODWAY

ARTHUR IN EARLY WELSH POETRY
EDITED BY
NERYS ANN JONES

MODERN HUMANITIES RESEARCH ASSOCIATION
LIBRARY OF MEDIEVAL WELSH LITERATURE

ALREADY PUBLISHED

Welsh Court Poems
edited by Rhian M. Andrews (2007)
(available from University of Wales Press)

Selections from Ystorya Bown o Hamtwn
edited by Erich Poppe and Regine Reck (2009)
(available from University of Wales Press)

Early Welsh Gnomic and Nature Poetry
edited by Nicolas Jacobs (2012)
(available from www.medwelsh.mhra.org.uk)

Historical Texts from Medieval Wales
edited by Patricia Williams (2012)
(available from www.medwelsh.mhra.org.uk)

A Selection of Early Welsh Saga Poems
edited by Jenny Rowland (2014)
(available from www.medwelsh.mhra.org.uk)

texts.mhra.org.uk

Arthur in Early Welsh Poetry

Edited by Nerys Ann Jones

Modern Humanities Research Association
2019

Published by

*The Modern Humanities Research Association
Salisbury House
Station Road
Cambridge CB1 2LA
United Kingdom*

© *Modern Humanities Research Association 2019*

Nerys Ann Jones has asserted her right under the Copyright, Designs and Patents Act 1988 to be identified as the author of this work. Parts of this work may be reproduced as permitted under legal provisions for fair dealing (or fair use) for the purposes of research, private study, criticism, or review, or when a relevant collective licensing agreement is in place. All other reproduction requires the written permission of the copyright holder who may be contacted at rights@mhra.org.uk.

First published 2019

*ISBN 978-1-78188-908-4 (HB)
ISBN 978-1-78188-909-1 (PB)*

Copies may be ordered from www.mhra.org.uk/series/LMWL

CONTENTS

	Acknowledgements	vii
	Abbreviations: Bibliographical and Grammatical	viii
	Bibliography	xii
	List of Figures	xxi
	Introduction	1
	Editorial Method	5
1	The Black Book of Carmarthen	7
	The Stanzas of the Graves	8
	Mi a wum …	15
	The Stanzas of Geraint son of Erbin	18
	Englynion by Cynddelw Brydydd Mawr for the warband of Madog son of Maredudd	28
	Pa gur …	29
2	The Book of Aneirin	60
	The Gwawrddur/Gorddur poem	64
3	The Hendregadredd Manuscript	70
	The poetry of Cynddelw Brydydd Mawr and his contemporaries	74
	Englynion by Cynddelw for the warband of Madog son of Maredudd	80
	The poetry of Llywarch Brydydd y Moch and his contemporaries	88
	Canu i Dduw attributed to Llywarch Brydydd y Moch	97
	The poetry of Bleddyn Fardd and his contemporaries	106
	Awdl by Bleddyn Fardd for Rhys ap Maredudd	113
4	The Book of Taliesin	122
	Kat Godeu	124
	Kadeir Teyrnon	127
	Song of the Steeds	133
	'The Elegy for Uthr Pendragon'	135
	Preideu Annwn	141
5	Poems in Other Manuscripts	167
	The Dialogue of Arthur and the Eagle	167
	Fragments of a Dialogue Between Melwas and Gwenhwyfar	184
	The Elegy for Cynddylan	212
	Index of Discussions of Arthurian Characters and Places	223

ACKNOWLEDGEMENTS

This volume is heavily indebted to the work of a great many scholars of the past and also to the generosity and kindness of a number of present-day scholars who I am privileged to regard as friends. It would not have been written had not Oliver Padel entrusted me with his working editions of *Pa gur …*, *Preideu Annwn*, the Dialogue of Arthur and the Eagle, and the fragments of a dialogue between Melwas and Gwenhwyfar. My co-editor of the Library of Medieval Welsh Literature, Erich Poppe, provided support and encouragement over many years. My students at the Celtic Department of the University of Edinburgh acted as 'guinea pigs' and gave valuable feedback. Rhian M. Andrews, Marged Haycock, Ceridwen Lloyd-Morgan, Oliver Padel and Patrick Sims-Williams offered suggestions and corrections, as did Erich Poppe and Simon Rodway, who also went through the whole volume with a fine-tooth comb. I am grateful to each one of them.

My thanks go to the Modern Humanities Research Association for their readiness to publish the volume and to Gerard Lowe for steering it to publication. For kind permission to reproduce photographs of manuscripts, acknowledgement is due to the following: the Principal and Fellows of Jesus College, Oxford, for Images 1.7 and 5.1, Cardiff County Council for Images 2.1 and 5.2, and to The National Library of Wales for all other images.

Finally, I must also thank my family, in particular my husband, Dauvit Broun, who is my anchor, and my parents, Bethan and the late Eddie Jones, whose passion for the Welsh language, its literature and its traditions ignited in me a lifelong interest in medieval Welsh poetry and a commitment to passing it on to future generations.

BIBLIOGRAPHICAL ABBREVIATIONS

ACL *Arthur in the Celtic Languages: The Arthurian Legend in Celtic Literatures and Traditions*, ed. by Ceridwen Lloyd-Morgan and Erich Poppe (Cardiff: University of Wales Press, 2019)
AMWL O. J. Padel, *Arthur in Medieval Welsh Literature* (Cardiff: University of Wales Press, 2000)
AstHen *Astudiaethau ar yr Hengerdd: Studies in Old Welsh Poetry*, ed. by Rachel Bromwich and R. Brinley Jones (Cardiff: University of Wales Press, 1978)
AW *The Arthur of the Welsh: The Arthurian Legend in Medieval Welsh Literature*, ed. by Rachel Bromwich, A. O. H. Jarman and Brynley F. Roberts (Cardiff: University of Wales Press, 1991)
AyG A. O. H. Jarman, *Aneirin, Y Gododdin: Britain's Oldest Heroic Poem* (Llandysul: Gomer Press, 1988)
BBGCC *Blodeugerdd Barddas o Ganu Crefyddol Cynnar*, ed. by Marged Haycock (Swansea: Barddas Publications, 1995)
BG *Beyond the Gododdin: Dark Age Scotland in Medieval Wales*, ed. by Alex Woolf (St Andrews: The Committee for Dark Age Studies, University of St Andrews, 2013)
CBT *Cyfres Beirdd y Tywysogion* I–VII, general editor R. Geraint Gruffydd (Cardiff: University of Wales Press, 1991–1996):
 I *Gwaith Meilyr Brydydd a'i ddisgynyddion, ynghyd â dwy awdl fawl ddienw o Ddeheubarth*, ed. by J. E. Caerwyn Williams et al. (1994)
 II *Gwaith Llywelyn Fardd I ac eraill o feirdd y ddeuddegfed ganrif*, ed. by Kathleen Anne Bramley et al. (1994)
 III *Gwaith Cynddelw Brydydd Mawr* I, ed. by Nerys Ann Jones and Ann Parry Owen (1991)
 IV *Gwaith Cynddelw Brydydd Mawr* II, ed. by Nerys Ann Jones and Ann Parry Owen (1995)
 V *Gwaith Llywarch ap Llywelyn 'Prydydd y Moch'*, ed. by Elin M. Jones (1991)
 VI *Gwaith Dafydd Benfras ac eraill o feirdd hanner cyntaf y drydedd ganrif ar ddeg*, ed. by N. G. Costigan (Bosco) et al. (1995)
 VII *Gwaith Bleddyn Fardd a beirdd eraill ail hanner y drydedd ganrif ar ddeg*, ed. by Rhian M. Andrews et al. (1996)
CCCC John T. Koch, *Cunedda, Cynan, Cadwallon, Cynddylan: Four Welsh Poems and Britain 383–655* (Aberystwyth: University of Wales Centre for Advanced Welsh and Celtic Studies, 2013)
CLLH *Canu Llywarch Hen*, ed. by Ifor Williams (Cardiff: University of Wales Press, 1935)

CO	*Culhwch and Olwen: An Edition and Study of the Oldest Arthurian Tale*, ed. by Rachel Bromwich and D. Simon Evans (Cardiff: University of Wales Press, 1992)
CP	J. E. Caerwyn Williams, *The Court Poet in Medieval Wales* (Lampeter: Edwin Mellen Press, 1997)
DMWL	Simon Rodway, *Dating Medieval Welsh Literature: Evidence from the Verbal System* (Aberystwyth: CMCS Publications, 2013)
EWGNP	*Early Welsh Gnomic and Nature Poetry*, ed. by Nicolas Jacobs (London: Modern Humanities Research Association, 2012)
EWP	*Early Welsh Poetry: Studies in the Book of Aneirin*, ed. by Brynley F. Roberts (Aberystwyth: National Library of Wales, 1988)
EWSP	Jenny Rowland, *Early Welsh Saga Poetry: A Study and Edition of the Englynion* (Cambridge: D. S. Brewer, 1990)
GMW	D. Simon Evans, *Grammar of Middle Welsh* (Dublin: The Dublin Institute for Advanced Studies, 1976)
GofA	John T. Koch, *The Gododdin of Aneirin: Text and Context from Dark-Age North Britain* (Cardiff: University of Wales Press, 1997)
GOSP	Kenneth Hurlstone Jackson, *The Gododdin: The Oldest Scottish Poem* (Edinburgh: University Press, 1969)
GPC	*Geiriadur Prifysgol Cymru: A Dictionary of the Welsh Language* (Cardiff: University of Wales Press, 1950–2002). For the online version, visit <http://www.geiriadur.ac.uk>
HCC	*The Horse in Celtic Culture: Medieval Welsh Perspectives*, ed. by Sioned Davies and Nerys Ann Jones (Cardiff: University of Wales Press, 1997)
IIMWL	Patrick Sims-Williams, *Irish Influence on Medieval Welsh Literature* (Oxford: University Press, 2011)
LHDd	*The Law of Hywel Dda*, ed. by Dafydd Jenkins (Llandysul: Gomer Press, 1986)
Llywelyn	J. Beverley Smith, *Llywelyn ap Gruffudd, Prince of Wales* (Cardiff: University of Wales Press, 1998)
LPBT	*Legendary Poems from the Book of Taliesin*, ed. by Marged Haycock (Aberystwyth: CMCS Publications, 2007)
Mab	Sioned Davies, *The Mabinogion* (Oxford: University Press, 2007).
Math	*Math uab Mathonwy: The Fourth Branch of the Mabinogi*, ed. by Ian Hughes (Dublin: The Dublin Institute for Advanced Studies, 2013)
MP	David Stephenson, *Medieval Powys: Kingdom, Principality and Lordships, 1132–1293* (Woodbridge: The Boydell Press, 2016)
MWM	Daniel Huws, *Medieval Welsh Manuscripts* (Cardiff: University of Wales Press and Aberystwyth: National Library of Wales, 2000)
Owein	*Owein, or Chwedyl Iarlles y Ffynnawn*, ed. by R. L. Thomson (Dublin: The Dublin Institute for Advanced Studies, 1968)
PBT	*Prophecies from the Book of Taliesin*, ed. by Marged Haycock (Aberystwyth: CMCS Publications, 2013)
PT	*The Poems of Taliesin*, ed. by Ifor Williams, English version by J. E. Caerwyn Williams (Dublin: The Dublin Institute for Advanced Studies, 1973)
TYP	*Trioedd Ynys Prydein: The Triads of the Island of Britain*, ed. by Rachel

	Bromwich (third edn, Cardiff: University of Wales Press, 2006)
VBA	Graham R. Isaac, *The Verb in the Book of Aneirin: Studies in Syntax, Morphology and Etymology* (Tübingen: Max Niemeyer Verlag, 1996)
WCP	*Welsh Court Poems*, ed. by Rhian M. Andrews (Cardiff: University of Wales Press, 2007)
WKC	*The Welsh King and his Court*, ed. by T. M. Charles-Edwards, Morfydd E. Owen and Paul Russell (Cardiff: University of Wales Press, 2000)
YG	*Ystoria Gereint Uab Erbin*, ed. by Robert L. Thomson (Dublin: The Dublin Institute for Advanced Studies, 1997)

GRAMMATICAL AND OTHER ABBREVIATIONS

adj.	adjective, adjectival
col.	column
conj.	conjunction
fem.	feminine
f., ff.	folio, folios
fut.	future
imper.	imperative
imperf.	imperfect
impers.	impersonal
indic.	indicative
l., ll.	line, lines
masc.	masculine
Mod W	Modern Welsh
MS, MSS	manuscript, manuscripts
MW	Middle Welsh
n.	noun
NLW	National Library of Wales, Aberystwyth
obj.	object
p., pp.	page, pages
pl.	plural
poss.	possessive
prep.	preposition
pres.	present
pret.	preterite
pron.	pronoun
r	recto
sing.	singular
subj.	subjunctive
v	verso
vb.	verb
v.n.	verb noun

BIBLIOGRAPHY

ANDREWS, RHIAN M., 'Y Bardd yn Llysgennad, Rhan II: Bleddyn Fardd yn Neheubarth', *Dwned*, 21 (2015), 49–68
—— 'Y Bardd yn Llysgennad, Rhan I: Llywarch Brydydd y Moch yn Neheubarth', *Dwned*, 20 (2014), 11–30
—— 'The Nomenclature of Kingship in Welsh Court Poetry 1100–1300: Part 1 The Terms', *Studia Celtica*, 44 (2010), 71–109
ANDREWS, RHIAN M., ed., *Welsh Court Poems* (Cardiff: University of Wales Press, 2007)
ANDREWS, RHIAN M., et al., ed., *Gwaith Bleddyn Fardd a beirdd eraill ail hanner y drydedd ganrif ar ddeg*, *Cyfres Beirdd y Tywysogion*, VII, general editor R. Geraint Gruffydd (Cardiff: University of Wales Press, 1996)
BARTRUM, PETER C., *Early Welsh Genealogical Tracts* (Cardiff: University of Wales Press, 1966)
—— *A Welsh Classical Dictionary: People in History and Legend up to about A.D. 1000* (Aberystwyth: National Library of Wales, 1993)
BOLLARD, J. K., 'The Earliest Myrddin Poems' in *Arthur in the Celtic Languages: The Arthurian Legend in Celtic Literatures and Traditions*, ed. by Ceridwen Lloyd-Morgan and Erich Poppe (Cardiff: University of Wales Press, 2019), pp. 35–50
—— *Englynion y Beddau: The Stanzas of the Graves: Verses on the Legendary Heroes of Wales from The Black Book of Carmarthen* (Llanrwst: Gwasg Carreg Gwalch, 2015)
BRAMLEY, KATHLEEN ANNE, et al., eds, *Gwaith Llywelyn Fardd I ac eraill o feirdd y ddeuddegfed ganrif*, *Cyfres Beirdd y Tywysogion*, II, general editor R. Geraint Gruffydd (Cardiff: University of Wales Press, 1994)
BROMWICH, RACHEL, 'Cyfeiriadau Traddodiadol a Chwedlonol y Gogynfeirdd' in *Beirdd a Thywysogion: Barddoniaeth Llys yng Nghymru, Iwerddon a'r Alban cyflwynedig i R. Geraint Gruffydd*, ed. by M. E. Owen and B. F. Roberts (Cardiff: University of Wales Press, 1996), pp. 202–18
—— 'Cynon fab Clydno' in *Astudiaethau ar yr Hengerdd: Studies in Old Welsh Poetry*, ed. by Rachel Bromwich and R. Brinley Jones (Cardiff: University of Wales Press, 1978), pp. 151–64
—— 'The "Tristan" Poem in the Black Book of Carmarthen', *Studia Celtica*, 14/15 (1979–1980), 54–65
BROMWICH, RACHEL, ed., *Dafydd ap Gwilym: A Selection of Poems* (Llandysul: Gomer Press, 1982)
—— *Trioedd Ynys Prydein: The Triads of the Island of Britain*, third edn (Cardiff: University of Wales Press, 2006)
BROMWICH, RACHEL, AND D. SIMON EVANS, eds, *Culhwch and Olwen: An Edition and Study of the Oldest Arthurian Tale* (Cardiff: University of Wales Press, 1992)

BROUN, DAUVIT, *Scottish Independence and the Idea of Britain from the Picts to Alexander III* (Edinburgh: Edinburgh University Press, 2007)
BULLOCK-DAVIES, CONSTANCE, ' *"Exspectare Arturum"*: Arthur and the Messianic hope', *Bulletin of the Board of Celtic Studies*, 29 (1981), 432–40
CARR, A. D., *Medieval Wales* (Basingstoke: St Martin's Press, 1995)
CHARLES-EDWARDS, GIFFORD, 'The Scribes of the Red Book of Hergest', *National Library of Wales Journal*, 21 (1977–1980), 246–56
CHARLES-EDWARDS, THOMAS, 'The Arthur of History' in *The Arthur of the Welsh: The Arthurian Legend in Medieval Welsh Literature*, ed. by Rachel Bromwich, A. O. H. Jarman and Brynley F. Roberts (Cardiff: University of Wales Press, 1991), pp. 15–32
—— *Wales and the Britons, 350–1064* (Oxford: University Press, 2013)
CHARLES-EDWARDS, T. M., AND PAUL RUSSELL, 'The Hendregadredd Manuscript and the Orthography and Phonology of Welsh in the Early Fourteenth Century', *National Library of Wales Journal*, 28 (1994), 419–62
CLANCY, JOSEPH P., *Medieval Welsh Poems* (Dublin: Four Courts Press, 2003)
COSTIGAN (BOSCO), N. G., et al., eds, *Gwaith Dafydd Benfras ac eraill o feirdd hanner cyntaf y drydedd ganrif ar ddeg, Cyfres Beirdd y Tywysogion*, VI, general editor R. Geraint Gruffydd (Cardiff: University of Wales Press, 1995)
DAVIES, CERI, ed., *Dr John Davies of Mallwyd: Welsh Renaissance Scholar* (Cardiff: University of Wales Press, 2004)
DAVIES, R. R., *The Age of Conquest: Wales 1063–1415* (Oxford: University Press, 1991)
DAVIES, SIONED, *The Mabinogion* (Oxford: Oxford University Press, 2007)
DAVIES, SIONED, AND NERYS ANN JONES, eds, *The Horse in Celtic Culture: Medieval Welsh Perspectives* (Cardiff: University of Wales Press, 1997)
DAY, JENNY, 'Shields in Welsh Poetry up to *c*.1300: Decoration, Shape and Significance', *Studia Celtica*, 45 (2011), 38–40
DIXON, NORMAN, 'The Place-Names of Midlothian', unpublished PhD thesis, University of Edinburgh, 1947, published 2009 in digital form <http://www.spns.org.uk>
DUNSHEA, PHILIP M., 'The Meaning of *Catraeth*: A Revised Early Context for *Y Gododdin*' in *Beyond the Gododdin: Dark Age Scotland in Medieval Wales*, ed. by Alex Woolf (St Andrews: The Committee for Dark Age Studies, University of St Andrews, 2013), pp. 81–114
EVANS, D. SIMON, *Grammar of Middle Welsh* (Dublin: Institute of Advanced Studies, 1976)
FEER, ESTHER, AND NERYS ANN JONES, 'The Poet and his Patrons: The Early Career of Llywarch Brydydd y Moch' in *Medieval Celtic Literature and Society*, ed. by Helen Fulton (Dublin: Four Courts Press, 2005), 132–62
FORD, PATRICK K., *The Celtic Poets: Songs and Tales from Early Ireland and Wales* (Belmont, Massachusetts: Ford and Bailie, 1999)
FORD, PATRICK K., ed., *Ystoria Taliesin* (Cardiff: University of Wales Press, 1992)
GOETINCK, GLENYS WITCHARD, ed., *Historia Peredur vab Efrawc* (Cardiff: University of Wales Press, 1976)
GREEN, THOMAS, 'A Note on *Aladur, Alator* and *Arthur*', *Studia Celtica*, 41 (2007), 237–41

GROOMS, C., *The Giants of Wales* (Lampeter: Edwin Mellen Press, 1993)
GRUFFYDD, R. GERAINT, 'Cynddelw Brydydd Mawr and the Partition of Powys', *Studia Celtica*, 38 (2004), 97–106
—— 'Marwnad Cynddylan', in *Bardos: Penodau ar y traddodiad barddol Cymreig a Cheltaidd*, ed. by R. Geraint Gruffydd (Cardiff: University of Wales Press, 1982), pp. 10–28
—— 'The Strathcarron Interpolation (*Canu Aneirin*, Lines 966–77)', *Scottish Gaelic Studies*, 17 (1996), 172–78
—— 'A Welsh "Dark Age" Court Poem' in *Ildánach Ildírech: A Festschrift for Proinsias Mac Cana*, ed. by John Carey et al. (Andover and Aberystwyth: Celtic Studies Publications, 1999), pp. 39–48
—— 'Where was *Rhaeadr Derwennydd* (Canu Aneirin, Line 1114)?' in *Celtic Language, Celtic Culture: A Festschrift for Erich P. Hamp*, ed. by A. T. E. Matonis and D. F. Melia (Van Nuys, California: Ford and Bailie, 1990), pp. 261–66
HAYCOCK, MARGED, 'Early Welsh Poets Look North' in *Beyond the Gododdin: Dark Age Scotland in Medieval Wales*, ed. by Alex Woolf (St Andrews: The Committee for Dark Age Studies, University of St Andrews, 2013), pp. 7–39
—— 'Llyfr Taliesin', *National Library of Wales Journal*, 25 (1988), 357–86
—— 'Metrical Models for the Poems in the Book of Taliesin' in *Early Welsh Poetry: Studies in the Book of Aneirin*, ed. by Brynley F. Roberts (Aberystwyth: National Library of Wales, 1988), pp. 155–77
—— '"Preiddeu Annwn" and the Figure of Taliesin', *Studia Celtica*, 18/19 (1983–1984), 52–78
—— 'The Significance of the "Cad Goddau" Tree-list in the Book of Taliesin', in *Celtic Linguistics/Ieithyddiaeth Geltaidd*, ed. by Martin J. Ball et al. (Amsterdam and Philadelphia: J. Benjamins Publishing Company, 1990), pp. 297–332
—— '"Some Talk of Alexander and Some of Hercules": Three Early Medieval Poems from the Book of Taliesin', *Cambridge Medieval Celtic Studies*, 13 (1987), 7–38
—— 'Taliesin's Questions', *Cambridge Medieval Celtic Studies*, 33 (1997), 19–79
HAYCOCK, MARGED, ed., *Blodeugerdd Barddas o Ganu Crefyddol Cynnar* (Swansea: Barddas Publications, 1995)
—— *Legendary Poems from the Book of Taliesin* (Aberystwyth: CMCS Publications, 2015)
—— *Prophecies from the Book of Taliesin* (Aberystwyth: CMCS Publications, 2013)
HIGLEY, SARAH LYNN, 'Forcing a Gap: The Stylistics of "amputation" in Marwnad Llywelyn by Gruffudd ab yr Ynad Coch', *Viator*, 19 (1988), 147–72
HOWLETT, DAVID, 'A Triad of Texts about St David' in *St David of Wales: Cult, Church and Nation*, ed. by J. Wyn Evans and Jonathan M. Wooding (Woodbridge: The Boydell Press, 2007), pp. 253–73
HUGHES, IAN, 'Camlan, Medrawd a Melwas', *Dwned*, 13 (2007), 11–46
HUGHES, IAN, ed., *Math uab Mathonwy: The Fourth Branch of the Mabinogi* (Dublin: Institute of Advanced Studies, 2013)
HUWS, DANIEL, 'John Davies and his Manuscripts' in *Dr John Davies of Mallwyd: Welsh Renaissance Scholar*, ed. by Ceri Davies (Cardiff: University of Wales Press, 2004), pp. 88–120
—— *Medieval Welsh Manuscripts* (Cardiff: University of Wales Press, and Aberystwyth: National Library of Wales, 2000)

—— 'Y Pedair Llawysgrif Ganoloesol' in *Canhwyll Marchogyon: Cyd-destunoli Peredur*, ed. by Sioned Davies and Peter Wynn Thomas (Cardiff: University of Wales Press, 2000), pp. 1–9
—— *A Repertory of Welsh Scribes* (forthcoming)
HUWS, DANIEL, ed., *Llyfr Aneirin: A Facsimile* (Aberystwyth: National Library of Wales, 1989)
INSLEY, CHARLES, 'The Wilderness Years of Llywelyn the Great' in *Thirteenth Century England IX: Proceedings of the Durham Conference 2001*, ed. by Michael Prestwich, Richard Britnell and Robin Frame (Woodbridge: The Boydell Press, 2003), pp. 163–73
ISAAC, GRAHAM R., 'An Indo-European Athematic Imperfect in Welsh? Middle Welsh *Gwant*', *Studia Celtica*, 35 (2001), 354–59
—— *The Verb in the Book of Aneirin: Studies in Syntax, Morphology and Etymology* (Tübingen: Max Niemeyer Verlag, 1996)
JACKSON, KENNETH HURLSTONE, *The Gododdin: The Oldest Scottish Poem* (Edinburgh: Edinburgh University Press, 1969)
JACOBS, NICOLAS, *Early Welsh Gnomic and Nature Poetry* (London: Modern Humanities Research Association, 2012)
JARMAN, A. O. H., 'The Delineation of Arthur in Early Welsh Verse' in *An Arthurian Tapestry: Essays in Memory of Lewis Thorpe*, ed. by K. Varty (Glasgow: published on behalf of the British branch of the International Arthurian Society at the French Department of the University of Glasgow, 1981), pp. 1–21
—— Aneirin, *Y Gododdin: Britain's Oldest Heroic Poem* (Llandysul: Gomer Press, 1988)
—— 'The Arthurian Allusions in the Black Book of Carmarthen' in *The Legend of Arthur in the Middle Ages*, ed. by P. B. Grout et al. (Cambridge: D. S. Brewer, 1983), pp. 99–112
JARMAN, A. O. H., ed., *Llyfr Du Caerfyrddin* (Cardiff: University of Wales Press, 1982)
—— *Ymddiddan Myrddin a Thaliesin* (Cardiff: University of Wales Press, 1967)
JARMAN, A. O. H., AND GWILYM REES HUGHES, eds, *A Guide to Welsh Literature*, I, revised edn (Cardiff: University of Wales Press, 1992)
JENKINS, DAFYDD, ed., *The Law of Hywel Dda* (Llandysul: Gomer Press, 1986)
JOHNSTON, DAFYDD, 'Bywyd Marwnad: Gruffudd ab yr Ynad Coch a'r Traddodiad Llafar' in *Cyfoeth y Testun: Ysgrifau ar Lenyddiaeth Gymraeg yr Oesoedd Canol*, ed. by Iestyn Daniel et al. (Cardiff: University of Wales Press, 2003), pp. 200–19
—— 'Hywel ab Owain a Beirdd yr Uchelwyr' in *Hywel ab Owain Gwynedd Bardd-Dywysog*, ed. by Nerys Ann Jones (Cardiff: University of Wales Press, 2009), pp. 134–51
JONES, E. D., 'Melwas, Gwenhwyfar, a Chai', *Bulletin of the Board of Celtic Studies*, 8 (1935–1937), 203–08
JONES, ELIN M., ed., *Gwaith Llywarch ap Llywelyn 'Prydydd y Moch'*, Cyfres Beirdd y Tywysogion, V, general editor R. Geraint Gruffydd, (Cardiff: University of Wales Press, 1991)
JONES, NERYS ANN, 'Ffynonellau Canu Beirdd y Tywysogion', *Studia Celtica*, 37 (2003), 118–24

—— 'Hengerdd in the Age of the Poets of the Princes' in *Beyond the Gododdin: Dark Age Scotland in Medieval Wales*, ed. by Alex Woolf (St Andrews: The Committee for Dark Age Studies, University of St Andrews, 2013), pp. 41–80

—— '*Marwysgafyn Veilyr Brydyt*: Deathbed Poem?', *Cambrian Medieval Celtic Studies*, 47 (2004), 17–39

—— 'The Warband and the Poets of the Welsh Princes', *Welsh History Review*, 29 (2018) 1–26

JONES, NERYS ANN, AND ANN PARRY OWEN, eds, *Gwaith Cynddelw Brydydd Mawr*, I, Cyfres Beirdd y Tywysogion, III, general editor R. Geraint Gruffydd (Cardiff: University of Wales Press, 1991)

—— *Gwaith Cynddelw Brydydd Mawr*, II, Cyfres Beirdd y Tywysogion, IV, general editor R. Geraint Gruffydd (Cardiff: University of Wales Press, 1995)

JONES, THOMAS, 'The Black Book of Carmarthen "Stanzas of the Graves"', *Proceedings of the British Academy*, 53 (1967), 97–137

—— *Brut y Tywysogyon or the Chronicle of the Princes: Peniarth MS. 20 Version* (Cardiff: University of Wales Press, 1952)

—— *Brut y Tywysogyon or the Chronicle of the Princes: Red Book of Hergest Version* (Cardiff: University of Wales Press, 1955)

—— 'The Early Evolution of the Legend of Arthur', *Nottingham Medieval Studies*, 8 (1964), 3–21

KOCH, JOHN T., 'Brân, Brennos: An Instance of Early Gallo-Britonnic History and Mythology', *Cambridge Medieval Celtic Studies*, 20 (1990), 1–20

—— *Celtic Culture: A Historical Encyclopedia* (Santa Barbara and Oxford: ABC-CLIO, 2006)

—— 'The Celtic Lands' in *Medieval Arthurian Literature: A Guide to Recent Research*, ed. by Norris J. Lacy (New York and London: Routledge, 1996), pp. 239–322

—— *Cunedda, Cynan, Cadwallon, Cynddylan: Four Welsh Poems and Britain 383–655* (Aberystwyth: University of Wales Centre for Advanced Welsh and Celtic Studies, 2013)

—— 'Further to *tongu do dia toinges mo thuath*, etc', *Études celtiques*, 29 (1992), 249–61

—— *The Gododdin of Aneirin: Text and Context from Dark-Age North Britain* (Cardiff: University of Wales Press, 1997)

—— A review of *The Arthur of the Welsh: The Arthurian Legend in Medieval Welsh Literature*, ed. by Rachel Bromwich, A. O. H. Jarman and Brynley F. Roberts (Cardiff: University of Wales Press, 1991), *Speculum*, 69 (1994), 1127–29

—— 'Thoughts on the Ur-Godoδin: Rethinking Aneirin and Mynyδawc Mŵynvawr', *Language Sciences*, 15 (1993), 81–89

LEWIS, BARRY, 'Arthurian References in Medieval Welsh Poetry, c. 1100–c. 1540' in *Arthur in the Celtic Languages: The Arthurian Legend in Celtic Literatures and Traditions*, ed. by Ceridwen Lloyd-Morgan and Erich Poppe (Cardiff: University of Wales Press, 2019), pp. 187–202

LLOYD J. E., *A History of Wales from the Earliest Times to the Edwardian Conquest*, II (London: Longmans, Green and Co., 1911)

LLOYD-JONES, J., 'Welsh *Palach*, etc.', *Ériu*, 16 (1952), 123–31

LLOYD-MORGAN, CERIDWEN, 'From Ynys Wydryn to Glastynbri: Glastonbury in Welsh Vernacular Tradition' in *Glastonbury Abbey and the Arthurian Tradition*, ed. by James P. Carley (Rochester, New York: D. S. Brewer, 2001), pp. 161-78

LLOYD-MORGAN, CERIDWEN, AND NERYS ANN JONES, 'Ymryson Melwas a Gwenhwyfar' (forthcoming)

LYNCH, PEREDUR I., 'Court Poetry, Power and Politics' in *The Welsh King and his Court*, ed. by T. M. Charles-Edwards, Morfydd E. Owen and Paul Russell (Cardiff: University of Wales Press, 2000), pp. 167-90

MCKEE, HELEN, ed., *The Cambridge Juvencus Manuscript Glossed in Latin, Old Welsh, and Old Irish: Text and Commentary* (Aberystwyth: CMCS Publications, 2000)

MCKENNA, CATHERINE, 'Learning Lordship: The Education of Manawydan' in *Ildánach, Ildírech: A Festschrift for Proinsias MacCana*, ed. by John Carey, John T. Koch and Pierre-Yves Lambert (Andover and Aberystwyth: Celtic Studies Publications, 1999), pp. 101-20

—— 'Performing Penance and Poetic Performance in the Medieval Welsh Court', *Speculum*, 82 (2007), 70-96

MCKENNA, CATHERINE, ed., *The Medieval Welsh Religious Lyric: Poems of the Gogynfeirdd, 1137-1282* (Belmont: Ford and Bailie, 1991)

MEYRRICK, S. R., *The History and Antiquities of the County of Cardigan* (London: Davies and Co., 1907, reprint, Rhaeadr, 2000)

MORRIS JONES, JOHN, *A Welsh Grammar Historical and Comparative* (Oxford: Clarendon Press, 1913)

MORRIS JONES, JOHN, AND JOHN RHŶS, eds, *The Elucidarium and Other Tracts in Welsh from Llyvyr Ackyr Llandewivrevi AD 1346 (Jesus College M.S. 119)* (Oxford: Clarendon Press, 1894)

O HEHIR, BRENDAN, 'What is the *Gododdin*?' in *Early Welsh Poetry: Studies in the Book of Aneirin*, ed. by Brynley F. Roberts (Aberystwyth: National Library of Wales, 1988), pp. 57-95

OWEN, GEORGE, *Description of Pembrokeshire*, Part IV (London: Chas Clark, 1936)

OWEN, MORFYDD E., 'Hwn yw e Gododin. Aneirin ae cant' in *Astudiaethau ar yr Hengerdd: Studies in Old Welsh Poetry*, ed. by Rachel Bromwich and R. Brinley Jones (Cardiff: University of Wales Press, 1978), pp. 123-50

—— 'Literary Convention and Historical Reality: The Court in the Welsh Poetry of the Twelfth and Thirteenth Centuries', *Etudes celtiques*, 29 (1992), 69-85

PADEL, OLIVER, 'Aneirin and Taliesin: Sceptical Speculations' in *Beyond the Gododdin: Dark Age Scotland in Medieval Wales*, ed. by Alex Woolf (St Andrews: The Committee for Dark Age Studies, University of St Andrews, 2013), pp. 115-52

—— *Arthur in Medieval Welsh Literature* (Cardiff: University of Wales Press, 2000)

—— *Cornish Place-Name Elements* (Nottingham: English Place-name Society, 1985)

—— 'Geoffrey of Monmouth and Cornwall', *Cambridge Medieval Celtic Studies*, 8 (1984), 13-14

—— 'A New Study of the *Gododdin*', *CMCS*, 35 (1998), 45-56

—— 'Oral and Literary Culture in Medieval Cornwall' in *Medieval Celtic Literature and Society*, ed. by Helen Fulton (Dublin: Four Courts Press, 2005), pp. 113–15

—— 'Some South-Western Sites with Arthurian Associations' in *The Arthur of the Welsh: The Arthurian Legend in Medieval Welsh Literature*, ed. by Rachel Bromwich, A. O. H. Jarman and Brynley F. Roberts (Cardiff: University of Wales Press, 1991), pp. 234–38

PEARCE, SUSAN M., 'The Cornish Elements in the Arthurian Tradition', *Folklore*, 85 (1974), 145–63

PRYCE, HUW, *Native Law and the Church in Medieval Wales* (Oxford: Clarendon Press, 1993)

PUTTER, AD, 'Arthur's Children in Le Petit Bruit and the Post-Vulgate Cycle', *Reading Medieval Studies*, 38 (2012), 25–42

ROBERTS, BRYNLEY F., 'Culhwch ac Olwen, the Triads, Saints' Lives' in *The Arthur of the Welsh: The Arthurian Legend in Medieval Welsh Literature*, ed. by Rachel Bromwich, A. O. H. Jarman and Brynley F. Roberts (Cardiff: University of Wales Press, 1991), pp. 73–95

—— 'Oral Tradition and Welsh Literature: A Description and Survey', *Oral Tradition*, 3 (1988), 61–87

—— 'Rhai o Gerddi Ymddiddan Llyfr Du Caerfyrddin' in *Astudiaethau ar yr Hengerdd: Studies in Old Welsh Poetry*, ed. by Rachel Bromwich and R. Brinley Jones (Cardiff: University of Wales Press, 1978), pp. 311–18

—— 'The Treatment of Personal Names in the Early Welsh Versions of *Historia Regum Britanniae*', *Bulletin of the Board of Celtic Studies*, 25 (1973), 274–90

ROBERTS, RICHARD GLYN, ed., *Diarhebion Llyfr Coch Hergest* (Aberystwyth: CMCS, 2013)

ROBERTS, TOMOS, 'Englynion Marwnad i Lywelyn ap Gruffudd', *Bulletin of the Board of Celtic Studies*, 26 (1974–1976), 10–12

RODWAY, SIMON, 'Absolute Forms in the Poetry of the Gogynfeirdd: Functionally Obsolete Archaisms or Working System?', *Journal of Celtic Linguistics*, 7 (1998), 63–84

—— 'The Date and Authorship of *Culhwch ac Olwen*: A Reassessment', *Cambrian Medieval Celtic Studies*, 49 (2005), 21–44

—— *Dating Medieval Welsh Literature: Evidence from the Verbal System* (Aberystwyth: CMCS Publications, 2013)

ROWLAND, JENNY, *Early Welsh Saga Poetry: A Study and Edition of the Englynion* (Cambridge: D. S. Brewer, 1990)

—— 'Genres' in *Early Welsh Poetry: Studies in the Book of Aneirin*, ed. by Brynley F. Roberts, (Aberystwyth: National Library of Wales, 1988), pp. 179–208

—— 'The Prose Setting of the Early Welsh *Englynion Chwedlonol*', *Ériu*, 36 (1985), 29–43

—— 'Trystan and Esyllt' in *Arthur in the Celtic Languages: The Arthurian Legend in Celtic Literatures and Traditions*, ed. by Ceridwen Lloyd-Morgan and Erich Poppe (Cardiff: University of Wales Press, 2019), pp. 51–63

—— 'Warfare and Horses in the *Gododdin* and the Problem of Catraeth', *Cambridge Medieval Celtic Studies*, 30 (1995), 13–40

RUSSELL, PAUL, 'Scribal (In)competence in Thirteenth-century North Wales: The Orthography of the Black Book of Chirk (Peniarth MS 29)', *Journal of the*

National Library of Wales, 29 (1995), 129–76
—— 'Scribal (In)consistency in Thirteenth-century South Wales: The Orthography of the Black Book of Carmarthen', *Studia Celtica*, 43 (2009), 135–74
SCHUMACHER, STEFAN, 'An Edition and Analysis of the Book of Aneirin B.39 (Including Preliminary Chapters on the Grammar and Poetics of Early Welsh Poetry)', *Zeitschrift für celtische Philologie*, 64 (2017), 299–420
SCOTT, JOHN, ed., *The Early History of Glastonbury: An Edition, Translation and Study of William of Malmesbury's De Antiquitate Glastonie Ecclesie* (Woodbridge: The Boydell Press, 1981)
SIMS-WILLIAMS, PATRICK, 'Clas Beuno and the Four Branches of the Mabinogi' in *150 Jahre "Mabinogion" — deutsch-walisische Kulturbeziehungen*, ed. by Bernhard Maier et al. (Tübingen: Max Niemeyer Verlag, 2001), pp. 116–22
—— 'Dating the Poems of Aneirin and Taliesin', *Zeitschrift für celtische Philologie*, 63 (2016), 163–234
—— 'The Early Welsh Arthurian Poems' in *The Arthur of the Welsh: The Arthurian Legend in Medieval Welsh Literature*, ed. by Rachel Bromwich, A. O. H. Jarman and Brynley F. Roberts (Cardiff: University of Wales Press, 1991), pp. 33–71
—— *Irish Influence on Medieval Welsh Literature* (Oxford: Oxford University Press, 2011)
—— 'Powys and Early Welsh Poetry', *Cambrian Medieval Celtic Studies*, 67 (2014), 41–43
SMITH, J. BEVERLEY, The "Cronica de Wallia" and the Dynasty of Dinefwr', *Bulletin of the Board of Celtic Studies*, 20 (1962–1964), 261–82
—— *Llywelyn ap Gruffudd, Prince of Wales* (Cardiff: University of Wales Press, 1998)
—— *The Sense of History in Medieval Wales* (Aberystwyth: University College of Wales, 1991)
STEPHENSON, DAVID, 'Mawl Hywel ap Goronwy: Dating and Context', *Cambrian Medieval Celtic Studies*, 57 (2009), 41–49
—— *Medieval Powys: Kingdom, Principality and Lordships, 1132–1293* (Woodbridge: The Boydell Press, 2016)
—— 'Welsh Chronicles' Accounts of the Mid-Twelfth Century', *CMCS*, 56 (2008), 45–57
THOMAS, GRAHAM C. G., 'From Manuscript to Print I. Manuscript' in *A Guide to Welsh Literature c. 1530–1700*, ed. by R. Geraint Gruffydd (Cardiff: University of Wales Press, 1997), pp. 241–62
THOMSON, ROBERT L., ed., *Owein, or Chwedyl Iarlles y Ffynnawn* (Dublin: Institute for Advanced Studies, 1968)
—— *Pwyll Pendeuic Dyuet* (Dublin: Institute of Advanced Studies, 1986)
—— *Ystoria Gereint Uab Erbin* (Dublin: Institute for Advanced Studies, 1997)
WILLIAMS, GRUFFYDD ALED, 'The Feasting Aspects of *Hirlas Owein*' in *Ildánach Ildírech: A Festschrift for Proinsias Mac Cana*, ed. by John Carey et al. (Andover and Aberystwyth: Celtic Studies Publications, 1999), pp. 289–302
WILLIAMS, HUGH, trans., *Two Lives of Gildas by a Monk of Ruys and Caradoc of Llancarfan* (1889, reprinted Felin-fach: Llanerch Press, 1990)
WILLIAMS, IFOR, *The Beginnings of Welsh Poetry*, ed. by Rachel Bromwich (Cardiff: University of Wales Press, 1980)
—— 'Dalen o Femrwn', *Bulletin of the Board of Celtic Studies*, 4 (1927–1929), 41–48

—— *Lectures on Early Welsh Poetry* (Dublin: Institute for Advanced Studies, 1954)
—— 'Marwnad Cynddylan', *Bulletin of the Board of Celtic Studies*, 6 (1932), 134–41
—— 'Ymddiddan Arthur a'r Eryr', *Bulletin of the Board of Celtic Studies*, 2 (1923-1925), 269–86
WILLIAMS, IFOR, ed., *Armes Prydein: The Prophecy of Britain from the Book of Taliesin*, trans. by Rachel Bromwich (Dublin: Dublin Institute of Advanced Studies, 1972)
—— *Canu Aneirin* (Cardiff: University of Wales Press, 1938)
—— *The Poems of Taliesin*, English version by J. E. Caerwyn Williams (Dublin: Institute of Advanced Studies, 1973)
WILLIAMS, J. E. CAERWYN, *The Court Poet in Medieval Wales: An Essay* (Lampeter: Edwin Mellen Press, 1997)
—— 'MlW *Neu, Neut* as Copula', *Celtica*, 11 (1976), 278–85
WILLIAMS, J. E. CAERWYN et al., eds, *Gwaith Meilyr Brydydd a'i ddisgynyddion, ynghyd â dwy awdl fawl ddienw o Ddeheubarth, Cyfres Beirdd y Tywysogion*, 1, general editor R. Geraint Gruffydd (Cardiff: University of Wales Press, 1994)
WILLIAMS, MARY, 'An Early Ritual Poem in Welsh', *Speculum*, 13 (1938), 38–51

LIST OF FIGURES

Chapter 1: The Black Book of Carmarthen

Figs. 1.1 and 1.2: NLW Peniarth MS 1, f. 32^r
Fig. 1.3: NLW Peniarth MS 1, f. 32^v
Fig. 1.4: NLW Peniarth MS 1, f. 34^r
Fig. 1.5.1: NLW Peniarth MS 1, f. 50^r
Fig. 1.5.2: NLW Peniarth MS 1, f. 50^v
Fig. 1.6: NLW Peniarth MS 1, f. 36^v
Fig. 1.7: Jesus College MS 111, f. 259^v, col. 1042
Fig. 1.8: NLW Peniarth MS 1, f. 52^r
Figs. 1.9–1.16.1: NLW Peniarth MS 1, f. 47^v
Figs. 1.16.2–1.18: NLW Peniarth MS 1, f. 48^v

Chapter 2: The Book of Aneirin

Fig. 2.1: Cardiff MS 2.28, p. 37

Chapter 3: The Hendregadredd Manuscript

Fig. 3.1: NLW MS 4973, f. 21^v
Fig. 3.2: NLW MS 6680, f. 7^r
Fig. 3.3: NLW MS 6680, f. 62^v
Fig. 3.4: NLW MS 6680, f. 116^r
Fig. 3.5: NLW 4973, f. 44^r
Figs. 3.6 and 3.10: NLW MS 6680, f. 117^r
Fig. 3.7: NLW MS 6680, f. 105^v
Fig. 3.8: NLW MS 6680, f. 112^v
Fig. 3.9: NLW MS 6680, f. 107^v
Fig. 3.11.1: NLW MS 6680, ff. 100^v
Fig. 3.11.2: NLW MS 6680, f. 101^r
Fig. 3.12: NLW MS 6680, f. 87^r
Fig. 3.13: NLW MS 6680, f. 28^r
Fig. 3.14: Peniarth MS 55, p. 188
Fig. 3.15: Peniarth MS 55, p. 189
Fig. 3.16: NLW MS 6680, f. 28^v

Chapter 4: The Book of Taliesin

Fig. 4.1: Peniarth MS 2, f. 13^r
Fig. 4.2: Peniarth MS 2, f. 16^v
Fig. 4.3: Peniarth MS 2, f. 23^v
Fig. 4.4: Peniarth MS 2, f. 34^r
Figs. 4.5 and 4.6.1: Peniarth MS 2, f. 25^v

FIGS. 4.6.2–4.10.1: Peniarth MS 2, f. 26^r
FIGS. 4.10.2–4.12: Peniarth MS 2, f. 26^v

Chapter 5: Other Manuscripts
FIG. 5.1.1 Jesus College MS 20, f. 1^r
FIG. 5.1.2 Jesus College MS 20, f. 1^v
FIG. 5.2.1 Cardiff MS 2.83, p. 89
FIG. 5.2.2 Cardiff MS 2.83, p. 90
FIG. 5.3 NLW Wynnstay MS 1, p. 212
FIG. 5.4.1 Llanstephan MS 122, p. 426
FIG. 5.4.2 Llanstephan MS 122, p. 427
FIG. 5.5 NLW MS 4973B, f. 108^v

INTRODUCTION

The aim of this volume is not to discuss the historicity of the figure of Arthur or the rise of Arthurian literature in medieval Wales, but to examine in context all the references to him in early Welsh poetry and to present the reader with the tools needed to interpret them.

The most immediate context of these poems is that of the manuscripts in which they are contained. In some cases, this is the only context about which anything can be said with certainty. It is for this reason that the texts in this volume have been ordered according to the earliest manuscripts in which they have been preserved. Any information gleaned about these manuscripts, which range in date from the mid-thirteenth century to the mid-seventeenth century, has been scrutinised for evidence as to when, where, by whom and for whom they were written.[1] The context of a particular text within its manuscript, its titles and attributions, the script and the orthography used, have also been carefully examined for any indications of the identity, date or nature of its sources. Finally, the content, form and language of the poem itself is explored and compared with others of the same genre or period.

According to Oliver Padel, who inspired this volume and laid the foundation for it, 'It is essential, when studying the portrayal of Arthur in a particular text, to try to understand the nature and purpose of that text'.[2] Despite the impression given in general studies of medieval Welsh literature, very little of this poetry can be described as 'Arthurian', and although some may be labelled 'legendary poems', none are, in fact, narrative texts.[3] Instead, they belong to a wide range of genres and are composed in a variety of metres. Some focus on or are spoken by other legendary or semi-historical characters or praise historical figures, some catalogue native lore, one contains religious instruction, and some are so obscure that it is difficult to be certain of their genre. What characterises them is their dramatic quality and an allusiveness which would have been appreciated by their intended audiences, familiar with the figures

---

[1] For a survey of the medieval manuscripts see Daniel Huws, 'Five Ancient Books of Wales' in *Medieval Welsh Manuscripts* [*MWM*] (Cardiff: University of Wales Press and Aberystwyth: National Library of Wales, 2000), pp. 65–83.
[2] Oliver Padel, *Arthur in Medieval Welsh Literature* [*AMWL*] (Cardiff: University of Wales Press, 2000), p. 1. Before his retirement, Oliver had started preparing editions of the more substantial texts aimed at students of medieval Welsh. It is from those notes that this volume grew.
[3] On the term 'legendary poems' see Marged Haycock, *Legendary Poems from the Book of Taliesin* [*LPBT*] (Aberystwyth: CMCS Publications, 2007), pp. 9–11.

and the incidents to which they refer.⁴ Although they were almost certainly oral compositions intended for oral communication, and were all probably transmitted orally for a period before being written down, it is not likely that any of them are popular works.⁵ Rather, as scholars like Jenny Rowland have shown, they are most probably aristocratic and literary productions, composed for courtly audiences by the most highly-trained and prestigious poets of their day.⁶

They do not add much to our knowledge of Arthur's character but they do portray him in a variety of roles: as a great leader of armies, a warrior with extraordinary powers, a slayer of magical creatures, a rescuer of prisoners from the Otherworld, a poet and the subject of prophecy. They testify also to the possibility of lost tales about him, his father, Uthr, his son, Llachau, his wife, Gwenhwyfar, and one of his companions, Cai, and associate him with a wide array of both legendary and historical figures. They also shed light on the possibility that characters like Modred (Welsh Medrawd) and Erec (Welsh Geraint) were regarded in the Welsh tradition as heroic figures and were the subjects of stories in their own right.

Whilst these poems enrich our understanding of native Arthurian traditions, it is not possible to claim that they were all composed before Geoffrey of Monmouth's highly influential *Historia Regum Britanniae*, which appeared around 1138. This is because, as Simon Rodway has pointed out in his important study of the dating of the corpus, 'it is often impossible to assign vernacular medieval Welsh texts to a particular century, let alone a year, without the heavy deployment of caveats and question marks'.⁷ Apart from the work of the court poets of the twelfth and thirteenth centuries collected together in the Hendregadredd Manuscript, none of these texts refer to datable events or are ascribed to a particular poet. Moreover, most have been preserved in three retrospective compilations belonging to the period of conservation of Welsh literature by medieval antiquaries between 1250 and 1350: the Black Book of Carmarthen, the Book of Aneirin and the Book of Taliesin.⁸

---

⁴ On the question of whether some of these were originally performed with a prose framework see Jenny Rowland, 'The Prose Setting of the Early Welsh *Englynion Chwedlonol*', *Ériu*, 36 (1985), 29–43.
⁵ See Brynley F. Roberts, 'Oral Tradition and Welsh Literature: A Description and Survey', *Oral Tradition*, 3 (1988), 61–87.
⁶ See Jenny Rowland, 'Genres' in *Early Welsh Poetry: Studies in the Book of Aneirin* [*EWP*], ed. by Brynley F. Roberts (Aberystwyth: National Library of Wales, 1988), pp. 179–208.
⁷ Simon Rodway, *Dating Medieval Welsh Literature: Evidence from the Verbal System* [*DMWL*] (Aberystwyth: CMCS Publications, 2013), p. 1.
⁸ See Daniel Huws, 'The Medieval Manuscript in Wales' and 'Welsh Vernacular Books, 1250–1400' in *MWM*, pp. 1–23, 36–56. The Red Book of Hergest, compiled in the late fourteenth century, contains variant versions of some of our poems but no additional references.

It is not possible to ascertain how many lost manuscripts lie behind an extant text or to what extent copyists changed their material, imposing their own spelling systems on older texts, sometimes modernising forms and possibly altering lines and even rhyme schemes in the process. In some cases, the existence of lost written exemplars can be determined from the evidence of occasional errors which can only be due to the misinterpretation of Insular script, which ceased to be used in Wales during the twelfth century.[9] There are also traces of older forms but because the language was changing so slowly at this time, and because so little is known of the chronology of the changes, it is difficult to give a precise dating on the basis of orthographic or linguistic analysis.[10]

During the last twenty-five years, authoritative editions of most of these poems have been published, in addition to general studies focussing on genre, language and metre, but instead of enabling a more accurate dating of undated texts, this work has brought into question some of the assumptions of previous generations of scholars.[11] Jenny Rowland, for example, has argued that differences in style and metre between the poetry of manuscripts like the Black Book of Carmarthen, the Book of Aneirin and the Book of Taliesin, designated by earlier scholars as the work of the *Cynfeirdd* (the earliest poets), and that of the twelfth- and thirteenth-century *Gogynfeirdd* (not so early poets) kept in the Hendregadredd collection, are not necessarily due to the antiquity of the former but to genre.[12] It is possible, for example, that metrical changes were not adopted in all kinds of poems at the same time. Whilst series of three-line stanzas (*englynion milwr* or *penfyr*) were replaced by four-line types in the praise poetry of the *Gogynfeirdd*, poets may have continued to use these older metres for other genres.[13]

The same may be true of linguistic developments, some of which have now

---

[9] Huws, 'Five Ancient Books of Wales' in *MWM*, pp. 65–83 (p. 68).
[10] See Patrick Sims-Williams, 'The Early Welsh Arthurian Poems' in *The Arthur of the Welsh: The Arthurian Legend in Medieval Welsh Literature* [*AW*], ed. by Rachel Bromwich, A. O. H. Jarman and Brynley F. Roberts (Cardiff: University of Wales Press, 1991), pp. 33–71 (pp. 35–36). Recent studies of the spelling systems in the different manuscripts have led to the conclusion that it is no longer possible to have a linear view of the development of Welsh orthography from Old Welsh to Middle Welsh since there is evidence of geographical variation and many scribes appear to have had their own individual systems; see Paul Russell, 'Scribal (In)consistency in Thirteenth-century South Wales: the Orthography of the Black Book of Carmarthen', *Studia Celtica*, 43 (2009), 135–74 (pp. 136–37).
[11] For a comprehensive discussion of the difficulties, see Patrick Sims-Williams, 'Dating the poems of Aneirin and Taliesin', *Zeitschrift für celtische Philologie*, 63 (2016), 163–234.
[12] Rowland, 'Genres', 179–208; on the terms *Hengerdd*, *Cynfeirdd* and *Gogynfeirdd* see J. E. Caerwyn Williams, *The Court Poet in Medieval Wales: An Essay* (Lampeter: Edwin Mellen Press, 1997), pp. 1–2.
[13] See Nicolas Jacobs, *Early Welsh Gnomic and Nature Poetry* [*EWGNP*] (London: Modern Humanities Research Association, 2012), pp. xliii–xlv.

been shown not to be dependable tools for the dating of these texts. Certain words and constructions in the largely datable corpus of the *Gogynfeirdd* were formerly considered to be obsolete in their period. When these appeared in other poems, they were used to date them earlier than the twelfth and thirteenth centuries. In recent years, however, some of these features have been shown to be still current during the *Gogynfeirdd* period. Simon Rodway's analysis of absolute forms, for example, suggests that this verbal system may have been still functional in the work of the Poets of the Princes at a time when it had disappeared from prose texts.[14] This may be true of other linguistic features thought to have become obsolete, and gives rise to the possibility that some of the poetry which has traditionally been classed as the work of the *Cynfeirdd* may have been composed as late as the twelfth or thirteenth centuries and is contemporaneous with the work of the *Gogynfeirdd*. No conclusive evidence has been found by Marged Haycock, for example, that the language of the legendary poems from the Book of Taliesin is particularly early. In fact, her close study of the diction of the corpus has shown that there seems to be an unusually close relationship between some of the poems and the work of a particular twelfth- to thirteenth-century court poet, Llywarch Brydydd y Moch.[15]

It is possible, then, that some of the poets who allude to Arthur and to characters, places and incidents connected to him were familiar with Geoffrey's transformative work. Yet the vast majority of their references appear to be free of its influence. In his reassessment of the date of the composition of the native prose tale *Culhwch ac Olwen*, Rodway has argued that the fact that it contains no definite echoes of the *Historia* does not necessarily mean that it antedates c. 1138, speculating that it may be a 'celebration of the native Arthur' by one of the court poets of Deheubarth during the reign of Lord Rhys, in the second half of the twelfth century.[16] The same may be true of the poetry composed in this period.[17] The poets may have chosen to eschew Geoffrey and adhere to the native traditions of Arthur in order to express their confidence in the conservative, independent political and cultural system to which they belonged. On the other hand, as practitioners of such a highly developed literary culture, it may simply have never occurred to them to draw on a text which belonged to a different milieu.

[14] Rodway, 'Absolute Forms in the Poetry of the Gogynfeirdd: Functionally Obsolete Archaisms or Working System?', *Journal of Celtic Linguistics*, 7 (1998), 63–84, updated in Rodway, *DMWL*, chapter 8.
[15] LPBT, pp. 21–36.
[16] Simon Rodway, 'The Date and Authorship of *Culhwch ac Olwen*: A Reassessment', *Cambrian Medieval Celtic Studies*, 49 (2005), 21–44 (pp. 43–44).
[17] This includes the Myrddin poems which, although they were composed in the twelfth and thirteenth centuries, show no influence of Geoffrey's work; see J. K. Bollard, 'The Earliest Myrddin Poems' in *Arthur in the Celtic Languages: The Arthurian Legend in Celtic Literatures and Traditions* [ACL], ed. by Ceridwen Lloyd-Morgan and Erich Poppe (Cardiff: University of Wales Press, 2019), pp. 35–50.

Editorial method

Twenty-six references to Arthur are discussed in this volume. Most of them are very short, consisting of a line, a couplet or a stanza at most. In each case, a photograph of the text in the earliest manuscript is provided along with a transliteration, an edition, a translation (where possible) and a comprehensive word-list. Nine texts are discussed in more detail with notes which attempt to interpret their meaning but which also comment on significant metrical, linguistic and stylistic features.

A basic knowledge of 'standard' Middle Welsh is assumed, but not of Modern Welsh. The poems are presented in the orthography of the earliest manuscript copy but with editorial capitalisation, punctuation and word division. Emendations to the text are shown in italic and additions in square brackets. Translations are as close as possible to the original Welsh. In the word-lists the head-words are given as far as possible as they occur in the manuscript with mutated forms listed under their originals. The word-lists follow the order of the English alphabet except that c-/k- and u-/v- are treated as interchangeable and listed together and, in some cases, ch- follows c-/k- and ff- follows f-. References to *Geiriadur Prifysgol Cymru: The University of Wales Dictionary* [*GPC*] and D. Simon Evans, *Grammar of Middle Welsh* [*GMW*] are given to enable more detailed study. Reference is confined to studies written in English except for the work of the Poets of the Princes where there is a lack of English editions. To avoid confusion and a proliferation of forms, the standard Modern Welsh forms of personal and place names are used as far as possible.

CHAPTER 1

The Black Book of Carmarthen

Peniarth MS 1, *Llyfr Du Caerfyrddin*, is the earliest extant manuscript to contain poems which allude to Arthur. The name, given to it in the sixteenth century or perhaps even earlier, refers to its black binding and that fact that it was from Carmarthen Priory that it was rescued at the dissolution of the monasteries.[1] A detailed study of its layout and script by E. D. Jones of the National Library of Wales suggested that it was produced at an ecclesiastical centre around 1250.[2] It may well have been compiled at the Augustinian priory of St John the Evangelist at Carmarthen or perhaps at a nearby religious house like the Cistercian abbey of Whitland. Many of its thirty-eight poems are religious, but it is interesting that those which are given pride of place and are written in the largest script are secular poems relating to the legendary figure of Myrddin, who is associated with the town of Carmarthen.[3]

Most of the poems fall into one of four categories: religious poems, eulogies and elegies, poems related to traditional lore, and poems containing legend and prophecy spoken by Myrddin. The court poetry included in the collection reflects the culture of the kingdom of Deheubarth during the reign of Lord Rhys in the second half of the twelfth century. Each of the praise poems it contains has associations with south-west Wales in this period but references in some of its prophetic poems to events in the early thirteenth century point to the compilation of the manuscript during the reign of one of Rhys' grandsons, perhaps Rhys Gryg (1204–1233). This still makes it the oldest extant manuscript written solely in the Welsh language and the oldest surviving collection of Welsh verse.

The striking irregularity in the size of the script caused earlier scholars to

---

[1] To view the manuscript and for an outline of its later history, visit the National Library of Wales website: <http://www.llgc.org.uk>.
[2] See A. O. H. Jarman, 'The Arthurian Allusions in the Black Book of Carmarthen' in *The Legend of Arthur in the Middle Ages*, ed. by P. B. Grout et al. (Cambridge: D. S. Brewer, 1983), pp. 99–112; *MWM*, pp. 70–72.
[3] Myrddin is the forerunner of Geoffrey of Monmouth's Merlin, but as these poems make no mention of Arthur, they are not discussed in this volume: see John K. Bollard, 'The Earliest Myrddin Poems' in *ACL*, pp. 35–50.

assume multiple authorship, but the study undertaken by Jones shows that it was produced by one scribe in various phases over a long period of time. There is no indication that it was a commissioned volume. Rather, it appears to be a selection of poems which reflect the compiler's personal taste and interests. This is confirmed by the fact that the collection does not have an obvious structure; it seems likely that the scribe added poems as he acquired them. It is difficult to know how many different sources he had as he used his own spelling system, which acts as a screen, hiding the original from the modern reader. Paul Russell's detailed and systematic analysis of the orthography, however, has shed some light on the exemplars the scribe was using, showing that they were numerous and varied.[4] It is also possible that some of the poems were written from memory or recitation.[5]

The earliest poems in the collection are thought by scholars to belong to the ninth and tenth centuries, but they are notoriously difficult to date. Poems containing references to Arthur are scattered throughout the manuscript and are not obviously from the same exemplar.

The Stanzas of the Graves

The first of these poems is known by the title given to it in the margin above the text by a late medieval hand: *Englynnionn y Beddev*, 'The Stanzas of the Graves'.[6]

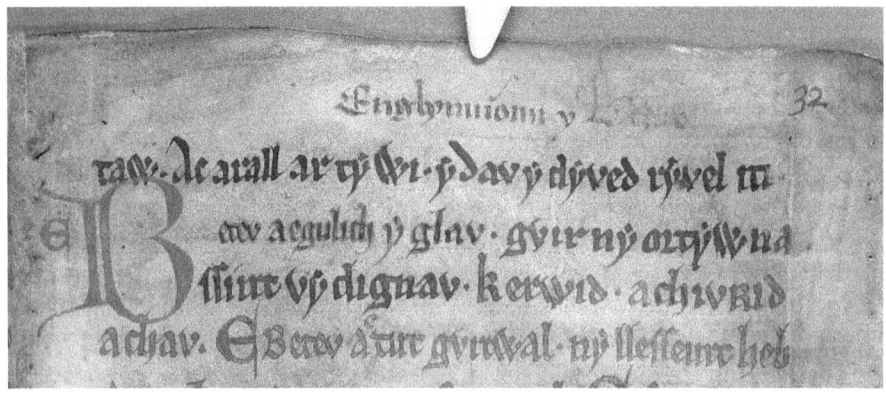

FIG. 1.1: NLW Peniarth MS 1, f. 32^r.

---

[4] Paul Russell, 'Scribal (In)consistency in Thirteenth-century South Wales: The Orthography of the Black Book of Carmarthen', *Studia Celtica*, 43 (2009), 135–74. Its distinctive orthographic features are the use of *t* for /ð/, *w* for /v/, and the predominance of *i*- spellings over *y*- spellings for /i/ and /ï/.
[5] See Chapter 3 below.
[6] NLW Peniarth MS 1, ff. 32^r–35^r.

It is a collection of 73 *englynion*, mostly three lines long, recording the traditional burial places of early Welsh heroes.[7] Each stanza refers to the graves of one to three figures, sometimes picturing them made wet by rain or covered with grass or a thicket, sometimes naming or describing the location, sometimes mentioning the heroic qualities of the dead warriors. It has traditionally been thought that the main purpose of the collection was antiquarian, but the use of techniques from saga and praise poetry gives these verses an elegiac quality and, in the words of Patrick Sims-Williams, 'unexpected poetic power'.[8] John K. Bollard has suggested that the collection can, in fact, be read as a 'meditation on mortality'.[9] Similar stanzas are found among the saga *englynion* of the Llywarch Hen and Heledd cycles, and smaller collections have been kept in later manuscripts.[10]

All the personal names which can be identified belong to legendary heroes associated with the fifth to the ninth centuries. Some feature in the eleven native prose-tales known as the *Mabinogion*, and in the collection of native lore, the Triads of the Island of Britain, others in the *Gododdin* and the early cycles of saga poetry.[11] The place names which can be located belong to all corners of Wales and the locations described, on hills, and near rivers and fords, suggest that standing stones and cairns were interpreted as the graves of ancient heroes. An analysis of the structure of a later collection compared with the Black Book stanzas led Sims-Williams to suggest that their common source contained a bias towards north-west Wales, especially Arfon, and that the original collection may have been produced at the ancient *clas* church of Clynnog.[12] Scholars agree that most of the stanzas in the Black Book collection appear to pre-date the manuscript by several centuries. Their first modern editor, Thomas Jones, claimed that 'their language and style, their metrical patterns, and their heroic mood, mellowed somewhat by a brooding sense of pity and sympathy, together with their textual corruptions and confusions reflecting errors in both oral and written transmission, point to their composition ... probably as early as the

---

[7] Most of the stanzas are either *englyn milwr* or *englyn penfyr*: see Jenny Rowland, *Early Welsh Saga Poetry: A Study and Edition of the Englynion* [*EWSP*] (Cambridge: D. S. Brewer, 1990), pp. 305–32.
[8] Patrick Sims-Williams, 'The Early Welsh Arthurian Poems' in *The Arthur of the Welsh: The Arthurian Legend in Medieval Welsh Literature* [*AW*], ed. by Rachel Bromwich, A. O. H. Jarman and Brynley F. Roberts (Cardiff: University of Wales Press, 1991), pp. 33–71 (p. 49).
[9] For a sensitive literary treatment of the text, see *Englynion y Beddau: The Stanzas of the Graves: Verses on the Legendary Heroes of Wales from The Black Book of Carmarthen*, ed. by John K. Bollard (Llanrwst: Gwasg Carreg Gwalch, 2015), pp. 116–19.
[10] The relationship between the Stanzas of the Graves and the saga *englynion* is explored by Jenny Rowland in *EWSP*, pp. 295–98.
[11] For introductions to these texts, see *A Guide to Welsh Literature*, I, ed. by A. O. H. Jarman and Gwilym Rees Hughes (revised edition, Cardiff: University of Wales Press, 1992).
[12] See Sims-Williams, 'Clas Beuno and the Four Branches of the Mabinogi' in *150 Jahre "Mabinogion" — deutsch-walisische Kulturbeziehungen*, ed. by Bernhard Maier et al. (Tübingen: Max Niemeyer Verlag, 2001), pp. 116–22.

ninth or tenth century'.[13] Sims-Williams is more cautious, suggesting that the bulk of the *englynion* date to the twelfth century or earlier. The loose structure of the series is such, however, that later additions could easily be made.[14] There is evidence that some of the *englynion* have been taken from sequences spoken by various figures, including the legendary Taliesin.[15] The three stanzas featuring well-known Arthurian characters may well have been added to the series, although there is no linguistic or metrical evidence to indicate that they are later than the rest.

Stanza 8 at the bottom of folio 32[r] is typical of the series, with its formulaic opening, followed by the naming of the heroes and the noting of the location of their graves. This is probably the earliest reference to Gwalchmai, who corresponds to Gawain of Arthurian romance and who also appears in *Culhwch ac Olwen*.[16] He is said to be buried *ym Peryton*, 'at' Peryddon, an old river name which appears in a number of medieval literary texts but whose location is uncertain.[17] Also mentioned is Cynon, possibly Cynon ap Clydno Eidyn, a warrior of the Old North (the Brythonic kingdoms in what is now northern England and southern Scotland) who took part in the expedition to Catraeth according to the *Gododdin*, and was later drawn into Arthurian legend, playing a prominent role in the Welsh romance of Owain.[18] He is said here to be buried at the *clas* church of Llanbadarn in Ceredigion.[19]

FIG. 1.2: NLW Peniarth MS 1, f. 32[r].

[13] Thomas Jones, 'The Black Book of Carmarthen "Stanzas of the Graves"', *Proceedings of the British Academy*, 53 (1967), 97–137 (p. 100).
[14] It is likely, for example, that the six four-line *englynion* in the series are later additions: see *EWSP*, p. 330.
[15] See Jones, 'The Black Book', pp. 103–06.
[16] For a summary of references to Gwalchmai in medieval Welsh literature, see *Trioedd Ynys Prydein: The Triads of the Island of Britain* [*TYP*], ed. by Rachel Bromwich (third edn, Cardiff: University of Wales Press, 2006), pp. 367–71, and for allusions to him in the court poems, see Chapter 3 below.
[17] See Bollard, *Englynion y Beddau*, p. 70.
[18] For the *Gododdin*, see Chapter 2 below. For other references to Cynon, see *TYP*, pp. 326–27, and Rachel Bromwich, 'Cynon fab Clydno' in *Astudiaethau ar yr Hengerdd: Studies in Old Welsh Poetry*, ed. by Rachel Bromwich and R. Brinley Jones [*AstHen*] (Cardiff: University of Wales Press, 1978), pp. 151–64, and for allusions to him in the court poems, see Chapter 3 below.
[19] This is the first of nine references to someone named Cynon in the Stanzas of the Graves. He is named as a son of Clydno Eidyn in stanzas 9 and 11, in a cluster of *englynion* about him.

Bet gwalchmei ymperyton. ir diliv. y dyneton. | in llan padarn bet kinon.

> Bet Gwalchmei ym Peryton
> ir diliv y dyneton;
> in Llan Padarn bet Kinon.
>
> The grave of Gwalchmai [is] at Peryddon
> as a reproach to men;
> at Llanbadarn [is] the grave of Cynon

Stanza 12 (f. 32ᵛ) records the location of the grave of Bedwyr (Bedivere) at *alld Tryvan*, possibly in Snowdonia, and contains a reference to Camlan, the site of Arthur's last battle.[20] The son of Osfran, who was buried there, has not been identified by modern scholars, but the first element of the father's name may be Anglo-Saxon and the second element Welsh.[21]

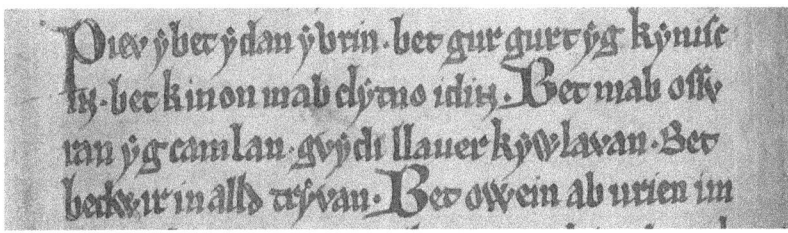

FIG. 1.3: NLW Peniarth MS 1, f. 32ᵛ.

Bet mab ossv|ran ygcamlan. gvydi llauer kywlavan. Bet | bedwir in alld tryvan.

> Bet mab Ossvran yg Camlan,
> gvydi llauer kywlavan;
> bet Bedwir in alld Tryvan.
>
> The grave of Osfran's son [is] at Camlan,
> after many a slaughter;
> the grave of Bedwyr [is] on the hillside of Tryfan.

Stanza 44 (f. 34ʳ) refers to Arthur himself along with three other well-known legendary figures who are all associated with him in later literature: March son of Meirchion, a character from the Trystan stories;[22] Gwythur, who may be identified with Gwythyr ap Greidyawl, a violent figure in *Culhwch ac Olwen*;[23]

---

[20] For further references to the Battle of Camlan, see Chapter 3 below and *TYP*, pp. 167–70. Its likely location is disputed by scholars: see O. J. Padel, 'Geoffrey of Monmouth and Cornwall', *Cambridge Medieval Celtic Studies*, 8 (1984), 13–14.
[21] See Sims-Williams, 'Arthurian Poems', pp. 50–51.
[22] See *TYP*, pp. 435–38.
[23] On Gwythyr ap Greidyawl, see *Culhwch and Olwen: An Edition and Study of the Oldest*

and Gwgawn Gledyfrudd, a king of Ceredigion who appears as a messenger in *Breuddwyd Rhonabwy* (The Dream of Rhonabwy).²⁴

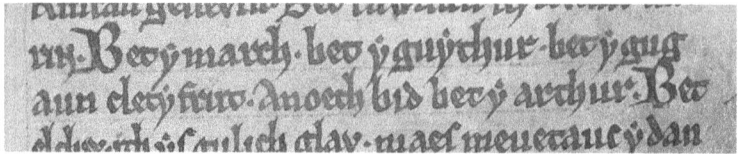

FIG. 1.4: NLW Peniarth MS 1, f. 34ʳ.

Bet y march. bet y guythur. bet y gug|aun cletyfrut. anoeth bid bet y arthur.

> Bet y March, bet y Guythur,
> bet y Gugaun Cletyfrut;
> anoeth bid bet y Arthur.
>
> A grave for March, a grave for Gwythur,
> a grave for Gwgawn Red-sword;
> the world's wonder a grave for Arthur.

The final line of this stanza has been the subject of much speculation.²⁵ The main difficulty has been to establish the meaning of the word *anoeth*, which occurs in prose only in *Culhwch ac Olwen*, where it appears in the plural, *anoetheu*, referring to the seemingly impossible tasks set by the giant Ysbyddaden.²⁶ It is, however, fairly well attested in the court poetry of the twelfth and thirteenth centuries with the meaning 'a wonder, a treasure'. It may have been an archaic term in these poems, which are characterised by their conservative language, suggesting an early date for this *englyn*. On the other hand, it may have been deliberately employed to bring the story of Culhwch to mind, as Patrick Sims-Williams has suggested.²⁷ Its use in all these texts suggests that the most likely

---

Arthurian Tale [CO], ed. by Rachel Bromwich and D. Simon Evans (Cardiff: University of Wales Press, 1992), l. 176n, and *TYP*, pp. 395–96, but note that in the poetry it is the form *Gwythur* rather than *Gwythyr* (< Lat. *victor*) that is used, often to rhyme with Arthur. Since the patronym does not appear in these instances, it is possible that the poets are alluding to a different figure. Gwythur is also named in the Song of the Steeds and 'the Elegy for Uthr Pendragon' from the Book of Taliesin (see Chapter 4 below), and in Cynddelw's elegy for Owain Gwynedd (see Chapter 3 below).
²⁴ *TYP*, p. 384.
²⁵ The stanza is an *englyn milwr* with generic end-rhyme (known by Welsh scholars as *odl Wyddelig*, 'Irish rhyme'), where the vowels are identical but the consonants vary according to certain classes; see *EWSP*, pp. 333–34. This is unusual but not an indicator of an early date as was once thought, since examples of generic rhyme are found in twelfth and thirteenth-century court poetry, gradually becoming rarer.
²⁶ CO, l. 827, and see pp. xvi–xvii.
²⁷ 'Arthurian Poems', p. 49.

sense in this stanza is 'a thing difficult (or even impossible) to find, a wonder'.[28] Taken with *byd*, *anoeth* can mean 'a wonder of the world' or 'the most difficult thing in the world to find'.

Ifor Williams suggested, based on the similar opening lines of two stanzas in the Urien cycle, *Anoeth byd Brawt bwyn kynnull*,[29] that this line should be emended to *Anoeth bid Brawt bet y Arthur*, 'a difficult thing to find until Judgement Day, a grave for Arthur'. This involves understanding *bid* as a mis-modernisation of the preposition *bed*, *fed*, 'as far as, up to, until', and adding *Brawt* 'Judgment (Day)'.[30] This emendation is rejected by Thomas Jones[31] because, in order to preserve the regular syllable count of the *englyn milwr*, the *y* before *Arthur* would need to be deleted and this would make this line different from the previous two: *Bet y March, bet y Guythur, | Bet y Gugaun Cletyfrut; | Anoeth bid brawt bet Arthur*.

Scholars may disagree as to the exact form of the line but its implication is commonly understood: the locations of all the other heroes' graves are well known, but that of Arthur cannot be found. It is possible that it alludes to early tradition which reflects or gave rise to the belief that Arthur did not die and would return as a deliverer of his people. There is evidence of this belief in the early twelfth century in an account of the journey of the canons of Laon in Brittany to Bodmin in 1113, and this is supported by William of Malmesbury, writing c. 1125 that 'Arthur's grave was nowhere to be found, wherefore ancient ditties prophecied his return'.[32]

Word-list

alld *n.* 'hillside, steep slope' (*GPC* allt) 12.2
anoeth *n.* 'a wonderful thing, a wonder, something difficult to find' 44.3
Arthur *personal name* 44.3
Bedwir *personal name* Bedwyr 12.2
bet *n.* 'grave' (*GPC* bedd) 8.1, 3, 12.1, 3, 44.1(2), 2, 3
bid *n.* 'world' 44.3
Camlan *place name* 12.1
Kinon *personal name* Cynon 8.3
kywlavan *n.* 'slaughter, battle' (*GPC* cyflafan) 12.2
diliv *n.* 'shame, reproach' (*GPC* diliw³) 8.2

---

[28] See *Geiriadur Prifysgol Cymru: A Dictionary of the Welsh Language* [*GPC*] (Cardiff: University of Wales Press, 1950–2002).
[29] 'Difficult until Judgment day would it be to gather us'; see *EWSP*, pp. 423, 479.
[30] See *EWSP*, p. 560, and for another possible example, see Chapter 4 below, *Preideu Annwn*, l. 8n.
[31] Thomas Jones, 'The Early Evolution of the Legend of Arthur', *Nottingham Medieval Studies*, 8 (1964), 3–21 (p. 18).
[32] See Sims-Williams, 'Arthurian Poems', pp. 49–50, and *AMWL*, p. 50.

dyneton *pl. of* **dyn**, 'man, human being, person' 8.2
Gugaun Cletyfrut *personal name* Gwgawn Gleddyfrudd, Gwgon Red-sword 44.2
Guythur *personal name* Gwythur, Gwythyr 44.1
gvydi *prep.* 'after, following' (*GPC* gwedi) 12.2
Gwalchmei *personal name* Gwalchmai 8.1
in *prep.* 'in, at' (causing nasal mutation, *GPC* yn^1) 8.3, 12.3, **yg** (form used before *c-*) 12.1, **ym** (form used before *p-*) 8.1
ir *prep.* 'causing, resulting in, (serving) as' (*GPC* er^1 1c) 8.2
Llan Padarn *place name* Llanbadarn Fawr in Ceredigion 8.3
llauer *adj.* 'many' 12.2
mab *n.* 'son' 12.1
March *personal name* 44.1
Ossvran *personal name* Osfran 12.1
Peryton *river name* Peryddon 8.1
Tryvan *place name* Tryfan 12.3
y *prep.* 'to' (causing lenition, *GPC* i^2) 8.2, 44.1(2), 2, 3
yg, ym see **in**

Mi a wum ...

It was Ifor Williams who first proposed that the last seven *englynion* of a rather obscure and clumsy dialogue between two well-known legendary characters, Gwyddno Garanhir, father of Elffin, and Gwyn ap Nudd, the otherworldly hunter, should be considered a separate poem.[33] Their modern editors, Brynley F. Roberts and Jenny Rowland, are less certain of this, and Rowland identifies possible links between the two sections.[34] In these verses, the dialogue has become a soliloquy by an unidentified speaker who, using the formula *mi a wum*, 'I have been',[35] states that he was present at the deaths in battle of various heroic figures from the past and, in the final two stanzas, claims to have been 'where all the warriors of Britain were slain, from the east to the north' and 'from the east to the south'. Sims-Williams, following A. O. H. Jarman, suggests that the speaker may be Gwyddno, but Rowland makes a strong case for Gwyn, a supernatural figure, and suggests that the sequence is similar to an addition to the Stanzas of the Graves where Taliesin uses his magical power to identify buried heroes.[36] Like the Stanzas of the Graves, this series is elegiac in tone, evoking a heroic past, but it seems to be primarily antiquarian in purpose, cataloguing the names of famous warriors, Gwenddolau, Brân, Llachau son of Arthur, Meurig and Gwallawg. A few textual errors reveal that it was probably first written down in Old Welsh spelling and is to be dated to c. 900–1100.

Llachau is a shadowy character despite the fact that he is named in a number of medieval Welsh texts: in the Triads of the Island of Britain and the Dream of Rhonabwy, where he is identified as a son of Arthur, and several times in pre- and post-conquest praise poetry where he is consistently referred to as a paragon of a warrior (see Chapter 3 below). Rachel Bromwich is probably right in suspecting that the frequent allusions to him in court poetry may not reflect his importance in the narrative tradition but that his name was useful to the poets for the purpose of alliteration.[37] In the *Pa gur ...* poem, we are told that Cai and Llachau 'performed battles', but it is not clear whether they fought alongside or against each other. The reference to Llachau in the third stanza of

---

[33] See Ifor Williams, *Lectures on Early Welsh Poetry* (Dublin: Institute for Advanced Studies, 1954), pp. 26–27. The first five stanzas are *englynion milwr*, the last two are *englynion penfyr*; see *EWSP*, pp. 319–28.

[34] Brynley F. Roberts, 'Rhai o Gerddi Ymddiddan Llyfr Du Caerfyrddin' in *AstHen*), pp. 311–18. For Rowland's edition and translation of the series, see *EWSP*, pp. 461–63, 506–07, 639–40. Rowland concludes that the relationship between the two poems remains problematical; *EWSP*, pp. 243–47.

[35] The same formula is used in Glewlwyd Gafaelfawr's boastful speech in *Culhwch ac Olwen*; see *CO*, ll. 114–28, discussed on pp. 58–59.

[36] Sims-Williams, 'Arthurian Poems', p. 44; Jarman, 'Arthurian Allusions', p. 107; *EWSP*, p. 247.

[37] See *TYP*, pp. 408–10, for a comprehensive discussion of these references. Bromwich dismisses the idea that there was an early association between Llachau and Loholt of French romance; see also Ad Putter, 'Arthur's children in Le Petit Bruit and the Post-Vulgate Cycle', *Reading Medieval Studies*, 38 (2012), 25–42 (pp. 26–27).

Mi a wum is also frustratingly vague.[38]

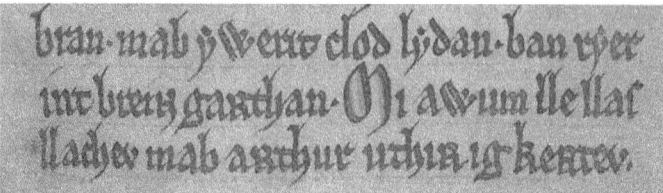

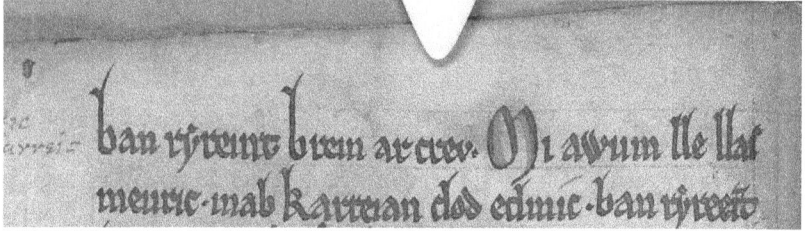

Fig. 1.5: NLW Peniarth MS 1, f. 50[r–v].

Mi awum lle llas | llachev mab arthur uthir ig kertev. || ban ryreint brein ar crev.

> Mi a wum lle llas Llachev,
> mab Arthur, uthir ig kertev,
> ban ryreint brein ar crev.
>
> I have been where Llachau was slain,
> son of Arthur, terrible in songs,
> when ravens rushed to gore [*or* croaked on gore].

The sequence is characterised by extensive use of *cymeriad geiriol*, which links not only the opening line of each stanza but the third line also in the case of the first four *englynion*.[39] In the second line of each stanza, the name of the hero's father is followed by an epithet which contains conventional material reminiscent of formal praise poetry. It is difficult, however, to know whether this phrase is intended to describe the father or the son or perhaps both. In this stanza, *uthir ig kertev*, 'terrible in songs', is probably a reference to the fame that Llachau or Arthur enjoyed amongst the poets for his ferocity or his might in battle.[40] The motif of ravens scavenging on battlefields and feasting on the blood of the slain in the third line is common in early and medieval Welsh

---

[38] Peniarth MS 1, f. 50.
[39] On this stylistic device, which involves the repetition of an opening word or phrase in a series of stanzas, and sometimes of words and phrases in other lines, see *EWSP*, pp. 351–52.
[40] It is unlikely that *uthir* here is the name of Arthur's father, Uthr, discussed below in *Pa gur*, 14n. It is nevertheless striking to find this word qualifying Arthur in this way. Oliver Padel (personal correspondence) wonders whether Geoffrey of Monmouth might possibly have invented Arthur's patronym from some phrase such as this.

panegyric. The verbal form *ryreint* (three syllables) is made up of the preverbal particle *ry-* (used here to express a customary action),[41] and the lenited third-person plural imperfect form of either *reaf*: *re*, 'to rise, go, set out', or *greaf*: *grëu*, a variant of *crëu*, 'to croak'. There are other examples in the poetry of *ar* being used to express the destination of a verb of motion ('ravens go *to* blood', *GMW*, p. 187) but the use of *ar* with the second verb is more problematic ('ravens croaked over (?)/beside (?) blood'). *Crëu*, *grëu*, however, is used in a similar context by two thirteenth-century court poets, Prydydd y Moch, *Y fort yd gertwyf, gwrt yd gre branhes*, 'the road I travel, confidently do ravens croak', and Einion ap Gwgon, *Oet tew peleidyr creu, creynt kicurein*, 'numerous were bloody spears, ravens were croaking'.[42]

We gather from the stanza that Llachau was a son of Arthur and was killed in battle. His burial place is not listed in the Stanzas of the Graves, but the thirteenth-century court poet Bleddyn Fardd refers to the spot where he was killed in an elegy to Dafydd, younger brother of Llywelyn the Last, preserved in the Hendregadredd Manuscript:[43]

> *Dewr a was ban llas, yn llassar — arueu,*
> *ual e llas Llacheu is Llech Ysgar.*
>
> [Dafydd was] a brave youth when he was slain, in blue-enamelled arms,
> as Llachau was slain below Llech Ysgar.

Llech Ysgar, named by Cynddelw Brydydd Mawr as one of the courts of his patron, Madog ap Maredudd, a prince of Powys who died in 1160, has been identified with Crickheath Hill, south of Oswestry in Shropshire. Dafydd ap Gruffudd was executed at nearby Shrewsbury in 1283, having been betrayed by his own men.[44] Llachau's name may have been used by Bleddyn Fardd simply for alliteration, as elsewhere in the court poetry, but this reference may suggest that as with Amr, another son of Arthur who met a violent end,[45] there was at one time a local tradition surrounding Llachau's death and this may also be reflected in the *englynion*.[46]

---

[41] See D. Simon Evans, *Grammar of Middle Welsh* [*GMW*] (Dublin: Institute of Advanced Studies, 1976), p. 168.
[42] *Cyfres Beirdd y Tywysogion* [*CBT*], general editor R. Geraint Gruffydd (Cardiff: University of Wales Press, 1991–1996), V 14.17, VI 18.65. (For the Prydydd y Moch poem, see *Welsh Court Poems* [*WCP*], ed. by Rhian M. Andrews (Cardiff: University of Wales Press, 2007), p. 30.)
[43] On the poet see Chapter 3 below.
[44] See David Stephenson, *Medieval Powys: Kingdom, Principality and Lordships, 1132–1293* [*MP*] (Woodbridge: The Boydell Press, 2016), p. 52.
[45] For the account of Amr's death and his marvellous grave in the *Historia Brittonum*, see Brynley F. Roberts, 'Culhwch ac Olwen, the Triads, Saints' Lives' in *AW*, pp. 73–95 (pp. 91–92).
[46] For a possible reference to Llachau's burial place in the church of Llandrinio at the

Word-list

a *preverbal particle* (causing lenition, *GPC* a¹) 1
ar *prep.* 'upon, to, ?over, ?beside' (*GPC* ar¹ 1a, 2b) 3
Arthur *personal name* 2
ban *conj.* 'when' (causing lenition, *GPC* pan¹, ban³) 3
brein *pl. of* **bran**, 'raven' 3
bum *1 sing.pret. of* **bod**, 'to be' 1
kertev *pl. of* **kert**, 'song' (*GPC* cerdd¹) 2
crev *n.* 'gore, blood' (*GPC* crau¹) 3
ig *form used before k- of prep.* **in, yn**, 'in' (causing nasal mutation) 2
Llachev *personal name* Llachau 1
llas *impers.pret. of* **llat**, 'to kill' (*GPC* lladdaf: lladd) 1
lle *conj.* 'where' 1
mab *n.* 'son' 2
mi *independent pron. 1 sing.* 'I' 1
ryreint *3 pl.imperf.indic. (with preverbal particle ry-) of either* **re**, 'to rise, go, set out' (*GPC* rheaf: rhe) *or* **grëu**, 'to croak' (*GPC* greaf: grëu) 3
uthir *adj.* 'fearful, dreadful, terrible' (with epenthetic vowel, see *GPC* uthr) 2

The Stanzas of Geraint son of Erbin

Another fleeting but intriguing reference to Arthur appears in a series of *englynion* featuring Geraint son of Erbin, a figure associated with Dumnonia in the south-west of Britain, who is also mentioned in a number of Welsh genealogies and tales and in the Triads, and may have originated as the well-known Cornish king Gerent named in the Anglo-Saxon Chronicle under the year 710.[47] In the later Welsh Arthurian romance which corresponds to Chrétien de Troyes' *Erec et Enide*, Geraint is depicted as a cousin of Arthur and one of his knights, but the earliest link between the two is in this text.[48]

The stanzas make extensive use of *cymeriad geiriol*, which is varied three times during the course of the series.[49] The short opening sequence depicts Geraint, victorious in battle, driving before him the unnamed enemy's bloodstained steeds:[50]

foot of Crickheath Hill in an *englyn* added to a poem by Cynddelw Brydydd Mawr in the Hendregadredd Manuscript, see Barry Lewis, 'Arthurian References in Medieval Welsh Poetry, *c.* 1100–*c.* 1540' in *ACL*, pp. 191–92.

[47] For a discussion of the numerous allusions to Geraint in medieval Welsh literature, see *TYP*, pp. 356–60, and for references to him in the work of Prydydd y Moch and Bleddyn Fardd, see Chapter 3 below. Bromwich lists references to historical figures bearing the name *Gerent*, associated with the south-west, in *TYP*, p. 359.
[48] See Susan M. Pearce, 'The Cornish Elements in the Arthurian Tradition', *Folklore*, 85 (1974), 145–63.
[49] On *cymeriad geiriol*, see footnote 41 above.
[50] The words and phrases which are repeated in the stanzas of each sequence are italicised.

> *Rac Gereint, gelin* kystut,
> *y gueleis-e meirch* can crimrut,
> *a gwidy gaur, garv* achlut.

> *Before Geraint, the enemy's* affliction,
> *I saw horses* white, bowed, blood-stained,
> *and after a battle-cry* (or *a battle*), *a rough* grave.

In the second sequence of stanzas, the unidentified speaker who had witnessed the conflict contrasts the attack led by Geraint and the resulting carnage:[51]

> *En llogborth y gueleis e* vitheint
> a geloraur mvy no meint,
> a *guir* rut rac ruthir Gereint.

> *In Llongborth*[52] *I saw* battle-fury,
> and biers beyond measure,
> and bloodstained *warriors* before the onrush of Geraint.

A change of metre from *englyn milwr* to *englyn penfyr* heralds a third sequence which describes stable-fed steeds ridden by Geraint rushing into battle like eagles of different hues:

> Oet re re[d]eint dan vortuid — Gereint
>   *garhirion graun* guenith,
>   *rution, ruthir eriron* blith.

> Swiftly there used to run under the thigh of Geraint,
>   long-legged horses [*fed on*] grains of wheat,
>   red [*with blood*], *with the onrush* of speckled *eagles*.

Jenny Rowland has suggested that this last section, where incremental repetition is used, may be a separate poem composed by a different poet.[53] This is not necessarily so as the opening stanzas also feature Geraint's horses, giving the series a sense of unity.

These *englynion* belong to a small number of texts from the Black Book

---

The word-order of the translation attempts to imitate that of the original.
[51] The repetition of *gweleis*, 'I saw', is a commonly-used device in praise poetry, especially in descriptions of battles. For examples, see *Legendary Poems from the Book of Taliesin* [*LPBT*], ed. by Marged Haycock (Aberystwyth: CMCS Publications, 2007), p. 279.
[52] Possibly Langport on the River Parret in Somerset, although *llongborth* (lit. ship harbour) could equally be a common noun, 'sea-port': see Sims-Williams, 'Arthurian Poems', p. 47. See also *EWSP*, p. 241, for the meaning 'camp, fortress', based on the use of Irish *longphort*. There is a tradition recorded in the eighteenth century locating the battle at Llanborth in Ceredigion, not far from a farm called Bedd Geraint, 'Geraint's grave'; see Peter C. Bartrum, *A Welsh Classical Dictionary: People in History and Legend up to about A.D. 1000* (Aberystwyth: National Library of Wales, 1993), p. 415.
[53] *EWSP*, pp. 240–41. Rowland (*EWSP*, pp. 351–52) is right to distinguish between the term *cymeriad geiriol*, which involves the repetition of individual words or phrases usually at the beginning of a stanza, and 'incremental repetition', where the variation is much less and is usually confined to the rhyming words. The first two sections of this series contain the former while this section uses the latter.

of Carmarthen which are also found in other medieval manuscripts. Only a few lines from the Geraint series survive in the White Book of Rhydderch, a compendium of medieval Welsh poetry and prose written in the mid-fourteenth century but with many sections now missing.[54] The series is complete, however, in an early modern manuscript whose copier, John Jones Gellilyfdy, writing in 1607, claims that it is a transcription of 'an old poem which old Richard Langford of Trefalun wrote out of the White Book of Rhydderch in AD 1573',[55] and also in the late fourteenth-century manuscript the Red Book of Hergest, which is not a copy of the White Book but contains a number of poems derived from a common source.[56] Whilst the White Book and Red Book versions of the poem are very close, there are substantial differences between them and the text preserved over a hundred years earlier in the Black Book.[57] In each version, that of the Black Book, which contains eighteen *englynion*, and that of the White/Red Book, which has twenty-four, there are stanzas not found in the other, and their order within the sequences is also substantially different, with the final *englyn* of the Black Book version used to open the White/Red Book text. The stanzas they have in common, however, are fairly similar, suggesting that much of the variation is probably due to oral and written transmission, the Black Book text being a shorter version of a longer original more fully preserved in the White/Red Book.[58]

The series has been edited by two scholars, Brynley F. Roberts and Jenny Rowland, who have taken different approaches to the problem of the variant texts. Roberts based his edition on the order of the stanzas in the Black Book because it is the older manuscript,[59] whilst Rowland followed the order of the White/Red Book version because it is 'much fuller and seems more consecutive'.[60] Both editors have created composite texts, grouping stanzas with a similar pattern in the two versions together.

These verses are generally dated between the ninth and the eleventh centuries.[61] It was traditionally thought that they belonged to a lost collection

---

[54] NLW Peniarth MS 4, f. 62^v. For more information see *MWM*, pp. 227–68, and to view the manuscript, visit <http://www.llgc.org.uk>.
[55] NLW Peniarth 111, pp. 117–21, and see *MWM*, pp. 247–48.
[56] Oxford, Jesus College MS 111, f. 259^v, cols 1042–43. On the Red Book, which has been described by Daniel Huws (*MWM*, p. 16) as 'a library of Welsh literature in one volume', see *MWM*, pp. 80–83. To view the Red Book, visit <http://image.ox.ac.uk>. For a discussion of the relationship between the early *englynion* series of the White Book and the Red Book, see *EWSP*, pp. 395–97.
[57] Peniarth MS 1, ff. 36^r–37^r.
[58] See *EWSP*, p. 240.
[59] 'Rhai o gerddi Ymddiddan Llyfr Du Caerfyrddin', pp. 286–96.
[60] For an outline of the structure of Rowland's composite reconstruction, see *EWSP*, pp. 636–39. For text and translation, see *EWSP*, pp. 457–61 and 504–05.
[61] This is mainly on stylistic grounds. There does not seem to be any linguistic evidence to date the series more precisely than sometime before the early twelfth century.

of poems about Geraint similar to the Llywarch Hen cycle, possibly with a prose element now lost.[62] They lack the emotional intensity of the saga poetry, however, and may perhaps be more usefully compared with the series of *englynion* on Cadwallon ap Cadfan which follows in the Red Book.[63] The opening stanzas in the White/Red Book version are not only full of extravagant praise for Geraint but also appear to express the poet's intention: 'Lord, I myself shall praise Geraint, | an enemy to an Englishman, a friend to Christians'.

The stanza which names Arthur appears at the end of the second sequence and seems to be closely related to an *englyn* referring to Geraint which follows it in the Black Book version:

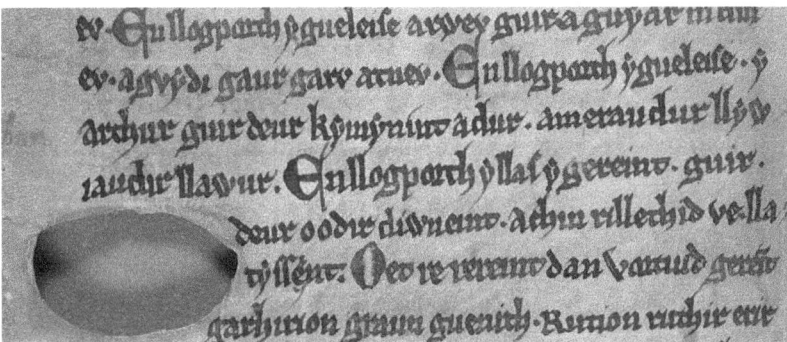

FIG. 1.6: NLW Peniarth MS 1, f. 36ᵛ.

En llogporth y gueleise. y | arthur guir deur kymynint a dur. ameraudur llyw-|iaudir llawur. En llogporth y llas y gereint. guir. | deur o odir diwneint. A chin rillethid ve.lla-|tysseint.[64]

> En Llogporth y gueleis-e y Arthur
> guir deur, kymynint a dur,
> ameraudur, llywiaudur llawur.
>
> En Llogporth y llas y Gereint
> guir deur o odir Diwneint,
> a chin rillethid-ve, llatysseint.

---

[62] See Sims-Williams, 'Arthurian Poems', pp. 48–49, who refers in particular to stanza 14 in Rowland's edition as evidence that the series is a speech-poem from a saga. For a discussion of Ifor Williams' theory of a lost prose framework to the saga *englynion*, see Jenny Rowland, 'The Prose Setting of the Early Welsh *Englynion Chwedlonol*', *Ériu*, 36 (1985), 29–43.
[63] See Jenny Rowland, 'Genres' in *EWP*, pp. 179–208 (p. 196). For text and translation see *EWSP*, pp. 446–47 and 495–96, and for a discussion see pp. 169–70.
[64] Note that the manuscript has *llatyssent* with an *i* added above, probably by the same hand, with an insertion sign below giving the form *llatysseint*. On this form, which is amended in the edited text, see below.

In Llongborth I saw to Arthur
brave warriors, they hewed with steel,
emperor, leader of battle.

In Llongborth was slain to Geraint
brave warriors from the region of Dyfnaint (Devon),
and although they had been killed, they killed.

In the White/Red Book version, the stanza which names Arthur is preceded by the stanza which mentions Geraint:[65]

FIG. 1.7: Jesus College MS 111, f. 259ᵛ, col. 1042.

Yn llongborth y llas gereint. Gwr deṽr o godir | dyfneint. wyntwy yn llad gyt asledeint. | Ynllongborth llas yarthur Gwyr deṽr kymy|nynt o dur. amheraṽdyr llywyaṽdyr llauur.

Yn Llongborth y llas Gereint,
gwr deṽr o godir Dyfneint,
wyntwy yn llad gyt as ledeint.

Yn Llongborth llas y Arthur
gwyr deṽr kymynynt a[66] dur,
amheraṽdyr, llywyaṽdyr llauur.

In Llongborth Geraint was slain,
a brave warrior from the region of Dyfnaint,
they were killing although they were killing them.

In Llongborth was slain to Arthur
brave warriors, they hewed with steel,
emperor, leader of battle.

---

[65] The text is from the Red Book of Hergest and is almost identical to that found in Peniarth MS 111. The ṽ symbol represents a *v* with the first stroke curled inwards, a characteristic of the Red Book. It is replaced in the edited version with *w*.

[66] Peniarth 111 *a*; Red Book *o*.

Both versions are unsatisfactory in places: words and phrases appear to be misremembered or mis-copied and there may also have been an effort to rationalise the text. It is impossible to reconstruct an 'original' with any certainty, but some suggestions can be made which would bring the two stanzas more in line with the rest of the series as regards form and meaning. The order of the stanzas in the Black Book seems the more likely, as Geraint's name at the end of the first line of the second *englyn* links it to the sequence which follows, where it is found in the same position in each verse.

The first lines of each of the two stanzas will be examined together:

BB	en Llogporth y gueleis-e y Arthur
W/RB	Llongborth llas y Arthur
BB	en Llogporth y llas y Gereint
W/RB	yn Llongborth y llas Gereint

The vast majority of the *englynion milwr* in the series consist of seven-syllable lines. In order to regularise the syllable count in the first lines of both stanzas in the Black Book version, the preverbal particle *y* can be omitted.[67] In the first stanza, the Black Book's *gueleis-e*, 'I saw', continues the *cymeriad* of the preceding *englynion*, but the line is still a syllable too long unless the preposition *y* which follows it is omitted. This would give 'In Llongborth I saw Arthur', which has no connection with the following line.[68] The White/Red Book's *llas*, 'was slain', connects the two stanzas, making them into a pair. There are, however, no other indications in the series that Geraint was killed in the battle, as is claimed in the White/Red Book version, and Rowland argues that the poem does not conform to the general pattern of *marwnadau* in the saga *englynion*.[69] The poem is often described by scholars as an elegy, but the title *Englynion marwnad Geraint* is found in early modern copies only.[70] This leaves us with *llas y Arthur* and *llas y Gereint*, which need to be taken with the second lines of each stanza:

BB	guir deur, kymynint a dur,
W/RB	gwyr de(v)r kymynynt a dur,
BB	guir deur o odir Diwneint,
W/RB	gwr de(v)r o godir Dyfneint,

These lines contain the object of the impersonal verb *llas*, the plural *gwyr*,

---

[67] The simple affixed pronoun (-*e*) is not usually included in the syllable count. For examples in the work of the Poets of the Princes, see *WCP* 10.13, 15.18, 19, 25.7, 11, 14, 22, etc.
[68] Sims-Williams suggests that *y gueleis-e* may be due to simple haplography, the scribe starting to copy another stanza with a similar opening and his eye jumping ahead to *y Arthur*; see 'Arthurian Poems', n. 82.
[69] *EWSP*, p. 242.
[70] The Red Book has no medieval title. The Black Book has the words *Gereint fil' Erbin* added by the rubricator and the White Book has *Englynnyon gereint vab erbin*.

'warriors', a word which is repeated in the second line of most of the stanzas of the sequence. In the Geraint verse of the White/Red Book version, *gwyr* may have been changed to the singular *gwr* so that it connects with *llas Gereint* of the previous line, 'Geraint was killed, a brave warrior ...', but this leaves the third line with its plural verb without a clear subject.

The use of the preposition *y* in the first line remains a problem. Sims-Williams describes it as syntactically tortuous but suggests that we may have a poetic inversion of *gwyr y Arthur*, 'warriors to (i.e. vassals of) Arthur', an idiom found in a previous *englyn* in the White/Red Book version: *a vo gwr y Ereint bryssyet*, 'he who would be a warrior to Geraint, let him make haste'.[71]

The first two lines of each stanza can be reconstructed as follows:[72]

> Yn Llongborth llas y Arthur
> wyr dewr, kymynynt a dur ...
>
> In Llongborth were slain brave warriors belonging to
> Arthur, they hewed with steel ...
>
> Yn Llongborth llas y Ereint
> wyr dewr o odir Dyfneint ...
>
> In Llongborth were slain brave warriors belonging to
> Geraint from the region of Dyfnaint ...

The final lines of both *englynion* appear to contain set phrases or ideas found in other poetic texts. That of the first *englyn* is almost identical in both versions and contains praise of Arthur:[73]

> BB   ameraudur, llywiaudir llawur
> W/RB   amhera(ỽ)dyr, llywya(ỽ)dyr llauur

In order to maintain the syllable count and have the internal rhyme with *llywyawdyr*, 'ruler, leader',[74] the first word needs to be *amherawdyr* with an epenthetic vowel, rather than the Black Book's *ameraudur* with a full vowel.[75] The description of Arthur as *amherawdyr* (from the Latin *imperator*) is not likely to be a reflection of the influence of the emperor figure of Geoffrey of Monmouth, as some scholars have suggested. It may be a foreshadowing of it, or, as suggested by Rhian M. Andrews, it may be a convenient metrical alternative for *Pen Teyrned*, 'Chief of Princes', the term used for Arthur in

---

[71] 'Arthurian Poems', p. 48.
[72] The reconstruction uses regular Middle Welsh orthography and shows initial mutations.
[73] Rowland, *EWSP*, p. 242, suggests that it may have replaced a different earlier line.
[74] Root of vb. *llywiaw*, 'to rule', + nominalising suffix *-yawdyr* from Lat. *-ātor*.
[75] Epenthetic vowels (*GMW*, pp. 12–13) were not recognised for metrical purposes in medieval Welsh poetry even though they were syllabic in speech and sometimes became assimilated to the preceding vowel.

Culhwch ac Olwen and in the Triads.[76] In the work of the Poets of the Princes, *amherawdyr* is used figuratively for powerful rulers like Lord Rhys, Llywelyn the Great and Llywelyn the Last, often in combination with *llywyawdyr*.[77]

The verbal forms in the two versions of the memorable final line of the second *englyn* differ, but they both express the same idea, that although they had been killed, Geraint's warriors had, during the course of the battle, valiantly killed others. A detailed analysis of these lines provides an insight into the activities of those who transmitted this text either orally or in writing and also enables a tentative reconstruction to be formed:

        BB   a chin rillethid ve, llatysseint

The form *cin* could be the preposition *cyn*, 'before (in time)', but it is more likely here to be a variant of the conjunction *cyd*, 'although', which is usually followed by a subjunctive (see *GMW*, p. 235). *Llethid* is an impersonal imperfect subjunctive of *llat*, the -*th*- caused by provection (see *GMW*, pp. 14, 128).[78] The preverbal particle *ry* gives a perfect meaning to the verb (*GMW*, pp. 166–69), 'had been killed'. Lenition usually follows *ry* unless it is combined with an infixed object pronoun 3 singular or plural, *'y*. The forms *rys* and *rwy* often express this combination (*GMW*, p. 55), but there are also examples where the pronoun is not visible in the text although the meaning demands it. It is likely that this is a case in point and that the *ve* that follows is not the third-person plural object, *wy* (*GMW*, p. 50), but an affixed pronoun which is not reckoned in the syllable count.

The line ends with the puzzling form *llatysseint*. The suffix -*eint* is crucial for the end-rhyme of this stanza. This is a third-person plural imperfect ending, used very rarely by the Poets of the Princes and their successors and in the medieval prose texts.[79] It is found, however, in the opening lines of the last nine stanzas of this poem: *Oed re redeint ... garhirion*, 'It was swiftly that the long-legged horses ran'. Here it appears, not with the root of the verb *llat* but with *llatys*-, found in the preterite and pluperfect forms of the verb. This appears to

---

[76] See Rhian M. Andrews, 'The Nomenclature of Kingship in Welsh Court Poetry 1100–1300: Part 1 The Terms', *Studia Celtica*, 44 (2010), 71–109 (p. 101). Andrews' suggestion that *amherawdyr* may be understood here as 'commander-in-chief' is rejected by Oliver Padel (private correspondence), who argues that 'although Latin *imperator* did etymologically mean simply "one who gives orders", hence "commander", it became specialised so early (1st century AD) in the sense "emperor", that one cannot plausibly plead that it could still carry its etymological meaning'.

[77] For example, Cynddelw in praise of Lord Rhys, *Ymerawdyr, llywyawdyr, llyw amniuer*, 'Ruler (lit. emperor), leader, lord of a multitude' (*CBT* IV 8.32), Prydydd y Moch to Llywelyn the Great, *Amherawdyr llywyawdyr llurycawc*, 'Ruler (lit. emperor), mail-clad leader' (V 24.62), and Bleddyn Fardd's elegy to Llywelyn the Last, where the prince is called *amerodr Kymro*, 'Welsh ruler (lit. emperor)' (VII 51.22).

[78] For further examples of -*th*- in subjunctive forms of *llat*, see *Pa gur*, ll. 32, 73 below.

[79] See *GMW*, p. 122, and *DMWL*, pp. 67–68.

be a hybrid or a corrupt form and may be amended to *lleteint*, a third-person plural imperfect of *llat*, giving a seven-syllable line: *A chin rillethid-ve, lleteint*, 'And although they had been killed, they were killing'.

This form is also found in the rhyming position in the White/Red Book version of this line: *Wyntwy yn llad gyt as [l]ledeint*.[80] *As* is the third-person singular or plural syllabic form of the infixed pronoun which often follows *kyt/gyt*, 'although', as in the elegy for Owain ap Urien, *kyt as cronyei*, 'although he hoarded them' (*PT* x, p. 21 and see *GMW*, p. 56). The line can therefore be tentatively translated as 'They were killing although they [the enemy] were killing them'.

Similar lines are found in the *Gododdin*, and in a series of *englynion* by Cynddelw Brydydd Mawr (see below) to the warband of Owain Gwynedd (d.1170) which seems to have been modelled on the *Gododdin*.[81] Cynddelw's poem has also been preserved in two versions, in the Hendregadredd Manuscript and the Red Book of Hergest. The verbal forms differ but the meaning of this line is almost identical:[82]

> H   a ched llated, llatessynt
> R   a chyt lledyt, lladyssynt
>
> and although they were killed, they had killed.

The two examples from the Book of Aneirin have similarities both with Cynddelw's line and that of the Black Book:[83]

> ket ryladet-wy, wy lladassant
>
> although they had been killed, they killed

and

> a chet llesseint, wy lladassan
>
> and although they were killed, they killed.

It is interesting to note that the unusual form *llesseint*, a plural passive preterite, is an emendation by modern editors of *lledessynt*, a confused or corrupt form

---

[80] Another possible example is found in a religious poem from the Book of Taliesin; see *DMWL*, p. 68 n. 210.
[81] See Nerys Ann Jones, 'Hengerdd in the Age of the Poets of the Princes', *BG*, pp. 41–80 (p. 68).
[82] There are differences in the verbal forms with the Hendregadredd scribe using an impersonal preterite form of *lladd* (see *GMW*, p. 126) and the Red Book scribe the impersonal imperfect form, followed by variant forms of the 3 pl. pluperfect.
[83] See A. O. H. Jarman, *Aneirin, Y Gododdin: Britain's Oldest Heroic Poem* [*AyG*] (Llandysul: Gomer Press, 1988), ll. 867 and 345. The first stanza is placed no earlier than the Old Welsh period by John T. Koch, *The Gododdin of Aneirin: Text and Context from Dark-Age North Britain* [*GofA*] (Cardiff: University of Wales Press, 1997), pp. 163–64. The second was added to the *Gododdin* at a late creative stage, between 1000 and 1350, according to Koch, pp. 203–04.

of the verb, similar to the final word of the Black Book line.[84] It seems that the scribes who committed the Geraint poem to parchment were not alone in struggling with obscure forms of the verb *lladd*. They may have been influenced by these other texts as they attempted to make sense of the line and perhaps, in the case of the White and Red Book version, to reconstruct it. Whether the original line was a deliberate echo of the *Gododdin*, or whether Cynddelw was familiar with this poem, is difficult to establish.[85]

What do these *englynion* tell us about Arthur's relationship with Geraint and his role in the battle of Llongborth? Other than the fact that both Arthur and Geraint lost a great number of their warriors, there is very little of which we can be certain. Rowland is probably correct in suggesting that the parallelism between the two stanzas indicates that Arthur and Geraint's men were allies rather than opponents,[86] but there is no certainty that Arthur himself was present at the battle or that Geraint was killed at it. Jarman has suggested that Arthur's name was introduced 'to embellish a scene of turmoil and bloodshed in the traditional style of earlier Welsh verse'.[87] A more common view, however, is that this poem should be understood against a background of legend containing traditions of the south-west into which Arthur has been introduced.

Word-list

a¹ *conj.* 'and' (causing spirant mutation) BB 6
a² *prep.* 'with' (*GPC* â¹ 1a) BB 2, W/RB 5
ameraudur (amherawdyr) *n.* 'emperor' (*GPC* ymherodr) BB 3, W/RB 6
Arthur *personal name* BB 1, W/RB 4
as *syllabic infixed 3 pl.obj.pron.* (*GPC* as²) W/RB 3
cin *conj.* 'although' (*GPC* cyd³, cyn³) BB 6
deur (dewr) *adj.* 'brave' BB 2 4, W/RB 2, 4
Diwneint (Dyfneint) *place name* Dyfnaint, Devon BB5, W/RB 2
dur *n.* 'steel, steel weapon' BB 2, W/RB 5
e *1 sing. dependent affixed pron.* (*GPC* i¹) BB 1

---

[84] See *AyG*, p. 100. A similar form, also amended to *llesseint*, is found in a rhyming position in the final *englyn* of the lament for Gwên in the Llywarch Hen Cycle: *Drwy vyn tauawt lledesseint* (*EWSP*, p. 208).
[85] Jones, 'Hengerdd', p. 52.
[86] *EWSP*, p. 48. It is not likely that the reference to Arthur is just a comparison, similar to that found in the Elegy for Cynddylan in Chapter 5 below, i.e. '[Geraint's men] were so valorous that they might be called/likened to "brave men of Arthur"', as suggested by Thomas Green, *Concepts of Arthur* (Stroud: Tempus, 2007), pp. 78-79.
[87] A. O. H. Jarman, 'The Delineation of Arthur in Early Welsh Verse' in *An Arthurian Tapestry: Essays in Memory of Lewis Thorpe*, ed. by K. Varty (Glasgow: published on behalf of the British branch of the International Arthurian Society at the French Department of the University of Glasgow, 1981), pp. 1-21 (p. 6).

en (yn) *prep.* 'in' (*GPC* yn¹) BB 1, 4, W/RB 1, 4
Gereint *personal name* Geraint BB 4, W/RB 1
godir *n.* 'region, area' BB5, W/RB 2
gueleis *1 sing.pret. of* **gweled**, 'to see' BB 1
gwr 'man, warrior' (*GPC* gŵr) W/RB 2; *pl.* **guir (gwyr)** BB 2, 4, W/RB 5
gyd *conj.* 'although' (*GPC* cyd³) W/RB 3
kymynint (kymynynt) *3 pl.imperf.indic. of* **kymynu**, 'to cut down, hew' (*GPC* cymynaf: cymynu) BB 2, W/RB 5
llad *v.n.* 'to kill' (*GPC* lladdaf: lladd) W/RB 3; **lleteint (lledeint)** *3 pl.imperf.indic.* BB 6, W/RB 3; **llas** *impers.pret.* BB 4, W/RB 1, 4; **rillethid** *impers.imperf. subj. with perfective preverbal particle containing infixed obj. pron. 3 pl.* (*GPC* rhy²) BB 6
llawur (llauur) *n.* '?battle' (*GPC* llafur) BB 3, W/RB 6
lledeint, lleteint see **llad**
Llogporth (Llongborth) *place name* Llongborth BB 1, 4, W/RB 1, 4
llywiaudir (llywyawdyr) *n.* 'leader' (*GPC* llywiawdr) BB 3, W/RB 6
o *prep.* 'from' (causing lenition, *GPC* o¹) BB5, W/RB 2
rillethid see **llad**
ve *3 pl. dependent affixed pron.* (*GPC* hwy¹, wy²) BB 6
wyntwy *3 pl. independent pron.* 'they' (*GPC* hwynt-hwy) W/RB 3
y *prep.* 'to, belonging to' (*GPC* i² 5a) BB 1, 4, W/RB 4
y *preverbal particle* (*GPC* y²) BB 1, 4, W/RB 1
yn¹ see **en**
yn² *participial particle* (causing no mutation, *GPC* yn²) W/RB 3

Englynion by Cynddelw Brydydd Mawr for the warband of Madog son of Maredudd

It is again Arthur's men rather than Arthur himself who are referred to in an unusual praise poem by the twelfth-century court poet Cynddelw Brydydd Mawr (Cynddelw the Great Poet). Three out of the six panegyric poems in the Black Book of Carmarthen were composed by Cynddelw, a native of Powys who in his old age sang at the court of Lord Rhys, ruler of Deheubarth (d.1197). Also included in the collection is part of a penitential ode entitled in other sources *Marwysgafn Cynddelw*, 'Cynddelw's Deathbed poem', probably composed towards the end of his life.[88] The praise poems consist of a series of *englynion* for Rhys and an *awdl* for his father-in-law, Madog ap Maredudd, prince of Powys, possibly sung by Cynddelw during a visit to the southern ruler soon after

---

[88] See Nerys Ann Jones, '*Marwysgafyn Veilyr Brydyt*: Deathbed Poem?', *Cambrian Medieval Celtic Studies*, 47 (2004), 17–39 (pp. 34–35), and Catherine McKenna, 'Performing Penance and Poetic Performance in the Medieval Welsh Court', *Speculum*, 82 (2007), 70–96.

Madog's death in 1160. Preceding the *awdl* (on f. 52ʳ) is a series of five four-line *englynion*, linked by *cymeriad geiriol*.

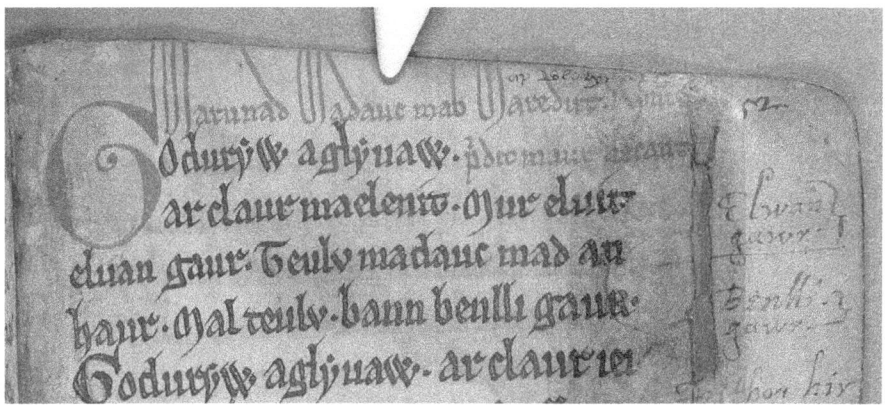

Fig. 1.8 NLW: Peniarth MS 1, f. 52ʳ.

The title is added by a rubricator: *Marunad Madauc mab Maredut, kyntelv prydit maur ae cant*, 'An elegy for Madog ap Maredudd, Cynddelw the Great Poet sang it'. The same title is given to the *awdl* but without the ascription. The latter is a formal elegy, opening and closing with prayers to God, lamenting Madog's death and praising his heroic qualities. The focus of the *englynion* is the *teulu* (warband) of Madog, which Cynddelw likens to those of Cynon ap Clydno Eidyn, Benlli Gawr of Powys and Arthur, before claiming that it is one of the three *Diwair Deulu*, the Three Faithful Warbands of the Island of Britain. The poem is also found in the Hendregadredd Manuscript with significant variation in line order and wording. It is fully discussed in Chapter 3 below, along with other poems containing references to Arthur by Cynddelw and his fellow court poets.

Pa gur …

It is interesting that each of the Black Book poems discussed above has a strong element of listing or cataloguing. This is also true of the untitled poem in *awdl* metre known by its opening words *Pa gur …*, 'What man …' — the only poem from the Black Book of Carmarthen which can be described as Arthurian.[89] It is often referred to as a dialogue poem, but the conversation between Arthur and the gatekeeper, Glewlwyd Gafaelfawr, is brief and most of the poem appears to be a monologue spoken by Arthur, listing the names of his followers, praising their heroic virtues and magical powers, and alluding to their exploits against

[89] Peniarth MS 1, ff. 47ᵛ–48ᵛ.

monsters, witches and giants as well as human enemies the length and breadth of the island of Britain. Some of these characters are totally obscure, some are known from native Welsh tradition but are not otherwise associated with Arthur, while over half are also found in *Culhwch ac Olwen*, leading Sims-Williams to suggest that the compilers of that tale may have had a vague memory of parts of *Pa gur*.[90] There are, however, a number of contradictions, not least in the role of Glewlwyd, who is Arthur's own gatekeeper in *Culhwch* but appears to be the guardian of a hostile fortress here. These inconsistencies have been interpreted by some scholars as evidence of the evolution of Arthurian traditions and by others as deliberate changes made for comic effect.[91]

Cai is the most prominent of Arthur's men in the poem, appearing together with Bedwyr as Arthur's closest companion, as he does in other medieval texts, *Culhwch ac Olwen*, the Triads and in the Latin Life of Saint Cadog by Lifris of Llancarfan which can be dated to around 1100. This and the fact that it contains forms which suggest an original text written in Old Welsh spelling have led most scholars to place the poem between 900 and 1100.[92] It could be a remnant of a saga, but it is more likely that the confrontation at the gate was used to provide a framework for a series of allusions to heroes and monsters and far-off places, their names evoking a wonderful world of magic and adventure, and, in the words of Sims-Williams, 'reminding the audience of half-forgotten stories and whetting their appetite for new ones'.[93] Its short lines and lively rhythm[94] may suggest that the poem is light-hearted and that Arthur is to be seen as a comic figure, the great war-leader having to endure the indignity of haggling with a gatekeeper in order to gain admission to a court. The fact that he refers to his followers' exploits using the past tense may suggest a garrulous old man harking back to former glories but a darker picture may have been intended of the great Arthur, having lost his court at Celli Wig and accompanied by only a handful of his most faithful followers, seeking shelter in a time of adversity.[95] Interpreting the poem is particularly difficult because it is incomplete, breaking

---

[90] See Sims-Williams, 'Arthurian Poems', pp. 39–40, and on the relationship between *Pa gur* and *Culhwch ac Olwen*, see *AMWL*, pp. 26–27, where a common author is suggested.
[91] See, for instance, John T. Koch, 'The Celtic Lands' in *Medieval Arthurian Literature: A Guide to Recent Research*, ed. by Norris J. Lacy (New York and London: Routledge, 1996), pp. 260–62, who concludes that the opening of *Pa gur* reflects an earlier stage in the development of the Arthurian material found in *Culhwch*, and *TYP*, p. 362, where Rachel Bromwich sees the episode at the gate in *Culhwch* as 'a burlesque of the poem's situation'.
[92] See below, notes on lines 16 and 25. John T. Koch has pointed out, in a review of *The Arthur of the Welsh*, *Speculum*, 69 (1994), 1127–29, that a date of composition in the eighth century is not implausible.
[93] 'Arthurian Poems', p. 38.
[94] The poem is made up of five-syllable lines, rhyming in sequences of irregular lengths. The metre corresponds to Marged Haycock's Class 1 line; see 'Metrical Models for the Poems in the Book of Taliesin', *EWP*, pp. 155–77 (pp. 162–68).
[95] See 'Arthurian Poems', p. 38.

off in mid-sentence due to the loss of a page or pages in the manuscript.

The poem will be presented a section at a time, accompanied by detailed discussion of matters of dating and interpretation and a full glossary.[96]

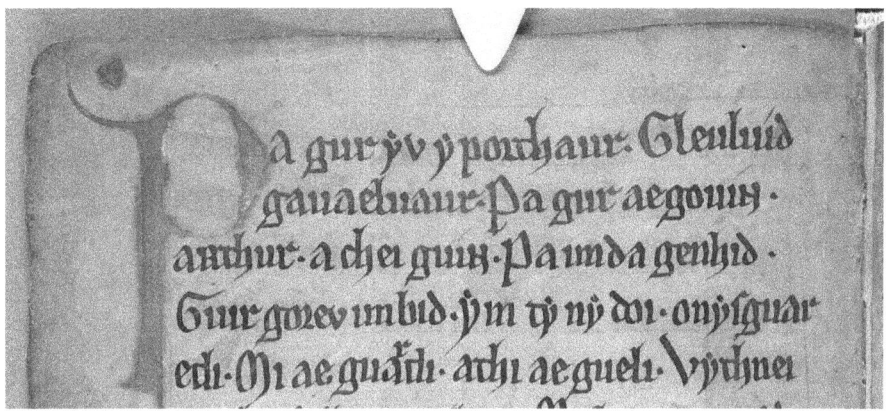

FIG. 1.9: NLW Peniarth MS 1, f. 47ᵛ.

Pa gur yv y porthaur. Gleuluid | gauaeluaur. Pa gur ae gouin. | arthur. A chei guin. Pa imda genhid. | Guir gorev im bid. Ym ty ny doi. Onysguar|edi.

        Pa gur yv y porthaur?
        Gleuluid Gauaeluaur.
        Pa gur a'e gouin?
4   Arthur, a Chei Guin.
        Pa imda genhid?
        Guir gorev im bid.
        Y'm ty ny doi
8   ony's guaredi.

        'What man is the gatekeeper?'
        'Glewlwyd Gafaelfawr.
        What man asks it?'
4   'Arthur and Cai Wyn.'
        'Who travels with you?'
        'The best men in the world.'
        'Into my house you will not come
8   unless you reveal [?]them.'

---

[96] I am indebted to Oliver Padel, on whose working edition of the poem this study is based. Padel, in turn, has drawn heavily on the first published edition of the poem by Brynley F. Roberts, 'Rhai o Gerddi Ymddiddan', pp. 296–309, and on the translations and discussion of Patrick Sims-Williams, 'Arthurian Poems', pp. 38–46, as well as the translation by Rachel Bromwich, *CO*, pp. xxxiv–vi.

This opening section of four rhyming couplets takes the form of a recognition dialogue between Glewlwyd, the gatekeeper, and presumably Arthur.

1 **Pa gur yv y porthaur?** The definite article is rare in early poetry and this is the only unambiguous instance in this poem; cf. l. 6 *im bid*, 'in [the] world'. After *yw*, the form *'r* might be expected (see *GMW*, p. 24). This would give the required five syllables to the line.

2 **Gleuluid Gauaeluaur** In *Culhwch ac Olwen*, *Glewlwyt Gauaeluawr* ('bold-grey of mighty grasp') is Arthur's own gatekeeper, but his role is essentially the same in both texts, refusing entry to the hero until he is given the assurances he requires. Similar exchanges with gatekeepers occur in a number of medieval texts, suggesting that the poet was perhaps drawing on a stock narrative formula well known to his audience. For parallels in texts written in Welsh, Irish and Latin, see Sims-Williams, 'Arthurian Poems', p. 40, and *TYP*, p. 362. John T. Koch, however, argues that this episode has its roots in Celtic mythology in 'Further to *tongu do dia toinges mo thuath*, etc', *Études celtiques*, 29 (1992), 249–61.

4 **Kei Guin** *Gwynn*, 'fair, fair-haired, blessed', is one of two epithets regularly applied to Cai in Welsh sources (again in lines 76 and 81), the other being *hir*, 'tall' (see 67n); *TYP*, p. 311. Note that there may be unwritten lenition here (compare line 81), though not necessarily so; see *GMW*, p. 19.

5 **Pa imda genhid?** It is unusual to see *pa*, *py* being used substantivally; see *GMW*, pp. 76–77. Its usual meaning is 'what (thing)?' or sometimes 'why?' but there are nine examples of it being used to mean 'who?' in an elegy by Cynddelw composed in 1179 (*CBT* III 21.21–32), and this is the most suitable meaning for the gatekeeper's question here; see *GPC* pa¹.

7 **Y'm ty ny doi** This is unexpected. In what sense was it Glewlwyd's house? It is interesting to note that it is the archaic form *doit* which is used in the other two examples of the 2 sing.pres.indic. of *dyuot* in the Black Book. Here we find the standard Middle Welsh form rhyming with *guaredi*: see *GMW*, pp. 115–16.

8 **ony's guaredi** The usual meanings of *gwaret* (< *gwo-*, *gwa-* + *red* (as in *redec*), lit. 'to run under') are 'to rescue, help; remove, get rid of, take off (clothing etc.)' but none of these work well here. Thomas Jones in 'Early Evolution', p. 17, suggests 'to disclose, reveal' and puts forward a theory that when his followers arrive at the gate they have been made invisible by Arthur.

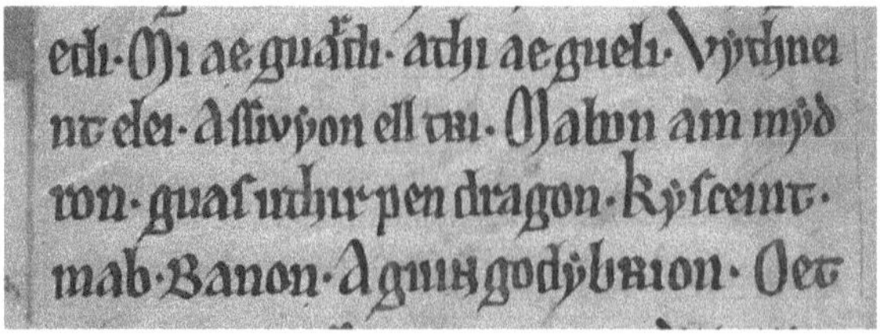

FIG. 1.10: NLW Peniarth MS 1, f. 47ᵛ.

Mi ae guardi. athi ae gueli. Vythnei|nt elei. Assivyon ell tri. Mabon am myd|ron. Guas uthir pen dragon. Kysceint. | mab. Banon. A guin godybrion.

        Mi a'e guar[e]di,
        a thi a'e gueli:
        vythneint Elei,
12   a ssivyon ell tri;
        Mabon am Mydron,
        guas Uthir Pendragon;
        Kysceint mab Banon,
16   a Guin Godybrion.

        I shall reveal them,
        and you shall see them:
        the … of Elái,
12   and able men all three:
        Mabon son of Modron,
        servant of Uthr Pendragon;
        Cysgaint (?) son of Banon,
16   and Gwyn Goddyfrion.

It is Arthur alone who speaks for most of the rest of the poem. He starts by listing three of his champions, Mabon, Cysgaint (?) and Gwyn.

9   **guar[e]di** In the MS the *r* is written above the word and the *e* is missing. The form can be understood as 3 sing.pres./fut. indicative of *gwaret* with an old relative ending -*y(δ)* (see *GMW*, p. 119). This means that the sentence has an emphatic construction (also possible in the following line): 'It is I who will reveal them and you who will see them'. There are also a very few examples of -*y(δ)* as a 1 sing.pres/fut.indic. ending (e.g. *EWSP* 'Gwyn ap Nudd', 3b *gogyuerchit*). which would give a more neutral meaning: 'I will reveal them'.

10   **gueli** Again, this form could be 2 sing. or 3 sing.pres./fut.indic. of *gweled* (see line 8n).

11   **vythneint Elei** The form *vythneint* (<*vyth*, 'eight', + *neint* pl. *nant*, 'stream') does not make much sense here. It is probably an error, as Sims-Williams suggests ('Arthurian Poems', n. 28), possibly influenced by a scribe's awareness that *Elei* was the name of a river or by confusion with the word *gwyth*, 'stream'. It can be emended to *wytheint*, 'birds of prey' (*GPC* wythaint), perhaps used figuratively for the three warriors named below, or a lenited form of *gwytheint*, 'anger, wrath, fury of war'.

Elei appears to be a place name or possibly a personal name derived from a place name. It may be the river name Elái (River Ely), near Llandaf in Glamorganshire, but cf. *eryr Eli*, 'the eagle of Eli' (*EWSP* 'Canu Heledd' 34b), referring possibly to a river in the old Powys.

12   **ssivyon** The doubling of initial *s* is unusual, but here it was probably felt to be in the middle of a word (MS *assivyon*), where doubling is common (e.g. *gueisson*, line 17).

13   **Mabon am Mydron** Mabon also features in *Culhwch ac Olwen* as one of Arthur's chief warriors who hunts the Twrch Trwyth, but he seems to be best known in Welsh tradition as a famous prisoner, incarcerated since the dawn of time: see *TYP* no. 52. His name derives from that of a Celtic god, *Maponus*, whose cult was particularly popular in North Britain in Roman times (*TYP*, pp. 424–28). *Mydron*, a variant form of *Modron*, the name of Mabon's mother, also derives from that of a deity (*TYP*, pp. 449–51). See l. 23 below for *Mabon am Melld*, who may have originated as a doublet of this figure.

14   **guas Uthir Pendragon** There is no other reference to Mabon as a servant of Uthr, who is best known as the father of Arthur in Geoffrey of Monmouth's *Historia Regum Britanniae*. He also appears as a great magician in the Triads, again in an Arthurian context (*TYP* no. 28) and is possibly named as the father of Arthur by thirteenth-century court poet Y Prydydd Bychan (see Chapter 3 below), and as the father of Madog in the Dialogue of Arthur and the Eagle (Chapter 5) and other sources. He may also be the speaker of the first part of a poem known as 'the Elegy for Uthr Pendragon' in the Book of Taliesin (Chapter 4). While none of these texts can be assumed to pre-date Geoffrey's *Historia*, the influence of the latter's delineation of Uthr is not obvious in any of them. See *LPBT*, introduction to poem 24.

15   **Kysceint mab Banon** This character does not appear elsewhere, but one of Arthur's men in *Culhwch ac Olwen* is called *Yscawin mab Panon* (< *ysgafn*, 'light', or perhaps the eponym of Porth Ysgewin (Portskewett in Gwent) and *banon*, 'queen'). *Kysceint* may be a corruption of this name, or it is possibly a scribal error for *Kysteint*, a derivative of the Latin *Constantinus*, Constantine; see Sims-Williams, 'Arthurian Poems', n. 31.

16   **Guin Godybrion** He is listed among Arthur's followers in *Culhwch ac Olwen*, and a corrupt form of his name appears in a late pedigree among the sons of Iaen, a kinsman of Arthur (see *CO*, p. 96). Nothing is known of him apart from his name. *Godybrion* is possibly a place name (< *go-*, 'under', + *dyfryon*, a rare plural form of *dwfyr*, 'water'). The spelling with *b* for [v] suggests an original written in Old Welsh orthography (cf. *Anguas*, line 25); see Sims-Williams, 'Arthurian Poems', pp. 39–40.

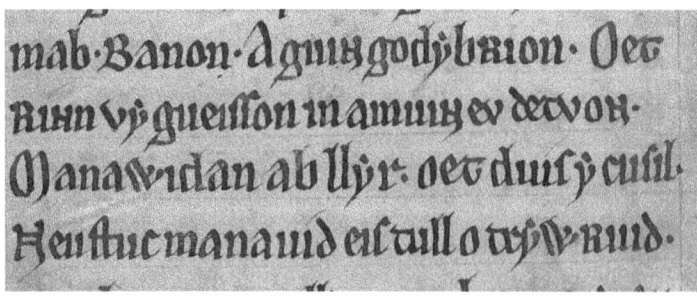

FIG. 1.11: NLW Peniarth MS 1, f. 47^v.

Oet | rinn vy gueisson in amuin ev detvon. | Manawidan ab llyr. Oet duis y cusil. | Neustuc manauid eis tull o trywruid

      Oet rinn vy gueisson,
      in amuin eu detvon.
      Manawid(an) ab Llyr,
   20 oet duis y cusil;
      neu's tuc Manauid
      eis tull o Trywruid.

      Steadfast were my men,
      defending their just claims/rights.
      Manawyd son of Llŷr,
   20 whose counsel was weighty;
      Manawyd brought back
      shattered spears from Tryfrwyd.

The poem is from now on couched entirely in the past tense, as Arthur reminisces about former glories achieved by his followers. It is not clear whether they are actually in Arthur's company; as Sims-Williams has suggested ('Arthurian Poems', p. 41), they may all be dead. Next on his list is Manawyd(an) son of Llŷr, a character who does not otherwise appear as a warrior figure.

18 **in amuin eu detvon** 'Fighting for' or 'defending' their 'customs' or 'rights'. The custom of his court is summed up by Arthur in *Culhwch ac Olwen* (*CO*, ll. 136–38): 'We are noblemen as long as others seek us out. The greater the gifts we bestow, the greater will be our nobility, and our fame and our honour'. According to Padel (*AMWL*, p. 30) these two references seem to foreshadow the chivalric ethos of later Arthurian romance.

19 **Manawid(an) ab Llyr** The metre suggests the form *Manawyd*, an attested variant (see *AyG*, l. 45, *LPBT*, 8.47, and below l. 22), without what might have been understood as a diminutive ending, which gives the more common form *Manawydan* (see Patrick Sims-Williams, *Irish Influence on Medieval Welsh Literature* [*IIMWL*] (Oxford: University Press, 2011), pp. 11–12). Manawydan son of Llŷr, a prominent figure in the Four Branches of the *Mabinogi* who also appears in the Triads, is named as one of Arthur's men who helps to hunt the Twrch Trwyth in *Culhwch ac Olwen*; see *TYP*, pp. 432–35.

20 **oet duis y cusil** Lit. 'who was weighty his counsel', with the relative pronoun omitted before *oeð*; see *GMW*, p. 61. Compare *deu unben degyn dwys eu kussyl*, 'two mighty chiefs, deep their counsel', referring to Cadwaladr and Cynan, saviours of Britain against the English (*Armes Prydein: The Prophecy of Britain from the Book of Taliesin*, ed. by Ifor Williams, trans. by Rachel Bromwich (Dublin: Dublin Institute of Advanced Studies, 1972), l. 165). Bromwich notes (*TYP*, p. 442n) how well this phrase describing Manawydan agrees with his behaviour in the Third Branch of the *Mabinogi*, where he is portrayed, not

as a warrior, but as a prudent nobleman; see Catherine McKenna, 'Learning Lordship: The Education of Manawydan' in *Ildánach, Ildírech: A Festschrift for Proinsias MacCana*, ed. by John Carey, John T. Koch and Pierre-Yves Lambert (Andover and Aberystwyth: Celtic Studies Publications, 1999), pp. 101–20.
Note the generic rhyme between *cusil* and *Llyr* in the previous line: see footnote 24 above.

21   **neu's tuc** The infixed object pronoun *'s* is proleptic, anticipating the true object *eis tull*. It causes the initial *d-* of the following verb to be unvoiced (provected) *d-* > *t-* and this is unusually shown in the spelling.

22   **eis tull** *Eis* is most probably the plural of *asen*, 'a rib; a lath', used figuratively for spears (see *GPC* asen²), cf. *AyG*, l. 265, *Heesid ais yng nghynnor trais*, 'He cast lances in the forefront of battle'. It has been suggested that it might be a rare plural form of *aes*, 'shield', as this would give a better meaning with the adj. *twll*, 'holed, pierced', but a line from the Black Book where *eis* is juxtaposed with *aessawr*, the usual plural form of *aes*, makes this unlikely; see *EWSP*, 'Gwyn' 11b. The reference to arms honourably damaged in battle is a common topos in medieval Welsh poetry and prose, used here to suggest the ferocity with which Manawyd fought. Manawyd[an] is not depicted as a warrior in any other source. In fact, in the Third Branch of the *Mabinogi* he avoids conflict on every occasion.

Trywruid This is possibly a reference to an unlocated battle listed in *Historia Brittonum* as one of Arthur's victories; see l. 28 below. There are examples, however, of the word being used as a common noun in poetry with the meaning 'battle, conflict' (see *GPC* tryfrwyd). In addition, it has been suggested that *o trywruid*, here and in another poem from the Black Book (*Ymddiddan Myrddin a Thaliesin*, ed. by A. O. H. Jarman (Cardiff: University of Wales Press, 1967), l. 4), can be interpreted as an adjective consisting of the prefixes *go-* and *try-* with *bruyd*, 'variegated, bloodstained, broken'. As Sims-Williams points out, however, the tense of the verb here, preterite not imperfect, implies a specific event rather than repeated habit, making a place name the more likely interpretation ('Arthurian Poems', p. 41).

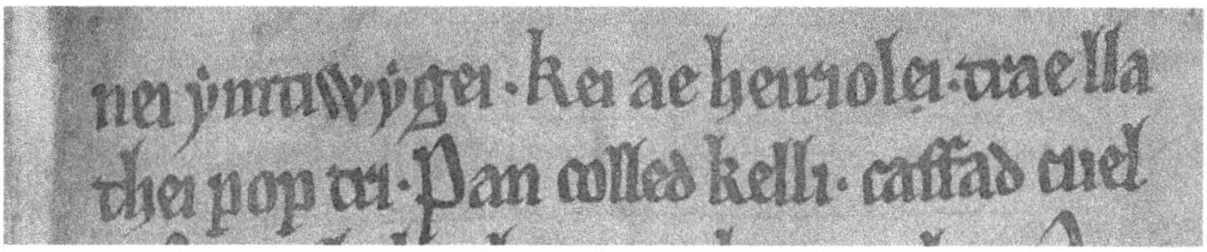

FIG. 1.12: NLW Peniarth MS 1, ff. 47ᵛ–48ʳ.

A mabon am melld. Maglei guaed ar | guelld. Ac anguas edeinauc. A lluch. | llauynnauc. Oetin diffreidauc ar ei-|din cyminauc. Argluit ae llochei my || nei ymtiwygei.

   A Mabon am Melld,
24 maglei guaed ar guelld.
   Ac Anguas Edeinauc,
   a Lluch Llauynnauc;
   oetin diffreidauc
28 ar Eidin cyminauc.
   Argluit a'e llochei,
   my nei ymtiwygei.

   And Mabon son of Mellt,
24 he used to stain grass with blood.
   And Anwas the Winged
   and Llwch Llaw-wynnog:
   they were accustomed to defend
28 at Edinburgh on the border.
   A lord would give them refuge,
   ?my nephew would avenge

Arthur goes on to name three mysterious warriors, Mabon son of Mellt, Anwas the Winged and Llwch Llawwynnog, who are also found in Culhwch's list of Arthur's followers. Nothing is known of the fighting at Edinburgh alluded to here and the identity of the lord who protects the three is uncertain.

23 **Mabon am Melld** Also named in *Culhwch ac Olwen* as one of Arthur's men involved in the hunt for the boar Ysgithrwyn but otherwise unknown. On the derivation of *Mellt* from the common noun meaning 'lightning' or from a root **meldo-*, 'gentle, mild, pleasant', see Jarman, 'Arthurian Allusions', p. 108. This Mabon was clearly regarded in medieval times as a distinct character from Mabon am Mydron of l. 13 above, but it is possible that they originated as names for the same person, with Mellt his father and Modron his mother.

24 **maglei guaed ar guelld** Lit. 'he spotted blood upon grass', cf. *The Poems of Taliesin* [PT], ed. by Ifor Williams, English version by J. E. Caerwyn Williams (Dublin: Institute of Advanced Studies, 1973), II 24, *a gwyar a uaglei ar dillat*, 'and blood he spotted on clothes', i.e. he stained clothes with blood. On *magl*, a

borrowing from Latin *macula*, 'a stain', see *GPC*.

25   **Anguas Edeinauc** He appears as *Anwas Edeinawc*, coupled with *Llwch Llawwynnyawc*, in Culhwch's list of Arthur's followers and, according to Sims-Williams (*IIMWL*, p. 174n241), *Henwas Edeinawc mab Erim*, whose fleetness of foot is celebrated in 'Culhwch', is probably the same character. *Anwas* is in origin an adjective with the meaning 'wrathful, fierce, agitated, turbulent, violent' (< *an-*, neg. prefix + *gwas*, 'rest, tranquillity'); see *GPC*. The form in the Black Book with the lack of mutation to the second element *-guas* probably reflects an exemplar in Old Welsh orthography. The epithet *Edeinawc*, 'winged one', derives from *adain*, 'wing', + adj. ending *-iawg* with penultimate affection (see *GPC* adeiniog) and is found as a personal name, *Edenawc*, 'The Winged One', in Triad no. 22.

26   **Lluch Llauynnauc** He is identified with *Lloch Llawwynnyawc* of *Culhwch ac Olwen*, the father of three men called Gwair from beyond *Mor Terrwyn* who are referred to as maternal uncles to Arthur: see *CO*, pp. 74, 97. Sims-Williams (*IIMWL*, p. 162) concludes that *Lluch* (*u* = /u/) is not likely to be a Welsh form of the Irish *Lug* but a native Welsh personal name, cognate with Gaulish names in *Lucc-* and Irish names in *Locc-*. For another example of *Lluch* with an alliterating epithet in the Black Book, see *Llwch Llawengin* (Jones, 'Stanzas of the Graves', verse 31). The epithet *Llauynnauc* may derive from *llaw*, 'hand', and *gwynnawc*, 'windy, stormy' (< *gwynt*, 'wind' + adj. ending *-awc*), or possibly *gwynawc*, 'painful; fierce' (< *gwŷn*, 'pain' + *-awc*) although this meaning is not found in medieval texts (see *GPC*). It does not appear other than as part of Lluch's name, and may be a corrupt form of a more common epithet like *llyminiog*; see Chapter 4, *Preideu Annwn* 19n below, and *IIMWL*, pp. 162–63.

28   **ar Eidin cyminauc** The name *Eidin*, identified by scholars with Castle Rock in Edinburgh, is rarely found in medieval texts other than the poems of the Book of Aneirin, except as the cognomens of characters like Clydno Eidyn (see *TYP*, pp. 313–14). *Ar*, 'upon', would work here if *Eidin* stands for *minit Eidin*, 'the hill of Edinburgh', as in line 43 below. *Ar* is also sometimes used with place names to mean 'beside, near; in the direction of, towards, facing' (see *GPC* ar¹ 1g, 2a).

This is the only example of *cyminauc*, 'bordering, neighbouring, ajacent'. Although its etymology is straightforward (see Glossary), its force is not clear — perhaps 'on the border'. The Firth of Forth and River Forth were frequently regarded in the middle ages as dividing Britain into two islands, with the northern island imagined as a kingdom (see Dauvit Broun, *Scottish Independence and the Idea of Britain from the Picts to Alexander III* (Edinburgh 2007), pp. 53–60). Because Edinburgh is located near the southern shore of the Firth of Forth, it could be conceived as standing near this border.

30   **my nei ymtiwygei** *My nei* could be the 1 sing.poss. pronoun *vy* (with Old

Welsh spelling) followed by *nei*, 'nephew', identifying the *argluit* of the previous line as a nephew of Arthur. This could perhaps be Medrawd (Modred of later tradition), although he is not referred to by name in this poem or claimed to be Arthur's nephew in Welsh sources before Geoffrey of Monmouth's *Historia Regum Britanniae* (see *TYP*, pp. 445–46). It is possible that this is an effort by a scribe to make sense of an obscure form. It may have been the conjunction *myn y*, 'where, wherever' (see *GPC* man¹) and a 3 pl. infixed object pronoun, spelt here *ei* but usually combined with the preverbal particle, as in *CBT* IV 18.68 *man y cefais*, 'wherever I received it'. If this is so, a *h-* would be expected before the initial vowel of the following verb as in l. 31 below (see *GMW*, p. 23).

Ymtiwygei is a hapax form but it can be interpreted as the 3 sing.imperf. of *diwygio*, 'to reform, improve, correct, amend, redress', with a reflexive prefix *ym-* giving a possible meaning 'to obtain amends for oneself', i.e. take vengeance. Another possibility is a form of the verb *difyngaf: difwng*, 'to rush, attack', but the reflexive force is unclear. A tentative meaning for the line is 'where he used to take vengeance for them' or 'my nephew would take vengeance'.

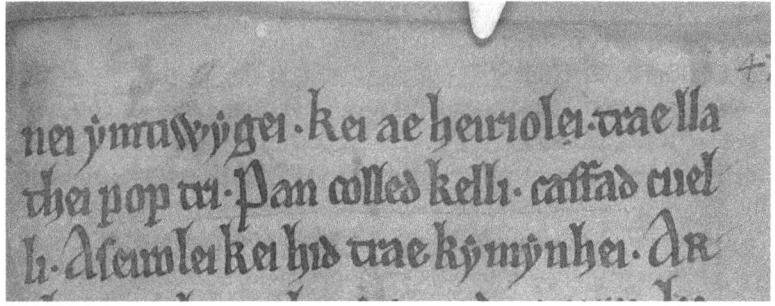

FIG. 1.13: NLW Peniarth MS 1, f. 48ʳ.

kei ae heiriolei. Trae lla|thei pop tri. Pan colled kelli. Caffad cuel-|li. Aseirolei kei hid trae kymynhei.

    Kei a'e heiriolei,
32 tra'e llathei pop tri.
    Pan colled Kelli,
    caffad cuelli.
    A's eirolei Kei
36 hid tra'e kymynhei.

    Cai would plead with them,
32 while he killed three at a time.
    When Celli was lost,
    fury was endured.
    Cai would plead with them
36 for as long as he cut them down.

This is the beginning of a section where the focus is on Cai. Could he be the *argluit* referred to in the previous section? It is not clear who his opponents are here. Could they be the four *gueisson* above? Lines 31–32 and 35–36, enclosing the couplet 33–34, suggest that the loss of Arthur's court, *Kelli Wic*, was connected with a story of Cai's attacks on Arthur's men, a story which is hinted at in *Culhwch ac Olwen* (*CO*, ll. 981–84). This would, as Sims-Williams suggests, make sense of the idea of Cai pleading with his opponents as he strikes them down: see 'Arthurian Poems', p. 41. Note that the main verb in both couplets, *eir(i)olei*, is imperfect, indicating continued or repeated action on Cai's part.

32   **llathei** The *-th-*, caused by provection (*GMW*, pp. 14, 128), suggests that this is an imperfect subjunctive form of *llat*. The subjunctive conveys uncertainty or indefiniteness and is commonly found following *tra*, cf. l. 73 below and see *GPC* tra³.

33   **pan colled Kelli** Understood as a reference to *Kelli Wic*, Arthur's court in Cornwall in *Culhwch ac Olwen*, the Triads and the work of the Poets of the Princes: see *TYP*, pp. 3–4; O. J. Padel, 'Some South-Western Sites with Arthurian Associations' in *AW*, pp. 234–38; id., 'Oral and Literary Culture in Medieval Cornwall' in *Medieval Celtic Literature and Society*, ed. by Helen Fulton (Dublin: Four Courts Press, 2005), pp. 113–15. As no tale of the court being 'lost' is known, it is possible but unlikely that *kelli* is a common noun here, 'grove, copse, woodland'.

34   **cuelli** A rare abstract noun formed from the adj. *cuall*, 'sudden, quick, hasty, rash' (with penultimate affection). The only other example is found in a poem by the thirteenth-century court poet Prydydd y Moch (*CBT* v 2.34). Note, however, that the names *Kelli* and *Cuel* appear together in the list of warriors of Arthur's court in *Culhwch ac Olwen* (ll. 297–98). Are these odd names due to faulty memory of this couplet or are they a deliberate echo of it with its meaning distorted?

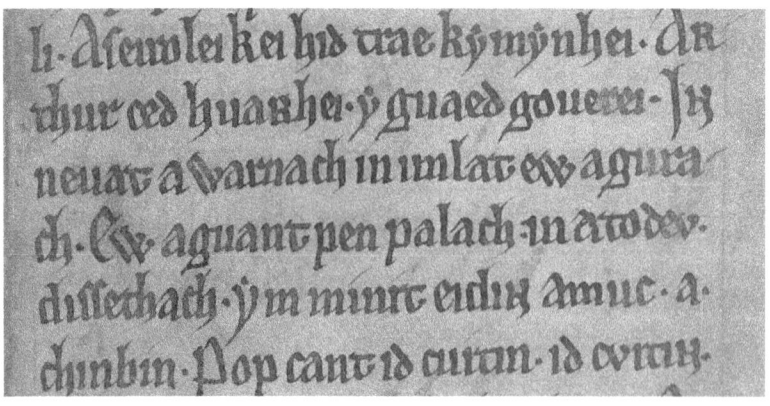

Fig. 1.14: NLW Peniarth MS 1, f. 48ʳ.

Ar-|thur ced huarhei. Y guaed gouerei. In | neuat a warnach in imlat ew a gura-|ch. Ew aguant pen palach. In atodev. | dissethach. Ym minit eidin amuc. a. | chinbin. Pop cant id cuitin.

        Arthur ced huar[t]hei,
        y guaed gouerei
        in neuat Awarnach
40   in imlat, ew a gurach.
        Ew a guant Penpalach
        in atodeu Dissethach.
        Ym Minit Eidin
44   amuc a chinbin:
        pop cant id cuitin.

        Though Arthur laughed,
        he caused her blood to flow
        in Afarnach's hall,
40   fighting, he and a hag.
        He stabbed Penpalach
        in the dwellings of Disethach.
        On the mountain of Edinburgh
44   he fought with dogheads:
        by the hundred they fell.

There is some uncertainty about the interpretation of this passage, and especially about the identity of its subject. Before discussing the possibilities and looking at parallels in *Culhwch ac Olwen* it is wise to focus on the text itself.

37   **Arthur ced huar[t]hei** The verbal form can be understood as 3 sing.imperf. subj. of *hwerthin, chwerthin* (stem *chwardd-*), 'to laugh, smile, be merry' (on the *chw-, hw-* variant, see *GMW*, p. 11, and on the *-th-*, see 32n above). The word-order, with the subject before the conjunction, is unusual but may be poetic. Alternatively, *Arthur* may here be an error for the adjective *aruthyr*, 'terrible, dreadful, frightening; fierce, cruel, harsh' (with an epenthetic *-y*) used adverbially: 'terribly though he/she laughed'. This error also occurs in the Red Book of Hergest text of Cynddelw's elegy for Rhirid Flaidd: Red Book version (col. 1430.25) *Ruthyr* **arthur** *eirthyan arthen unbenn*; Hendregadredd version (see *CBT* III 24.95) *Ruthyr* **aruthyr** *eirthya6 Arthen unbenn*.

38   **y guaed gouerei** The verb can be intransitive, 'to gush, stream, run', or transitive, 'to cause to flow, pour'. The second is the most likely with the *y* preceding the object, *guaed*, understood as a 3 sing.fem. possessive pronoun referring to the hag of l. 40: 'he made her blood flow'. The word-order is object + verb (without particle *a*), an order common in early poetry though there are no other clear examples in this poem.

For a similar idea, see Stanzas of the Graves no. 49 (the name of the hero is lost): *tra'th lathei, chvartei vrthid*, 'while he killed/struck you, he would laugh at you'.

39   **Awarnach** There are no other examples of this form. Since the line has six syllables, the word could be emended to *Wrnach*, the name of the giant who is slain by Cai in his own hall in *Culhwch ac Olwen* (*CO*, l. 747n).

40   **in imlat, ew a gurach** The fight between Arthur and a hag in the hall of Afarnach (or Wrnach) is not known elsewhere, but it is reminiscent of the final marvel achieved by Arthur in *Culhwch ac Olwen*, to collect the blood of *Y Widon Ordu*, 'The Very Black Witch' (see *CO*, ll. 652–53n). This happened, not in a hall as here, but in her cave at *Pennant Gouut*, 'the head of Grief Valley', in the uplands of Hell (*CO*, pp. 1207–08n).

41   **Ew a guant Penpalach** If *ef* is to be understood as an independent pronoun, it could be the subject of the verb, 'he stabbed Penpalach', or the object, 'it is he whom Penpalach stabbed'. To give a five-syllable line, the preverbal particle *a* may be omitted (cf. l. 38 above) and the pronoun understood as a rather early example of a particle (*GMW*, p. 172), but ambiguity regarding the subject of the verb remains.

Penpalach is thought to be a combination of the noun *pen*, 'head', and the rare word *palach* containing the element *pal-*, 'to dig, pierce, wound, hit, scratch, claw', found in *pâl*, 'spade', *paladr*, 'spear shaft', and *pladur*, 'scythe', and the nominalising ending *-ach*, which often has unpleasant connotations (see Sims-Williams, *IIMWL*, pp. 183–84). It is understood as the name of 'an intrinsically unsavoury character or a monster of some kind, not known elsewhere', cf. below 84n *Cath Paluc*, and see also J. Lloyd-Jones, 'Welsh *Palach*, etc.', *Ériu*, 16 (1952), 123–31.

42   **Dissethach** Another unknown name with an *-ach* ending. A slightly similar personal name, *Bryssethach*, occurs in Culhwch's list of Arthur's men.

43   **minit Eidin** See above l. 28n. On the North in the literary imagination of medieval Wales, and especially as a place where monsters dwelt, see Marged Haycock, 'Early Welsh Poets Look North' in *Beyond the Gododdin: Dark Age Scotland in Medieval Wales* [*BG*], ed. by Alex Woolf (St Andrews: The Committee for Dark Age Studies, University of St Andrews, 2013), pp. 7–39 (p. 13). The 'mountain' may be Castle Rock in Edinburgh or Arthur's Seat. There is no evidence, however, that the latter's association with Arthur is earlier than the sixteenth century according to Norman Dixon, 'The Place-Names of Midlothian' (unpublished PhD thesis, University of Edinburgh, 1947, published 2009 in digital form <http://www.spns.org.uk>), p. 42.

44   **amuc a chinbin** The *cinbin* are probably the *Cynocephali*, dog-headed monsters who were thought to inhabit remote parts of the world (< *cyn-* the original root of *ci*, 'hound', + *pin*, rare plural form of *pen*, 'head', cf. Middle Irish *conchend*). The only other example of this word is found in *Kat Godeu* in the Book of Taliesin. For more on the *cinbin* see *LPBT* 5.209n and Sims-Williams, 'Arthurian Poems', p. 42.

If Arthur is the subject of this section, then the speaker may be his companion, Cai. If the emendation from *Arthur* to *aruthyr* is accepted, then this is a continuation of Arthur's listing of Cai's exploits. Another possibility is that Arthur is talking about himself in the third person in line 37 but that Cai is the subject of the rest of the section: 'Although Arthur laughed (mocked?), [Cai] caused her blood to flow ...'. Comparison with *Culhwch ac Olwen* is not particularly helpful as it is Cai who kills the giant Wrnach and Arthur who kills the hag.

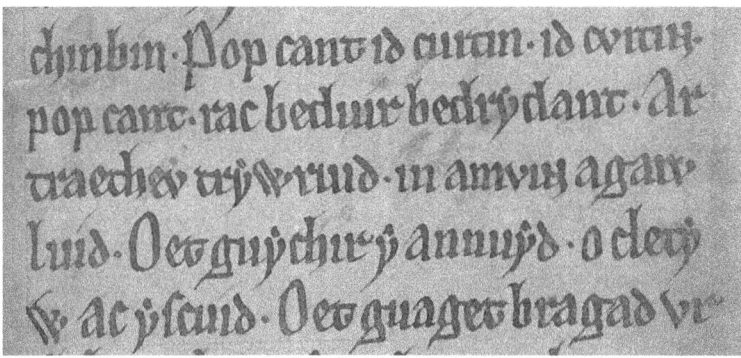

FIG. 1.15: NLW Peniarth MS 1, f. 48ʳ.

Id cvitin. | pop cant. Rac beduir bedrydant. Ar | traethev trywruid. In amvin agarv|luid. Oet guychir y annuyd. o clety|w. ac yscuid.

            Id cuitin pop cant,
            rac Beduir Bedrydant.
48   Ar traetheu Trywruid,
            In amuin a Garuluid,
            oet guychir y annuyd
            o cletyw ac yscuid.

            They fell by the hundred
            before Bedwyr ? the Powerful.
48   On the shores of Tryfrwyd,
            fighting with Garwlwyd,
            violent was his nature
            with sword and shield.

This section, which is linked to the previous one by repetition, focusses on Bedwyr (Bedivere), who often appears as Cai's companion in medieval Welsh Arthurian literature. A short statement in *Culhwch ac Olwen* conveys concisely the courage with which he acts in these texts and also his subordinate role to Cai: *nyt arswydwys y neges yd elhei Gei idi*, 'he never feared the quest upon which Cai went' (see *CO*, ll. 393–94 and *TYP*, p. 287).

45-46 Pop cant id cuitin. | Id cuitin pop cant Mirror verbal repetition is fairly common in the short-line *awdlau*; see, for example, *Angar Kyfundawt LPBT* 4.106-18, *Kadeir Teyrnon* 9.18-19, *Eg gorffowys PT* IV. It is not clear, however, whether we should take lines 45 and 46 together as referring to the same occasion, or separately as making the same observation about two different battles. For examples of similar numerical exaggeration using multiples of a hundred and of three hundred (see below ll. 159-60) in praise poetry as well as prose, see Jones, 'Early Evolution', pp. 10-11.

47 rac Beduir Bedrydant Although there are a number of examples of *pedrydant* in the poetic corpus, its derivation and meaning are obscure. It appears to contain the prefix *pedr(y)-* from the numeral *pedwar*, 'four', which is also used to give a favourable meaning, e.g. *pedrylaw*, 'dextrous' (with *llaw*, 'hand'). The second element is uncertain; it may be *tant*, 'string, sinew', giving the adjective the meaning 'well-sinewed, strong, powerful'. This would suit the examples which refer mostly to warriors or to their fame; see *LPBT* 5.60n. There are, however, no instances of *tant* being used with this meaning before the early modern period; see *GPC* tant.

If *pedrydant* is an epithet for *Beduir* as suggested by its lenition (see 4n above), then it brings to mind the patronymic given him in Triad no. 21 and the Romance of Gereint, *Bedwyr mab Bedrawc* or *Bedrawt*, which also contains the element *pedr(y)-*; see *TYP*, p. 286.

48 ar traetheu Trywruid This phrase closely echoes the wording of the *Historia Brittonum*: *Decimum gessit bellum in litore fluminis quod vocatur Tribruit*, 'He [Arthur] waged the tenth battle on the shore of the river which is called Tribruit' (Sims-Williams, 'Arthurian Poems', p. 41). On *Tryfrwyd* see above 22n.

49 in amuin a Garuluid This is probably an allusion to *Gwrgi Garwlwyd*, whose killing is listed in Triad no. 32 as one of the *Teir Mat Gyflauan*, 'the Three Fortunate Slaughters'. He is described as an evil character who 'used to make a corpse of the Cymry every day, and two on each Saturday so as not to (slay) one on the Sunday'. For the suggestion that the etymology of his name, 'Man-Hound', and that of the epithet, 'rough-grey', might indicate that he was imagined as a werewolf or one of the 'dog-heads' of line 44, see *TYP*, p. 385. On the fact that the sons of Gwrgi's slayer are named 'the Three Chieftains of Deira and Bernicia', placing Gwrgi in the Old North, see Sims-Williams, 'Arthurian Poems', pp. 42-43. In order to have a five-syllable line, the preposition *a* may be deleted.

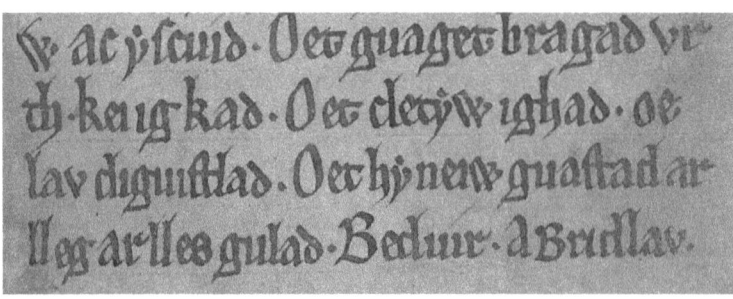

The Black Book of Carmarthen

Fig. 1.16: NLW Peniarth MS 1, f. 48^{r–v}.

Oet guaget bragad vr|th.kei ig kad. Oet cletyw ighad. Oe | lav diguistlad. Oet hyneiw guastad ar|lleg ar lles gulad. Beduir. A Bridlav. || nau cant guarandau. Chuechant y eirth|au. A talei y ortinav.

52 Oet guaget bragad
    vrth Kei ig kad;
    oet cletyw ighad;
    o'e lav diguistlad;
56 oet hyneiw guastad,
    arlleg ar lles gulad.
    Beduir a Bridlav:
    nau cant guarandau,
60 chuechant y eirthau
    a talei y ortinav.

52 Useless was an army
    compared with Cai in battle;
    he was a sword in battle;
    into his hand pledges were given;
56 he was a steadfast chief,
    a defender for the good of the land.
    Bedwyr ...
    the submitting of nine hundred
60 [and] six hundred for scattering
    was the value of his attack.

Both Cai and Bedwyr are praised in turn for their military prowess, with the idea that they were victorious against vast numbers of both human and monstrous opponents again coming to the fore. The opening section, which focusses on Cai, is linked by initial repetition of *oet*, 'was', giving, in the words of Sims-Williams, 'elegiac colour' to Arthur's boasting ('Arthurian Poems', p. 38).

54 **oet cletyw ighad** It is very unusual for a weapon to be used as a metaphor for a warrior in medieval Welsh poetry, but cf. Cynddelw's eulogy for Owain Cyfeiliog (*CBT* II 16.161–68) where the ruler of southern Powys is likened to a shield, a blade and a sword.

Ighad is another way of expressing the nasal mutation in the combination *yn*, 'in', + *cad*, 'battle', cf. line 53 above, *ig kad*; but *kad* here rhymes with itself, which is metrically poor, and it is tempting to see the form *ighad* as a corruption of some adjective qualifying *cletyw*.

55 **o'e lav diguistlad** An almost identical line appears in a fragment of an elegy for Madog ?son of Uthr in the Book of Taliesin: *LPBT* 20.5–6, *Mab Vthyr cyn lleas, o'e law dywystlas*, 'Before the son of Uthr was slain, he pledged himself by his hand'. Here the *o'e* may contain the preposition *o*, 'from' or 'by' (denoting the agent of the impersonal verb; see *GPC* o^1 4b); 'from/by his hand pledges are given'. It is more likely, however, to be an example of *o*, 'to', which is found only in combination with the infixed possessive pronoun (*GPC* o^5): 'to his hand pledges are given'.

56–57 **oet hyneiw guastad Arlleg | ar lles gulad** The syntax is ambiguous: the subject could be contained in *oet* ('he was…'), with *hyneiw guastad* the complement in the first line and *arlleg ar lles gulad* in the second; or else *hyneiw guastad* could be the subject, with *arlleg ar lles gulad* as the complement: 'The steadfast chief was a defender for the good of the land'.

57 **arlleg** The word is divided across a line end in the manuscript. As the scribe has not consistently indicated word-divisions with a hyphen, it is impossible to know whether *arlleng*, 'defender', was intended or *ar lleng*, 'over a legion'. The use of *lleng* in the poetry for an army, other than for a host of angels, is, however, very rare (see *GPC*).

58 **Beduir a Bridlav** This line appears to be corrupt. The personal name *Bridlav* (perhaps containing the element *llaw*, 'hand') is otherwise unknown and seems out of place here. Sims-Williams ('Arthurian Poems', p. 43) suggests that *a Bridlau* could be seen as a patronymic name, *ab Bridlau* or *ab Ritlau*, although that would conflict with Bedwyr's usual patronym in Welsh (see 47n above). Another possibility is that it might be a reference to the fact that Bedwyr was one-handed (see *CO*, l. 396): *Beduir a br[u]idlav*, 'Bedwyr with a shattered hand' (see *GPC* $brwyd^2$).

59 **nau cant guarandau** It is likely that the sense of *guarandau* here is stronger than 'to listen'. The meanings 'to consider, to submit to persuasion or reproof' may be more appropriate (see *GPC* gwrandawaf: gwrando). The syntax of this line appears to be *nau cant* as a preceding possessive governing *guarandau* (which therefore has unwritten lenition): 'nine hundred (of the enemy)'s reconsidering'.

60 **chuechant y eirthau** The unusual construction of this line is subject + prep. *y*, 'to, for', used for expressing purpose (*GPC* i^2 9b) + verb noun: 'six hundred (people) for scattering, for being scattered'. Compare *Godeu a Reget y ymdullu*, 'Goddeu and Rheged for preparing' (*PT* vi.4) and see *GMW*, pp. 162–63n for further examples.

61 **a talei y ortinav** It appears that *y ortinav*, 'his attacking', is the subject of the verb and that the previous two lines are the object. The verb *talu* is used here with the meaning 'to be worth, to be of benefit', cf. *AyG* l. 32 *medd a dalai*, lit. 'he was worthy of mead'. This gives the meaning 'his attacking was worth six hundred's reconsidering and nine hundred's scattering', i.e. the hero's onslaught in battle had the value or effect of causing six hundred of the enemy to think again and nine hundred to scatter before him. If we assume that *y*, 'his', refers to Bedwyr (line 58), then Brydlaw seems redundant.

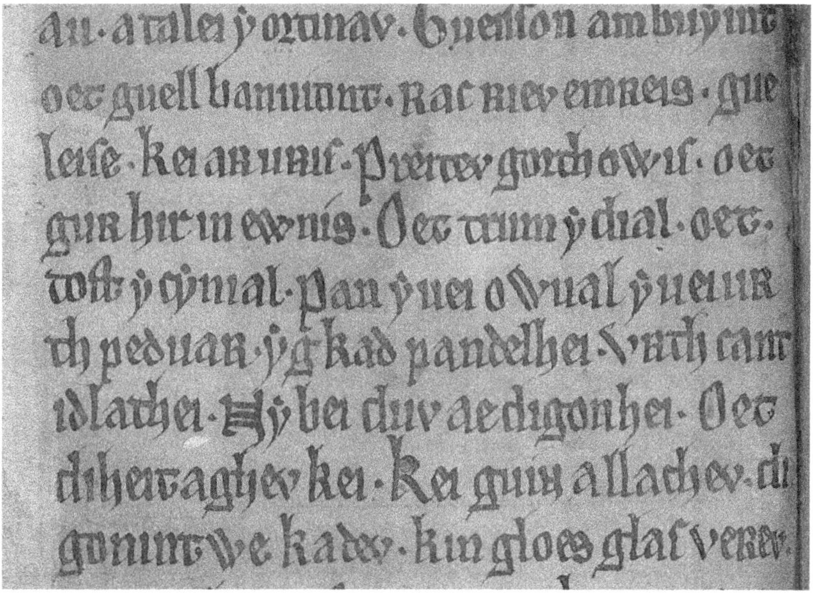

FIG. 1.17: NLW Peniarth MS 1, f. 48^v.

Gueisson am buyint | oet guell banuitint. Rac riev emreis. Gue|leise. Kei ar uris. Preitev gorthowis. oet | gur hir in ewnis. Oet trum y dial. Oet. | tost y cynial. Pan yuei o wual yuei ur|th peduar. Ygkad pandelhei. Vrth cant | id lathei. Ny bei duv ae digonhei. Oet | diheit aghev kei. Kei guin a llachev. Di|gonint we kadev. Kin gloes glas verev.

    Gueisson a'm buyint,
    oet guell ban uitint.
64 Rac riev Emreis
    gueleis-e Kei ar uris.
    Preitev gorthowis,
    oet gur hir in ewnis.
68 Oet trum y dial,
    oet tost y cynial.
    Pan yuei o wual
    yuei urth peduar.

72	Yg kad pan delhei,
	vrth cant id lathei.
	'Ny bei Duv a'e digonhei,
	oet diheit aghev Kei.
76	Kei Guin a Llachev,
	digonint-we kadev
	kin gloes glas verev.

	I used to have men,
	it was better when they were alive.
64	Before/against the lord(s) of Emrys
	I saw Cai in haste.
	Prince of plunder,
	the tall man was hostile / he was a warrior long-lasting as an enemy.
68	Severe was his vengeance,
	harsh was his fury.
	When he would drink from a horn,
	he would drink enough for four.
72	Whenever he came into battle,
	he would slay enough for a hundred.
	Unless God should achieve it,
	Cai's death were unattainable.
76	Cai the Fair and Llachau,
	they performed battles
	before the anguish of silvery spears.

From here on Arthur seems to have lost all track of the original question, the digression of lines 31–61 prompting further reminiscences. The remainder of the poem, from line 64, becomes a panegyric of Cai's prowess. Note the tone of departed glory in lines 62 to 63, contrasting with the tone of heroic bravado elsewhere in the poem, and in *Culhwch ac Olwen*.

62 **Gueisson a'm buyint** A form of the verb 'to be' preceded by an infixed dative pronoun is used here to denote possession, 'men there were to me' (*GMW*, p. 57, and cf. Chapter 5 below, Elegy for Cynddylan l. 4). The verbal form, *buyint*, is a variant of *bitint*, a 3 pl. consuetudinal (habitual) past form of *bod*; see *GMW*, p. 137, and cf. *EWSP* 'Marwnad Gwên' 26a *Pedwarmeib ar hugaint a'm bwyn* (< *bwy-yn*), 'Twenty-four sons there were to me'.

63 **oet guell ban uitint** The second form of the verb 'to be', *bitint*, is probably used here to express existence. It could be a 3 pl. consuetudinal past form like *buyint* above, 'it was better when they used to be [alive]', or a 3 pl.imperf.subj. (*GMW*, p. 138), 'it was better at such at time as they might be [alive]', adding a wistful tone. In either case, Arthur is clearly not listing his present companions at the gate.

64 **Rac riev Emreis** This simple line can be interpreted in a number of different

ways. *Riev* was originally the plural form of *ri*, 'king', but it is commonly used in poetry as an alternative singular; see Andrews, 'Nomenclature of Kingship Part 1', p. 90. The preposition *rac* has a range of suitable meanings here, as in line 47 above, including 'against' and also 'before, in front of, in the presence of'.
In court poetry addressed to four generations of the royal dynasty of Gwynedd, the name of *Emrais* is mostly used as a way of referring to the land and the people of Gwynedd, or sometimes Arfon: e.g. *CBT* I 9.84, *Emreis eryr*, 'eagle (lord) of Emrais'; V 10.34, *O dragon tud Emreis*, 'From among the dragons (heroes) of the land/people of Emrais'; VI 6.13, *dreic Emreis*, 'dragon (ruler) of Emrais'. It is likely that it is used in a similar way here; cf. especially Meilyr Brydydd's elegy for Gruffudd ap Cynan (d.1137), which speaks of the prince of Gwynedd fighting 'at the head of the army of Emrais', *rac bytin Emreis* (I 3.52). In *Historia Brittonum*, Emrais or Emrys is identified with the great Romano-British leader Ambrosius Aurelianus, and also with the gifted fatherless boy in the story of Vortigern of Gwynedd and the fight between the two dragons later developed by Geoffrey of Monmouth (see *TYP*, pp. 347–48). It is difficult to be sure which *Emreis* was intended by the poets as both are connected with Dinas Emrys, a hill-fort in Snowdonia, Gwynedd. The end-rhyme in -*is* suggests the form *Emrys* which is rare in poetry.

65   **gueleis-e Kei** The device of a first-person narrative account, which imparts vividness to a description of a battle, was frequently used in poetry from the earliest period onwards, see footnote 36 above.

66   **preiteu gorthowis** It is a convention in Welsh praise poems for warrior-kings to refer to the booty they have amassed from cattle-raids or from battle. The literal meaning of *preiteu*, 'herds', is possible here, with *gorthowis*, 'leader' (derived from *gor-*, 'over' + the root of *tywysaf*: *tywys*, 'to lead, guide', *GPC gorthywys*) as well as a more general 'prince of plunder'. In both cases, *preiteu* acts as a preceding possessive causing lenition in *gorthowis* which is not shown in the text.

67   **oet gur hir in ewnis** There are at least two ways of interpreting this line, depending on whether *ewnis* is understood as an adjective, 'hostile, wrathful', or a noun, 'enemy' (*GPC efnys*). The first would give the meaning 'the tall warrior was hostile', an appropriate description for Cai who is called Cai Hir in the Romance of Peredur and described as being 'as tall as the highest tree in the wood when he wished' in *Culhwch* (*TYP*, p. 309, and see C. Grooms, *The Giants of Wales* (Lampeter: Edwin Mellen Press, 1993), pp. 148–49, on the traditions of Cai Hir as a giant). Sims-Williams, however, has proposed a different translation, while suggesting that the poet is playing on the meanings of *hir*: 'he was a warrior long (i.e. unrelenting) as an enemy' ('Arthurian Poems', p. 44).

74   **'Ny bei Duv a'e digonhei** Lit. 'were it not God who might achieve it'.

75   **oet diheit aghev Kei** An example of *oet* used modally to mean 'would be'

rather than 'was, used to be'; see *GMW*, pp. 110–11. The etymological sense of *diheit* (*di-* negative prefix + *haeδ*, 'success', *GPC* dihaidd), 'unattainable, impossible', seems more appropriate here than its dictionary meaning, 'immovable, intractable, wretched'. Sims-Williams has suggested that an additional quality possessed by Cai might have been that, like Lleu of the Fourth Branch of the *Mabinogi*, he could only be killed in special circumstances ('Arthurian Poems', p. 44).

76 **Kei Guin a Llachev** On Arthur's son, Llachau, see the Stanzas of the Graves above. Sims-Williams ('Arthurian Poems', p. 44) suggests that this is an oblique echo of a story of the killing of Llachau by Cai or by Arthur himself, but it is impossible to know from l. 77 whether he and Cai were fighting on the same side or against each other.

78 **kin gloes glas verev** In the court poetry, the adjective *glas* with the meaning 'steel coloured, silvery, bright' is commonly found with *ber* to convey the shine or perhaps the sharpness of a hero's spears or those of his opponents (cf. the compound *glasfer*, *CBT* III 16.199, 29.10). The alliterating noun *gloes*, 'pain, anguish', is also used with this combination in Heledd's lament for her brother (*EWSP* 'Canu Heledd' 101b, *a gloes glas uereu*) and by Einion ap Gwalchmai, referring to the suffering of Christ (*CBT* I 27.37, *Portheist yr pym hoes gloes glas uereu*).

FIG. 1.18: NLW Peniarth MS 1, f. 48^v.

The Black Book of Carmarthen 51

Y guarthaw ystawingun. Kei a guant | nav guiton. Kei Win a aeth von y dilein | lleuon. Yiscuid oet mynud erbin cath | paluc. Pan gogiueirch tud. Puy guant | cath paluc. Nau ugein kinlluc. a cuyt|ei in y buyd. Nau ugein kinran. a

      Yguarthaw Ystawingun,
80   Kei (a) guant nav guiton;
      Kei Win a aeth Von
      y dilein lleuon;
      y iscuid oet mynud
84   erbin Cath Paluc.
      Pan gogiueirch tud,
      puy guant Cath Paluc?
      Nau ugein kinlluc
88   a cuytei in y buyd;
      nau ugein kinran
      A …

      In the uplands of ?Ystafnwn,
80   Cai pierced nine witches.
      Cai the fair went to Anglesey
      to destroy lions.
      His shield was ?fragmented/polished
84   against Palug's Cat.
      When people ask,
      who stabbed Palug's Cat?
      Nine score ?warriors
88   used to fall as its food;
      Nine score champions
      used to …

Arthur continues to recount the exploits of Cai, who appears to range over the whole of Wales fighting witches and wildcats.

79 **yguarthaw Ystawingun** The combination *yguarthaw* is often used with place names, cf. *ygwarthaf Keredigyawn*, 'in the uplands of Ceredigion' (*Math uab Mathonwy: The Fourth Branch of the Mabinogi* [*Math*], ed. by Ian Hughes (Dublin: Institute of Advanced Studies, 2013), l. 89n). *Ystawingun*, ?Ystafnwn, however, has not been identified. Sims-Williams ('Arthurian Poems', p. 45) has suggested that it might be a corrupt form for (Porth) Ysgewin (Portskewett in Gwent), a name often used in contrast with Anglesey in the extreme north-west (see, for example, *TYP*, p. 254, 'The Names of the Island of Britain', no. 9), perhaps through an Old Welsh form such as **Scauguin*.

80 **Kei (a) guant nav guiton** To give a five-syllable line, the preverbal particle *a* may be omitted (cf. l. 38 above). On references to nine witches and nine maidens in the Romance of Peredur, *Preiddeu Annwn*, and also in an early version of the Life of St Samson, see Sims-Williams, 'Arthurian Poems', p. 45.

81   **aeth Von** For the lenition of *Mon*, an object of destination after a verb of motion, cf. *AyG*, l. 78, *gwŷr a aeth Gatraeth*, 'warriors went to Catraeth'; see *GMW*, p. 19.

83   **y iscuid oet mynud** To give a five-syllable line, *iscuid* may be emended to *scuid*, the earlier monosyllabic form without a prosthetic vowel, cf. *AyG*, ll. 887, 940, and see *GMW*, p. 11, *GPC* ysgwyd³. For the dating implications of this, see *EWSP*, p. 316, but note that the only pre-twelfth century example of a prosthetic vowel before *sc*- cited by Jackson (to whom Rowland refers) is doubtful (see *The Cambridge Juvencus Manuscript Glossed in Latin, Old Welsh, and Old Irish: Text and Commentary*, ed. by Helen McKee (Aberystwyth: CMCS Publications, 2000), p. 520).

The usual meaning of *mynud*, 'courteous', is not appropriate here. Its original meaning, as a borrowing from Latin *minutus*, was probably 'minute, tiny', as in its Middle Breton and Cornish cognates (see *GPC* mynud²). It may therefore have developed the sense 'in tiny pieces, fragmented, shattered, broken', an indication of Cai's ferocity in battle (see *eis tull*, l. 22n above). Another meaning, suggested by a description of Cai destroying wildcats by using a glass shield in a fifteenth-century English text, is 'smooth, polished' (see Sims-Williams, 'Arthurian Poems', p. 45). Note the generic rhyme between *mynud* and *Paluc* below; see footnote 24 above.

84   **Cath Paluc** For the element *pal*-, 'digging, clawing, scratching', see *Penpalach* above, l. 41n. The -*uc* ending is thought to be adjectival as in *sarruc* and *seithuc*. The name may have been understood here as 'the clawing cat', but in an account of the monster's origin in the later version of Triad 26, *Paluc* is understood as the name of those who fostered it, *meibion Paluc*, 'the sons of Palug'. Since *Cath Paluc* is associated with Anglesey in the triad, it is possible that it was one of the 'lions' which Cai went to destroy. For other monster cats in medieval Welsh poetry and in later Arthurian romance, see *TYP*, pp. 473–76, and *Prophecies from the Book of Taliesin* [*PBT*], ed. by Marged Haycock (Aberystwyth: CMCS Publications, 2013), 6.23n.

85   **Pan gogiueirch tud** Because the end of this section is lost, it is difficult to be sure of the meaning of *pan*. It may be the conjunction 'when' (*GPC* pan¹) or possibly the interrogative *pan* which sometimes has the meaning 'how, why' (*GPC* pan⁴ d).

87   **Nau ugein kinlluc** A compound consisting of *cyn*-, 'first', + *llug*, 'light, radiance', used figuratively for a 'warrior, leader' (cf. *GPC* gwawr). It has been suggested that it should perhaps be emended to *kinlluyd*, 'grey-headed (person)' (*GPC* cynllwyd). This would rhyme with *buyd* in the following line. The scribal error (-*uc* for -*uyd*) could easily have arisen under the influence of *Paluc* in the previous line.

89–90   **nau ugein kinran a …** The poem breaks off here, through loss of one or more folios, so it is not known how much more of it existed in the manuscript. The one word *a* indicates that l. 90 would have contained a verb, probably imperfect, matching the construction of l. 88 ('nine score warriors used to ...'). We cannot know how the soliloquy ended, and whether or not the conversation with the porter was resumed, or its outcome.

Word-list

a^1 *preverbal particle* (causing lenition, *GMW*, pp. 172–73) 41, 61, 80, 81, 88, 90; *with infixed obj.pron. 1 sing.* **a'm** 62; *with infixed obj.pron. 3 sing. or pl.* **a'e** 3, 9, 10, 29, 31, 74; *with infixed obj.pron. 3 pl.* (*GMW*, p. 55) **a's** 35
a^2 *prep.* (causing spirant mutation, *GMW*, p. 21) 'with' 44, 49
a^3 *conj.* (causing spirant mutation, *GMW*, p. 21) 'and' 4, 10, 12, 16, 23, 26, 40, 58n, 76; (before vowels) **ac** 25, 51
ab see **mab**
ac see **a**^{2}
aeth *3 sing.pret. of* **myned**, 'to go' 81
agheu *n.* 'death' (*GPC* angau) 75
am see **mab**
amuin *v.n.* 'to contend, attack, fight (for); defend, protect' (*GPC* amygaf: amwyn^1) 18, 49; *3 sing.pret.* **amuc** (for the suffixless preterite, see *GMW*, p. 124) 44
Anguas Edeinauc *personal name* Anwas Edeinawg 25n
annuyd *n.* 'nature, temperament, emotion' (*GPC* annwyd^1) 50
ar *prep.* 'on, upon' (*GMW*, pp. 183–89, causing lenition), 24, 48; 'beside, near; in the direction of, towards, facing' (with place name) 28n; 'for' (conveying intention in the combination **ar lles**, 'for the good or benefit of', *GMW*, p. 187, and on lack of lenition after *ar*, see *GMW*, p. 20n) 57; 'in' (conveying manner in the combination **ar vris**, 'in haste, quickly', *GMW*, p. 184), 65
argluit *n.* 'a lord' (*GPC* arglwydd) 29
arlleg *n.* 'defence, refuge', used figuratively for a person, 'defender' (*GPC* arlleng) 57n
Arthur *personal name* 4, 37n
atodeu *pl. of* **atawd** *n.* 'a home, residence, dwelling-place' (*GPC* addod) 42
Awarnach *personal name* Afarnach 39n

ban see **pan**
Beduir Bedrydant *personal name* Bedwyr ?the Powerful 47n, 58
bei see **bod**
bereu *pl. of* **ber** *n.* 'a spear, lance' (*GPC* bêr) 78
bid *n.* 'world' (*GPC* byd^1) 6
bitint see **bod**

bod *vb.* 'to be' (*GMW*, pp. 136–38) *3 sing.pres.indic.* **yv** 1; *3 sing.imperf.indic.* **oet** 17, 20n, 50, 52, 54, 56, 63, 67, 68, 69, 75n, 83; *3 pl.imperf.indic.* **oetin** (on *-nt* > *-n*, see *GMW*, p. 120 n. 2) 27; *3 pl. consuetudinal past* **buyint** 62n, **bitint** 63n; *3 sing.imperf.subj.* **bei** 74

bragad *n.* 'an army, host' 52

Bridlau *personal name?* Brydlaw 58n

bris see **ar vris**

bual *n.* 'a drinking-horn' 70

buyd *n.* 'food' (*GPC* bwyd) 88

buyint see **bod**

kad *n.* 'battle' 53, 72; **ighad** (*combined with prep.* **in**¹) 'in battle' 54n; *pl.* **kadeu** 77

caffad *impers.pret. of* **caffael**, 'to get, obtain, receive' (*GMW*, p. 149) 34

cant *numeral* 'a hundred' 45, 46, 59, 73

Cath Paluc *proper name* 'The Clawing Cat; Palug's cat' 84n, 86

ced *conj.* 'although, even though' (*GPC* cyd³) 37

Kei Guin *personal name* Cai Wyn, Cai the Fair 4n, 76, **Kei Win** 81; **Kei** 31, 35, 53, 65, 75, 80

Kelli *place name* Celli, Celli Wig 33n

chuechant *numeral* 'six hundred' (with *chwech* causing spirant mutation, *GMW*, p. 21) 60

kin *prep.* 'before (in time), previous to' (*GPC* cyn¹) 78

kinbin *pl. of* **kinben** *n.* 'dog-head, dog-headed monster' (*GPC* cynben) 44n

kinlluc *n.* 'warrior, leader' (*GPC* cynllug¹) 87n

kinran *n.* 'prince, leader, warrior' (*GPC* cynran) 89

cletyw *n.* 'sword' (*GPC* cleddyf) 51, 54

colled *impers.pret. of* **colli**, 'to lose' (*GMW*, p. 126) 33

cuelli *n.* 'fury, fierceness' 34n

cuitau *v.n.* 'to fall, fall in battle, die' (see *GPC* cwyddaf: cwyddo) *3 sing.imperf. indic.* **cuytei** 88; *3 pl.imperf.indic.* **cuitin** (on *-nt* > *-n*, see *GMW*, p. 120 n. 2) 45, 46

cusil *n.* 'advice, counsel' (from Low Latin *cōsilium* < *consilium*, see *GPC* cysul) 20n

cyminauc *adj.* 'bordering, neighbouring, adjacent' (< prefix *cy(f)-*, which often denotes relationship, + *min*, 'lip; margin, side; boundary, border', + adj. ending *-awc*) 28n

cynial *n.* 'ferocity, anger' (a hapax formation with *gal*, an element commonly found in compounds, *GPC* gâl¹) 69n

kymynhei *3 sing.imperf.subj. of* **cymynu**, 'to hew, fell, cut down' (on *-h-* as an indication of the subj., see *GMW*, p. 128) 36n

Kysceint mab Banon *personal name, possibly corrupt* 15n

delhei 3 *sing.imperf.subj.* of **dyvod**, 'to come' (*GMW*, p. 133–35) 72n

detvon *pl.* of **detyf** *n*. 'custom, right, a just claim, privilege' (see *GPC* deddf) 18n

dial *n*. 'vengeance, retribution' 68

diffreidauc *adj*. 'defending, protecting, supporting' (*GPC* diffreidiog) 27n

digoni *vb*. 'to do, perform, achieve, accomplish', 3 *pl.imperf.indic.* **digonint** 77; 3 *sing.imperf.subj.* **digonhei** 74

diguistlad *impers.pret. of* **dywystlaw**, 'to give a pledge or assurance' (< affirmative prefix (*GPC* dy-¹) + *gwystlaw*) 55n

diheit *adj*. 'immovable, intractable, ?unattainable' (*GPC* dihaidd) 75n

dilein *v.n.* 'to destroy, annihilate, get rid of' (*GPC* dileaf: dileu) 82

Dissethach *personal name*? 42n

doi (do-i) 2 *sing.pres./fut.indic.* of irregular *vb.* **dyvod**, to come (*GMW*, p. 133) 7n

duc 3 *sing.pret.* of **dwyn**, 'to bring; bear, carry; take away, carry off' (suffixless preterite, see *GMW*, p. 124) 21n

duis *adj*. 'serious; earnest; profound, weighty' (*GPC* dwys) 20n

Duv *n*. 'God' (*GPC* duw¹) 74

-e *affixed pron.* 1 *sing.* (not usually included in the syllable count, *GMW*, p. 57) 65

'e¹ *infixed obj.pron.* 3 *sing.* or *pl.* (*GMW*, p. 55) 3, 9, 10, 29, 31, 74 (with **a¹**); 32, 36 (with **tra**)

'e² *infixed poss.pron.* 3 *sing.masc.* (*GMW*, p. 53), see **o'e**

Eidin *place name* Eidyn, Edinburgh 28n, 43n

eiriolei, eirolei 3 *sing.imperf.indic.* of **eir(i)ol**, 'to plead, entreat, beseech, exhort' 31, 35

eirthau *v.n.* 'to scatter, disperse' (*GPC* eirthiaf: eirthio) 60

eis *pl.* of **asen** *n*. 'a rib, a lath, *fig.* a spear' 22n

Elei *place name or personal name* Elái 12n

ell *pl.* or oblique form of pron. **oll**, 'all', *used with numerals* (see *GPC* ill) 'all [three] of them' 12

Emreis *personal name* Emrais, Emrys 64n

erbin *prep*. 'against' (usually in the compound *yn erbyn*, *GMW*, p. 217); 'in preparation for' (*GMW*, p. 193) 84n

eu *prefixed poss.pron.* 3 *pl.* 'their' 18

ew *independent pron.* 3 *sing.masc.* 'he' (*GPC* ef, *GMW*, p. 49) 40, 41n

ewnis *adj. and n*. 'hostile, wrathful; enemy' (*GPC* efnys) 67n

Garuluid *personal name* (< *garw*, 'rough' (counted as one syllable in poetry), + *llwyd*, 'grey') 49n

genhid *conjugated prep.* 2 *sing.* of **gan**, 'with' (*GMW*, p. 60) 5

glas *adj.* 'iron or steel-coloured, bright' (for weapons, *GPC* glas¹) 78

Gleuluid Gauaeluaur *personal name* 'Bold-grey' (< *glew*, 'brave, daring', + *llwyd*, 'grey, grey-haired'), 'Great-grasp, of mighty grasp' (< *gavael n.*, 'a grasp', or *v.n.*, 'to grasp', + *mawr*, 'great') 2n

gloes *n.* 'pain, agony, anguish' 78

gogiveirch 3 *sing.pres.indic.* of **gogyvarch**, 'to ask' (*GPC* gogyfarchaf: gogyfarch) 85

gorev *adj.* 'best' *superlative grade of* **da**, 'good' (*GMW*, p. 40), 6

gorthowis *n.* 'leader, prince, chieftain, lord' (*GPC* gorthywys) 66n

gortinau *v.n.* 'to attack, drive' (*GPC* gorddinaf: gorddino) 61n

gouerei 3 *sing.imperf.indic.* of **goferu**, 'to gush, flow; cause to flow, pour' 38n

gouin *vb.* 3 *sing.pres.indic.* of **govyn**, 'to ask' 3

guaed *n.* 'blood' 24, 38

guaget *n.* 'vanity, emptiness, uselessness' (< *gwag*, 'empty, vain, useless', + abstract noun suffix *-eδ*) 52

guant 3 *sing.pret.* of *vb.* **gwanu**, 'to pierce, stab' (for the suffixless preterite, see *GMW*, p. 124) 41, 80, 86

guarandau *v.n.* 'to listen, to reconsider, to submit to persuasion' (*GPC* gwrandawaf: gwrando) 59n

guared *vb.* (?) to disclose, reveal 1/3 *sing. pres./fut.indic.* **guar[e]di** 9n; 2 *sing. pres./fut.indic.* **guaredi** 8n

guarthaw *n.* 'topmost part, summit, uplands' (*GPC* gwarthaf²) 79n

guas *n.* 'lad, young man, servant, follower, man' (*GPC* gwas¹) 14; *pl.* **gueisson** 17, 62

guastad *adj.* 'consistent, steadfast' 56

gueisson see **guas**

gwelet *vb.* to see 2/3 *sing.pres./fut.indic.* **gueli** 10n; 1 *sing.pret.* **gueleis** 65n

guell *adj.* 'better', *comparative grade of* **da**, 'good' (*GMW*, p. 40) 63

guelld *n.* 'grass' (*GPC* gwellt) 24

guin *adj.* fair, fair-haired, blessed (*GPC* gwyn¹) 4n, 76, [g]**win** 81

Guin Godybrion *personal name* Gwyn Goddyfrion 16n

guir see **gur**

guiton *n.* 'giantess; hag, witch' (*GPC* gwiddon¹) 80n

gulad *n.* 'country, land' 57

gur *n.* man, warrior 1, 3, 67n; *pl.* **guir** 6

gurach *n.* 'hag, witch' 40n

guychir *adj.* 'violent, fierce, brave' (with epenthetic vowel, *GPC* gwychr) 50

gvytheint *n.* 'anger, battle-fury' 10n

heiriolei see **eiriolei**

hid tra *compound conj.* (*GMW*, pp. 238–39) 'while, as long as, all the time that'; see also **tra**

hir *adj.* 'long, tall, long-lasting' 67n
huar[t]hei 3 *sing.imperf.subj. of* **hwerthin, chwerthin,** 'to laugh, smile, be merry' 37n
hyneiw *n.* 'chief, lord' (a form of *hynaf,* superlative of *hen,* 'senior' (see *GPC*), more often found in prose texts than in poetry, where *hynefydd* is more common) 56

id *preverbal particle* **yd** (causing lenition, rare in prose, but quite common in poetry, see *GMW*, p. 171n) 45, 46, 73
ig, ighad, im see **in**[1]
imda 3 *sing.pres.indic.* of **ymdeith,** 'to travel, go around' (*GMW*, p. 156) 5
imlat *v.n.* 'to fight' (mutual prefix *ym-* + *llað,* 'to strike') 40
in[1], **yn** *prep.* (*GPC* yn¹, causing nasal mutation, see *GMW*, p. 21), 'in' 39, 42; **im, ym** 6 (before **bid**), 43 (before **minit**); **ig, yg** 53, 72 (before **kad**), **ighad** 54n; **yguarthaw** (combined with **guarthaw,** *GMW*, p. 217f) 79
in[2] *particle with v.n.* (*GPC* yn², *GMW*, p. 215, causing no mutation) 18, 40, 49
in[3] *predicative particle* 'as' (*GPC* yn³, *GMW*, p. 139, causing lenition except in *ll-* and *-rh*) 67, 88
iscuid see **yscuid**

Llacheu *personal name* Llachau 76n
llathei 3 *sing.imperf.subj. of* **lladd,** 'to kill, slay, strike' 32n, 73
llau *n.* 'hand' (*GPC* llaw¹) 55
lles see **ar lles**
lleuon *pl. of n.* **llew,** 'a lion, wildcat, monster' 82
llochei 3 *sing.imperf. of* **llochi,** 'to shelter, protect, nurture, support' 29
Lluch Llauynnauc *personal name* Llwch Llaw-wynnog 26n

'm[1] *infixed obj.pron. 1 sing.* 'me' (*GMW*, p. 55) see **a'm**
'm[2] *infixed poss.pron. 1 sing.* 'my' (*GMW*, p. 53) see **y'm**
mab *n.* 'son' 15; *in patronymics* **ab** 19, **am** (before *M-*), 13, 23
Mabon am Melld *personal name* Mabon son of Mellt 23n
Mabon am Mydron *personal name* Mabon son of Modron 13n
maglei 3 *sing.imperf.indic. of vb.* **maglu,** 'to spot, cause to stain' 24n
Manawid ab Llyr *personal name* Manawyd son of Llŷr 19n, **Manauid** 21
mi *independent pron. 1 sing.* 'I' 9
Minit Eidin *place name* Mynydd Eidyn, the Mountain of Eidyn 43n
Mon *place name* Ynys Môn, Anglesey 81
my *1 sing.poss.pron.* 'my' 30n (see also **vy**)
mynud *adj.* 'courtly, courteous', here possibly 'fragmented' or 'smooth' 83n

nau *numeral* 'nine' (*GPC* naw¹) 59, 80, 87, 89
nei *n.* 'nephew' (*GPC* nai¹) 30n
neuat *n.* 'hall' (*GPC* neuadd¹) 39
neu's *a combination of the preverbal particle* **neu** (*GMW*, pp. 169–70) + *infixed obj.pron. 3 pl.* 's 21n
ny *negative preverbal particle* (*GPC* ni²) 7 (on lack of lenition, see *GMW*, pp. 61–62)
'ny *conj.* 'if not, unless, except' (abbreviated form of **ony**, *GMW*, p. 241), 74

o *prep.* 'of, from' 22, 70; 'carrying, with' (*GPC* o¹19) 51
o'e *a combination of prep.* **o**, 'to', + *infixed poss.pron. 3 sing.masc.* 'e, 'to his' 55n
oet, oetin see **bod**
ony's *a combination of conj.* **ony**, 'unless, if not' (*GMW*, p. 241), + *infixed obj. pron. 3 pl.* 's, 'them' 8
ortinau see **gortinau**

pa *interrogative adj.* (causing lenition, *GMW*, p. 21) what? (*GMW*, pp. 75–76, *GPC* pa¹, py¹) 1, 3, who? 5n
pan *conj.* 'when' (*GMW*, p. 242, causing lenition, *GMW*, p. 21) 33, 70, 72, 85n; **ban** (lenited as an unstressed proclitic, *GMW*, p. 17 n. 3) 63
peduar *numeral* 'four' (*GPC* pedwar) 71
Penpalach *personal name* 41n
pop *pronominal adj.* 'each, every', with numerals, 'in (twos, threes, etc.), (two, three etc.) at a time' (*GPC* pob¹), 32, 45, 46 (the initial p- is lenited in each of these cases because the expression is adverbial, *GMW*, p. 98)
porthaur *n.* 'porter, gatekeeper' (< *porth*, 'gate, door', + *-awr*, nominalising agent suffix) 1
preiteu *pl. of n.* **preit**, 'herd of cattle; spoils, booty, plunder' (*GPC* praidd) 66n
puy *interrogative pron.* 'who?' (normally followed by relative *a*, see *GMW*, p. 74n) 86n

rac *prep.* 'before, in front of; because of' (*GPC* rhag, *GMW*, pp. 206–07) 47n, 64n
rieu *pl. of* **ri**, 'a lord, king', *sometimes used as an alternative sing.* (*GPC* rhiau¹) 65n
rinn *adj.* 'rigid, stiff, unyielding, steadfast, brave' (*GPC* rhyn¹) 17

's *infixed obj.pron. 3 sing. or pl.* 'him, them' (*GMW*, p. 55) *combined with* **a** 35, **neu** 21n, **ony** 8
ssiuyon *pl. of adj.* syw, 'excellent, splendid; wise, skilful' (probably a borrowing from Irish, see *GPC*), *used substantively*, 'splendid or wise ones' 12n
talei 3 *sing.imperf.indic. of* talu, 'to be worth, to be of value' 61n
ti *independent pron. 2 sing.* 'you' (*GMW*, p. 49) 10

tost *adj.* 'sharp, severe, harsh' 69

tra *conj.* 'while' (*GMW*, p. 244); **hid tra**, 'while, as long as' (see **hid**); *with infixed 3 pl.obj.pron.* **tra'e** 32, **hid tra'e** 36

traetheu *pl. of* **traeth** *n.* 'a shore, strand, beach' 48n

tri *numeral* 'three' 12, 32

trum *adj.* 'heavy, oppressive, severe' (*GPC* trwm¹) 68

Trywruid *unidentified place name* Tryfrwyd 22n, 48n

tuc see **duc**

tud *n.* 'people, folk' 85

tull *n. used as adj.* 'holed, pierced, broken' (*GPC* twll¹) 22

ty *n.* 'house' 7

ugein *numeral* 'twenty' 87, 89

vrth *prep.* 'compared with, beside' (*GPC* wrth 1e) 53 71, 73

Uthir Pendragon *personal name* Uth(y)r (with epenthetic vowel, *GMW*, pp. 12–13) P/Bendragon ('Chief Dragon', i.e. 'foremost leader' or 'chief or warriors', see *TYP*, pp. 512–13) 14n

vy *poss.pron. 1 sing.* 'my' (*GMW*, p. 53, causing nasal mutation, *GMW*, p. 22) 17, see also **my**

vythneint *n.* see 11n

-we *affixed pron. 3 pl.* (not usually included in the syllable count, *GMW*, p. 57 wy) 77

y¹ *definite article* 'the' 1n

y² *prefixed poss.pron. 3 sing.masc.* 'his' (causing lenition, *GPC* ei¹) 20, 50, 61, 68, 69, 83; *3 sing.fem.* 'her' (causing spirant mutation) 38n, 88

y³ *prep.* 'to, in order to' (with v.n.) 60n, 82

yg, yguarthaw, ym see **in¹**

y'm a combination of either **y³**, 'to', or a form of **in¹** (*GMW*, p. 199) + *infixed poss. pron. 1 sing.* 'm, 'to my, into my' 7

ymtiwygei *3 sing.imperf.indic. of* ***ymddiwygio** *or* ***ymddifwng** 30n

yscuid, iscuid *n.* 'shield' (*GPC* ysgwyd³) 51, 83

Ystawingun *unidentified place name* Ystafngwn, Ystafnwn 79n

yv see **bot**

yvei *3 sing.imperf.indic. of vb.* **yved**, 'to drink' 70, 71

CHAPTER 2

The Book of Aneirin

Cardiff Manuscript 2.81 is a small book containing only nineteen leaves of parchment with a few stubs at the end indicating that it is incomplete. It was written by two unnamed scribes whose hands can be dated to the second half of the thirteenth century, a generation later than the Black Book of Carmarthen. Scribe A copied eighty-eight short *awdlau*[1] and four longer poems in Medieval Welsh orthography called *gwarchanau*. Scribe B filled the blank spaces left by Scribe A and added some pages of his own, contributing forty-two *awdlau* in total. About half of these are variants of *awdlau* already copied by Scribe A. Scribe B's texts appear to have been taken from two sources; the last nineteen *awdlau* in the manuscript may be in a more archaic spelling than the rest.[2] Two other manuscripts written by Scribe B have been identified. One contains the Life of Gruffudd ap Cynan, a Gwynedd text, suggesting that our manuscript is of north-Wales origin, compiled perhaps at the Cistercian house of Aberconwy.[3]

It opens with the rubric *Hwn yw e gododin. Aneirin ae cant*, 'This is the Gododdin. Aneirin sang it'. It is this ascription which led Edward Lhuyd to give the manuscript its modern name, *Llyfr Aneirin*, 'The Book of Aneirin', in his *Archaeologia Britannica* of 1707. Aneirin is also named in two *awdlau* in the collection, one of which refers to him as a poet who sang the *Gododdin*.[4] In that *awdl* and also in *Anrec Urien*, 'The Gift of Urien', a twelfth or thirteenth-

---

[1] This is the term used in the manuscript itself for the units of verse, which vary in length and are marked by a large initial.
[2] There is uncertainty because Paul Russell has shown that characteristics which traditionally place this hand in the Old Welsh period (from the eighth to the early twelfth centuries) would not be out of place in a manuscript written in the mid thirteenth-century: 'Scribal (In)consistency in Thirteenth-century South Wales: The Orthography of the Black Book of Carmarthen', *Studia Celtica*, 43 (2009), 135–74 (p. 172).
[3] See *MWM*, pp. 72–75, and for detailed treatment of the manuscript see *Llyfr Aneirin: A Facsimile*, ed. by Daniel Huws (Aberystwyth: National Library of Wales, 1989). To view the manuscript, which is now housed at the National Library of Wales, visit <https://www.llgc.org.uk>.
[4] See *AyG* poems 1 and 49, and for a consideration of the references to Aneirin in medieval Welsh literature, see Morfydd E. Owen, 'Hwn yw e Gododin. Aneirin ae cant' in *AstHen*, pp. 123–50.

century anonymous poem from the Red Book of Hergest, Aneirin's name is linked to that of Taliesin, and there are suggestions of traditions which had developed about him as a seer and a prophet. Two of the Triads seem to allude to a story about his violent death[5] but, compared to Taliesin, references to Aneirin in medieval Welsh literature are scarce.[6] Among the Poets of the Princes, it is only Dafydd Benfras, composing in Gwynedd at about the time the Book of Aneirin was being compiled, who mentions him by name, when, in the formal opening of a praise poem for Llywelyn the Great, he calls on God for inspiration so that he can sing 'like Aneirin long ago, the day he sang the *Gododdin*'.[7] There are echoes of the *Gododdin* and allusions to it in a few twelfth-century poems, but it appears that knowledge of it and of Aneirin was scarce among the professional poets of independent Wales.[8] Daniel Huws is probably right in suggesting that the purpose of creating the Book of Aneirin was 'to rescue treasured texts ... which had probably almost passed from oral currency, and which were perhaps no longer entirely understood'.[9] Some of its rubrics, however, suggest that the manuscript was intended to be used by poets to prepare for competitive performances.

Aneirin has been identified with Neirin, the famous sixth-century Brythonic poet mentioned along with Taliesin in a section of *Historia Brittonum* thought to be based on early sources.[10] There is no early evidence, however, to corroborate this, and the question of whether any of the *awdlau* attributed to him in the Book of Aneirin could have been produced in the sixth century is the subject of a long-running debate between scholars. The text largely consists of series of short elegies for warriors who died heroically in battle. Many are identified as members of the army of Gododdin, a Brythonic kingdom centred on Din Eidyn (Edinburgh) which was annexed by the Anglian kingdom of Bernicia in 638. Some are also said to have been slain at Catraeth (identified as Catterick in North Yorkshire) within territory which in the period belonged to the Anglian kingdom of Deira. This battle, however, is unrecorded in sources relating to the period.[11]

Scholars agree that the *Gododdin* is more of an anthology than a single work, with *awdlau* added at different stages as the material was handed down orally

---

[5] *TYP* nos 33 and 34, and see pp. 278–79.
[6] See discussion on Book of Taliesin poems below.
[7] *CBT* VI 25.5–6.
[8] For an exploration of the court poets' knowledge of him, see Jones, 'Hengerdd', pp. 49–52.
[9] *MWM*, p. 75.
[10] See John T. Koch, *Celtic Culture: A Historical Encyclopedia* (Santa Barbara and Oxford: ABC-CLIO, 2006).
[11] On Catraeth's place within the *Gododdin* and the possibility that it was originally used in the text as a kenning, 'battle-shore', rather than a place name, see Philip M. Dunshea, 'The Meaning of *Catraeth*: A Revised Early Context for *Y Gododdin*' in *BG*, pp. 81–114.

or in written form. The A text starts with an elegy for a young warrior called Owain son of Marro which has no mention of Catraeth or Gododdin. It has been suggested that it was composed in Wales sometime after 900 as a contemporary elegy, at a time when Gododdin poems might have been performed at funerals or commemorations of the dead.[12] The B text is prefixed by a short poem celebrating the victory of the Britons of the kingdom of Alclud at the Battle of Strathcarron (dated to 642). Since it too has nothing to do with the *Gododdin*, it has been argued that it may mark the occasion of the formation of the B version, but it is also possible that it originated as an addition in the margin of a source used by Scribe B.[13] The same could be true of *Peis Dinogat* …, 'Dinogad's Tunic …', a poem copied by Scribe A, spoken perhaps in the voice of a mother of a young child, as a lament for her dead husband, or an old bard, with the child on his knee, and which has been located in the kingdom of Rheged.[14] It has been argued that the Strathcarron poem might have been incorporated into the B version in Alclud soon after the fall of the Gododdin, and that the A version (which also contains the Strathcarron poem) went from Alclud to Rheged sometime before its fall in the mid-seventh century, before arriving in Gwynedd. It is also possible, however, that these poems independently found their way to Wales in oral or written form and were collected together with the Gododdin poems at a much later date.[15]

The second poem in the A text, in the voice of a reciter of the *Gododdin* singing after the death of Aneirin, provides a prologue to the collection. It is followed by a dozen *awdlau* linked by incremental repetition, which contain some of the most powerful and poignant poetry in the collection. They portray Catraeth as a disastrous defeat by a vast English army which was threatening the Brythonic kingdoms. The Gododdin force of three hundred young warriors, who had been feasted by their lord for a year before being sent to battle, was wiped out with the exception of very few survivors, including the poet. The Catraeth legend which can be gathered from these verses appears to be more suited to medieval Wales under threat from the English than to the northern kingdoms, where temporary alliances between different ethnic groups appear to

---

[12] See Brendan O Hehir, 'What is the *Gododdin*?' in *EWP*, pp. 57–95 (pp. 73–74).
[13] See R. Geraint Gruffydd, 'The Strathcarron Interpolation (*Canu Aneirin*, Lines 966–77)', *Scottish Gaelic Studies*, 17 (1996), 172–78.
[14] See Ifor Williams, *The Beginnings of Welsh Poetry*, ed. by Rachel Bromwich (Cardiff: University of Wales Press, 1980), p. 63; R. Geraint Gruffydd, 'Where was *Rhaeadr Derwennydd* (Canu Aneirin, Line 1114)?' in *Celtic Language, Celtic Culture: A Festschrift for Erich P. Hamp*, ed. by A. T. E. Matonis and D. F. Melia (Van Nuys, California: Ford and Bailie, 1990), pp. 261–66.
[15] See Thomas Charles-Edwards, *Wales and the Britons, 350–1064* (Oxford: University Press, 2013), pp. 364–78; O. J. Padel, 'A New Study of the *Gododdin*', *CMCS*, 35 (1998), 45–56; John T. Koch, 'Thoughts on the Ur-Gododdin: Rethinking Aneirin and Mynyδawc Mŵynvawr', *Language Sciences*, 15 (1993), 81–89.

have been the norm. These two chains of *awdlau* are not found in the B version, and are possibly additions or a later reworking of older material to reflect a very different political situation.[16] The B version has fewer references to the expedition to Catraeth, celebrating instead warriors who died fighting against Picts and Scots as well as Deirans, on the borderlands of the Gododdin.

Detailed work on the language of the *Gododdin* has concluded that most of it conforms to that of thirteenth-century Wales, with some linguistic archaisms which can be taken back to about the tenth or the ninth centuries.[17] The last nineteen *awdlau* of the B text are written in Old Welsh orthography, but it is difficult to date them with any precision based on spelling alone as some of the characteristics of this system are seen in manuscripts as late as the thirteenth century.[18] John T. Koch, in his reconstruction of the text into the language of the sixth or seventh centuries, has uncovered features in some verses which suggest that they cannot be older than the later Old Welsh period (after c. 900).[19] He also claims to have recovered archaisms which go back to the sixth and seventh centuries, and argues that the later part of the B version reflects a seventh-century written text which remained in the Old North until the ninth century without much textual change.[20] It is extremely difficult, however, to isolate a core of early material if one exists, and the case has been made, most notably by Graham R. Isaac and O. J. Padel, that the whole corpus might be no earlier than the ninth or the tenth centuries.[21] A convincing context for the composition of this poetry in Wales in this period, however, is yet to be outlined.[22]

---

[16] For the suggestion by Saunders Lewis that these may have been created as 'exercises or competition-pieces upon a common theme', see Padel, 'New Study', p. 54

[17] The first modern edition is *Canu Aneirin*, edited with notes and an introduction in Welsh by Ifor Williams in 1938. His work has been made accessible to English readers by Kenneth Hurlstone Jackson in *The Gododdin: The Oldest Scottish Poem* [*GOSP*] (Edinburgh: Edinburgh University Press, 1969) and by A. O. H. Jarman in *Aneirin, Y Gododdin: Britain's Oldest Heroic Poem* [*AyG*] (Llandysul: Gomer Press, 1988).

[18] See Paul Russell, 'Scribal (In)competence in Thirteenth-century North Wales: The Orthography of the Black Book of Chirk (Peniarth MS 29)', *Journal of the National Library of Wales*, 29 (1995), 129–76.

[19] A striking example is the rhyming pairs in the elegy for Owain ap Marro mentioned above, which would probably not have rhymed in the language of the sixth or seventh century; see *GofA*, p. lxxii.

[20] For a critique of Koch's approach and a summary of his theory of the history of the text, see Padel, 'New Study', pp. 45–55.

[21] See O. J. Padel, 'Aneirin and Taliesin: Sceptical Speculations' in *BG*, pp. 115–52.

[22] See Stefan Schumacher, 'An Edition and Analysis of the Book of Aneirin B.39 (Including Preliminary Chapters on the Grammar and Poetics of Early Welsh Poetry)', *Zeitschrift für celtische Philologie*, 64 (2017), 299–420, and Patrick Sims-Williams, 'Dating the Poems of Aneirin and Taliesin', *Zeitschrift für celtische Philologie*, 63 (2016), 163–234.

64   THE BOOK OF ANEIRIN

The Gwawrddur/Gorddur poem

Morfydd E. Owen has described the contents of the Book of Aneirin as 'perhaps the most puzzling corpus of poetry which has survived from early Welsh'.[23] On the penultimate page of the manuscript as it is today is an eight-line *awdl* written by Scribe B, which appears to contain a reference to Arthur.[24] Its subject is a warrior called Gwawrddur, or perhaps Gorddur, who is praised for his superiority both in battle and as a generous host. Because of textual ambiguities and corruptions it is difficult to produce a definitive translation of the whole poem, but it is clear that conventional motifs are used: the hero leading the host and fighting in the van of battle, attacking both the centre of the opposing army and its wing, and generously giving away gifts of steeds in times of peace. As is common in the *Gododdin*, the focus is on the heroic actions of the deceased. There is no expression of grief; in fact, his death is not mentioned. There is no specific reference either to the conflict at Catraeth, but the 'three hundred' of the opening line is probably an allusion to the warband of the Gododdin.

The lines which contain the reference to Arthur are linguistically fairly straightforward: 'He ?fed black ravens on/before the rampart of a fortress although he was no Arthur'. This motif of the warrior providing carrion for ravens through his extreme ferocity in battle is common in medieval Welsh praise poetry. It also brings to mind the reference in the *Historia Brittonum* to the single-handed killing of 960 men by Arthur at Badon, and may allude to similar traditions. The couplet is a typical example of what Oliver Padel describes as 'the grim understatement' often used in the *Gododdin* for praising its heroes.[25] In an earlier *awdl* the son of Golystan is extolled using a similar construction:[26]

> Gnaut mab Golistan, cen n(e)i bei guledic
> i tat, indeuit a lauarei.
>
> It was usual for the son of Golystan — although his father was no lord — that what he said was heeded.

Scholars have shown that the form of the comparison with Arthur is highly unusual in Welsh praise poetry.[27] In fact, any kind of reference to figures other than the fathers of the deceased heroes is extremely rare in the *Gododdin*. The only other is a comparison with Elffin in the first of a short chain of *awdlau* found only in the A text, which is usually understood as a later intrusion.[28]

---

[23] *AstHen*, p. 124.
[24] See Cardiff MS 2.28, p. 37.
[25] *AMWL*, p. 6.
[26] *AyG*, ll. 951–52; *GofA*, pp. 8–9.
[27] For speculation on whether this reference sheds any light on the question of the historicity of Arthur, see *AyG*, pp. 147–48, and *AMWL*, pp. 6–7.
[28] *AyG*, ll. 405–06; *GofA*, pp. 93–94. It is said of Eithinyn, that 'he ?pressed forward with

There is no evidence to suggest that either this couplet or the *awdl* as a whole are later interpolations. It has orthographical features (discussed below) which point to the Old Welsh period, but detailed study and a reconstruction by Koch has revealed no convincing linguistic evidence to place it either earlier or later than this.[29] An edited text with detailed notes and a comprehensive word-list follows.

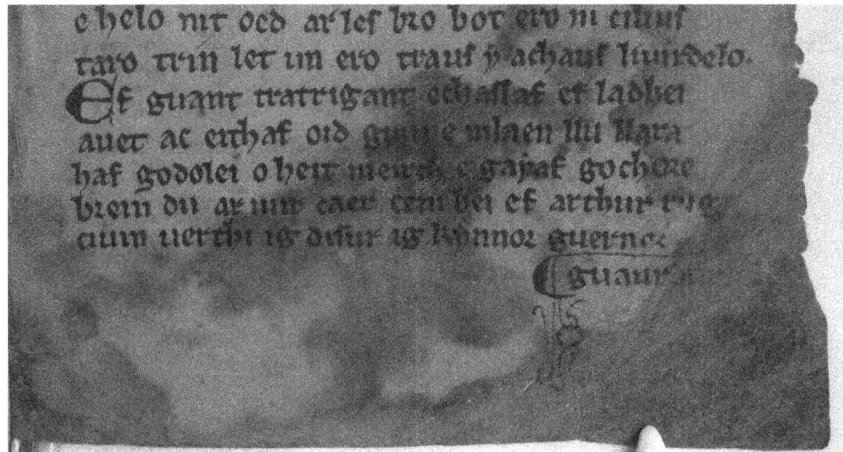

FIG. 2.1: Cardiff MS 2.28, p. 37.

Ef guant tratrigant echassaf ef ladhei | auet ac eithaf oid guiu e mlaen llu llara|haf godolei o heit meirch e gayaf gochore | brein du ar uur caer ceni bei ef arthur rug | ciuin uerthi ig disur ig kynnor guernor | guaur[dur]

          Ef guant tra tricant echassaf,
          ef ladhei a [per]uet ac eithaf,
          oid guiu e mlaen llu llaryhaf,
4   godolei o heit meirch e gayaf.
          Gochore[i] brein du ar uur
          caer ceni bei-ef Arthur.
          Rug ciuin uerthi ig [cl]isur,
8   ig kynnor guernor Guaur[...].

1   **Ef guant tra trigant echassaf** The form *guant*, prefixed by a subject pronoun (a common construction in early poetry, cf. *AyG*, ll. 774–75), can be understood as the 3 sing.pret. of *gwanu*. A range of meanings are appropriate: 'to stab,

courage in the manner of Elffin'. This may be Elffin son of Urien Rheged or Elffin ap Gwyddno, Taliesin's patron, both popular figures in the Welsh literary tradition from the ninth century onwards; see *LPBT* 4.56n. Another possible comparison is *eil Nedic nar*, 'a lord second to Nedig' (*AyG*, l. 570), but there is much textual uncertainty surrounding this *awdl*.
[29] *GofA*, pp. 22–23, 147–49.

pierce, kill, strike, charge, attack', depending on the meaning of the preposition *tra*. It is usually found with place names and words for rivers and seas with the sense 'over, beyond'.

The manuscript form *trigant* is a hapax and probably a mis-modernisation of Old Welsh *tricant* = Middle Welsh *trichant*, *trychant*, 'three hundred', the numeral *tri* causing a spirant mutation; see *GMW*, p. 21. 'Three hundred' is used often in the collection to refer to the host of the Gododdin. Another possibility put forward by Graham R. Isaac in *The Verb in the Book of Aneirin: Studies in Syntax, Morphology and Etymology* [*VBA*] (Tübingen: Max Niemeyer Verlag, 1996), p. 407, is a form containing *cant*, 'periphery', which has a cognate in a Celtiberian inscription. Translated as 'boundary' it would give a good meaning with *tra*, 'beyond'.

Echasaf, a superlative, is a rare form (see *PT* IX 1n), and is tentatively understood as an adjective used substantively for the warriors, 'finest or bravest ones'. The preposition *tra* might be used here with the unusual meaning 'beyond, surpassing': 'he attacked beyond (i.e. in a way that surpassed) three hundred of the finest [warriors]', i.e. the whole of the Gododdin army. For a similar use of *tra*, see *LPBT* 10.32, *Aranrot drem clot tra gwawr hinon*, 'Arianrhod, famed for her appearance surpassing the radiance of fair weather'; *CBT* II 24.18, *a glyw tra glyw, a llyw tra llyw, trillu rhagddaw*, 'and [he was] a lord beyond [any other] lord, and a leader beyond [any other] leader, with three hosts before him'. According to *GPC*, *tra* may also be used with the meaning 'over, more than'. If *tricant echassaf* is understood as the object of *guant* and a reference to the enemy, the line can be read as follows: 'he attacked more than three hundred of the finest [warriors]' (cf. *GOSP*, p. 112). A. O. H. Jarman's interpretation, 'he charged before three hundred of the finest' (*AyG*, l. 967), is less likely, as it stretches the meaning of *tra* to 'before', and John Koch's suggestion (*GofA*, l. 1237n) that *guant* may be passive is possible but would require omitting *ef*.

2   **ef ladhei a [per]uet ac eithaf** The *-h-* in the verbal form *lladhei* suggests an imperfect subjunctive but this is unexpected following *guant* in the previous line. According to Isaac (*VBA*, p. 250), this second clause may express a final sense, 'He charged ... so that he might kill ...'. The form may, however, be better understood as an error or an unusual spelling for *lladei*, the imperfect indicative form, especially since *guant* may still have its original imperfect sense here (see Isaac, 'An Indo-European Athematic Imperfect in Welsh? Middle Welsh *Gwant*', *Studia Celtica*, 35 (2001), 354–59). (For examples of <dh> for /ð/ in the A-text of the manuscript, see, for example, *ny dheli* (*Canu Aneirin*, l. 1438 (*Gwarchan Maeldderw*).) The form *uet* may be understood as a mutated form of *met*, a rare word with the meaning 'authority, power' (see *GPC* medd^2) but this does not make much sense. Koch (*GofA*, p. 148), for metrical reasons, restores it to *ue(i)* < *mei(ð)*, 'middle', which is only attested as a prefix in forms like *meiau*, 'middle-

yoke', and *meiwr*, 'a mediocre man, coward' (*GPC* mei-). This is possible, but the emendation to *a peruet ac eithaf* is suggested by the examples in the Book of Taliesin of *perueδ*, 'middle, centre', and *eithaf*, 'extremity, wing (of an army)', used together, and especially the lines *ef lladei a pherued | ac eithaf a diwed*, 'he slashed the centre [of the army] and the wing and the rear' (see *LPBT* 5.104n). Patrick Sims-Williams (personal correspondence) has suggested that the first syllable of *peruet* may have been omitted by a copier who was unfamiliar with the Latin abbreviation for *per*.

3   **oid guiu e mlaen llu llaryhaf** MS *llarahaf*. It appears that Old Welsh **largham*, the superlative degree of the adjective **larg*, 'generous', a borrowing from Latin *largus*, may have been mis-modernised here. In the medieval period, the non-syllabic *y*, which represented a final *g* following *r* or *l*, was either vocalised as *a* or dropped (*llary > llara, llar*, see *GMW*, p. 10). When a syllable was added, the non-syllabic *y* was retained (*llary + -haf*). *Llarahaf*, however, contains the syllabic form. It is possible to understand *llaryhaf* as an adjective complimenting *llu*, 'he was most splendid [even] at the head of the most generous host', or used substantively as the subject of the sentence, 'the most generous one was splendid at the front of a host'. In these lines, then, the contrasting virtues of ferocity in battle and generosity towards followers are praised.

4   **godolei o heit meirch e gayaf** It would be a sign of great generosity and great wealth for a lord to give away gifts of horses from his stud during the harsh winter months. On horses as valuable commodities, see *The Horse in Celtic Culture: Medieval Welsh Perspectives* [*HCC*], ed. by Sioned Davies and Nerys Ann Jones (Cardiff: University of Wales Press, 1997). *E gayaf* may be understood as an adverbial phrase, 'in winter time', very common in the Welsh law texts and the chronicles (see *GMW*, p. 226). Although the definite article is rare in early poetry there are a number of examples of it with *gayaf* and it is more likely here than Isaac's suggestion (*VBA*, p. 169) of preposition *yn* + *gaeaf*, of which there are no examples.

5   **Gochore[i] brein du** A 3 sing.imperf. form is expected here. The *-e* is probably the Old Welsh spelling of the ending, which had not been modernised to *-ei* as the scribe was not familiar with the verb. There are no other examples of *gochoraf*: *gochori* (< ?*go-*, 'under; rather' + unknown element). Koch (*GofA*, p. 148) has drawn attention to *fo-cuirethar*, a regular cognate in Old Irish, but its literal meaning, 'to throw or send forth', is not appropriate here. The meaning 'to feed, satisfy, glut' given by Jackson (*GOSP*, p. 112) and Jarman (*AyG*, l. 971n), is based on the common motif of the warrior providing food for ravens in battle. According to Sims-Williams (personal correspondence), *gochori* may be connected with the noun *gogawr* (*GPC* gogor[1]), 'fodder', with *g ~ ch* as in the variant forms *gogel* and *gochel*.

5–6   **ar uur | caer** One can imagine the fighting happening on the ramparts of a fort or, using a more unusual meaning of the preposition *ar* found in the poetry (*GMW*, p. 184), 'in front of, facing' the defensive wall of a fortress or a fortified town. The use of enjambment is common throughout the collection.

7   **Rug ciuin(u)erthi ig [cl]isur** This line requires emendation and is very difficult to interpret with any certainty. The MS forms *ciuin uerthi* may be understood as one word, with *ciuin* an error for prefix *cyf-* in its Old Welsh form *cum-*, and *uerthi* an error for *nerth*, 'force, strength, power' and the suffix *-i*. The only other example of *cyfnerthi* (*CBT* I 26.39) is an abstract noun, 'strength, firmness, support, aid'. If *i-* were a plural ending here, it could refer to the mighty warriors among whom the hero was fighting. The form *ig*, a form of the preposition *yn* which occurs before *c-/g-*, indicates that the d- of *disur* is probably a copying error for *cl-*. *Clisur*, an element which is found in the compounds *gochlysur* (*LPBT* 9.9n), *goglysur* (*AyG*, p. 718), and *echlysur* (*LPBT* 24.9, 13) may be understood as having the same root as *achles*, 'refuge, shelter', or compared to Old Irish *cless*, 'feat', with *-ur*, which may be an agent ending or an abstract ending. Various meanings have been deduced, including 'armour, defence; feats, deeds; a shower of spears'.

8   **ig kynnor guernor Guaur[dur]** The form *guernor* is a hapax legomenon (a form which occurs only once) in the Welsh language. It contains the element *or*, 'limit, boundary', which is also found in *kynnor*, 'the van, the front'. Its first element is *gwern*, 'alder', and it refers either to a wooden rampart or palisade or a line of wooden shields joined together and overlapping to form a defensive battle-fold or phalanx (*GPC* gwernor). Here it may be used literally, 'at the front of the alder defence was Gwawrddur', or figuratively for the hero, 'at the van [of battle], a palisade was Gwawrddur'. The last three letters of the subject's name are not clear in the MS but the rhyme requires *-ur*, and the name occurs in an *awdl* belonging to the A version where the members of the warband who fell at Catraeth are listed; see *AyG*, l. 343. The elements of the name appear to be *gwawr*, 'dawn; lord', and *dur*, 'steel'. Koch (*GofA*, p. 148) argues, however, that *guaur-* is not a common element in male names and suggests that it is a false modernisation of *Guordur* with *guor-* (later *gor-*), a much more common initial element in compound names, which also gives three rhymes in the line, a regular pattern in the *Gododdin*. Even if the exemplar read *guordur*, however, the first element would correspond ambiguously either to Middle Welsh *gwawr* or to Middle Welsh *gwor-*, *gor-*. If the latter, *Gwardur* in the Song of the Steeds, Chapter 4 below, could be a variant, since *gwar-* is a variant of *gwor-*.

Word-list

a *conj.* 'and' *in the combination* **a ... a(c)**, 'both and' 2(2)
ar *prep.* 'upon; in front of, facing' (causing soft mutation) 5n

Arthur *personal name* 6
blaen 'front' (*GPC* ymlaen, ym mlaen) 3
brein *pl. of* **bran** *n.* 'crow, rook, raven' 5
caer *n.* 'fortress, fortified town' 6
ceni *conj.* 'although not' (< **cyn**, **cyd** + *negative* **ny**, *GMW*, pp. 235–36, causing soft mutation) 6
ciuinerthi *n.* 'strength, might, support' (*GPC* cyfnerthi) *or* ?*pl.adj. used nominatively* 'mighty ones' 7n
clisur *n.* '?armour, defence; feats, deeds; a shower of spears' 7n
du *adj.* 'black' 5
e *definite article* 'the' 4
echassaf *superlative adj. used nominatively* '?the finest, the most brave' (*GPC* echas) 1
ef^1 *3 sing.masc. independent pron.* 'he' 1, 2 (for the syntax, see *LPBT* 5.104n)
ef^2 *3 sing.masc. affixed pron.* 6
eithaf *n.* 'extreme, wing [of an army]' 2
e mlaen *compound prep.* 'at the front (of)' (< *prep.* **yn**, 'in' (causing nasal mutation) + *n.*
gayaf *n.* 'winter' (*GPC* gaeaf) 4n
gochorei *3 sing.imperf.indic. of* *gochori, 'to feed, satisfy, glut' 5n
godolei *3 sing.imperf.indic. of* **goddolaf**: **goddoli** (a variant of **gwaddoli**, see *GPC*) 'to endow, divide, distribute, give' 4
guant *3 sing.pret. of* **gwanu** (*t-* preterite, *GMW*, pp. 123–24) 'to charge, attack; stab, pierce, kill, strike' 1n
Guaurdur *personal name* Gwawrddur, Gworddur 8n
guernor *n.* 'a defence made of alder' (*GPC* gwernor) 8n
guiu *adj.* 'fine, excellent, handsome, good' (*GPC* gwiw) 3
heit *n.* 'herd or stud of horses' (*GPC* haid) 4
ig *form of prep.* **in**, **yn**, 'in' *used before c-* (*GPC* yn^1) 7, 8
kynnor *n.* 'front, van' 8n
lladhei *3 sing.imperf.subj. of* **llad**, 'to kill, cut down, strike' 2n
llaryhaf *superlative degree of adj.* **llary**, 'generous' 3n
llu *n.* 'a host, army' 3
meirch *pl. of* **march**, 'horse' 4
mur *n.* 'wall, rampart' 5
o *prep.* 'from' 4
oid *3 sing.imperf.indic. of* **bot**, 'to be' 3
pei *3 sing.imperf. subj. of* **bot**, 'to be' 6
peruet *n.* 'centre, middle' (*GPC* perfedd) 2n
rug *prep.* 'between, among' (*GMW*, p. 208, rwng) 7
tra *prep.* (causing spirant mutation) 'over, beyond, surpassing, more than' 1n
tricant *numeral* 'three hundred' (*GPC* trichant) *or n.* 'boundary' 1n

CHAPTER 3

The Hendregadredd Manuscript

National Library of Wales manuscript 6680B was discovered in 1910 in a wardrobe at Hendregadredd, a mansion near Porthmadog, after having been lost from Robert Vaughan's library in Hengwrt in the eighteenth century.[1] It is called a 'manuscript' rather than a 'book' because it was named in the twentieth century and not earlier. Intended as an anthology of the work of the court poets who sang during the two centuries before the death of Llywelyn the Last in 1282,[2] it is the most carefully planned of all the medieval collections containing Welsh poetry.

Daniel Huws has shown that it was written mostly by one hand, which he called Alpha.[3] This compiler gathered the work of each of the main court poets of the period, a total of some 130 poems, into separate quires or sequences of quires, creating a mixed quire for those represented by only a few poems. He was clearly a master of *ordinatio* and *compilatio*, arts which he may have learnt, along with his distinctive heavy rounded script, at a university in Paris.[4] Alpha left spaces at the end of a number of quires for more poetry. These were filled by nineteen near-contemporary scribes who added another fifty poems to the collection, following the scheme set out by Alpha. The large number of hands working in collaboration, in addition to the high standard of the rubrication and decoration of the work of Alpha, suggests a sizeable monastic scriptorium. Another group of about twenty hands added a third stratum to the manuscript's text, filling the spaces that remained with twenty-five poems for Ieuan Llwyd ap Gruffudd Foel, his relatives and friends.[5] Ieuan, a nobleman descended from

---

[1] To view the manuscript, and for an outline of its later history, visit the National Library of Wales website <www.llgc.org.uk>.
[2] These poets are referred to by modern scholars as Poets of the Princes or the *Gogynfeirdd*; see J. E. Caerwyn Williams, *The Court Poet in Medieval Wales: An Essay* [*CP*] (Lampeter: Edwin Mellen Press, 1997); Peredur I. Lynch, 'Court Poetry, Power and Politics' in *The Welsh King and his Court* [*WKC*], ed. by T. M. Charles-Edwards, Morfydd E. Owen and Paul Russell (Cardiff: University of Wales Press, 2000), pp. 167–90.
[3] Daniel Huws, 'The Hendregadredd Manuscript' in *MWM*, pp. 193–226.
[4] Ibid., p. 226.
[5] On the possibility that Dafydd ap Gwilym, the best-known poet of fourteenth-century Wales, contributed a poem in his own hand to the manuscript, see Huws, 'The Transmission

the princes of Deheubarth, was one of the most prominent patrons of poets in Ceredigion during the second quarter of the fourteenth century. The haphazard way in which these poems were added and the lack of skill in their writing suggests that, at this time, the manuscript may have been used as a 'house-book' at Ieuan's home, Glyn Aeron, not far from the Cistercian Abbey of Strata Florida where it had probably been produced.

The latest poem copied by Alpha is an elegy for Llywelyn the Last composed soon after his death in 1282. The earliest datable poem is an elegy for Llywelyn's ancestor, Gruffudd ap Cynan of Gwynedd, who died in 1137. The scribe may have spent many years collecting poems from all parts of Wales. He was probably responsible for ordering them and may also have modernised their spelling and added some titles, possibly writing some poems from memory.[6] What compelled him to go to such lengths to preserve the poetry of the recent past? J. E. Caerwyn Williams has suggested that the collection was commissioned by a descendant of Maredudd ab Owain, the most powerful of the princes of Ceredigion in the mid-thirteenth century, and the subject of a number of poems kept in the manuscript.[7] Members of his family were famous as patrons of learning: it was one of his sons who commissioned Madog ap Selyf to translate the Chronicle of Turpin into Welsh, and it was for his daughter, Efa, that Gruffudd Bola translated the Athanasian Creed.[8] It is also possible that the impulse to produce the manuscript originated in the monastery itself. We know very little about the abbots of this period, but it may be significant that the original Latin version of *Brut y Tywysogyon*, a chronicle of independent Wales based on monastic annals, was also complied in Strata Florida around this time.[9] According to A. D. Carr, 'it may have been intended by its author as a kind of elegy on the age of the princes'.[10] Could it be that this collection was created at Strata Florida with a similar intention?

It is not possible to be sure of the original order of the quires in the manuscript but if the pagination made by Wiliam Llŷn in the sixteenth century is followed, it opens with an extensive collection of the work of Cynddelw Brydydd Mawr

---

of a Welsh Classic: Dafydd ap Gwilym' in *MWM*, pp. 88–89.
[6] See T. M. Charles-Edwards and Paul Russell, 'The Hendregadredd Manuscript and the Orthography and Phonology of Welsh in the Early Fourteenth Century', *National Library of Wales Journal*, 28 (1994), 419–62.
[7] *CP*, pp. 65–67.
[8] Ibid., pp. 58–61.
[9] Thomas Jones, *Brut y Tywysogyon or the Chronicle of the Princes: Peniarth MS. 20 Version* (Cardiff: University of Wales Press, 1952), pp. xxxv–xliv. The relationship between the lost Latin original of the Brut and earlier annalistic texts is under revision: see, for example, David Stephenson, 'Welsh Chronicles' Accounts of the Mid-Twelfth Century', *CMCS*, 56 (2008), 45–57.
[10] A. D. Carr, *Medieval Wales* (Basingstoke: St Martin's Press, 1995), p. 5.

(Cynddelw the Great Poet),[11] organised according to subject matter. Poems addressed to God and to Tysilio, patron saint of the poet's native Powys, come first, followed by three quires of secular poetry in *awdl* metre for the princes of twelfth-century Wales, Owain Gwynedd, Madog ap Maredudd of Powys and Lord Rhys of Deheubarth, and for their noblemen, and a quire of *englynion* arranged in similar fashion but also including poems for the princes' warbands. Three quires of the poetry of Llywarch Brydydd y Moch (Llywarch Poet of the Pigs),[12] court poet to Llywelyn the Great, are also organised according to metre and subject, chronologically and by kingdom, with precedence given to God and then the rulers of Gwynedd. Quires are dedicated to the work of the two twelfth-century poet-princes Owain Cyfeiliog of Powys and Hywel ab Owain Gwynedd, to the *awdlau* of Meilyr Brydydd of Gwynedd, his son Gwalchmai and grandson Einion ap Gwalchmai, to the *awdlau* of Gwynfardd Brycheiniog and the *englynion* of Y Prydydd Bychan (the Minor or Junior Poet) of Deheubarth,[13] and there is also a miscellany containing *awdlau* by nine different Gwynedd poets. The only sign of confusion in the ordering of the poems surrounds the work of Bleddyn Fardd, who sang elegies for Llywelyn the Last and his brothers.[14]

Daniel Huws has shown that at least one quire and many individual pages are missing from the manuscript today.[15] Some of the now lost poems were preserved by the seventeenth-century scholar Dr John Davies of Mallwyd in a manuscript now known as NLW 4973B.[16] Others are found in the late fourteenth-century Red Book of Hergest along with variant versions of existing Hendregadredd poems.[17] Unlike Alpha and his successors, the scribes of the

[11] The accent in Cynddelw's name is on the first syllable. His cognomen *Prydydd Mawr* may have referred to his physical size if it was used during his lifetime, as is suggested by an *englyn* attributed to Seisyll Bryffwrch (*CBT* IV 12.21–24), but it may also reflect his stature as a court poet.

[12] It has been suggested that his unusual cognomen may derive from a provocative warning he gives to one of his patrons: 'For you, let the casting of my poem not be like the casting of pearls before swine', *CBT* V 8.13–14.

[13] If this cognomen was used during the poet's lifetime it may have been because he was a son of Phylip Brydydd, who sang praise poetry to members of the same noble family in Deheubarth. It is also possible that it was used later to distinguish between him and Cynddelw the Great Poet.

[14] It appears that Alpha's original plan was to include poems by Bleddyn in a mixed quire. As more poems came to hand, he dedicated two quires to *awdlau* and *englynion* by the poet. For an overview of the poems in the Hendregadredd Manuscript, see Nerys Ann Jones, 'Ffynonellau Canu Beirdd y Tywysogion', *Studia Celtica*, 37 (2003), 118–24.

[15] For his outline of the collation of the manuscript, see Huws, 'Hendregadredd', p. 197. It is likely that a quire containing religious poems by Cynddelw is missing, but the manuscript may also have included a quire of *awdlau* by Y Prydydd Bychan and more poems by Gwilym Rhyfel.

[16] See Chapter 5 below.

[17] On the Red Book, see Chapter 1.

Red Book created their vast compendium of medieval Welsh poetry and prose by copying material as it came to hand.[18] Because of this, some light is shed on the source of the works of the Poets of the Princes common to both manuscripts and on the original form of some series of poems possibly distorted by the Hendregadredd scribes, who were keen to set poetry in *awdl* metre, apart from the *englynion*.[19]

The subject matter of the poems contained in the Hendregadredd Manuscript is quite limited compared with those of the Black Book, the Red Book and the Book of Taliesin.[20] The great majority are eulogies or elegies for princes or noblemen, praising their qualities as warriors, rulers and benefactors. Within the confines of genre, however, there is huge variety of expression according to the status of the subject and the nature of the occasion. Some poems are clearly intended for great ceremonial gatherings, a prince's inauguration, a diplomatic visit by the poet to the court of an ally or a subject of his patron, or the commemoration of a ruler's death. These are stately odes running to two or three hundred ornate and highly formulaic lines, with archaic vocabulary, complex syntax and rhetorical devices.[21] Others are concise and immediate expressions of loyalty or loss, short *awdlau*, or chains of *englynion*, often containing an element of drama or movement and the same delight in creating lists as was seen in some of the Black Book poems above.

All these poems have in common a desire on the part of the poets to display their knowledge and learning. They do this by enumerating and evoking their patrons' greatest victories, tracing their ancestry, and listing the lands and peoples they ruled. The poems are characterised by a prolific use of epithets and a vast range of terms related to warfare and feasting, and an echoing of the vocabulary, imagery and motifs used by their immediate predecessors and poets of earlier centuries. They also allude to figures from the past, historical kings and legendary heroes, with whom the subjects of their praise are compared or identified.

---

[18] See Gifford Charles-Edwards, 'The Scribes of the Red Book of Hergest', *National Library of Wales Journal,* 21 (1977–1980), 246–56.
[19] This source is discussed further in Jones, 'Ffynonellau', 109–11.
[20] The corpus has been edited in *Cerddi Beirdd y Tywysogion* [*CBT*], general editor R. Geraint Gruffydd (7 volumes, Cardiff: University of Wales Press, 1991–1996). The texts and translations included in this chapter are based on this edition. I am grateful to Rhian M. Andrews for many suggestions regarding making the translations more accessible and clear.
[21] For an outline of the commonest metres, the various kinds of *cymeriad* used, and the patterns of internal rhyme and consonantal correspondence (*cynghanedd*), see WCP, pp. xl–li.

The poetry of Cynddelw Brydydd Mawr and his contemporaries

It is not surprising that it is in the work of Cynddelw, which constitutes about a quarter of the corpus, that most of these are found: some eighty references in thirty eulogies and elegies. They include allusions to kings and heroes of classical literature like Hector, Hercules, Achilles and Alexander, rulers and champions of the Brythonic kingdoms of the Old North and early Gwynedd like Cynon ap Cynwyd, Urien, Maelgwn, Rhun and Hiriell, characters from the Four Branches of the *Mabinogi* like Brân fab Llŷr, Lleu, Pryderi, Teyrnon and Matholwch, and a number of figures who are otherwise unknown like Gwrfan, Alaswy, Hilig and Heilyn. Most of these appear once or twice only, with the exception of metrically useful names like Heilyn and Teyrnon.[22] There is only one reference to Arthur himself, but Cynddelw names some fourteen figures who are associated with him in texts like *Culhwch ac Olwen*, the Welsh romances, the Dream of Rhonabwy and the Triads. They are Cai and his father, Cynyr, Cynon fab Culfanawyd, Dillus fab Efrai, Elifry, Graid fab Eri, Gwair, Gwalchmai, Gwythur, Llachau, March, Medrawd, Ogrfan and Owain.

Almost a half of these Arthurian characters are named in one poem towards the beginning of Alpha's collection of secular poetry attributed to Cynddelw, an elegy for Owain who died in 1170 after thirty-three years on the throne of Gwynedd. In a majestic sequence of seven *awdlau* reaching to almost 300 lines,[23] Owain's life as a ruler, military leader, patron and friend is celebrated. Each mono-rhyming section has a different emphasis. The sixth contains praise of Owain's military might, focussing in particular on a great victory of his youth, the famous Battle of Crug Mawr near the River Teifi in 1136. It is in this section that Owain is compared with a number of legendary figures, most of them Arthurian:[24]

> Gwerssyll toruoet teƿ, lleƿ llatei,
> gorsaf taryf, taerualch ual Gwalchmei,
> goruaran Gƿruan goruytei,
> gƿr yn aer yn aros gwaetuei.
> ...
> Gwythur naƿs, ual traƿs a'e treissei,
> gwytuid Eigyl, yg clat a'e trychei,
> gwytgƿn coed, colled a'e porthei.

---

[22] On these two names see below, Chapter 4, *Kadeir Teyrnon*.
[23] The metre is *Byr a Thoddaid*, a combination of eight-syllable lines (*Cyhydedd Fer*) and a unit of sixteen syllables (written as two lines) consisting of three equal sections linked together by consonantal correspondence or internal rhyme (*Toddaid Byr*); see *WCP*, p. xliii.
[24] For the poem see NLW MS 6680B 'The Hendregadredd Manuscript', ff. 38ʳ–39ᵛ. The edition and translation given below are based on *CBT* IV 4.181–84 and 196–208.

Gwytwal Dyfneual dyfnassei — uy mot,
    uy metyant a gaffaei,
colleis arglwyt call ny'm collei,
coryf eurdoryf, eurdal a'm rotei;
cof cadulawt (a'm cawt a'm carei)
car kertawr, kerteu a'e kyrchei,
gryd wasgar lluchuar a'm llochei,
grym dillut Dullus uab Eurei,
gretyf Greidwyr a Chynyr a Chei,
glew defawd, glyw oestrawd aestrei.

The refuge of great multitudes, [Owain] the lion would slay,
a bulwark amidst confusion [in battle], eager and imposing like Gwalchmai,
his [wrath] exceeded the great wrath of Gwrfan,
a warrior in battle awaiting the call to fight.
…
The nature of Gwythur [was his], his attacker was like a powerful warrior,
buried are those of the Angles' army who struck at him,
it was the dead that gave sustenance to the wild dogs of the forest,
Dyfneual [i.e. Owain] was a wild leader who used to satisfy me,
he had authority over me,
I lost a wise lord who would never lose me,
the upholder of a splendid host, he gave me splendid payment;
memories of a battle-stirrer (he who loved me causes me grief),
beloved of poets, poems came to him,
[the one of] flashing anger, scattering [the enemy] in battle, used to nurture
                                                                            me,
[he had] the unopposed authority of Dillus ap Efrai,
and the nature of Greidwyr and Cynyr and Cai,
brave was his manner, a lord of constant attack with a shattered shield.

The first to be mentioned is *Gwalchmei*, famous in later Welsh literature as one of Arthur's knights. His name is found only once more in the corpus but it is also borne by Cynddelw's contemporary, Gwalchmai ap Meilyr, suggesting that he was already well known in the Welsh tradition before Geoffrey of Monmouth.[25] In a section dominated by the sound /gw-/, the prince is also compared with *Gŵruan* and *Gwythur*. The first may be *Gwruan Gwallt Auwyn*, 'Gwrfan of the Beautiful Hair', listed in *Culhwch ac Olwen*;[26] another reference to him by Cynddelw may suggest that he was a giant.[27] The second may be Gwythyr son of

---

[25] The name is used by Y Prydydd Bychan to praise his patron, Rhys Ieuanc of Deheubarth, for his prowess in battle (*CBT* VII 2.15n). For the reference to Gwalchmai in the Stanzas of the Graves and in other medieval Welsh texts, see Chapter 1 above. It is likely that the poet Gwalchmai was born in the early years of the twelfth century, as he mentions that he received patronage from Cadwallon ap Gruffudd ap Cynan, who died in 1132.
[26] *CO*, l. 294.
[27] For the other two references to him by Cynddelw, see *CBT* IV 5.33 and 9.94. In the latter

Greidawl, who appears in a number of episodes of *Culhwch ac Olwen*, where he is portrayed as a violent character.[28] Nothing is known about the fierce warrior *Dyfneual*, who is mentioned again by Cynddelw in a praise poem for Owain's son, Hywel.[29] It is interesting to note that in both lines, *Dyfneual*'s name is used by the poet for alliteration and rhyme. *Dullus uab Eurei* may also have been chosen for metrical reasons, but he does appear in *Culhwch ac Olwen* as the giant *Dillus Varchawc* (the horseman) or *Dillus Uaruawc* (the bearded).[30] Owain is likened to *Cei* in the subsequent line along with his father, *Kynyr*, and an otherwise unknown figure, *Greidwyr*.

The proximity of the references to Cai and Dillus suggests that Cynddelw may have been familiar with the episode recounted in *Culhwch ac Olwen* where the bearded giant is slain by Cai and Bedwyr.[31] Further evidence of the poet's knowledge of some of the legendary material gathered together in the tale is found in Cynddelw's poem of praise for Hywel ab Owain, which was probably commissioned soon after his father's death. In lines linked by the repetition of forms of the verb *caffael*, 'to receive', which talk mostly of his great generosity, Hywel is also praised for providing scavenging dogs and carrion birds with food in battle, and is identified with *Trwyd*, the fierce boar-king hunted by Arthur, known in *Culhwch ac Olwen* and later Welsh literature as *Twrch Trwyth*:[32]

> Keffid eu keinllith kỽn kunllwyd,
> keffynt ueryon voreuwyd,
> keffitor ymdwr am Drwyd — heuelyt,
> tỽrch teryt y ar uwyd,
> caffaỽd beirt eu but yn yt wyd,
> keffid noeth noted rac anwyd ...

Lord Rhys is likened to *Gỽrvan gaỽr*, which may be understood as 'Gwrfan the giant' (< *cawr*) or 'Gwrfan [in] battle' (< *gawr*). It is possible, but not likely, that *gỽrvan* is an adjective; see *GPC* gwrfan for its derviation and further examples of its use as a personal name.

[28] For other references to Gwythur in the Welsh bardic tradition, see Chapter 1 above, Stanzas of the Graves.

[29] *CBT* IV 6.145, *Fwyr dyfynurys Dyfneual*, '[He who instils] terror [arising out of] intense speed [like] Dyfneual'.

[30] See *CO*, l. 700n.

[31] *CO*, ll. 953-74. Oliver Padel draws attention to the fact that the two names are found again in rhyming position in the *englyn* Arthur uses to mock Cai in *Culhwch*; see *CO*, l. 977n; *AMWL*, pp. 57-58.

[32] On the name *Trwyd*, which is also used for the boar hunted by Arthur in *Historia Brittonum*, see *CO*, pp. lxv-vi. On the form *teryt* (*GPC* terydd) in the following line of the poem, which appears as the boar's name in an eleventh-century recension of the *Historia*, suggesting that Cynddelw may have drawn on written sources, see Sims-Williams, *IIMWL*, pp. 40-44. For the poem, see NLW MS 6680B, f. 42ʳ. For these lines, see *CBT* IV 6.204-09 and *AMWL*, pp. 58-59. For a discussion of the 3 pl pres.indic. verbal form *keffynt*, which is not otherwise found in the corpus, and the suggestion that this and *keffid* in the previous line may be interpreted as imperfect forms, see Rodway, *DMWL*, pp. 57-58.

Wild dogs in a grey pack receive their splendid nourishment,
birds of prey receive a morning meal,
there is mustering around the one like Trwyd,
the fierce boar at his food,
poets receive their gift wherever you are,
the naked receive shelter from cold ...

In both the elegy for Owain and the eulogy for Hywel, two extremely ambitious poems composed shortly before Hywel's untimely death, Cynddelw three times identifies father and son with Arthur without naming him. In the fifth section of Owain's elegy he praises the abundance of the prince's Christmas feasts, picturing crowds of guests visiting his court at Llanbeblig near Caernarfon, just like the warriors on their wonderful warhorses coming to receive Arthur's patronage at his court in *Kelliwyc*.[33] Towards the end of the elegy, Owain, 'splendid dragon of Snowdonia', is said to have exhibited in his lifetime military action like that seen at *Gweith Uadon*, the Battle of Badon, where Arthur slew 960 warriors according to *Historia Brittonum*.[34] An earlier reference to the battle in an anonymous poem in the Black Book of Carmarthen praises Hywel ap Goronwy, a ruler of Brycheiniog who died in 1106, as *Baton vetveint*, '[a provider of] drunkenness [as in] Badon', alluding perhaps to the celebration that followed the great victory over the English.[35] In the other poems in the Hendregadredd collection, however, Badon is compared with specific military encounters: the Battle of Crug Mawr (1136) in an inaugural poem by Cynddelw for Owain Gwynedd, the burning of the castle at Aberystwyth (1143) in his poem of praise for Hywel, and an attack led by Llywelyn the Great on Porthaethwy in Anglesey (1194) in a series of *englynion* attributed by John Davies of Mallwyd to Cynddelw but more likely to be the work of Llywarch Brydydd y Moch.[36] Arthur's final battle at Camlan is used in a similar way by Llywarch, as he compares its ferocity with that of the taking of Mold in 1199 in a catalogue of the victories of Llywelyn.[37] Bromwich claims that stories about this battle were prominent in the early Arthurian tradition,[38] but there does not seem to be an awareness of the disastrous nature of Camlan in this reference or in a poem by Llywelyn Fardd II to a thirteenth-century prince of southern

---

[33] *CBT* IV 4.167–70. On Celli Wig see Chapter 1 above, *Pa gur*, l. 33n, and on the depiction of royal courts in the corpus, see Morfydd E. Owen, 'Literary Convention and Historical Reality: The Court in the Welsh Poetry of the Twelfth and Thirteenth Centuries', *Etudes celtiques*, 29 (1992), 69–85.
[34] *CBT* IV 4.236–39. On the battle, first associated with Arthur in *Historia Brittonum*, see Thomas Charles-Edwards, 'The Arthur of History' in *AW*, pp. 15–32.
[35] *CBT* I 1.42. On the dating of the poem, see David Stephenson, 'Mawl Hywel ap Goronwy: Dating and Context', *Cambrian Medieval Celtic Studies*, 57 (2009), 41–49.
[36] See *CBT* IV 1.39–40, 6.98–99, 13.19–20.
[37] See *CBT* V 23.79–80.
[38] *TYP*, pp. 167–68, and see *AMWL*, pp. 58–59, 87–88.

Powys where the booty which he has amassed is likened to that taken from Camlan.[39] Cynddelw, likewise, simply praises Hywel ab Owain for his custom of causing his opponents to flee, 'disappearing as at the great assault at the Battle of Camlan'.[40] Gruffudd ab yr Ynad Coch, however, makes a poignant comparison between Camlan and the skirmish in which Llywelyn the Last was killed in 1282, implying, perhaps, that the two were similar in their devastating consequences: *Llawer llef druan, ual ban vu Gamlan*, 'Many pitiful cries, as it was in Camlan'.[41]

Although only one reference to Arthur himself (discussed below) can be confidently attributed to Cynddelw, the numerous allusions in his poetry to Arthurian characters, places and events give us an idea of his enthusiasm for and knowledge of the traditions and stories surrounding him. A similar impression cannot be gained from the work of the other poets of the twelfth century. This is largely due to the paucity of allusions to any figures other than ancestors in their surviving compositions. In a total of sixteen eulogies or elegies by his predecessor, Meilyr Brydydd, his contemporaries, Gwalchmai ap Meilyr, Llywelyn Fardd I, Daniel ap Llosgwrn Mew, Peryf ap Cedifor, Seisyll Bryffwrch, Gwynfardd Brycheiniog, and the two poet-princes Owain Cyfeiliog and Hywel ab Owain, we find only eleven references, most of them consisting simply of an epithet containing an abstract noun or an adjective and the name of the hero, often linked by alliteration or rhyme: *cyfeisior Echdor, Cadarnfael hael, menwyd Medrawd* etc.

The two allusions to Arthur furnish us with very little direct information about the way he was perceived in the middle years of the twelfth century. The reference in an elegy by Seisyll Bryffwrch for Owain Gwynedd is difficult to interpret because of a missing line and may even be due to an editorial emendation by John Davies of Mallwyd, whose seventeenth-century copy of a lost portion of Hendregadredd is the earliest text of this poem.[42]

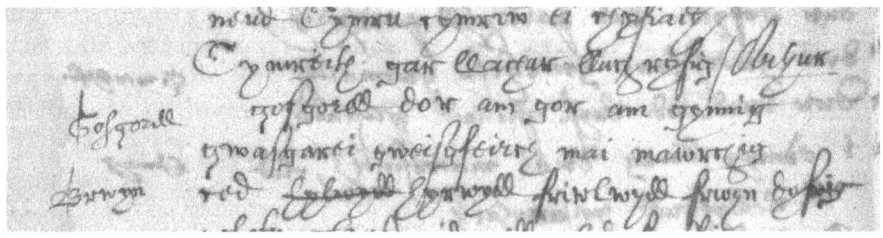

FIG. 3.1: NLW 4973B, f. 21ᵛ.

[39] *CBT* VI 8.5.
[40] *CBT* IV 6.266–67.
[41] *CBT* VII 36.57.
[42] NLW MS 4973B, f. 22ʳ; *CBT* II 22.27–30. I am grateful to Rhian Andrews for suggesting to me that this excerpt probably consists of the first line of a *Toddaid Byr* with its second line missing, followed by two lines of *Cyhydedd Fer*. (For the metre see n. 23 above.) Errors in John Davies' modernised text are noted in italic script in the edited version.

Cymreith gar llachar luch ryfig / Arthur | gosgordd dor am gor am gynnig | gwasgarei gweisgfeirch mai mawrchig

> Cyfiaith gar llachar, lluch ryfig — Arthur,
> [   ]
>   gosgordd dor am gor, am gynnig,
>   gwasgarei gweisgfeirch mai mawrthig.
>
> Bright benefactor of his fellow-countrymen, of the lightning boldness of
>   Arthur,
> ...
> protector of the warband around the assembly, around those who sought
>   [him],
> he distributed swift steeds of the plain, trained for war.

In Gwalchmai's *arwyrain* (exaltation) poem, which may have been composed to mark the beginning of his professional relationship with Madog ap Maredudd, prince of Powys, *c.* 1150, Arthur is again presented in a military context.[43]

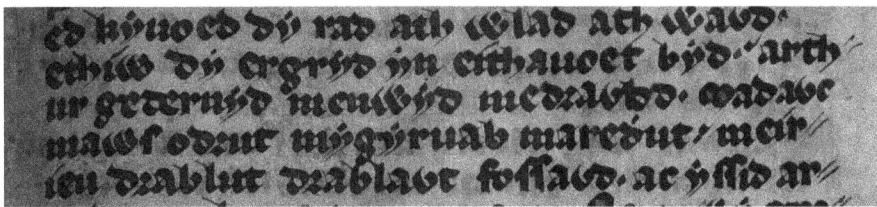

FIG. 3.2: NLW MS 6680B, f. 7ʳ.

ethiw dy ergryd yn eithauoet byd. arth-|ur geternyd menwyd medrawṭd. madaƲc | maws odrut mygyruab maredut. meir-|ieu drablut drablaut fossaƲd.

> Ethiw dy ergryd yn eithauoet byd,
>   Arthur gedernyd, menwyd MedraƲd;
> MadaƲc maws odrut, mygyruab Maredut,
>   meirieu drablut, drablaƲt fossaƲd.
>
> Fear of you has reached the ends of the earth,
> [you have] the strength of Arthur, the disposition of Medrawd;
> impetuous, gentle Madog [*or* Madog, the delightful inciter], splendid
>   son of Maredudd,
> a cause of agitation to stewards, one who inspires great fear in battle.

---

[43] NLW MS 6680B, f. 7ʳ; *CBT* I 6.7–10. *Arwyrain* poems were addressed almost exclusively to rulers. The variety of the content suggests that they were probably composed for a number of different circumstances, including the inauguration of a *brenin* and the initiation or resumption of the relationship between poet and patron.

Arthur is paired here with Medrawd who, in an entry in the *Annales Cambriae*, a chronicle written towards the end of the thirteenth century but based on earlier records, is said to have fallen at the Battle of Camlan. In later Welsh literature, Medrawd is identified with Modredus or Modred, who is presented in Geoffrey of Monmouth's *Historia Regum Britanniae* as Arthur's nephew and mortal enemy, a treacherous and malicious character. In Gwalchmai's poem as in three other twelfth-century praise poems in the Hendregadredd collection, including an elegy by his father, Meilyr Brydydd, for Gruffudd ap Cynan of Gwynedd who died in 1137, Medrawd is presented favourably as a standard of comparison to the greatest princes of the day.[44] It is thought that Geoffrey attributed some of the character traits of Melwas, the abductor of Gwenhwyfar, to Medrawd in order to make him Arthur's antagonist at the Battle of Camlan.[45] It seems likely, then, that in the native tradition, Medrawd played some part at the battle of Camlan, but was not responsible for the treachery which led to Arthur's defeat.

Englynion by Cynddelw for the warband of Madog son of Maredudd

The only poem by Cynddelw in which Arthur himself is named is a short series of *englynion* linked by the repetition of the words *godŵryf a glywaf*, 'I hear great tumult'.[46] The series is entitled by Alpha *Eglynyon a cant Kyndelŵ y deulu Madaŵc mab Maredut pan vu uarŵ Madaŵc am glybod eu godŵryf*, '*Englynion* which Cynddelw sang for the warband of Madog ap Maredudd when Madog died because of hearing their great tumult'.[47] A different version is found in the Black Book of Carmarthen under the heading *Marunad Madauc mab Maredut, kyntelv prydit maur ae cant*, 'An elegy for Madog ap Maredudd, Cynddelw the Great Poet sang it'.[48] The order of the first three *englynion* is not the same in both manuscripts[49] and there is an extra *englyn* at the end of the series in Hendregadredd.[50] It is unusual to have such significant differences between two manuscript versions in the court poetry of this period. Both scribes may

---

[44] Medrawd is not mentioned in *Culhwch ac Owen* or by the Welsh court poets of the thirteenth century, but appears again as a heroic figure in fourteenth-century praise poetry; see *TYP*, pp. 445–46. Of significance is the fact that the name Medrawd is not cognate with Modred, which may be Cornish or Breton in origin; see Oliver Padel, 'Geoffrey of Monmouth and Cornwall', *Cambridge Medieval Celtic Studies*, 9 (1984), 15–16.

[45] On Melwas, see Chapter 5 below.

[46] The metre is *Englyn Unodl Union*, a four-line stanza consisting of a *Toddaid Byr* or one of its variants and a rhyming couplet of seven-syllable lines; see *WCP*, p. xliii.

[47] NLW MS 6680B, f. 62^v; *CBT* III 9.

[48] NLW Peniarth MS 1 'Black Book of Carmarthen', f. 52^{r-v}; see Chapter 1 above.

[49] This is enabled by the fact that it is repetition that links these stanzas rather than the more common *cyrch-gymeriad*, where the last word of an *englyn* is repeated at the beginning of the following one.

[50] See the note to l. 21 below.

have been dealing with defective texts which they or others 'corrected', but the variants could also be the product of oral transmission, that is, scribes copying from memory or recitation.[51] In addition to the structural variation facilitated by the loose pattern of incremental repetition, there are also variant readings which are difficult to explain as copying errors.[52]

The titles in both manuscripts agree that the poem was composed after Madog's death, and yet there is no expression of loss or grief in this joyful celebration of the exploits of the warband and its lord in Maelienydd, an area to the south of Powys.[53] It is only the use of the past tense in a line expressing Madog's ownership of the land (line 18 below) which suggests that the prince is no longer alive. It is difficult to imagine the circumstances in which this poem was first performed. Was it perhaps an informal piece composed to encourage the warband of Madog at a difficult time?[54] Or was it originally part of a longer, more formal, sequence of poems, as is suggested by Cynddelw's use of a similar series of dramatic *englynion* as the prelude to a long *awdl* for Lord Rhys of Deheubarth?[55]

It is Madog's warband rather than the prince himself which is the main focus of the poem.[56] The poet hears its battle-cry and likens it to that of three famous warbands of the past, those of Cynon, Benlli and Arthur, before claiming also that it is one of the Three Faithful Warbands of the Island of Britain. The *Tri Diweir Deulu* is listed in the collection the Triads of the Island of Britain which was, according to its editor Rachel Bromwich, probably first brought together in the twelfth century, possibly by Cynddelw himself.[57] They are named as the warbands of Cadwallawn son of Cadfan, Gafran son of Aeddan and Gwenddolau son of Ceid(i)aw, three early rulers with historical connections.[58] Cynon would also probably have been regarded as a historical figure from the distant past. He may be Cynon ap Clydno Eidin, a hero of the *Gododdin* who is listed in the Stanzas of the Graves.[59] Another possibility is Cynon fab Culfanawyd, whose attack in battle is praised by Cynddelw and the thirteenth-

---

[51] See Russell, 'Scribal (In)consistency', p. 170.
[52] See the notes to the edition below.
[53] For the political background, see Stephenson, *MP*, p. 43.
[54] For another series of *englynion* by Cynddelw, probably composed in similar circumstances, see R. Geraint Gruffydd, 'Cynddelw Brydydd Mawr and the Partition of Powys', *Studia Celtica*, 38 (2004), 97–106.
[55] See *WCP*, p. 16.
[56] See Nerys Ann Jones, 'The Warband and the Poets of the Welsh Princes', *Welsh History Review*, 29 (2018) 1–26.
[57] Bromwich puts forward this possibility in 'Cyfeiriadau Traddodiadol a Chwedlonol y Gogynfeirdd' in *Beirdd a Thywysogion: Barddoniaeth Llys yng Nghymru, Iwerddon a'r Alban cyflwynedig i R. Geraint Gruffydd*, ed. by M. E. Owen and B. F. Roberts (Cardiff: University of Wales Press, 1996), pp. 202–18 (p. 215).
[58] See further *TYP* no. 29.
[59] See Chapter 1 above. Cynon is also referred to as a great warrior by two thirteenth-century court poets, Llywelyn Fardd II and Dafydd Benfras; see *TYP*, pp. 326–27.

century poet Gwgon Brydydd.[60] Benlli Gawr most famously appears in *Historia Brittonum* as a wicked king of Powys foiled by St Germanus. Cynddelw alludes to his tyranny in an elegy for the lord of Maeliennydd, Cadwallon ap Madog, but it is for his courage that Llywelyn the Great is compared with him by Llywarch Brydydd y Moch. Gwilym Rhyfel refers to him as a giant in a poem for Dafydd ab Owain Gwynedd, and a generation later Bleddyn Fardd suggests a connection with Arthur, comparing Dafydd ap Llywelyn's spear with that of Arthur at the fort of Benlli.[61]

Unfortunately, no traditions have survived about the warbands of any of these figures and *teulu Arthur* is not mentioned in any other source, although the idea of his band of companions is central to *Pa gur ...* and is played with in *Culhwch ac Olwen*.[62] A. O. H. Jarman is probably right, however, to suggest that Arthur's appearance in this poem shows that Cynddelw thought of him as 'inhabiting the unidentified borderland between history and legend'.[63]

The edited text below is based on the Hendregadredd version, with significant variants from the Black Book also discussed.

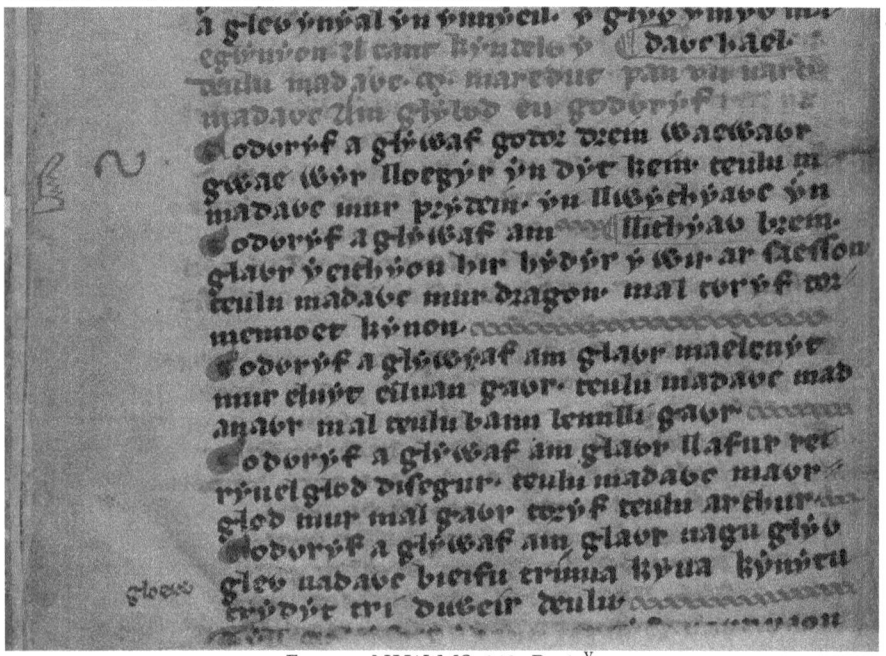

FIG. 3.3: NLW MS 6680B, 62^v.

---

[60] Again there is an Arthurian connection, as this Cynon is named as father of Esyllt in the list of the ladies at Arthur's court in *Culhwch ac Olwen* and in a late Triad; see *TYP*, p. 316.
[61] See *CBT* III 21.61, V 20.21, II 18.25. For the reference by Bleddyn Fardd, see below.
[62] See, however, *Kadeir Teyrnon* from the Book of Taliesin, Chapter 4 below, which may contain a picture of Arthur *ymplith goscord nur*, 'in the midst of a lordly warband'.
[63] Jarman, 'Arthurian Allusions', p. 102.

Godỽryf a glywaf godor drein waewaỽr | gwae wyr lloegyr yn dyt kein. Teulu m | madaỽc mur prydein. Yn llwythyaỽc yn | Godỽryf a glywaf am /llithyaỽ brein. | glaỽr yeithyon hir hydyr y wir ar saesson | teulu madaỽc mur dragon. Mal tỽryf tor-|mennoet kynon. | Godỽryf a glywyaf am glaỽr maelenyt | mur eluyt eiluan gaỽr. Teulu madaỽc mad | anaỽr mal teulu bann bennlli gaỽr |Godỽryf a glywaf am glaỽr llafur rei | ryuelglod disegur. Teulu madaỽc maỽr|glod mur mal gaỽr toryf teulu arthur. | Godỽryf a glywaf am glaỽr magu glyỽ | gleỽ uadaỽc bieifu trinua kyua kynytu | trydyt tri diweir deulu | Tyll eu hysgwydaur teruysc uaỽr uaon

        Godỽryf a glywaf, godor drein — waewa6r.
            Gwae wyr Lloegyr yn dyt kein!
            Teulu Madaỽc, mur Prydein,
4   yn llwythyaỽc yn llithyaỽ brein.   (BB verse 3)

        Godỽryf a glywaf *ar* glaỽr Yeithyon — hir,
            hydyr y wir ar Saesson,
            teulu Madaỽc, mur dragon,
8   mal tỽryf tormennoet Kynon.   (BB verse 2)

        Godỽryf a glywaf *ar* glaỽr — Maelenyt,
            mur eluyt, eiluan gaỽr,
            teulu Madaỽc mad anaỽr,
12   mal teulu bann Bennlli Gaỽr.   (BB verse 1)

        Godỽryf a glywaf *ar* glawr llafur — rei,
            ryuelglod disegur,
            teulu Madaỽc, maỽrglod mur,
16   mal gaỽr toryf teulu Arthur.   (BB verse 4)

        God6ryf a glywaf *ar* glaỽr uagu — glyỽ,
            gleỽ Uadaỽc bieifu,
            trinua kyua kynytu,
20   trydyt Tri Diweir Deulu.   (BB verse 5)

        Tyll eu hysgwydaur, teruyscuaỽr — uaon … (Absent from BB)

        I hear a great tumult, an impediment for thorn[-like] spears.
        Woe betide the warriors of England on [that] splendid day!
        The warband of Madog, defence of Britain,
4   [heavy-]laden, feeding ravens.

        I hear a great tumult over the surface [of the land] of long River] Ithon,
        mighty is its claim against the English,
        the warband of Madog, a defence of/against dragons,
8   like the war-cry of the hosts of Cynon.

        I hear a great tumult over the surface [of the land] of Maelienydd,
        defence of a country, a well-defended site [in] battle,

the warband of Madog, fortunate [their] ?might/praise,
12 like the exalted warband of Benlli the Giant.

I hear a great tumult over the surface [of a land ?where] certain ones are striving,
[subjects of] unceasing praise in battle,
the warband of Madog, a greatly praised defence,
16 like the clamour of the multitude of Arthur's warband.

I hear a great tumult over the surface [of a land ?where] brave men are nurtured,
It was brave Madog who owned it,
gaining the entire battlefield,
20 one of the Three Faithful Warbands.

With their pierced shields, hosts causing great commotion ...

1 **godor drein — waewaʋr** This is the first of many descriptive phrases used to praise Madog's warband as mighty defenders in battle. Most consist of a noun used figuratively followed by a genitive noun (e.g. l. 3 *mur Prydein*, lit. 'rampart of Britain'), but in this example, *godor*, 'hindrance, impediment', is followed by two nouns, as *gwaewaʋr*, which refers to the enemy's spears, is complemented by *drein*, 'thorns', used adjectivally perhaps to convey the shape and sharpness of the tips of the spears.

2 **Gwae wyr Lloegyr** Despite the fact that he had built sound relationships with Earl Ranulf of Chester and with King Henry II, Madog is consistently depicted as an adversary to 'the men of England' in the court poetry. For an account of his reign, see *MP*, pp. 39–57.

3 **mur Prydein** The princes of twelfth-century Wales are commonly praised by the poets as rulers or defenders of the whole of the island of Britain: see *WCP* 2.68n.

4 **llithyaʋ brein** On the motif of warriors feeding ravens and other scavengers by the ferocity of their fighting, see the Gwawrddur/Gorddur poem, Chapter 2 above, l. 5.

5 **am** (H); **ar** (BB) This variant happens in four of the verses. Both versions are possible, but the Black Book reading is more likely here as the phrase *ar glawr* is found in other medieval Welsh texts: see *LPBT* 8.18n.

7 **mur dragon** (H) lit. 'a rampart for/against dragons'; **mur galon** (BB) lit. 'a rampart [against] enemies' (plural of *gal*, see *GPC* gâl¹). Both readings give a suitable meaning and are metrically acceptable. *Dragon*, a borrowing from Latin (see *GPC*), is commonly used in the court poetry with a singular meaning for a courageous leader and with a plural meaning for valiant warriors.

10 **eiluan gaʋr** (H); **eluan gaur** (BB) The second was probably understood as a personal name *Eluan*, with the lenited form of *caur*, 'giant'. It could be a reference to Elfan Powys, one of the sons of Cyndrwyn listed in 'Canu

THE HENDREGADREDD MANUSCRIPT 85

Heledd' and in the genealogical tract *Bonedd yr Arwyr* (see *EWSP*, p. 587). The Hendregadredd form, *eiluan*, may be a variant of this name, as in Llywelyn Fardd's description of Meirionnydd, *eluyt Eiluann*, 'the land of Eilfan' (*CBT* II 1.167). This would mean, however, that two giants are named in the same *englyn*, with the word *cawr* happening twice in rhyming position. *Gawr* may be an error for *Vawr*, giving 'E(i)lfan the Great', but it is strange for the same error to be found in both manuscript traditions. In light of this, it may be better to understand the Hendregadredd version as the common noun *eiluan*, 'well-defended site or height', used figuratively with *gaỽr*, 'battle' (see *GPC* eilfan¹).

11   **anaỽr** (H); **anhaur** (BB) Its form, derivation and meaning are uncertain: see *LPBT* 4.155n. It is complemented by the adjective *mad* and is in genitival relationship with *teulu Madaỽc*: lit. 'the warband of Madog of fortunate ?might/?honour'.

13   **ar glawr llafur — rei** Lit. 'over the surface [of a land] of the labour of some', i.e. '?where some labour'. The line may be corrupt as a place name is expected here, but cf. l. 17.

14   **ryfelglod disegur** It is assumed that this clause is an epithet for the warband. Compounds containing *clod-*, referring to the amount or quality of the praise they receive, are common in contemporary poems addressed to princes.

15   **maỽrglod mur** (H) Lit. 'a rampart of great praise' (with the lenition to *mur* not shown); **mur eglur** (BB) 'conspicuous/illustrious rampart'. According to Russell ('Scribal (In)consistency', p. 165), the two readings may have arisen because of a copying error in the Hendregadredd version, but oral variation is also possible. Note the repetition of the element *clod* in the Hendregadredd version, which weakens the stanza.

17   **ar glaỽr uagu — glyỽ** Lit. 'over the surface [of a land] of the nurturing of brave men', i.e. '?where warriors are nurtured', but it is difficult to explain the lenition of *magu* if this interpretation is correct.

18   **gleỽ** (H); **gloev** (BB) 'bright' (*GPC* gloyw). It is again difficult to decide between the two very similar forms, but there may be an etymological relationship between *glyw* in the previous line and *glew*; see *GPC* glyw³.

gleỽ Uadaỽc bieifu On the formation of *pieufu*, a form of *pieu*, see *GMW*, pp. 80–81. Its object is thought to be Madog's warband, described in the next two lines but not named.

21   **Tyll eu hysgwydaur, teruyscuaỽr — uaon** Lit. 'pierced their shields', a phrase complementing *teruyscuaỽr uaon*. On broken shields and other weapons as signs of warriors' bravery in the poetry, see above *Pa gur*, l. 22, *eis tull*. This line is found in the Hendregadredd MS only; the rest of the englyn is missing because the bottom of the page has been torn away. This *englyn*, which is linked to the fifth by a weak *cyrch-gymeriad*, may be a later addition. Alpha does have

a tendency of incorporating marginal lines or stanzas into his text. It is difficult to be sure that this is an addition, however, as the custom of varying a pattern of repetition towards the end of a poem is not uncommon in the work of the Poets of the Princes.

Word-list

a *preverbal particle* (causing lenition, *GMW*, pp. 172–73) 1, 5, 9, 13, 17
anaѵr *n.* '?might; ?honour, praise' 11n
ar *prep.* 'upon, over, against' 5n, 6, 9, 13, 17
Arthur *personal name* 16

bann *adj.* 'of high status, exalted, renowned' 12
Bennlli *personal name* Benlli 12
brein *pl. of n.* **bran**, 'raven' 4

caѵr *n.* 'giant' 12
kein *adj.* 'splendid' 2
clawr *n.* 'face, surface (of country, sea etc.)' 5, 9, 13, 17
clywaf *1 sing.pres.indic.* **clybot**, 'to hear' 1, 5, 9, 13, 17
Kynon *personal name* Cynon 8
kynytu *v.n.* 'to gain, to occupy' 19
kyua *adj.* 'whole, entire' 19

disegur *adj.* 'without idleness, ceaseless' 14
diweir *adj.* 'faithful' 16
dragon *pl.n.* 'valiant warriors' 7n
drein *sg./pl. n.* 'thorn(s)' (*GPC* draen¹, drain) 1n
dyt *n.* 'day' 2

eiluan *n.* 'a well-defended site or height' (*GPC* eilfan¹) 10n
eluyt *n.* 'land, country, world' (*GPC* elfydd¹) 10
eu *prefixed poss.pron. 3 pl.masc.* (causing Sandhi h- to occur before vowels, see *GMW* 23c) 'their' 21

g- see also **c-**
gaѵr *n.* 'battle' 10n, 'clamour' (see *GPC* gawr¹) 16
glew *adj.* 'brave', 18n
glyѵ *pl.n.* 'mighty ones, brave men, warriors' 17n
godor *n.* 'a fault, hindrance, impediment' 1
godѵryf *n.* 'great tumult' 1, 5, 9, 13, 17
gwae *interjection* 'woe betide!' 2

gwaewa{r *pl. of n.* **gwaew**, 'spear' 1
gwir *n.* 'claim' 6
gwyr *pl. of n.* **gwr**, 'man, warrior' 2

hir *adj.* 'long' 5
hydyr *adj.* 'mighty, powerful' (see *GPC* hydr^1) 6

llafur *n.* 'labour' 13
llithya{ *v.n.* 'to feed' (*GPC* llithiaf: llithio) 4
Lloegyr *place name* Lloegr, England 2
llwythya{c *adj.* '[heavy-]laden, burdened [with booty?]' (see *GPC* llwythog) 4

mad *adj.* 'fortunate' 11
Mada{c *personal name* Madog (ap Maredudd) 3, 7, 11, 15, 18
Maelenyt *place name* Maelienydd 9
magu *v.n.* 'to rear, nurture' 17n
mal *prep.* 'like' 8, 12, 16
maon *pl.n.* 'hosts' 21
ma{rglod *n.* 'great praise' 15n
mur *n.* 'wall, rampart, *fig.* defender' 3, 7, 10, 15

pieifu *verbal form (past tense)* 'whose was, who owned' (see *GPC* piau 2a) 18n
Prydein *place name* Britain 3

rei *pl.pron.* 'some people, certain ones' (*GPC* rhai) 13
ryuelglod *n.* 'praise or fame in battle' 14

Saesson *pl. of n.* **Seis**, 'English person' 6

teruyscua{r *adj.* 'causing great commotion' 21
teulu *n.* 'warband' 3, 7, 11, 12, 15, 16, 20
tormennoet *pl. of n.* **torment**, 'host, army' 8
toryf *n.* 'multitude' 16
tri *numeral* 'three' 20
trinua *n.* 'battlefield' 19
trydyt *ordinal* 'third, one of three' (see *GMW*, p. 48) 20
t{ryf *n.* 'clamour, war-cry' (see *GPC* twrf, twrw) 8
tyll *pl. of adj.* **twll**, 'holed, pierced' 21n

w- see **gw-**

y *prefixed poss.pron. 3 sing.masc.* 'his, its' (causing lenition) 6
Yeithyon *place name* Ieithion, River Ithon (25 miles long) which runs through the cantref of Maelienydd 5
yn¹ *prep.* (*GPC* yn¹, causing nasal mutation, see *GMW*, p. 21) 'in' 2
yn² *particle with v.n.* (*GPC* yn², *GMW*, p. 215, causing no mutation) 4
yn³ *predicative particle* (*GPC* yn³, *GMW*, p. 139, causing lenition except in *ll-* and *rh-*) 4
ysgwydaur *pl. of* ysgwyd *n.* 'shield' 21n

The poetry of Llywarch Brydydd y Moch and his contemporaries

The next largest collection of poetry in the Hendregadredd Manuscript after that of Cynddelw belongs to Llywarch, who sang for the descendants of Owain Gwynedd in the turbulent years after his death and then served his grandson, Llywelyn the Great, who took the throne of Gwynedd in 1202, eventually uniting the whole of Wales under his rule.[64] In his twenty-six eulogies and elegies, allusions to legendary or historical figures are less frequent than in the praise poems of Cynddelw, and the range of characters used is narrower. He compares or identifies his patrons with four classical heroes, three biblical figures, three characters from the Four Branches of the *Mabinogi*, thirteen early historical figures from Wales and the Old North, the Irish hero Cú Chulainn, and eight characters whose names are found in Arthurian texts (Benlli, Cibddar, Elifri, Garwy, Geraint, Godiar, Gwair fab Gwestl and Ogrfan). Amongst the total of forty-four references to thirty-two different names, however, Arthur is mentioned five times, the only figure to appear more than twice in the corpus.

It would be natural to assume that this reflects an increased interest in Arthur in the late twelfth century and the first half of the thirteenth century, due perhaps to the popularity of Geoffrey of Monmouth's *Historia Regum Britanniae* and the Arthurian romances of Chrétien de Troyes.[65] There are, however, very few signs of the influence of Geoffrey or of the romances on the portrayal of Arthur in Llywarch's praise poems.

It is for his qualities as a military leader who caused fear in his enemies that Llywelyn is compared with Arthur in an *englyn* series probably composed to

[64] See Esther Feer and Nerys Ann Jones, 'The Poet and his Patrons: The Early Career of Llywarch Brydydd y Moch' in *Medieval Celtic Literature and Society*, ed. by Helen Fulton (Dublin: Four Courts Press, 2005), 132–62, and Charles Insley, 'The Wilderness Years of Llywelyn the Great' in *Thirteenth Century England IX: Proceedings of the Durham Conference 2001*, ed. by Michael Prestwich, Richard Britnell and Robin Frame (Woodbridge: The Boydell Press, 2003), pp. 163–73.

[65] For an introduction to these texts, see chapters in *AW*. On what is thought to be the earliest reference in the court poetry to a character from *Brut y Brenhinedd*, the thirteenth-century adaptation of the *Historia* into Welsh, in the work of Elidir Sais, a contemporary of Llywarch Brydydd y Moch, see *TYP*, p. lxvi n. 92.

celebrate a successful attack on the Anglo-Norman castle at Mold in January 1199.[66]

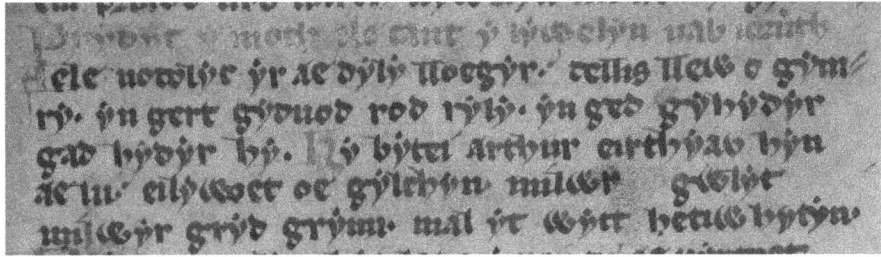

FIG. 3.4: NLW MS 6680B, f. 116ʳ.

Aele nodolyc yr ae dyly lloegyr. dellis llew o gym-|ry. yn gert gyduod rod ryly. yn ged gyhydyr | gad hydyr hy. Hy bytei Arthur eirthyaỽ hyn | ae lu. eilywoet oe gylchyn. milwr gwlyt | milwyr gryd grynn. mal yt wytt hetiw hytyn.

>   Aele Nodolyc y'r a'e dyly — Lloegyr,
>   dellis llew o Gymry,
>   yn gert gyduod, rod ryly,
>   yn ged gyhydyr, gad hydyr hy.
>
>   Hy bytei Arthur, eirthaỽ hyn — a'e lu,
>   eilyw oet o'e gylchyn,
>   milwyr glyd, milwr gryd grynn,[67]
>   mal yt wytt hetiw, hytyn.

> A wretched Christmas for those whom the men of England claim,
> the lion from Wales has seized them,
> associating with poets, a ?defending shield,
> of equal power [regarding his] gift, powerful and audacious one in battle.
>
> Thus was Arthur, scattering these with his host,
> grief was all around him,
> ? the refuge of warriors, a warrior [in] the thrust of battle,
> as you are today, audacious man.

A similar comparison is made between Llywelyn and Arthur in a series of *englynion* addressed to the prince and his warband, composed soon after his first successful campaign in south Wales in 1215. There is no attribution in John Davies of Mallwyd's copy of a lost page from the Hendregadredd Manuscript or in the Red Book of Hergest, but metrical and stylistic features suggest that

---

[66] NLW MS 6680B, f. 116, with a very similar version in the Red Book, Oxford, Jesus College MS 111, f. 352ʳ, col. 1403–04; *CBT* v 20.1–8. For the dating of the poem, see Feer and Jones, 'The Poet and his Patrons', pp. 156–57.
[67] Rhian Andrews has suggested to me on the basis of ornament that both the Hendregadredd and Red Book versions of this line are incorrect.

this is Llywarch's work.[68] Some twelve battles or attacks on both native and Anglo-Norman castles are listed, with echoes of the antiquarian *englynion* enumerating the victories of Cadwallon ap Cadfan, a famous king of Gwynedd who was killed in 635.[69] The comparison with Arthur occurs in a stanza where the poet speaks as a member of the warband.[70]

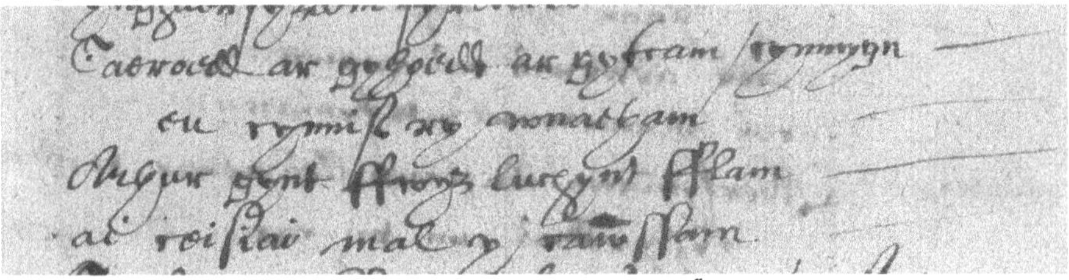

FIG. 3.5: NLW 4973B, f. 44^r.

Caeroedd ar gyhoedd ar gytcam / cynnygn | eu cynnif ry wnaetham | Arthur gynt ffwyr luchynt fflam | ai ceisiai mal y cawssam

>   Caeroedd ar gyhoedd, ar gytcam — cynnygn,
>   eu cynnif rywnaetham,
>   Arthur gynt ffwyr luchynt fflam
>   a'*u* ceisiai mal y cawsam.

>   [Whilst] playing with [our] adversaries,
>   we attacked castles openly,[71]
>   Arthur in times past, in a terrible, flaming lightning rush,
>   would have sought them as we did.

Similarly, it is because he was a 'bear of battle' that Maredudd ap Cynan, another grandson of Owain Gwynedd, is likened to Arthur in an elegy composed soon after his death in 1212.[72]

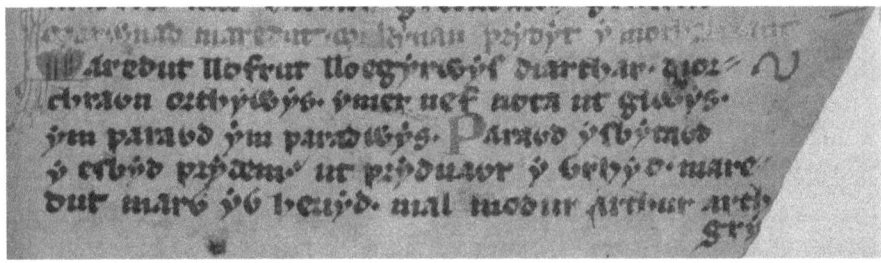

FIG. 3.6: NLW MS 6680B, f. 117^r.

---

[68] NLW MS 4973B, ff. 43^v–44^v, and Oxford, Jesus College MS 111, f. 353^v, col. 1404–05; *CBT* VI 20.81–84 (an edition based on the Red Book).
[69] For an edition of 'Englynion Cadwallon', see *EWSP*, pp. 169–73, 446–47, 495–96, 613–16.
[70] NLW MS 4973B, ff. 44^r.
[71] Lit. 'Castles publicly, [whilst] playing with [our] adversaries, | we attacked them'.
[72] NLW MS 6680B, f. 117; *CBT* V 15–18.

Para𝑣d ysbyta𝑣d | y esbyd prydein. ut prydua𝑣r y wrhyd. mare-|dut mar𝑣 y𝑣 heuyd. mal modur Arthur arth gry

> Para𝑣d ysbyta𝑣d y esbyd — Prydein,
> ut prydua𝑣r y wrhyd,
> Maredut, mar𝑣 y𝑣 heuyd:
> mal modur Arthur arth gry[d].
>
> One whose feast was prepared for guests from [the whole of] Britain,
> a lord whose courage was greatly praised,
> Maredudd, he is also dead:
> like the lord Arthur he was a bear in battle.

Llywarch again juxtaposes *Arthur* and *arth*, 'bear', possibly playing with the derivation of his name,[73] in an *awdl* of exuberant praise for Rhodri ab Owain Gwynedd composed some twenty years earlier.[74] Here the poet claims that his lord is a superior warrior to both Arthur and Eiddol.[75]

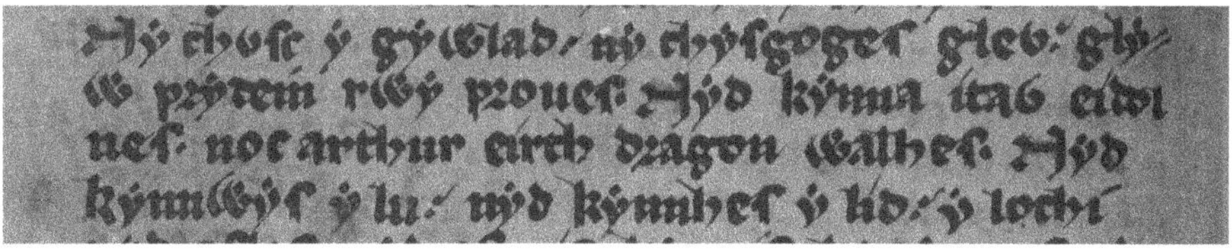

FIG. 3.7: NLW MS 6680B, f. 105ᵛ.

Nyd kynna ita𝑣 eidol | nes. noc Arthur eirth dragon walhes.

> Nyd kynna ita𝑣 Eidol, nes
> noc Arthur, eirth dragon walhes.
>
> Eiddol[76] is not an equal of his, [any] more
> than Arthur, a refuge for the leaders of fierce warriors [lit. bears].

And it is in a variant on this common topos of the superiority of the poet's patron over all others that Arthur is again named at the climax of a section of praise for Llywelyn, towards the end of a lengthy *awdl* series for his ally Rhys Gryg of Deheubarth, composed in 1220.[77]

---

[73] In the work of the Poets of the Princes there are only five examples of *arth* and one of the plural form *eirth*. All are used for warriors, figuratively or in comparisons.
[74] NLW MS 6680B, ff. 105ʳ–06ʳ; *CBT* v 5.11–12; see Feer and Jones, 'The Poet and his Patrons', pp. 140–42.
[75] NLW MS 6680B, f. 105ᵛ.
[76] *GPC* eidol¹ lists this example as a common noun, 'shout, cry, praise', but it is difficult to make sense of the couplet with these meanings. Alpha's spelling system suggests that the form *Eidol* contains /-d-/ but /-ð-/ would give alliteration with *itaw*. On Eiddol's identity, see below.
[77] NLW MS 6680B , ff. 111ᵛ–13ʳ (112ᵛ); *CBT* v 26.95–96. See further discussion of this reference below.

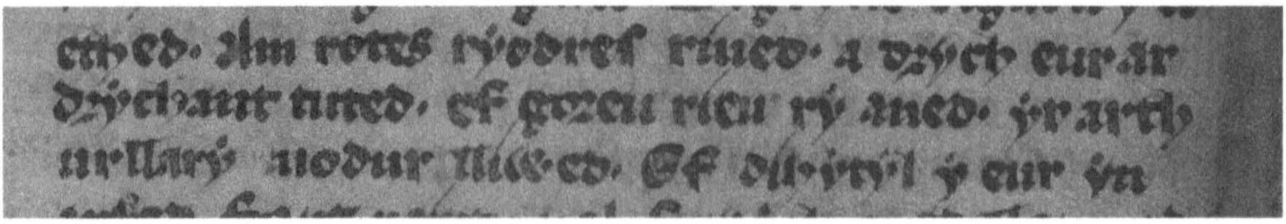

FIG. 3.8: NLW MS 6680B, f. 112ᵛ.

Ef goreu rieu ry aned. yr arth|ur llary uodur lliwed.

> Ef goreu rieu ryaned
> yr Arthur, llary uodur lliwed.

> He is the best king who has been born
> since Arthur, generous lord of a host.

Here for the first time in the court poetry, we find Arthur depicted as a ruler rather than a soldier.[78] The term *modur*[79] is used again for him in a magnificent *awdl* for Llywelyn probably sung during 1213, a year of many victories for the prince.[80]

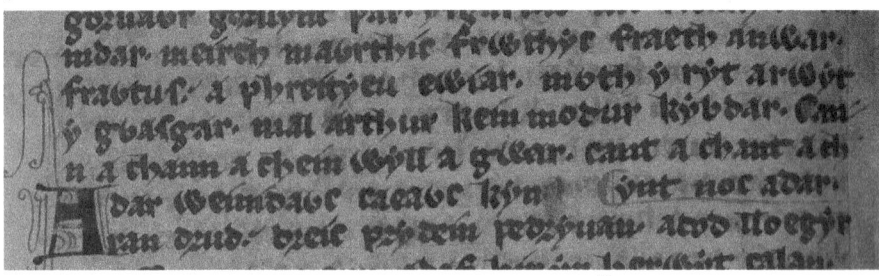

FIG. 3.9: NLW MS 6680B, f. 107ᵛ.

meirch maꟳrthic frwthyc fraeth anwar | fraꟳtus. a phreityeu ewiar. mꟳth y ryt arwyt | y gꟳasgar. mal Arthur kein modur kybdar. can-|n a chann a chein wyll a gwar. cant a chant ach|ynt noc adar.

> Meirch maꟳrthic, frwythyc, fraeth, anwar, — fraꟳtus,
>   a phreityeu ewiar,
> mꟳth y ryt arwyt yg gꟳasgar,
> mal Arthur, kein modur Kybdar,
> cann a chann a cheinwyll a gwar,
> cant a chant a chynt noc adar.

[78] For the term *rieu*, see Andrews, 'Nomenclature of Kingship Part 1', p. 90.
[79] For the meanings of *modur*, which is used three times by Prydydd y Moch to rhyme with Arthur, see *GPC* modur¹.
[80] NLW MS 6680B, ff. 107ʳ–09ʳ (107ᵛ) with a variant version in the Red Book, Oxford Jesus College MS 111, f. 356, col. 1419–22; *CBT* v 23.61–66.

> War-trained steeds, prosperous, swift, wild and eager,
> and ?desirable herds,
> swiftly does he give the signal in their distribution,
> like Arthur, fair lord of Cibddar,[81]
> a grey and a grey and a fair, wild one and a tame one,
> a hundred and [another] hundred, swifter than birds.

Llywelyn is here compared with Arthur as a distributer of warhorses, probably taken as booty from battlefields. Generosity is also the quality praised in the final *englyn* of Llywarch's elegy for Gruffudd ap Cynan, brother of Maredudd, who died in 1200.[82] It contains one of the earliest references to the Triad of the Three Generous Men, a triad which became a cliché in later praise poetry, but with the addition of the name of Arthur and also Gruffudd, who is claimed to be more generous than them all.[83]

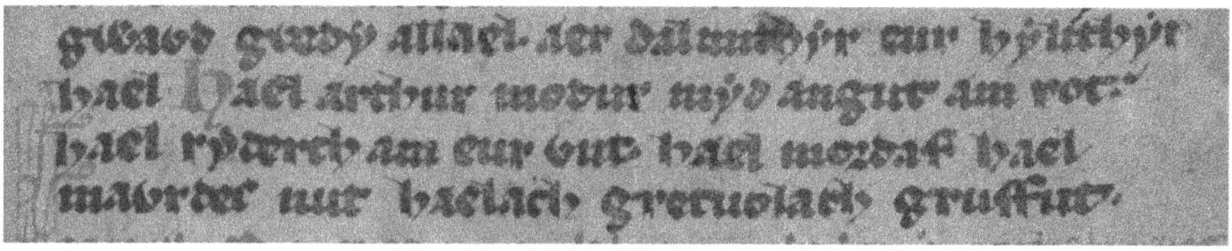

FIG. 3.10: NLW MS 6680B, f. 117ʳ.

Hael arthur modur myd angut am rot.| hael ryderch am eur 6ut. hael mordaf hael | ma6rdec nut haelach gretuolach gruffut.

> Hael Arthur, modur, myd angut, — am rot;
>   hael Ryderch am eur6ut;
>   hael Mordaf, hael ma6rdec Nut:
> haelach, gretuolach Gruffut.
>
> Generous was Arthur — a lord conspicuous in battle — in giving;
>   generous was Rhydderch for golden bounty;
>   generous was Mordaf, generous was great and fair Nudd:
> more generous, more powerful, was Gruffudd.

---

[81] If the personal name Cibddar is intended here, it might be a reference to the father of *Drych eil Kibdar*, who is named in *Culhwch ac Olwen* as one who, along with Arthur, was as handsome as Bedwyr; see *CO*, l. 395.

[82] NLW MS 6680B, ff. 116ᵛ–17ʳ, also in the Red Book, Oxford, Jesus College MS 111, f. 352ᵛ, col. 1401–02, where this *englyn* opens the series; *CBT* v 11.53–56.

[83] *TYP* no. 2, and for allusions to the triad by other twelfth and thirteenth-century court poets, see pp. 5–6. Arthur's name is also added to that of Rhydderch, Nudd and Mordaf in a fifteenth-century text of the Triad of the Three Generous Men with the claim that he was 'more generous than the three' (*Ac Arthur ehun oedd haelach no'r tri*). This is not the only instance where Prydydd y Moch displays his knowledge of the Triads and makes imaginative use of them: see, for example, *WCP* no. 4, which contains a reference to a pair of triads, *TYP* nos 47 and 48, and *TYP*, pp. 120–30.

Arthur is named in this *englyn* alongside three rulers regarded as historical figures who lived in the Old North in the sixth century, but in other praise poems by Llywarch he appears with characters whose names are found in Welsh versions of Geoffrey's *Historia* and the romances. This may be taken as evidence that the poet was drawing on contemporary Arthurian literature. In many cases, however, he may be referring to older native heroic figures.

Ambiguity surrounds references by Llywarch to three characters who appear in the Romance of Geraint — Elifri, Odiar and Geraint himself. In a praise poem for Dafydd ab Owain composed around 1175, the prince is said to act 'in the manner of Elifri'.[84] This is one of five allusions in the corpus to the figure who appears in the Romance of Geraint as an official in Arthur's court.[85] Barry Lewis has suggested that the high number of references may be a measure of Elifri's importance.[86] Unfortunately, they are too terse and general to identify him as the romance character or to reveal any earlier traditions, Arthurian or otherwise, that might have circulated about him. Indeed, the fact that his name occurs in rhyming position each time might suggest that, like that of Llachau, its popularity with the poets may be due to its form.[87] He appears in a different guise, however, in Einion ap Gwalchmai's elegy for Nest, a noblewoman of Tywyn in Meirionnydd who probably died in the early years of the thirteenth century:[88]

> Keintum gert y Nest kyn no'e tregi,
> cant y molyant mal Eliuri
>
> I sang a poem for Nest before she died,
> a hundred sang her praises like Elifri.

Elifri the poet brings to mind the epithet used with the name in the catalogue of Geraint's escort, *Elifry Anaw Kyrd*, which may be translated as 'abundance of poems', although the translation favoured by the editor of the text is 'abundance of skills'.[89]

As we have seen, Llywelyn the Great's military prowess is compared several times with that of Arthur by Llywarch Brydydd y Moch, but he is also twice

---

[84] *CBT* V 2.49.
[85] See *Ystoria Gereint Uab Erbin*, ed. by Robert L. Thomson [*YG*] (Dublin: Institute for Advanced Studies, 1997), l. 46n. Cynddelw compares the generosity of Lord Rhys with that of Elifri in a long *awdl* sung between 1189 and 1195 (*CBT* IV 9.82); Hywel Foel ap Griffri compares Owain ap Gruffudd's courage with that of Elifri in the middle years of the thirteenth century (VII 23.20), and his contemporary, Bleddyn Fardd, in an elegy for Owain's brother, Dafydd, in 1283 compares his passion in battle with that of Elifri (VII 53.30).
[86] 'Arthurian References in Medieval Welsh poetry, c. 1100 — c. 1540' in *ACL*, p. 192.
[87] See *AMWL*, p. 56.
[88] *CBT* I 26.15–16; see *WCP*, p. 25.
[89] *YG*, ll. 601–08n. On the meanings of *kyrd*, see *GPC* cerdd¹.

said to be a fierce opponent of the English like Godiar.⁹⁰ This could be *Odiar Franc* (Odiar the Frenchman), named as the steward of Arthur's court in the Romance of Geraint,⁹¹ but, as Patrick Sims-Williams has shown, despite the fact that the name is French, other references suggest that a much older native hero is also possible.⁹²

Rachel Bromwich has argued that *llid Geraint* in a short *awdl* for Rhodri, an epithet which can be interpreted as 'the passion of Geraint', may be an allusion to the protagonist of the romance.⁹³ This is disputed by Barry Lewis, as the term *llid* is commonly used in the poetry to express a warrior's fury in battle.⁹⁴ Geraint, moreover, is a hero well established in Welsh tradition, as the Triads and the Black Book stanzas testify.⁹⁵

It is equally difficult to be sure whether Eiddol, paired with Arthur in a praise poem for Rhodri ab Owain Gwynedd discussed above, is to be identified as the Earl of Gloucester, depicted as a ferocious warrior in a Welsh version of *Historia Regum Britanniae*, or as the warrior named in an early twelfth-century anonymous praise poem from the Black Book of Carmarthen and other sources.⁹⁶ Likewise, Ogrfan, who is named by Llywarch as well as by Cynddelw and Einion Wan as a courageous warrior from the past, may be a Powysian hero who gave his name to the giant who was Gwenhwyfar's father, *Gogrfan Gawr*, in *Brut y Brenhinedd*. In a love poem attributed to Hywel, son of Owain Gwynedd, Ogrfan is named along with another native figure who had been drawn into Arthur's orbit. The poet opens by expressing the poet's desire to journey on horseback to the home of the unnamed girl in order to praise her great beauty and proclaim his great sorrow, caused by love for one who is 'of the colour of snow of glittering frostiness on a high peak'. The poem closes with a report of the unfortunate result of the visit:⁹⁷

---

⁹⁰ *CBT* v 20.19, *cymrawd Gotyar*, 'one equal to Godiar'; cf. also v 23.8, *rwysc Odyar*, 'one of the attack/authority of Godiar'.
⁹¹ See *YG*, l. 13n.
⁹² See *IIMWL*, pp. 157–59.
⁹³ *TYP*, pp. 359–60. See *CBT* v 7.9, and for a reference to Geraint by Bleddyn Fardd, a member of the next generation of poets, see *CBT* VII 51.31.
⁹⁴ Lewis, 'Arthurian References', and see *GPC* llid¹.
⁹⁵ See Chapter 1 above.
⁹⁶ See *CBT* I 2.16 (Eulogy for Cuhelyn Fardd), *Gur oet eitoel* (recte *Eitol*), *gorvy reol, gordethol doeth*, 'he was a warrior [like] Eiddol, he established rule, a chosen, wise one'. *Eidoel mab Ner* (or *mab Aer*), a famous prisoner in *Culhwch ac Olwen*, and the warrior *Eidal*, with whom Hywel ab Owain is compared by Cynddelw (*CBT* IV 6.150), are also possible. The name of Geoffrey's Eldol Earl of Gloucester is probably taken from one of these earlier figures, according to Brynley F. Roberts, 'The Treatment of Personal Names in the Early Welsh Versions of *Historia Regum Britanniae*', *Bulletin of the Board of Celtic Studies*, 25 (1973), 274–90 (see n. 5).
⁹⁷ *CBT* II poem 9. Dafydd Johnston has suggested that Cynddelw is the author of the poems attributed to Hywel; see 'Hywel ab Owain a Beirdd yr Uchelwyr' in *Hywel ab Owain*

> Chweris o'e hata(v)d-hi atoed kynrann,
> ethi(v) a'm eneid-y, athwyf yn wann;
> neud athwyf o nwyf yn eil Garwy Hir,
> y wenn a'm llutir yn llys Ogyruann.
>
> In her home misfortune befell [this] distinguished warrior,
> she took away my soul, I have become weak;
> I have become, because of desire, like Garwy the Tall,
> for the sake of the fair one who is forbidden to me in the court of (G)ogrfan.

The poet likens himself to Garwy Hir, who is named in the Triads as the father of Indeg, one of Arthur's lovers,[98] and identifies the father of the maiden with (G)ogrfan.[99] Oliver Padel suggests that, as Hywel refers to the girl as *gwenn*, he may be subtly comparing himself with Arthur, also a poet according to the Triads, and alluding to a lost tale of the wooing of Gwenhwyfar.[100] If so, this would be the earliest datable reference to Gwenhwyfar and her father.[101]

Finally, whilst there are no references to Uthr, Arthur's father, in the work of Llywarch or his contemporaries,[102] Oliver Padel has drawn attention to the use of the term *pendragon* in their poems and has proposed that it might reflect 'the growing influence of Geoffrey's History towards the end of the twelfth century'.[103] Close scrutiny of the examples suggests, however, that the poets are generally more concerned with playing with the elements of the word, used as a common noun with the meaning 'chief leader' or 'chief of warriors', than with evoking the epithet given to Uthr in the *Historia*.[104] Similarly, just as Llywarch's reference to Camlan shows no awareness of later stories surrounding the battle,[105] there is not a hint of an allusion in his praise of Gwenllïan, daughter of the lord of Caerleon, to Geoffrey's use of the town as the site of Arthur's chief court.[106]

There seems to be no unambiguous evidence, then, of the influence of Arthurian literature on the praise poetry produced by Llywarch Brydydd y

---

Gwynedd Bardd-Dywysog, ed. by Nerys Ann Jones (Cardiff: University of Wales Press, 2009), pp. 134–51.

[98] *TYP*, p. 356. Garwy is renowned as a lover in the poetry of the fourteenth century, but in other references by the Poets of the Princes it is his wisdom and courage which are praised.

[99] As *llys* can be a masculine or feminine noun it is impossible to know whether the name is Ogrfan or a lenited form of Gogrfan.

[100] See *AMWL*, pp. 56–57, and on Arthur as a poet, see *TYP* no. 12. For a different understanding of the reference, see Barry Lewis, 'Arthurian References'.

[101] Rachel Bromwich holds, however, that 'the evidence for an authentic pre-Geoffrey tradition of *Gwenhwyfar* in Wales is highly doubtful'; see *TYP*, pp. 376–80 (p. 377).

[102] For the only reference to Uthr in the corpus, see below.

[103] *AMWL*, p. 54.

[104] See *GPC* pendragon for examples.

[105] See p. 77 above.

[106] See *WCP* no. 24.

Moch. In light of this, it is interesting to note that Arthurian characters are extremely scarce in the work of his contemporaries in the courts of Llywelyn the Great. Of some forty-five references to figures from the past in thirty praise poems by Einion ap Gwalchmai, Elidir Sais, Einion Wan, Llywelyn Fardd II, Llywarch ap Llywelyn, Gwgon Brydydd, Einion ap Gwgon, Einion ap Madog ap Rhahawd and Dafydd Benfras, most of which were preserved in the Hendregadredd collection, there are none to Arthur himself and only six to characters associated with him, namely Bedwyr, Cai, Elifri, Gwair fab Gwestl, Llachau and Ogrfan.

Canu i Dduw attributed to Llywarch Brydydd y Moch

It has been argued, however, that the poem which opens the collection of Llywarch's work in the Hendregadredd Manuscript, a series of *awdlau* entitled *Canu i Dduw*, 'A song for God',[107] sets Arthur alongside the great empire-builders, Alexander and Julius Caesar, indicating that its author was aware of the new dimension which had been given to the Arthurian legend by Geoffrey of Monmouth and was influenced by it.[108] Unfortunately, the authorship of this poem is disputed, as it is to Cynddelw that it is attributed in the Red Book of Hergest, where it appears sandwiched between two of his religious poems.[109] Some of the variant readings in the latter indicate that they derive from the same source, probably produced at an ecclesiastical centre in Gwynedd. It is also likely that only the first poem of the three bore a title in that manuscript. The attribution of the second to Cynddelw or Llywarch was probably made by the scribes of the extant collections. Most scholars would give priority to the evidence of hand Alpha over that of Hywel Fychan, the scribe of this portion of the Red Book, but it is difficult to confirm the authorship of the poem by means of a stylistic comparison alone because of the lack of religious works by Llywarch.[110]

In many ways, this work is typical of the religious poems of the court poets of both the twelfth and the thirteenth centuries.[111] With their message of the sinner's need for remorse and repentance in the face of death and judgment, they were probably intended to be performed during the penitential season

[107] *Canu* is a metrical term used in manuscript titles for series of between three and thirteen *awdlau*.
[108] See *AMWL*, p. 54.
[109] On the variants of the Red Book and Hendregadredd texts, see below.
[110] The poem is included with Cynddelw's work in *CBT* IV but its editor, Ann Parry Owen, suggests that more work needs to be done to establish its authorship.
[111] On the corpus, which traditionally consists of thirty-three poems, see *The Medieval Welsh Religious Lyric: Poems of the Gogynfeirdd, 1137–1282*, ed. by Catherine A. McKenna (Belmont: Ford and Bailie, 1991).

of Lent.¹¹² This particular poem, presented as a contemplation of Heaven and Hell, is unusual in that it contains, in its third section, a list of great leaders of world history and heroes of legend, some native and others classical, starting with Arthur.¹¹³ It has been suggested that this catalogue of three native figures alternating with three classical ones is a precursor of what became known as the Nine Worthies Scheme.¹¹⁴ This list of the bravest and most noble warriors in the world, three pagans, three Jews and three Christians (one of which was Arthur), was especially popular in the literature of fifteenth and sixteenth-century Wales, but it appears that the court poets were already familiar with such frameworks in the twelfth and thirteenth centuries.¹¹⁵

The six famous rulers and heroes of the past are named here to emphasise the transience of human life and the vanity of worldly power and glory in a variation of the *ubi sunt?* theme, where the form *rybu*, literally 'he has been', is used to introduce each figure in turn. Arthur is presented as a courageous warrior, attacking like a whirlwind, although *kyfraŏd gŏynt* may be deliberately ambiguous, perhaps bringing to mind a simile from Psalm 144. 4, 'Man's life is like a breath'. Brân son of Llŷr is also characterised by his military might, as in the praise poetry of both Cynddelw and Llywarch, but it is difficult to be sure whether his 'feat in a neighbouring land' is a reference to a specific tradition.¹¹⁶ The allusion in the previous lines seems to be to an episode in a lost tale consisting of a love triangle between Julius Caesar, the British prince Caswallon son of Beli, and a maiden called Fflur, which led to his 'costly' invasion of Britain.¹¹⁷ Hercules, who appears as a standard of courage and strength in eulogies by both poets, is here likened to an otherwise unknown Greiddur, another example perhaps of an obscure figure from the past whose

---

¹¹² See Nerys Ann Jones, '*Marwysgafyn Veilyr Brydyt*: Deathbed Poem?', *Cambrian Medieval Celtic Studies*, 47 (2004), 22–32; Catherine McKenna, 'Performing Penance and Poetic Performance in the Medieval Welsh Court', *Speculum*, 82 (2007), 70–96.

¹¹³ The Hendregadredd Manuscript, ff. 100ʳ–01ᵛ (100ᵛ–101ʳ); Red Book of Hergest, f. 292, col. 1169–72 (1171); *CBT* IV 17.67–90. The edition below is based on the Hendregadredd version. The metre is known as *Gwawdodyn*, a combination of alternating *Toddeidiau* and couplets of *Cyhydedd Nawban*; see *WCP*, pp. xl–xlii.

¹¹⁴ *LPBT*, pp. 409–10, and see *TYP*, p. 131.

¹¹⁵ See *TYP*, pp. 129–30 for Llywarch's triple triad of biblical and classical heroes based on an early version of *TYP* nos 47–49, 'The Three Men who Received the Might, the Beauty and the Wisdom of Adam', in a eulogy for Rhodri ab Owain Gwynedd, and his combining of the *Tri Hael* with triads 47 and 48 in a poem for Rhys Gryg (see below). There is also, according to Marged Haycock, a hint of the scheme in a religious poem from the Book of Taliesin in which Alexander, King David, Solomon and other biblical figures are named; see *Blodengerdd Barddas o Gann Crefyddol Cynnar* [*BBGCC*], ed. by Marged Haycock (Swansea: Barddas Publications, 1995), pp. 80–91.

¹¹⁶ See *TYP*, p. 291.

¹¹⁷ Another enigmatic reference to Flora (Fflur) in *TYP* no. 67 may recall a later episode in the now lost story; see *TYP*, p. 354.

name was useful for metrical purposes.[118] The identity of 'iniquitous Madog', the only one of the six to be criticised by the poet, is also uncertain. Marged Haycock is probably right to argue that Madog ab Uthr, brother of Arthur and father of Eliwlad, is more likely here than a contemporary historical figure such as Madog ap Maredudd or Madog ap Gruffudd Maelor.[119] Despite being the subject of a fragment of an elegy in the Book of Taliesin, very little is known about Madog ab Uthr. The warning he receives in this poem is that even Alexander the Great, despite the fact that he had travelled to the stars, was not immune from death.[120]

What is most striking about the way these figures are presented is that there is no sign of the influence of *Historia Regum Britanniae*. Rather than drawing on Geoffrey's account of Julius Caesar's invasion of Britain, for example, the poet alludes to a story of unknown origin reminiscent of *Breudwyt Maxen Wledic*. It is interesting to contrast these lines with Latin metrical verses composed on the death of Lord Rhys in 1197.[121] The names of Arthur, Julius Caesar and Alexander the Great are again invoked to convey the greatness of the prince, but he is also identified with the three sons of Brutus — Camber, Locrinus and Albanactus — characters created by Geoffrey of Monmouth. Geoffrey's influence is also very apparent in the portrayal of Arthur as saviour of the Britons in *Trucidare Saxones*, a poem exhorting the Britons to overthrow the Saxons, thought to have been composed in Wales during Llywelyn ap Iorwerth's reign.[122]

The edited text presented here is based on the Hendregadredd version, with significant variants from the Red Book also discussed.

---

[118] For the poets' references to Hercules, see *TYP*, p. 350, and for likely sources of information about him in medieval Wales, see *LPBT*, pp. 453–54.
[119] *LPBT*, pp. 459–60, and see Chapter 5, Dialogue of Arthur and the Eagle, below.
[120] It is Haycock's interpretation of the line which is followed here, based on another reference to Alexander's celestial flight in a poem in the Book of Taliesin; see *LPBT*, pp. 423–27. The only other reference in the corpus to Alexander is found in a eulogy by Cynddelw for Lord Rhys, *kynnifyad kynnetyf Alexander*, 'a warrior with the qualities of Alexander'; see *LPBT*, p. 410 n. 34.
[121] These lines are included in the Peniarth 20 Manuscript version of the Chronicle of the Welsh Princes and were probably composed either in St David's or Strata Florida. For the text, see Thomas Jones, *Brut y Tywysogyon or the Chronicle of the Princes: Peniarth MS. 20 Version* (Cardiff: University of Wales Press, 1952), pp. 77-78.
[122] See David Howlett, 'A Triad of Texts about St David' in *St David of Wales: Cult, Church and Nation*, ed. by J. Wyn Evans and Jonathan M. Wooding (Woodbridge: The Boydell Press, 2007), pp. 253–73 (pp. 258–61). A thirteenth-century Latin poem attributed to Madog of Edeirnion, who may have been an author of religious poetry in Welsh, also draws on the *Historia* to celebrate the achievements of the Britons; see J. Beverley Smith, *The Sense of History in Medieval Wales* (Aberystwyth: University College of Wales, 1991), pp. 5–6.

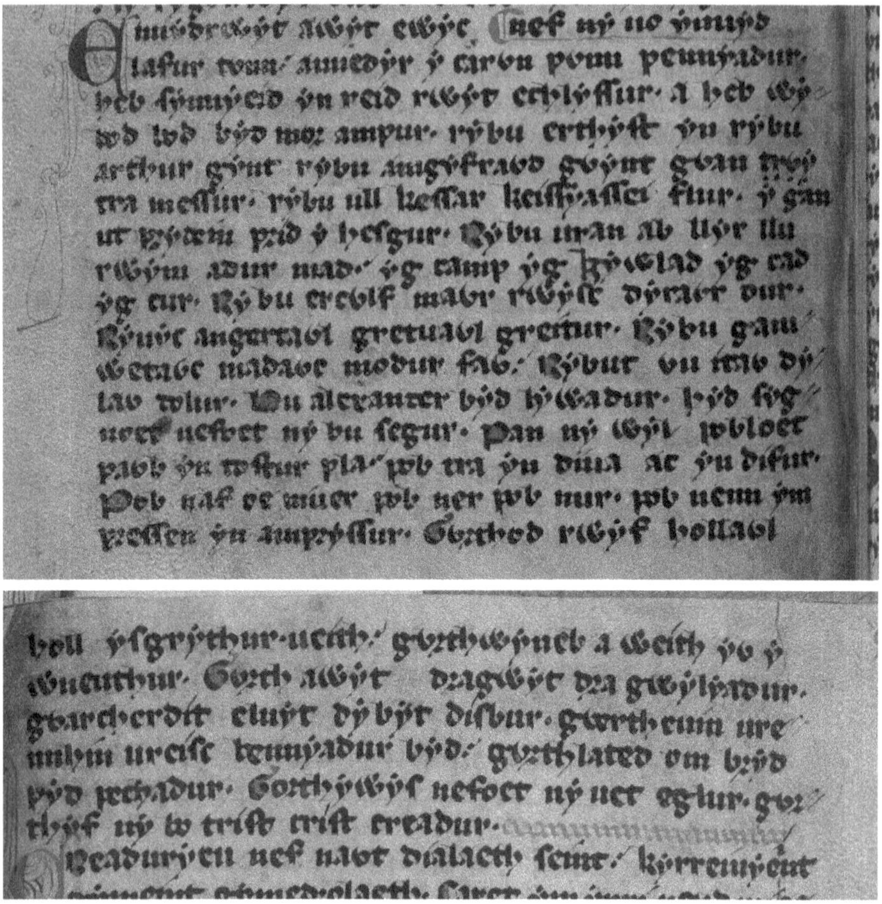

FIG. 3.11: NLW MS 6680B, ff. 100ᵛ–101ʳ.

rybu erthyst yn rybu | arthur gynt rybu amgyfra6d g6ynt g6an t̶r̶v̶y̶ | tra messur. rybu ull kessar keissyassei flur. y gan | ut prydein prid y hesgur. Rybu uran ab llyr llu | rwym adur mad. yg camp yg kywlad yg cad | yg cur. Ry bu erc6lf ma6r rwysc dyra6r dur. | Ryuyc angerta6l gretua6l greitur. Rybu gam-|weta6c mada6c modur fa6. Rybut 6u ita6 dy-|la6 dolur. Bu alexander byd lywadur. hyd syg-|noet nefoet ny bu segur. Pan ny wyl pobloet | pa6b yn tostur pla. pob tra yn diua ac yn difur. | Pob naf oe niuer pob ner pob nur. pob nenn ym | pressen yn ampryssur. G6rthod rwyf holla6l ‖ holl ysgrythur ueith. g6rthwyneb a weith y6 y | wneuthur. G6rth awyt dragwyt dra gwylyadur. | gwarcherdit eluyt dybyt disbur. gwrtheuin ure-|nnhin ureisc bennyadur byd. g6rthlated om bryd | pyd pechadur. Gworthywys nefoet ny uet eglur. g6r-|thyf ny bo trist crist creadur.

The Hendregadredd Manuscript

Rybu erthyst yn: rybu Arthur — gynt,
rybu amgyfraỽd gỽynt, gỽan tra messur;
rybu Ull Kessar, keissyassei Flur
4   y gan ut Prydein, prid y hesgur.
Rybu Uran [u]ab Llyr, llu rwymadur — mad
yg camp yg kywlad, yg cad, yg cur;
rybu Ercỽlf maỽr, rwysc dyraỽr dur,
8   ryuyc angertaỽl gretuaỽl Greitur.
Rybu gamwetaỽc Madaỽc, modur — faỽ,
rybut ỽu itaỽ, dylaỽ dolur:
bu Alexander, byd lywadur,
12 hyd sygnoet nefoet, ny bu segur.
Pany wyl pobloet paỽb yn tostur — pla,
pob tra yn diua ac yn difur,
pob naf o'e niuer, pob ner, pob nur,
16 pob nenn ym pressen yn ampryssur?
Gỽrthod Rwyf hollaỽl holl ysgrythur — ueith,
gỽrthwyneb a weith yỽ y wneuthur;
gỽrth awyt dra gwyt dra gwylyadur
20 gỽartherdyt eluyt, dybyt disbur.
Gỽertheuin Urennhin, ureisc Bennyadur — byd,
gỽrthlated o'm bryd pyd pechadur;
gorthywys nefoet, nyued eglur,
24 gỽrthyf ny bo trist Crist Creadur.

We have received a lesson: Arthur lived in times past,
he was an agitation of the wind, attacking beyond measure;
Julius Caesar lived; he had sought Fflur
4   from the lord of Britain, claiming her [was] costly.
Brân son of Llŷr lived, one who bound an army well
as a feat in a neighbouring land, in battle, in conflict;
great Hercules lived, [with his] fierce, cruel attack,
8   [with] the passionate, mighty boldness of ?Greiddur.
Iniquitous was Madog, celebrated lord,
he received a warning, wretched grief:
Alexander, ruler of the world, went
12 as far as the signs of the heavens, [even] he was not ?safe.
Do not the peoples see, everyone in the misery of adversity,
[that] everything is destroyed and ruined,
every leader with his host, every prince, every chieftain,
16 every lord in this world is ?transitory?
To refuse the absolute Lord of the whole of lengthy scripture,
to do that is a perverse undertaking;
by means of a desire beyond sight, beyond the watcher
20 [on] the day of triumph [over] the world, the very pure will come.
Supreme King, mighty Ruler of the world,
may he drive out of my mind the danger of the sinner;

prince of heaven, bright ?refuge,
24   may Christ the Creator not be sorrowful because of me.

1   **Rybu erthyst yn** Lit. 'There has been a lesson to us', and cf. l. 10 below for the same syntax denoting possession. The force of the verbal form with the preverbal particle *rhy-* may be to create immediacy.

2   **rybu amgyfraỽd gỽynt** As the line is too long by a syllable, *amgyfraỽd* may be emended to *gyfraỽd*; see *GPC* amgyffrawd¹, cyffrawd. For the meaning of the phrase, see the discussion above.

4   **prid y hesgur** Lit. 'costly her claiming'. For the significance of this phrase, see the discussion above.

5   **llu rwymadur — mad.** The noun *rwymadur*, which contains the agent ending *-adur* (cf. l. 11 below, *llywadur*), does not occur elsewhere, but Llywarch Brydydd y Moch uses *rwym* several times for a warrior who binds or shackles his enemy in battle. *Rwymadur* is complemented by an adjective, *mad*, and a preceding genitive noun, *llu*, which causes lenition, giving the literal meaning 'good binder of an army'.

8   **ryuyc angertaỽl gretuaỽl Greitur** It is thought that the boldness (*ryuyc*) of Hercules is identified with that of *Greitur*, an otherwise unknown hero. The form may, however, be an error for a compound containing *graid*, 'burning zeal, ferocity, warfare; ardent, fierce'. The rhyming adjectives *angertaỽl* and *gretuaỽl* may complement either of the two nouns.

13   **pan ny** (H) 'when not'; **pam na** (R) 'why not'. It appears that neither scribe has recognised the unusual negative interrogative form *pany*, which gives a better meaning; see *GMW*, pp. 175–76.

19   **dra gwyt** The Hendregadredd Manuscript's reading, *dragwyt*, is likely to be the preposition *tra*, *dra*, 'beyond', and the noun *gwyt*, 'sight', run together. The Red Book's interpretation of the form as *dragywyd*, 'eternal', does not make much sense and adds a syllable to the line.

20   **gỽartherdyt** The MSS forms *gỽarcherdit* (H) and *gỽarchedid* (R) suggest that both scribes struggled to modernise the spelling of their source and to make sense of a unique compound form probably consisting of *gwarther*, lit. 'summit', fig. 'honour, pride' (*GPC*), and *dyt*, 'day'.

27   **nyued** The MSS forms *ny uet* (H) and *nyued* /nyveð/ (R) again appear to be attempts by scribes to interpret an unfamiliar form, /nyved/, a word given the meaning 'strength' in a fifteenth-century bardic word-list (see *GPC* nyfed), but which was thought by Ifor Williams to mean 'refuge, sanctuary' in the Fourth Branch of the *Mabinogi* (see *Math*, p. 105), and 'hall' in the *Gododdin* (see *AyG*, l. 649). Koch, however, suggests that the Gododdin example is close in meaning to its Irish cognate *ne(i)med*, 'privileged person or thing' (see *GofA*, pp. 11, 137). It is used again with a word containing the element *nef*, 'heaven', in a religious ode by Elidir Sais (*CBT* I 22.24).

Word-list

a *prep.* 'of' (causing lenition, see *GPC* a⁴ and *GMW*, p. 37) 18
ac *conj.* 'and' 14
Alexander *personal name* Alexander (the Great) 11
amgyfraⱴd *n.* 'raid, attack, tumult' (*GPC* amgyffrawd¹) 2n
ampryssur *adj.* '?transitory' (< *am-* negative prefix + *pryssur*, '?constant, continual', see *GPC* amhrysur) 16
angertaⱴl *adj.* 'passionate' (*GPC* angerddol) 8
Arthur *personal name* 1
awyt *n.* 'desire' (*GPC* awydd) 19

bo *3 sing.pres.subj.* of **bod**, 'to be' 24
Bran [u]ab Llyr *personal name* Brân fab Llŷr, Brân son of Llŷr 5
breisc *adj.* 'large, mighty' (*GPC* braisg) 21
brennhin *n.* 'king' 21
bryd *n.* 'mind' 22
bu *3 sing.pret.* of **bod**, 'to be' 10, 11, 12 (see also **rybu**)
byd *n.* 'the world' 11, 21

cad, cat *n.* 'battle, conflict' 6
camp *n.* 'feat' 6
camwetaⱴc *adj.* 'iniquitous, evil' (*GPC* camweddog) 9
keissyassei *3 sing.pluperfect* of **keissyaw**, 'to seek' (*GPC* ceisiaf) 3
creadur *n.* 'creator' (< Lat. *crēatōrem*, see *GPC* creadur²) 24
Crist *personal name* Christ 24
cur *n.* 'a thrashing, conflict, battle' 6
kywlad *n.* 'bordering country, other country' 6

difur *adj.* 'ruined' 14
disbur *adj.* 'very pure' (used as pl.n.) 20
diua *adj.* 'destroyed' (*GPC* difa) 14
dolur *n.* 'pain, suffering, grief' 10
dra see **tra**
dur *adj.* 'of steel, hard, cruel' *GPC* 7
dybyt *3 sing.fut.* of **dyuod**, 'to come' (see *GMW*, p. 133) 20
dylaⱴ *adj.* 'wretched' 10
dyn *n.* 'man' 17
dyraⱴr *adj.* 'fierce, violent' 7

eglur *adj.* 'conspicuous, illustrious, bright' 23
eluyt *n.* 'land, country, world' (*GPC* elfydd¹) 20

Ercvlf *personal name* Ercwlff, Hercules 7
erthyst *n.* 'a (monitory) lesson, a warning' 1
esgur *v.n.* 'to seek, claim' (*GPC* esguraf: esguro) 4

fav *adj.* 'celebrated' (*GPC* ffaw¹) 9
Flur *personal name* Fflur, Flora 3

gan see **y gan**
gorthywys *n.* 'prince' 23
Greitur *?personal name* Greiddur 8n
gretuavl *adj.* 'strong, mighty' (*GPC* greddfol) 8
gwan *v.n.* 'to rush or push forward, attack' (*GPC* gwanaf¹: gwanu, gwân 2) 2
gvartherdyt *n.* 'day of triumph or victory' (*GPC* gwartherddydd) 20n
gweith *n.* 'task, undertaking, workmanship' 18
gvertheuin *adj.* 'highest, supreme' (*GPC* gwerthefin) 21
gwneuthur *v.n.* 'to do' 18
gvrth *prep.* 'by means of' (see *GPC* wrth 6.a) 19
gvrthlated 3 *sing. imperative* of **gwrthlat**, 'to expel, drive out' 22
gvrthod *v.n.* 'to refuse' 17
gvrthwyneb *adj.* 'peverse' 18
gvrthyf *conjugated prep. 1 sing.* 'because of me' (*GPC* wrth) 24
gwyl 3 *sing.pres.indic.* of **gweled**, 'to see' 13
gwyladur *n.* 'watcher' 19
gwynt *n.* 'wind' 2
gwyt *n.* 'sight' (*GPC* gŵydd¹) 19n
gynt *adverb* 'formerly, in times past' 1

hesgur see **esgur**
holl *pron.* 'all, the whole of' (*GPC* oll) 17
hollavl *adj.* 'whole, absolute' 17
hyd *prep.* 'as far as' 12

itav *conjugated prep. 3 sing.masc.* 'to him' (*GMW*, p. 60) 10

llu *n.* 'host, army' 5
llywadur *n.* 'ruler' (*GPC* llywiadur) 11

mad *adj.* 'good' 5
Madavc *personal name* Madog (ap Uthr?) 9
mavr *adj.* 'great' 7
meith *adj.* 'lengthy' (*GPC* maith) 17
messur *n.* 'measure' 2

modur *n.* 'lord' 9

naf *n.* 'leader, lord' 15
nefoet *pl.n.* 'heaven(s)' 12, 22
nenn *n.* 'lord' 16
ner *n.* 'prince' 15
niuer *n.* 'host' 15
nur *n.* '?lord, chieftain' 15
ny *neg.* 'not' 12, 24
nyued *n.* '?refuge' 22n

o'e *combination of prep.* **o** *and infixed poss.pron. 3 sing.* **'e**, 'with his' 15
o'm *combination of prep.* **o** *and infixed poss.pron. 1 sing.* **'m**, 'from my' 22

pany *negative interrogative particle* (causing soft mutation, *GPC* poni¹) 'not?' 13n
paѵb *pron.* 'everyone' 13
pechadur *n.* 'sinner' 22
pennyadur *n.* 'ruler, chief' (*GPC* penadur) 21
pla *n.* 'plague, affliction, adversity' 13
pob *pron. (with adjectival force)* 'every' 14, 15(3), 16
pobloet *pl. of n.* **pobyl**, 'people' 13
pressen *n.* 'this world' 16
prid *adj.* 'costly' 4
Prydein *place name* Britain 4
pyd *n.* 'danger' 22

rwyf *n.* 'lord' 17
rwymadur *n.* 'one who binds' (*GPC* rhwymadur) 5n
rwysc *n.* 'attack' (*GPC* rhwysg) 7
rybu *3 sing.preterite of* **bod**, 'to be, to live' combined with **ry**, *preverbal perfective particle* (*GPC* rhy²; on the lack of mutation after **ry** in a principal clause, see *GMW*, pp. 61–62 n. 1) 1(2)n, 2, 3, 5, 7, 8, 9
rybut *n.* 'warning' (*GPC* rhybudd¹) 10
ryuyc *n.* 'boldness' (*GPC* rhyfyg) 8

segur *adj.* 'secure; idle' (< Lat. *sēcūrus*, see *GPC* segur 1 and 3) 12
sygnoet *pl. of n.* **sygyn**, 'sign (usually of the Zodiac)' 12

tostur *n.* 'misery' 13
tra¹, dra *prep.* 'beyond' (*GPC* tra²) 2, 19(2)
tra² *n.* 'thing' (*GPC* tra¹) 14

trist *adj.* 'sorrowful' 24

u-, v- see **b-**
Ull Kessar *personal name* Ul Cesar, Julius Caesar 3
ut *n.* 'lord' 4

w- see **gw-**

y¹ *prefixed poss.pron. 3 sing.masc.* 'his, its' (causing lenition) 18
y² *prefixed poss.pron. 3 sing.fem.* 'her' (causing spirant mutations and Sandhi h-, GMW, pp. 22–23) 4
yg see **yn**¹
y gan *compound prep.* 'from' (GPC i⁴) 4
yn¹ *prep.* (GPC yn¹, causing nasal mutation, see GMW, p. 21) 'in' 13 **yg** (before c-, k-) 6(4), **ym** (before p-) 16
yn² *predicative particle* (GPC yn³, GMW, p. 139, causing lenition except in *ll-* and *-rh*) 14(2), 16
yn³ *conjugated prep. 1 pl.* of *y, i* 'to' (GMW, p. 60) 1
ysgrythur *n.* 'Scripture' 17
yv *3 sing.pres.indic.* of **bod**, 'to be' 18

The poetry of Bleddyn Fardd and his contemporaries

The Hendregadredd manuscript also contains twenty-three complete praise poems by Phylip Brydydd and Y Prydydd Bychan, who sang mostly in the courts of the southern kingdom of Deheubarth during the thirteenth century. The fact that the great majority of these poems are short series of *englynion* may account for the paucity of references to heroic figures, only twelve in all, including Gwalchmai[123] and an intriguing allusion to a son of Uthr:[124]

> Oesuyrr dy alon, aesuriw — Uaredut,
> travsualch ut treiswlad wiw,
> pwyll mab Uthyr, rwyf aruthyr riw,
> pwyllavc par dryllyavc, drilliw.

> Short-lived are your enemies, Maredudd of the broken shield,
> the proud and mighty lord of a fine, mighty land,
> one with the deliberation of the son of Uthr, a frightening leader on a slope,
> deliberately broken is the three-coloured spear.

His ferocity on the battlefield is the main quality for which Maredudd ab Owain, a great-grandson of Lord Rhys who held lands in Ceredigion during the middle

---
[123] See above.
[124] *CBT* VII 10.1–4. On Uthr, see above *Pa Gur*, l. 14n.

years of the thirteenth century, is praised by Y Prydydd Bychan,[125] but it may be for his prudence that the prince is likened to *mab Uthyr*, perhaps Arthur. The word *pwyll*, however, is also used by the poets with the more general meaning 'nature, temperament', and, although unlikely, it is not impossible that Pwyll is a proper noun here.[126]

Powys, like Deheubarth, was for most of the thirteenth century under the sway of the princes of Gwynedd. It is impossible to know whether it is due to this political situation or the hazards of transmission that so little of the work of thirteenth-century Powys poets was kept in the Hendregadredd manuscript. An exception is that of Llygad Gŵr ('Warrior-eye'), who served the princes of Northern Powys for two generations. The subjects of his five praise poems are compared with nine figures from the past, including the obscure Gwalhafed, named as a brother of Gwalchmai in *Culhwch ac Olwen*,[127] Arthur's son Llachau,[128] and Arthur himself.

It is in the closing lines of an imposing series of five *awdlau* for Llywelyn the Last, probably commissioned by his vassal Gruffudd ap Madog of Powys, to celebrate the victories of 1257 which brought Gwynedd, Powys and Deheubarth under his rule, that the reference to Arthur appears.[129]

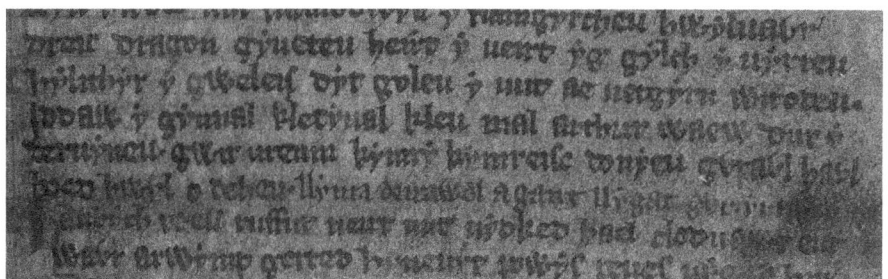

FIG. 3.12: NLW MS 6680B, f. 87ʳ.

jddaw y gynnal kletyual kleu mal arthur waew dur y | deruyneu. gwir urenin kymry kymreisc donyeu gṏraṏl haṏl | boed hwyl o deheu.

> Iddaw y gynnal, kletyual kleu,
> mal Arthur waew dur, y deruyneu,

---

[125] For the *topos* of the broken shield or spear representing a warrior's ferocity in battle, see above *Pa Gur*, l. 23n.
[126] See *GPC* pwyll. The only Pwyll in Welsh literary tradition is the protagonist of the First Branch of the *Mabinogi*, who was probably given the name in order to exemplify the quality of *pwyll*, 'prudence', but there is no evidence to suggest that he was a son of Uthr.
[127] See *CO*, l. 345n.
[128] See Chapter 1 above.
[129] NLW MS 6680B, f. 87ʳ, copied by hand J of Stratum II (see *MWM*, pp. 201–07); *CBT* VII 24.153–56.

> gwir urenin Kymry kymreisc donyeu,
> gẁraẁl haẁl, boed hwyl odeheu.

> To him, [Llywelyn], in order to uphold (swift his sword stroke),
> his borders, like Arthur of the steely spear,
> true king of Wales of powerful abilities,
> splendid his right, let there be a successful progress for him [Llywelyn]!

Here, in an exuberant celebration of the new-found unity of Wales under Llywelyn, *gwledic rieu*, 'overlord of kings', Arthur is presented not only as a mighty warrior but as a defender of the nation.[130]

A heightened sense of national identity also characterises the work of the other representatives of the last generation of poets who sang the praises of members of the royal dynasty of Gwynedd and lamented their deaths. The verse of Hywel Foel and Bleddyn Fardd is particularly rich in allusions to great figures from the past, with some thirty references in sixteen poems. All the Arthurian references except for one, however, are to be found in the work of Bleddyn.[131] These include an allusion to Caerleon, which may have been intended to evoke the splendour of Arthur's court in *Historia Regum Britanniae*. It occurs in an elegy for Llywelyn the Last, whose authority is said to have extended over the whole of Wales.[132]

> Gẁr kywirgoeth doeth, detholaf — o Uon
>   hyd yg Caer Llion, y lle teccaf.

> Faithful, fine and wise warrior, the most excellent from Anglesey
>   to Caerllïon, the fairest place.

Bleddyn's work also contains the earliest references in the corpus to Peredur, the counterpart of Perceval;[133] Drystan, the Welsh form of Tristan, a character who may have deep roots in the early traditions of Cornwall and the Old North as a heroic figure and a lover;[134] and Eliwlad, Arthur's nephew, who features in the Dialogue of Arthur and the Eagle,[135] in addition to Bedwyr, Elifri and Llachau.[136] It is interesting to note that it is in order to praise the courage and military skills of their patrons rather than their more courtly qualities that Arthur's companions are named by the court poets, even in the closing years

---

[130] For a detailed examination of the historical and political context of this poem and the poet's understanding and interpretation of it, see Lynch, 'Court Poetry'.
[131] For Hywel's reference to Elifri, see above.
[132] *CBT* VII 50.31–32.
[133] See *TYP*, pp. 477–80. As Barry Lewis points out ('Arthurian References'), this is, in fact, the earliest of all references to Peredur in the Welsh tradition.
[134] See *TYP*, pp. 331–34, and Jenny Rowland's chapter in *ACL*, pp. 51–63.
[135] See Chapter 5 below.
[136] For a discussion of his reference to Llachau, see Chapter 1.

of the thirteenth century,¹³⁷ but that Arthur himself is depicted in a variety of roles.

Gwaewddur, 'steely spear' again rhymes with *Arthur* in the elegy for the three brothers, Owain, Llywelyn and Dafydd, whose deaths brought about the end of the royal dynasty of Gwynedd.¹³⁸

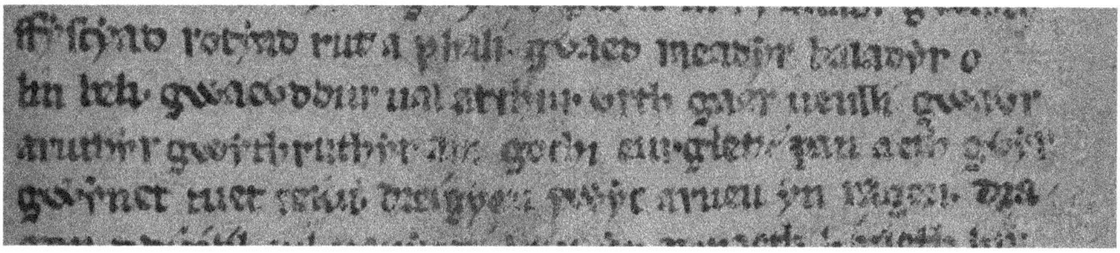

FIG. 3.13: NLW MS 6680B, f. 28ʳ.

G6aed raeadyr blaldyr o | lin beli. gwae6ddur ual arthur 6rth gaer uenlli gwa6r | aruthyr gwythruthyr am gochi eurglet. pan aeth g6yr | gwynet tuet teiui.

> G6aed raeadyr baladyr, o lin Beli,
> gwae6ddur ual Arthur 6rth Gaer Uenlli,
> gwa6r aruthyr gwychruthyr am gochi — eurglet
> pan aeth g6yr Gwynet tuet Teiui.

> [With his] spear [causing] a torrent of blood, of the lineage of Beli,
> with a steely spear like Arthur near Caer Fenlli,
> terrible lord of the mighty attack to redden a splendid sword
> when the men of Gwynedd went to the lands of Teifi.

It is Dafydd, the youngest of the three, who led the men of Gwynedd to victory at Cilgerran on the banks of River Teifi in 1258, whose spear is likened to that of Arthur here. Lost onomastic traditions from Dafydd's lordship of the Vale of Clwyd may explain Arthur's otherwise unknown involvement in an attack on the giant Benlli.¹³⁹

It is for his military prowess also that Dafydd's brother, Llywelyn, is commemorated in a striking series of *englynion* where Arthur is named twice. Only the last seven lines of this poem are to be found in the Hendregadredd Manuscript due to a lost page, but the poem is complete in the late fifteenth-century manuscript Peniarth 55A, and in some sixteenth and seventeenth

---

¹³⁷ Note in particular the use of the word *arfod*, 'blow, attack, assault', with the names of Cai and Bedwyr in an elegy by Elidir Sais for two notable warriors (*WCP* no. 21), and with the names of Geraint and Peredur in poems by Bleddyn Fardd (*CBT* VII 46.15, 51.31).
¹³⁸ NLW MS 6680B, f. 28, Hand A of Stratum II (see *MWM*, pp. 201–07); *CBT* VII 54.29–32.
¹³⁹ For Benlli, see above. It may be significant that Caerfenlli ('The Fort of Benlli') stands on Moel Fenlli not far from Moel Arthur in the Vale of Clwyd, which was at the time under Dafydd's rule; see *AMWL*, p. 9.

century copies of two lost exemplars from the same period.[140] The hand of the Peniarth 55 text has been identified as that of Dafydd Epynt, a poet from Brecon, and a study of the variant readings by Dafydd Johnston suggests that he probably wrote it down from memory, having perhaps seen it in the Hendregadredd Manuscript.[141] Although the poem is not attributed to Bleddyn in any of the manuscripts, his authorship of it has been convincingly argued by Tomos Roberts, based on its location in the Hendregadredd Manuscript, its content and its style.[142] The composite edition below is based on the Peniarth 55 version, incorporating some readings from the later manuscripts noted in italics.[143]

The poem opens with a sequence reminiscent of that in the religious poem attributed to Llywarch Brydydd y Moch in the Hendregadredd Manuscript. Arthur's death is again set alongside that of Bendigeidfran (Brân the Blessed).

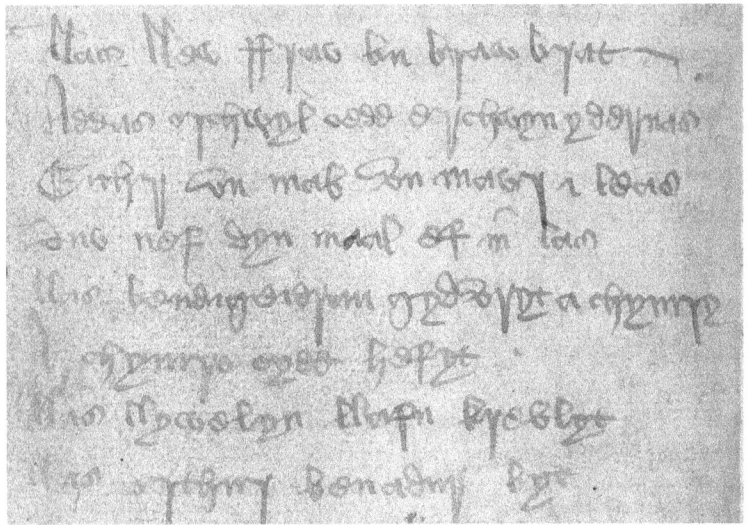

FIG. 3.14: Peniarth MS 55, p. 188.

Llas llew ffrav bu braw brat | Addas orchwyl oedd erchwyn y deyrnas | Eithr vn mab vn mawr i leas | duv nef dyn mal ef ni las | llas bendigeidran gydvryt a chymry | A chymro oydd hefyt | llas llywelyn llafn krevlyt | llas arthur benadur byt.

[140] NLW MS 6680B, f. 30^r, and see the manuscript notes for *CBT* VII poem 51.
[141] Dafydd Johnston, 'Bywyd Marwnad: Gruffudd ab yr Ynad Coch a'r Traddodiad Llafar' in *Cyfoeth y Testun: Ysgrifau ar Lenyddiaeth Gymraeg yr Oesoedd Canol*, ed. by Iestyn Daniel et al. (Cardiff: University of Wales Press, 2003), pp. 200–19 (pp. 212–15).
[142] Tomos Roberts, 'Englynion Marwnad i Lywelyn ap Gruffudd', *Bulletin of the Board of Celtic Studies*, 26 (1974–1976), 10–12.
[143] NLW Peniarth MS 55A, pp. 188–90; for a digital copy of the MS, visit < http://digidol.llgc.org.uk>.

Lladd llew Ffrav! Bu braw *bryt* addas — orchwyl
  erchwyniog teyrnas;
eithr *Vn Mab Mair, mawr lias*
Duv nef, dyn mal ef ni las.

Llas Bendigeidran gydvryt — a chymri,
  a *chymraw* oydd hevyt;
llas Llywelyn llafngrevlyt,
llas Arthur, benadur byt.

The lion of Ffraw has been killed![144] Fear was the appropriate employment
                                                                of the mind
[regarding] the upholder of the kingdom;
apart from the only Son of Mary (great was His death),
God of Heaven! no man like him has ever been killed.

Bendigeidfran was killed, [one] familiar with sorrow,
and there was terror [then] also;
Llywelyn, his blade bloody, was killed,
Arthur was killed, ruler of the world.

The terror expressed in these *englynion*, which also characterises the opening of the famous elegy by Bleddyn's contemporary, Gruffudd ab yr Ynad Coch, was largely due to the circumstances of Llywelyn's untimely death.[145] He was the first prince of Gwynedd to be slain in battle against the English for a number of generations. His severed head was taken to Edward I at Rhuddlan before being put on display on the Tower of London. J. Beverley Smith is probably right to suggest that the reference to Bendigeidfran, who, according to the Second Branch of the *Mabinogi*, was also decapitated after death and had his head taken to London, places the loss of Llywelyn against a mythological background and signals that it was to bring about the end of an era.[146] The epithet given to Arthur is similar to that used by Llywarch Brydydd y Moch for Alexander, portraying him as a world leader. The use of the term *penadur*, however, also brings to mind the play on the meanings of *pen*, 'head', and 'chief' in Gruffudd ab yr Ynad Coch's elegy. Moreover, the reference to Arthur's death, like Gruffudd's allusion to the Battle of Camlan,[147] may also have reminded listeners that it was by treachery that both he and Llywelyn were killed, and that

---

[144] For the emendation, see *GMW*, p. 161n.
[145] It is likely that Gruffudd's elegy for Llywelyn (*CBT* VII 36), which follows that of Bleddyn in Peniarth 55, was once in the Hendregadredd Manuscript as well in as the Red Book of Hergest. For a translation, see Joseph P. Clancy, *Medieval Welsh Poems* (Dublin: Four Courts Press, 2003), pp. 171–74.
[146] See J. Beverley Smith, *Llywelyn ap Gruffudd, Prince of Wales* [*Llywelyn*] (Cardiff: University of Wales Press, 1998), pp. 568–69, and John T. Koch, 'Brân, Brennos: An Instance of Early Gallo-Britonnic History and Mythology', *CMCS*, 20 (1990), 1–20.
[147] See above p. 78.

his death had long-lasting consequences for the nation.[148]

The short reference to Arthur in the fifth stanza of the poem is ambiguous. It may have been intended to bring to mind the image of the soldier Arthur so common in the corpus, but a different reading may suggest a similar figure to the national ruler of Llygad Gŵr's eulogy for Llywelyn above.

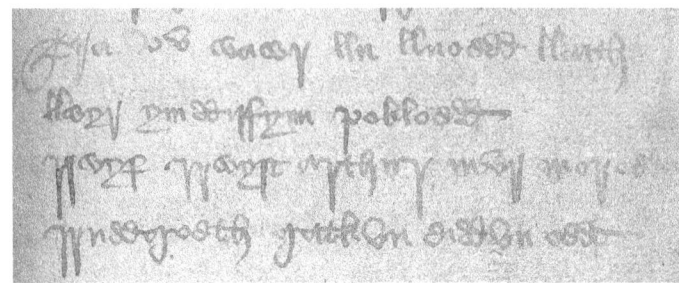

FIG. 3.15: Peniarth MS 55, p. 189.

Tra vv vawr wawr llu lluoedd llaith | llwyr ymddiffynn pobloedd | rrwyf rrwysc arthur mvr moroedd | rruddgoeth gatkvn eiddvn oedd

> Tra vv vawr *yn llawr mewn* lluoedd — *a llaw*,
>   llwyr ymddiffyn pobloed[d],
>   rrwyf rrwysc Arthur, mvr moroedd,
>   *rruddgo*ch gatkvn eiddvn oedd.

> While our champion was great amongst hosts with authority,
> [and a] complete defence of [his] people,
> a lord with the attack/authority of Arthur, a rampart [against] the seas,
> he was a choice/eager, blood-red battle-chief.

Although *rwysc* is commonly employed with personal names in the corpus, it is difficult to know whether it is used here in a military context or as a reference to Arthur's great power.[149] The significance of the epithet *mvr moroedd* is also unclear, but in the following stanza Llywelyn is called *amerodr Kymro*, 'Welsh ruler (lit. emperor)'.[150]

---

[148] For a discussion of the evidence that Llywelyn was killed by treachery, see *Llywelyn*, pp. 551–56, and on the play on *pen* also found in *EWSP*, pp. 420–22, 'Pen Urien', see Sarah Lynn Higley, 'Forcing a Gap: The Stylistics of "amputation" in Marwnad Llywelyn by Gruffudd ab yr Ynad Coch', *Viator*, 19 (1988), 147–72.
[149] See *GPC* for the meanings of rhwysg.
[150] For other examples of *amherawdyr* in the corpus, see Chapter 1, p. 25, above.

Awdl by Bleddyn Fardd for Rhys ap Maredudd

There is no such ambiguity in Bleddyn's *awdl* of praise for Rhys ap Maredudd,[151] the ruler of a portion of Cantref Mawr in Ystrad Tywi, part of the old kingdom of Deheubarth.[152] The poem was probably performed during a visit by the poet to the court of Rhys in 1277 in order to ensure the continuing allegiance of the prince to his patron, Llywelyn. He skilfully echoes the work of his predecessors, in particular Llywarch Brydydd y Moch's *canu* for Rhys' grandfather, Rhys Gryg, an ally of Llywelyn's grandfather, Llywelyn the Great, a poem probably composed for a similar diplomatic mission to south Wales in 1220.[153] It is called an *awdl* in a title in the margin of the Hendregadredd Manuscript but it starts like an *arwyrain*, bringing to mind the opening words of Cynddelw's *arwyrain* for Rhys' great-grandfather, the Lord Rhys, suggesting perhaps that he was a worthy descendant of the greatest ruler of Deheubarth.[154]

Although it is composed on a smaller scale, the structure of this poem is very similar to that of Llywarch Brydydd y Moch for Rhys Gryg, with the penultimate section in each case dedicated to praise for the poet's Gwynedd patron. Both poets use references to figures of history and legend, including Arthur, to enrich their eulogies, but their approach is quite different. Llywarch, like Cynddelw in his elegy for Owain Gwynedd above, chooses to use the device in one section of his long poem only. He draws on a wide array of figures, including a pair of triads, using them as 'bardic short-hand' to convey the many worthy qualities of Llywelyn and Rhys Gryg.[155] Bleddyn, on the other hand, appears to be more deliberate and selective, limiting his allusions to Arthurian characters only. Just as Elidir Sais identified Ednyfed Fychan and Tegwared ab Iarddur, two of Llywelyn the Great's supporters in Gwynedd, with Cai and Bedwyr,[156] Bleddyn likens Rhys to Arthur's beloved nephew, Eliwlad, and to Peredur son of Efrog, a knight of his court. The significance of the poet's choice of Peredur has been outlined by Rhian Andrews with reference to the contemporary Romance of Peredur, where he is depicted as a great champion of

---

[151] NLW MS 6680B, f. 28ᵛ, copied by hand C of Stratum II; *CBT* VII 46.
[152] On the lands held by Rhys, see J. Beverley Smith, 'The "Cronica de Wallia" and the Dynasty of Dinefwr', *Bulletin of the Board of Celtic Studies*, 20 (1962–1964), 261–82 (272–74), and on his career, see R. R. Davies, *The Age of Conquest: Wales 1063–1415* (Oxford: University Press, 1991), pp. 380–81.
[153] *CBT* V 26. See Rhian M. Andrews' detailed analysis of both poems in 'Y Bardd yn Llysgennad, Rhan I: Llywarch Brydydd y Moch yn Neheubarth', *Dwned*, 20 (2014), 11–30; 'Y Bardd yn Llysgennad, Rhan II: Bleddyn Fardd yn Neheubarth', *Dwned*, 21 (2015), 49–68.
[154] llyma aȟdyl a gant bledyn ȟard y rys am maredud ap rys, 'Here is an *awdl* which Bleddyn Fardd sang for Rhys ap Maredudd ap Rhys'. The poem for Lord Rhys (*CBT* IV 8) opens: *Ardwyreaf dreic fwyr, feleic fer*, 'I exhalt a dragon [fig. warrior], a terrible, steadfast leader'.
[155] See Marged Haycock, '"Some Talk of Alexander and Some of Hercules": Three Early Medieval Poems from the Book of Taliesin', *Cambridge Medieval Celtic Studies*, 13 (1987), 7–38 (p. 32). On Llywarch's use of triads, see above.
[156] See *CBT* I 18.18.

the whole of Wales.[157] Andrews has also suggested that play on the element *pâr*, 'spear', in his name, and his epithet *Paladr Hir*, 'Long Lance', may have led to the use of *arf*, 'weapon', in these lines, and also the reference to Rhôn Ofyniad, Arthur's spear according to *Culhwch ac Olwen*.[158] Despite the repetition of the element *tëyrn*, 'king', it is as a soldier that Rhys 'brave dragon of Deheubarth' is compared to Eliwlad and Peredur. It is Llywelyn, the defender of the whole of Wales, who is identified with Arthur.

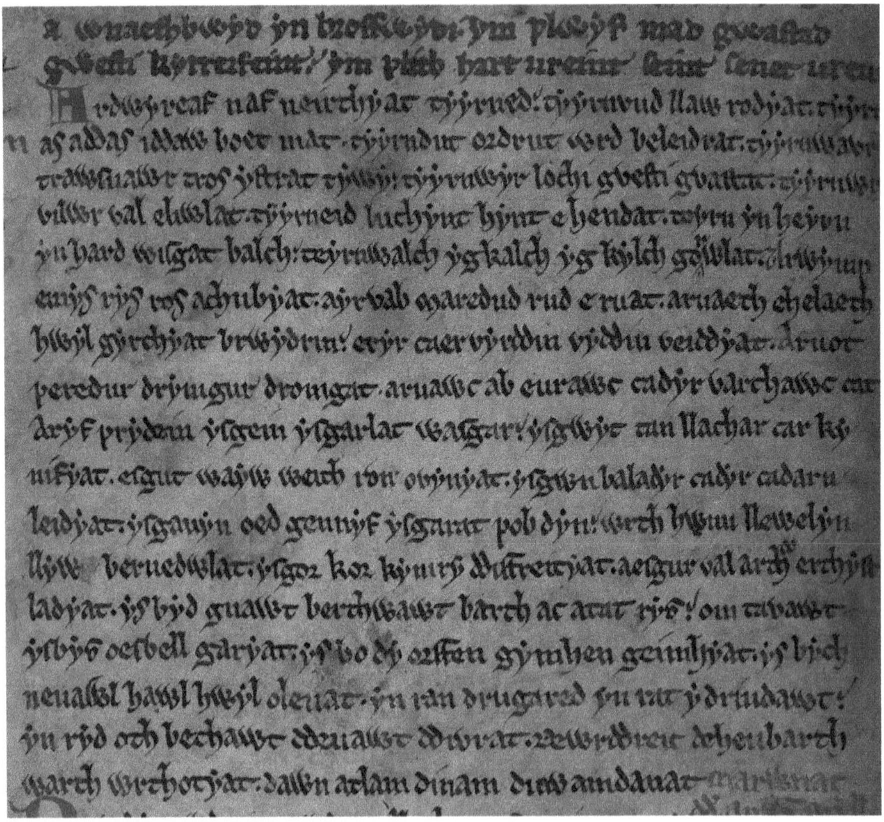

FIG. 3.16: NLW MS 6680B, f. 28^V

---

[157] See *Historia Peredur vab Efrawc*, ed. by Glenys Witchard Goetinck (Cardiff: University of Wales Press, 1976). On the dating of various versions of the tale, see Daniel Huws, 'Y Pedair Llawysgrif Ganoloesol' in *Canhwyll Marchogyon: Cyd-destunoli Peredur*, ed. by Sioned Davies and Peter Wynn Thomas (Cardiff: University of Wales Press, 2000), pp. 1–9. As Barry Lewis has suggested ('Arthurian References'), the use of the word *marchawc*, 'knight', for Peredur makes a connection with the Romance of Peredur very likely.

[158] CO, ll. 159–60. See above for other references to Arthur's spear in the work of Bleddyn and Llygad Gŵr.

Ardwyreaf naf neirthyat tyyrned. tyyrn6ud llaw rodyat. tyyrn|as addas iddaw boet mat. tyyrndut ordrut wrd beleidrat. tyyrnwa6r | trawsuawr tros ystrat tywy. tyyrnwyr lochi g6esti g6astat. tyyrnwr | 6ilwr 6al eliwlat. tyyrneid luchyynt hynt e hendat. teyrn yn heyrn | yn hard wisgat balch. teyrnwalch yg kalch yg kylch gorwlat. arwymp | emys rys ros achubyat. Ayr6ab maredud rud e ruat. aruaeth ehelaeth | hwyl gyrchyat brwydrin eryr caervyrddin vyddin veiddyat. aruot | peredur drymgur dromgat. aruawc ab eurawc cadyr 6archawc cat | aryf prydein ysgein ysgarlat wasgar. ysgwyt tan llachar car ky|nifyat. esgut wayw weith ron o6ynyat. ysgwn baladyr cadyr cadarn | leidyat. ysgauyn oed gennyf ysgarat pob dyn. wrth hwnn llewelyn | llyw beruedwlat. ysgor kor kymry ddiffreityat. aesgur 6al arthur erthyst | ladyat. ys byd guawt berthwawt barth ac atat rys. om ta6awt | ysbys oesbell garyat. ys bo dy orffen gymhen geimhyat. ys bych | neuawl hawl hwyl oleuat. yn ran drugared yn rat y drindawt. | yn ryd oth bechawt ddeuawt ddi6rat. dewrddreic deheubarth | warth wrthotyat. dawn atlam dinam duw amdanat

        Ardwyreaf naf, neirthyat — tyyrned,
           tyyrn6ud, llawrodyat,
         tyyrnas addas iddaw boet mat,
4   tyyrndut, ordrut wrd beleidrat.
        Tyyrnwa6r trawsuawr tros Ystrat — Tywy,
         tyyrnwyr lochi g6esti g6astat,
         tyyrnwr, 6ilwr 6al Eliwlat,
8   tyyrneid luchynt, hynt e hendat.
        Teyrn yn heyrn, yn hard wisgat — balch,
         teyrnwalch yg kalch ygkylch gorwlat,
         arwymp emys: Rys, Ros achubyat,
12   ayr6ab Maredud, rud e ruat.
        Aruaeth ehelaeth, hwyl gyrchyat — brwydrin,
         eryr Caer6yrddin, 6yddin 6eiddyat,
         aruot Peredur drymgur dromgat,
16   aruawc [u]ab Eurawc, cadyr 6archawc cat.
        Aryf Prydein ysgein, ysgarlat — wasgar,
         ysgwyt tanllachar, car kynifyat,
         esgut wayw, weith Ron O6ynyat,
20   ysgwn baladyr cadyr, cadarn leidyat.
        Ysgauyn oed gennyf ysgarat — pob dyn
         wrth hwnn: Llewelyn, llyw Beruedwlat,
         ysgor kor, Kymry ddiffreityat,
24   aesgur 6al Arthur, erthyst ladyat.
        Ys byd guawt berthwawt barth ac atat, — Rys,
         o'm ta6awt ysbys oesbell garyat;
         ys bo dy orffen, gymhen geimhyat,
28   ys bych neuawl hawl hwyl oleuat,
        yn ran drugared, yn rat — y Drindawt,
         yn ryd o'th bechawt ddeuawt ddi6rat;

dewrddreic Deheubarth, warth wrthotyat,
32 dawn atlam dinam Duw amdanat

I exalt a lord, sustainer of kings,
[one of] royal riches, a giver of gifts,
may the kingdom [which is] worthy of him be blessed/fortunate,
4 [a man of] royal people with a most bold [and] powerful spear blow.
A royal lord, mighty and powerful, over Ystrad Tywi,
supporting royal warriors [with] continual sustenance,
a royal warrior, a soldier like Eliwlad,
8 [on] a royal lightning assault like his grandfather's assault.
A ruler in iron armour, in fine, splendid clothing,
a royal hero in coloured armour around a bordering country,
[on] excellent warhorses: Rhys, the attacker of Rhos,
12 warlike son of Maredudd, bloodthirsty his roar.
[A man with a] far-reaching plan, an attacker on an incursion in battle
the eagle of Carmarthen, challenger of an army,
[he has] the blow of Peredur of the hard struggle [causing] severe affliction,
16 the armed son of Efrog, mighty knight in conflict.
[He is] the weapon of the men of Britain scattering [sparks], distributing
                                                         scarlet cloth,
[a man with] a shield emitting sparks, a warrior's friend,
[with his] swift spear [of the same] workmanship [as that of] Rhôn Ofyniad,
20 [with] a ready [and] mighty lance, a strong slayer [is he].
It would be light work for me to abandon every [other] man
beside this one: Llywelyn, the lord of Perfeddwlad,
[he is the] stronghold of the host, the defender of the Welsh,
24 shield-shattering like Arthur in an admonitory slaughter.
A poem of glorious praise will come to you, Rhys,
from my well-known tongue with long-lasting love;
may your end be, accomplished champion,
28 (may you be a heavenly claimant on a bright journey)
in the place of mercy, in the grace of the Trinity,
free of your sin through the true rite;
Brave dragon of Deheubarth, rejector of shame,
32 [may] the blessing of God's faultless abode surround you!

2 **tyyrnѵud** ... The first in a sequence of nine lines beginning with the element *tëyrn-*, 'kingly, royal', which had two syllables in MW, weakened to one in ModW. On its use by the poets, see Andrews, 'Nomenclature', pp. 91–94, 106–09. The compound noun *tyyrnѵud*, 'royal bounty', is understood as an attribute of Rhys, cf. l. 4, *tyyrndut*, but the form may be an error for *tyyrnud*, 'royal lord' (*CBT* v 9.8).

8 **hynt e hendat** A reference to Rhys Gryg (d.1233), the last prince to rule the whole of Ystrad Tywi.

10 **Yg kalch** 'wearing limewashed or decorated armour'. For *calch* used for shields, see below, the Elegy for Cynddylan, 8n.

11   **Ros** A reference perhaps to an attack by Llywelyn ap Gruffudd and his allies on the cantref of Rhos, Pembrokeshire, in 1257; see J. E. Lloyd, *A History of Wales from the Earliest Times to the Edwardian Conquest* (London: Longmans, Green and Co., 1911), II, p. 721.

13   **hwyl gyrchyat — brwydrin** The main element is *cyrchyat*, 'attacker', preceded and followed by genitive nouns.

14   **eryr Caer(v)yrddin** There is no record of Rhys ap Maredudd attacking the royal borough of Carmarthen. The purpose of the epithet may be to bring to mind Llywarch Brydydd y Moch's praise poem to Rhys Gryg, who was involved in Llywelyn ap Iorwerth's attack on Carmarthen in 1215.

15   **Aruot Peredur drymgur dromgat** '[he has] the blow of Peredur of the hard struggle [causing] severe affliction'. *Trymgur dromgat* is treated as a compound adjective complementing *Peredur*. The main element of the compound is the noun *tromgat*, 'hard struggle', with the adjective *trymgur*, 'severe affliction', preceding it and causing it to lenite.

17   **Aryf Prydein ysgein** This is the only example of *Prydein* in the extant poetry of Bleddyn Fardd. He frequently refers to Llywelyn as leader or defender of the *Cymry* as in l. 23 below. This may be a deliberate echo of epithets used by Cynddelw of the Lord Rhys and by Llywarch Brydydd y Moch of Rhys Gryg. The verb noun *ysgein* is unusual and its relationship to the preceding nouns is uncertain, but it could be connected to *aryf*, 'weapon', commonly used as a metaphor for a warrior, with the idea that he scattered sparks (cf. l. 18 below) through his ferocious fighting.

22   **llyw Beruedwlat** Y Berfeddwlad, 'the middle country', consisted of the four cantrefi of Rhos, Rhufoniog, Tegeingl and Dyffryn Clwyd in north-east Wales. The same epithet is used for Llywelyn ap Iorwerth by Dafydd Benfras (*CBT* VI 30.10). The definite article is omitted here but the lenition it causes in a feminine noun is retained.

Word-list

ac see **parth ac at**
achubyat *n.* 'seizer' (*GPC* achubiad[1]) 11
addas *adj.* 'suitable, worthy' 3
aesgur *adj.* 'shield-shattering' 24
amdanat *conjugated prep. 2 sing.* 'around you' 32
ardwyreaf 1 *sing.pres.indic.* of **ardwyrein**, 'to exalt, to praise' (*GPC* arddwyreaf: arddwyrain) 1
Arthur *personal name* 24
aruaeth *n.* 'intention, plan' (*GPC* arfaeth) 13
aruawc *adj.* 'armed' (*GPC* arfog) 16
aruot *n.* 'blow' (*GPC* arfod) 15

arwymp *adj.* 'splendid' 11
aryf *n.* 'weapon' (*GPC* arf) 17n
atat *conjugated prep. 2 sing.* 'to you' 25 (see **parth ac at**)
atlam *n.* 'abode' (*GPC* adlam¹) 32
ayrṽab *n.* 'warlike son' (*GPC* aerfab) 12
balch *adj.* 'splendid' 9
beiddyat *n.* 'challenger' 14
berthwawt *n.* 'glorious praise' 26
bo *3 sing.pres.subj.* of **bot**, 'to be' 27
boet *3 sing.imper.* of **bot**, 'to be' 3
brwydrin *n.* 'battle' 13
bych *2 sing.pres.subj.* of **bot**, 'to be' 28
byd *3 sing.fut.indic.* of **bot**, 'to be' 25
byddin *n.* 'army' 14

cadarn *adj.* 'strong' 20
cadyr *adj.* 'mighty' (*GPC* cadr) 16, 20
Caerṽyrddin *place name* Caerfyrddin, Carmarthen 14
kalch *n.* 'coloured armour' (see *GPC* calch) 10
car *n.* 'friend, companion' (*GPC* câr) 18
caryat *n.* 'love' (*GPC* cariad) 26
cat *n.* 'battle, conflict' 16
keimhyat *n.* 'champion' (*GPC* ceimiad) 27
kor *n.* 'host' (*GPC* côr¹ a) 23
kymhen *adj.* 'accomplished' 27
Kymry *pl. of* **Kymro**, 'Welshman' (*GPC* Cymro) 23
kynifyat *n.* 'warrior' (*GPC* cynifiad) 18
kyrchyat *n.* 'attacker' (*GPC* cyrchiad²) 13

dawn *n.* 'gift, blessing' 32
Deheubarth *place name* 31
deuawt *n.* 'custom, practice, rite' 30
dewrddreic *n.* 'brave dragon, *fig.* warrior' 31
diffreityat *n.* 'defender' (*GPC* diffreidiad) 23n
dinam *adj.* 'faultless' 32
diṽrat *adj.* 'just, true' (*GPC* difrad) 30
Duw *name* God 32
dy *2 sing. possessive pron.* 'your' 27
dyn *n.* 'man, person' 21

e *prefixed poss.pron. 3 sing.masc.* 'his, its' (causing lenition, see *GPC* ei¹) 8, 12

ehelaeth *adj.* 'broad, far-reaching' 13
Eliwlat *personal name* Eliwlad (son of Madog ap Uthr) 7
emys *pl. of n.* **amws**, 'warhorse' 11
erthyst *n.* 'a warning' *as adj.* 'cautionary, admonitory' 24
eryr *n.* 'eagle, *fig.* hero' 14
esgut *adj.* 'swift' 19
Eurawc *personal name* Efrog 16

g- see also **c-, k-**
gennyf *conjugated prep. 1 sing. of* **gan** *denoting possession* (see *GPC* gan¹) 21
goleuat *n.* 'light' 28
gorffen *n.* 'end' 27
gordrut *adj.* 'very bold' (*GPC* gorddrud) 4
gorwlat *n.* 'a bordering country' 10
guawt *n.* 'poem' (*GPC* gwawd) 25
gwarth *n.* 'shame' 31
gwasgar *v.n.* 'to distribute' 17
gvastat *adj.* 'continual' 6
gwayw *n.* 'spear' 19
gweith *n.* 'workmanship' (*GPC* gwaith¹ 1c) 19
gvesti *n.* 'sustenance' 6
gwisgat *n.* 'clothing' 9
gwrd *adj.* 'powerful' (*GPC* gwrdd) 4
gwrthotyat *n.* 'rejector' 31

hard *adj.* 'fine' 9
hawl *n.* 'claim, claimant' 28
hendat *n.* 'grandfather' 8
heyrn (hëyrn) *pl.n.* 'iron armour' (see *GPC* haearn) 9
hwnn *demonstrative pron.* 'this one' 22
hwyl *n.* 'course, journey, incursion' 13, 28
hynt *n.* 'course, assault' 8

iddaw, itav *conjugated prep. 3 sing.masc.* 'to him' (*GMW*, p. 60) 3

lladyat *n.* 'slaughter' (*GPC* lladdiad¹) 24
llawrodyat *n.* 'giver of gifts, generous giver' (*GPC* llawroddiad) 2
lleidyat *n.* 'slayer' (*GPC* lleiddiad) 20
Llewelyn *personal name* Llywelyn (the Last) 22
llochi *v.n.* 'to protect, support' 6
lluchynt *n.* 'assault, *lit.* lightning rush' 8

llyw *n.* 'leader, lord' 22

mab *n.* 'son of' 16
marchawc *n.* 'horseman, knight' 16
Maredud *personal name* Maredudd (ap Rhys) 12
mat *n.* 'fortunate, blessed' (*GPC* mad¹) 3
milwr *n.* 'soldier' 7

naf *n.* 'leader, lord' 1
neirthyat *n.* 'sustainer' 1
neuawl *adj.* 'heavenly' (*GPC* nefol) 28

o- see **go-**
oed 3 *sing.imperf.indic.* **bot**, 'to be' 21
o'm *combination of prep.* **o** *and infixed poss.pron. 1 sing.* **'m**, 'from my' 26
oesbell *adj.* 'long-lasting' 26
o'th *combination of prep.* **o** *and infixed poss.pron. 2 sing.* **'th**, 'from your' 30

paladyr *n.* 'lance' (*GPC* paladr) 20
parth ac at *compound prep.* 'towards' 25
pechawt *n.* 'sin' (*GPC* pechod) 30
peleidrat *n.* 'spear blow' 4
Peredur *personal name* 15
Peruedwlat *place name* Perfeddwlad 22n
pob *pron. (with adjectival force)* 'every' 21
Prydein² *pl.n.* 'men of Britain' 17n

ran *n.* 'region, place' (*GPC* rhan¹ i.) 29
rat *n.* 'grace' (*GPC* rhad) 29
Ron Oṽynyat *name of Arthur's spear* Rhôn Ofyniad 19
Ros *place name* Rhos 11n
ruat *n.* 'roar' (*GPC* rhuad) 12
rud *adj.* 'bloodthirsty' (*GPC* rhudd) 12
ryd *adj.* 'free' (*GPC* rhydd) 30
Rys *personal name* Rhys (ap Maredudd) 11, 25

tanllachar *adj.* 'fire-bright, emitting sparks' 18
taṽawt *n.* 'tongue' (*GPC* tafod) 26
teyrn (tëyrn) *n.* 'king, ruler' 9; *pl.* **tyyrned** (teÿrnedd) 1
teyrnwalch (teÿrnwalch) *n.* 'royal hero' 10
trawsuawr *adj.* 'mighty and powerful' 5

Trindawt, y *name* 'the Trinity' 29
tromgat *n.* 'an intense battle, a hard struggle' 15
tros *prep.* 'over' 5
trugared *n.* 'mercy' 29
trymgur *n.* 'severe affliction' 15
tyyrnas (teÿrnas) *n.* 'kingdom' (*GPC* teyrnas) 3
tyyrndut (teÿrndud) *n.* 'royal people' 4
tyyrned see **teyrn**
tyyrneid (teÿrnaidd) *adj.* 'royal' (*GPC* teyrnaidd) 8
tyyrnwavr (teÿrnwawr) *n.* 'royal lord' 5
tyyrnwr *n.* (teÿrnwr) 'royal warrior' 6; *pl.* **tyyrnwyr** 5
tyyrnvud (teÿrnfudd) *n.* 'royal riches' 2n

v- see **b-**
val *prep.* 'like' (*GPC* fal) 7, 24
w- see **gw-**
wrth *prep.* 'beside, except for' (see *GPC* wrth e) 21

y *definite article* 'the' 29
ygkylch *prep.* 'around' (*GPC* ynghylch) 10
yn¹ *prep.* (*GPC* yn¹, causing nasal mutation, see *GMW*, p. 21) 'in' 9(2), 29(2) **yg** (before **c-**) 10
yn² *predicative particle* (*GPC* yn³, *GMW*, p. 139, causing lenition except in *ll-* and *-rh*) 30
ys *preverbal particle* (*GPC* ys²) 25, 27, 28
ysbys *adj.* 'well-known' (*GPC* hysbys) 26
ysgarat *v.n.* 'to separate from, abandon' (*GPC* ysgaraf¹: ysgaru, ysgarad) 21
ysgarlat *n.* 'scarlet cloth, costly material' 17
ysgauyn *adj.* 'light, easy' (*GPC* ysgafn¹) 21
ysgein *v.n.* 'to scatter' (see *GPC* ysgeiniaf: ysgain²) 17n
ysgor *n.* 'stronghold' 23
ysgwn *adj.* 'ready' 20
ysgwyt *n.* 'shield' 18
Ystrat Tywy *place name* Ystrad Tywi 5

CHAPTER 4

The Book of Taliesin

NLW Peniarth MS 2, which was probably given its modern name, *Llyfr Taliesin*, 'The Book of Taliesin', by its seventeenth-century owner, Robert Vaughan of Hergest, has been described as 'a small, plain, incomplete manuscript'.[1] Written in a script dated to the first half of the fourteenth century, it is a copy made by a single scribe of an older manuscript (or manuscripts) containing poetry drawn from a variety of sources.[2] The fact that the same scribe was also responsible for copies of the Romance of Geraint, two law texts and a copy of a translation of *Historia Regum Britanniae*, suggests that he was a professional, working in the scriptorium of a religious establishment at a time when many volumes of vernacular literature were being produced to order in Wales. The southern associations of the law tracts he copied, the southern dialect features in the modernised orthography of the Book of Taliesin texts and the fact that the manuscript was in the possession of a Radnorshire family towards the end of the middle ages, all point to a monastery in south or mid-Wales, possibly the Cistercian house of Cwm Hir.

Very little can be gleaned from the manuscript about the original compiler of the anthology as the regularity of the spelling system tends to mask features which might date or locate him or his sources. Many of the surviving sixty-one poems, however, are concerned with north Wales. According to Marged Haycock, on whose seminal work this chapter is based, the arrangement of the poems in the manuscript is more orderly than that of the Black Book of Carmarthen, with some individual poems arranged in pairs and others in blocks according to subject matter.[3] It is also a more exclusive collection,

---

[1] *Prophecies from the Book of Taliesin* [*PBT*], ed. by Marged Haycock (Aberystwyth: CMCS Publications, 2013), p. 1. The name first appears in a list of medieval manuscripts compiled by Edward Lhuyd in his *Archaeologia Britannica* of 1707. To view the manuscript and for a summary of its later history, visit the National Library of Wales website: <www.llgc.org.uk>.

[2] What follows is based on a detailed study of the manuscript by Marged Haycock ('Llyfr Taliesin', *National Library of Wales Journal*, 25 (1988), 357–86), summarised in *Legendary Poems from the Book of Taliesin* [*LPBT*], ed. by Marged Haycock (Aberystwyth: CMCS Publications, 2007), pp. 1–5, and in Daniel Huws, 'Five Ancient Books of Wales' in *MWM*, pp. 77–79.

[3] See *LPBT*, pp. 5–6, and the Conspectus on pp. 558–59.

containing verse in *awdl* metres only and none of the acknowledged court poetry of the Poets of the Princes. It does, nevertheless, include a wide range of genres, including religious poetry, prophetic material, eulogies and elegies, and a broad class termed by Haycock 'legendary poems'.[4] It is this mixed group which holds the key to understanding the collection, as most of these poems are spoken by the fictional figure of Taliesin, an extraordinary warrior-poet with supernatural knowledge and abilities.

Haycock is probably right to propose that the compiler has created a 'layered anthology', where poems concerned with Taliesin, as he was envisaged in different periods, have been brought together. Apart from the political prophecy *Armes Prydein*, which can be placed on historical grounds in the tenth century,[5] very few of the poems can be dated with any precision. Whether the poetry in praise of Urien Rheged and other sixth-century kings are in fact contemporary with the 'historical' Taliesin of *Historia Brittonum* is uncertain and has been the subject of much debate by modern scholars.[6] Most of the other poems in the collection are assigned the broad date of between the tenth and the thirteenth centuries by Haycock. Her detailed study of the diction of the legendary poetry has revealed that, although there are some indications of a much older layer of composition, the language of some of the texts is very similar to that of the court poetry of the twelfth century and early thirteenth century. In fact, a high number of correspondences with words and phrases in the work of Llywarch Brydydd y Moch has led her to propose that it was the thirteenth-century poet of Gwynedd who composed or reworked many of them, in some cases perhaps adapting or incorporating earlier material.[7] If this is so, one can only speculate as to the role of these poems in the life of the courts of Llywelyn the Great and his supporters, whether they had a political motive or were intended purely as entertainment. Their allusive character suggests that their first audiences were familiar with the native bardic tradition but could also appreciate the more exotic learning displayed by the figure of Taliesin.[8]

It is not surprising, then, that the poems contained in the Book of Taliesin are populated by a dazzling array of historical and fictional figures. Among them are the sixth-century Brythonic chieftains Brochfael Powys, Urien Rheged, Ynyr Gwent and Maelgwn Gwynedd, national deliverers Cynan and Cadwaladr,

---

[4] See LPBT, pp. 9–11.
[5] For a summary of the latest arguments for the dating of *Armes Prydein*, see *PBT*, pp. 2–3.
[6] For a useful discussion of the issues surrounding the dating of these poems, see O. J. Padel, 'Aneirin and Taliesin: Sceptical Speculations' in *BG*, pp. 115–51.
[7] See LPBT, pp. 21–36. There are, for example, over forty words, phrases and collocations in the text of *Kat Godeu*, discussed below, which are also found in the work of Prydydd y Moch.
[8] Much of this learning is explored in Haycock, 'Taliesin's Questions', *Cambridge Medieval Celtic Studies*, 33 (1997), 19–79.

characters also found in the Four Branches of the *Mabinogi*, heroes of classical literature, biblical figures, and legendary Irish heroes. Arthurian references are scarce, however, possibly because, as Patrick Sims-Williams has suggested, he may have been, in the mind of the poets, too important to appear side-by-side with Taliesin, or perhaps because the Taliesin figure belonged to the traditions of Gwynedd and Arthur to those of south Wales and Cornwall.[9]

There are five poems containing references to Arthur scattered throughout the manuscript. As many of these are obscure, it is sometimes difficult to assess how central Arthur is to them.

Kat Godeu

The title of the first of these, added by the main scribe in red ink, has been taken from the poem itself, like most of the titles in the collection.[10] *Kat Godeu* can mean 'Battle of the Trees' or 'The Battle of Goddau', referring to the name of a region in the Old North mentioned twice in poems attributed to the historical Taliesin.[11] The fact that it is listed in the Triads as one of the Three Futile Battles of the Island of Britain, along with the Battle of Arfderydd and the Battle of Camlan, suggests that it came to be regarded as a historical battle.[12] In the poem, however, the battle is fought by trees which have been brought to life by the magician Gwydion at Nefenhyr's Fort to oppose an unnamed enemy. At its core is an extensive catalogue of trees and shrubs, accompanied by some of the stock phrases of early praise poetry, a parody perhaps of the catalogues of heroes found in poems like *Mi a wum* and the Stanzas of the Graves discussed above, and of the diction of heroic poetry.

This central list is surrounded by sections containing elements common in the other legendary poems spoken by Taliesin: an account of his creation and of the many transformations he underwent, and boasts of his accomplishments and his exploits as a poet and a warrior. Arthur is mentioned explicitly only once, towards the end of the long poem, where Taliesin calls on wise men to sing their prophecies about him or possibly to him.[13]

---

[9] Sims-Williams, 'Arthurian Poems', p. 51. Taliesin and Arthur are associated in the Court List in *Culhwch ac Olwen*, where Taliesin is named as *Teliessin Penn Beird*, 'Chief of Poets' (*CO*, l. 214), and in *TYP* no. 87 (in a seventeenth-century MS) where he is named as one of the 'Three Skilful Bards' at Arthur's court.

[10] NLW Peniarth MS 2, ff. 11^r–13^r (pp. 23–27); *LPBT* poem 5. See GPC goddau^2 and for a discussion of other possibilities, see Haycock, 'The Significance of the "Cad Goddau" Tree-list in the Book of Taliesin', in *Celtic Linguistics/Ieithyddiaeth Geltaidd*, ed. by Martin J. Ball et al. (Amsterdam and Philadelphia: J. Benjamins Publishing Company, 1990), pp. 297–332 (pp. 307–09).

[11] *PT* VI.4 and VII.44.

[12] See *TYP* no. 84.

[13] NLW Peniarth MS 2, f. 13^r (p. 27); *LPBT* no 5.238–49.

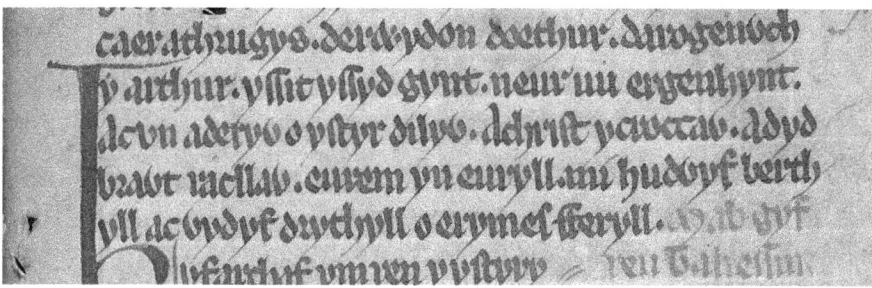

Fig. 4.1: NLW Peniarth MS 2, f. 13ʳ.

derwydon doethur. darogenŵch | y arthur. yssit yssyd gynt. neur uu ergenhynt. | ac vn aderyŵ o ystyr dilyŵ. achrist y croccaŵ. a dyd | braŵt racllaŵ.

Derwydon, doethur,
darogen(v)ch y Arthur!
Yssit yssyd gynt
4 neur uu ergenhynt:
ac vn a deryŵ
o ystyr Dilyŵ,
a Christ y croccaŵ,
8 a dyd Braŵt rac llaŵ.

Sages, wise men,
prophesy to Arthur! *or* prophesy [the return of] Arthur!
There is something which / someone who ?has been before *or* there is someone
                                                                      who is swifter still
4 [and] of that which has been they sang/perceived
and one came about
as a result of the story of the Flood,
and [the second was] Christ's Crucifixion
8 and [the third is] The Day of Judgment to come.

It is the ambiguity of the second line of this extract which makes Arthur's role in the poem uncertain. The most straightforward reading of it would be to understand the *y* as a preposition following the verb *darogan*, 'prophesy to Arthur'. This would suggest that Arthur was present, waiting to hear the wise men speak to him. He may, therefore, be the lord mentioned towards the beginning of the poem as the one before whom Taliesin sang on the advent of the battle:[14]

Keint yg (kat) godeu bric
rac Prydein Wledic.

I sang in the [battle of the] tree tops
before the ruler of Britain.

---

[14] *LPBT* 5.26–27. *Kat* is excised by Haycock to give a five-syllable line. The title of the poem may have been taken from these lines.

Prydein wledic is an epithet not used of Arthur or any other ruler in the surviving native literature of medieval Wales, despite the fact that both elements are very common. In *Culhwch ac Olwen*, however, Arthur is styled *Penn Teyrned yr Ynys honn*, 'the Chief of the Kings of this Island', and in the Life of Gruffudd ap Cynan he is *regum totius Britanniae rex* or *brenhin brenhined enys Brydein*, 'the king of the kings of the island of Britain'.[15]

The seven-syllable line is, however, unusually long.[16] It could be given syllabic regularity by understanding the *y* as representing -*chwi*, a non-syllabic affixed pronoun:

> Darogenwch-y Arthur!   Prophesy [the coming *or* return of] Arthur!

This reading would imply that Arthur, the subject of the wise men's prophecy, is absent from the poem.[17] The lines that follow can be tentatively interpreted to refer to Arthur's return. It is difficult to be sure of the meaning of *yssit yssyd gynt* since *gynt* can be read as either an adverb, 'formerly, in time past', or a comparative adjective, 'swifter'. Haycock suggests that if the former is understood, the poet could be alluding to an event which has been foretold or to a person, Arthur perhaps, who is returning to fulfil a prophecy. The latter reading may suggest a comparison between Arthur's return and that of Christ, whose birth may have been foretold by the legendary Taliesin along with the *Teir Aryfgryt*, 'the three Cataclysms', the Flood, the Crucifixion and Doomsday.

Word-list

a *preverbal particle* (causing lenition) 5
a *conj.* (causing spirant mutation) 'and' 7, 8 (before vowels) **ac** 5
Arthur *personal name* 2
Brawt *n.* 'judgment' (*GPC* brawd²) 8
bu 3 *sing.pret. of* **bot**, 'to be' 4
Crist *personal name* 'Christ' 7
croccaw *v.n.* 'to hang, to crucify; (*as a n.*) crucifixion (*GPC* crogaf: crogi, crogaw) 7
darogenwch 2 *pl. imper. of* **darogan**, 'prophesy' 2
derwydon *pl. of* **derwyd** *n.* 'sage, wise man, prophet' (*GPC* derwydd¹) 1
deryw 3 *sing.pres.indic.* of **daruot** *with perfect meaning* 'has come about' 5
Dilyw *n.* 'flood, deluge; the Great Flood' (< Latin *diluvium*, see *GPC* dilyw) 6

---

[15] See Andrews, 'Nomenclature', pp. 92, 97.
[16] For the simple short line, usually five syllables in length, which is the metre of this poem and many others in the Book of Taliesin, see *LPBT*, pp. 37–38.
[17] Arthur is not the subject of any of the prophetic poems of the Book of Taliesin, but see Constance Bullock-Davies, '"*Exspectare Arturum*": Arthur and the Messianic hope', *Bulletin of the Board of Celtic Studies*, 29 (1981), 432–40.

doethur *sing./pl. n.* (< Latin *doctorem* or *doctores*) 'learned man/men' 1
dyd *n.* 'day' 8
ergenhynt 3 *pl.imperf.indic. of* **arganuot**, 'to perceive', *or a vb. containing* **canu**, 'to sing' (see *LPBT* 5.245n) 4
gynt *adv.* 'formerly, in time past' *or comparative degree of adj.* **cynnar**, 'swifter' (*LPBT* 5.240n) 3
neur *preverbal particle* (*GMW*, p. 166) 4
o *prep.* 'because' 6
rac llaw *adv.* 'after this, later, to come' (*GMW*, p. 208) 8
vn *numeral* 'one' 5
y *definite article* 'the'
y *prep.* 'to' *or 2 pl. affixed pron.* **-chwi** (*LPBT* 5.239n) 2
yssit *impers.pres.indic. of* **bot** *as a copula* (*GMW*, p. 142) 'there is' 3
yssyd 3 *sing.pres. relative form of* **bot**, 'who/which is' 3
ystyr *n.* 'story' (< Latin *historia*, see *GPC* ystyr¹) 6

Kadeir Teyrnon

The next poem which contains an allusion to Arthur is found in a group with similar titles, *Kadeir Taliessin*, *Kadeir Teyrnon* and *Kadeir Kerrituen*.[18] These titles appear to have been taken from lines in the poems where, according to Haycock, *kadeir* has the meaning 'song, poem' rather than the usual 'chair, throne'.[19] In the case of this poem, the title may have come from a passage of prophetic discourse spoken by Taliesin:[20]

> *Kadeir Teyrnon,*
> *keluyd rwy katwo*

> The song of ?Teÿrnon — may it be the skilful poet who perpetuates it.

It is difficult to know how the title relates to the poem as a whole. Haycock suggests that *teyrnon* may be best understood here, as in many instances in the work of the Poets of the Princes, as the name of a hero.[21] Apart from one example in a poem of praise for Hywel ap Goronwy, however, the identity of Teÿrnon is uncertain in the court poetry.[22] Moreover, he does not appear to be the speaker or the subject of this poem. Its second half is clearly spoken by Taliesin, who

---

[18] *LPBT*, pp. 7–10.
[19] *LPBT*, pp. 263–64.
[20] *LPBT* 9.59–60. Note the lack of end rhyme, which suggests that the lines may be corrupt.
[21] There are also a few examples of *teyrnon* as a plural noun and also a possibility that it could have been used as a singular with the meaning 'monarch'; see *LPBT*, p. 299, and *GPC* teyrnon.
[22] See Andrews, *WCP*, 1. 46n, which is thought to be an allusion to Teÿrnon Twrf Liant, a character from the First Branch of the *Mabinogi*.

boasts of his prowess as a poet, asks challenging questions and utters words of prophecy. Although he is not named, his identity is confirmed by the final line, which alludes to the releasing of his patron, Elffin, from captivity.

The first half is presented as a praise poem for a descendant of Aladur, a mysterious figure who does not appear elsewhere in medieval Welsh literature but who may have originated as a native deity identified with Mars, the Roman god of war.[23] Haycock has suggested that the initial repetition in *a-* may point to Arthur, who is mentioned twice towards the end of the section. The end rhyme in *-ur* may also have indicated to the listener the identity of the subject of this part of the poem.[24]

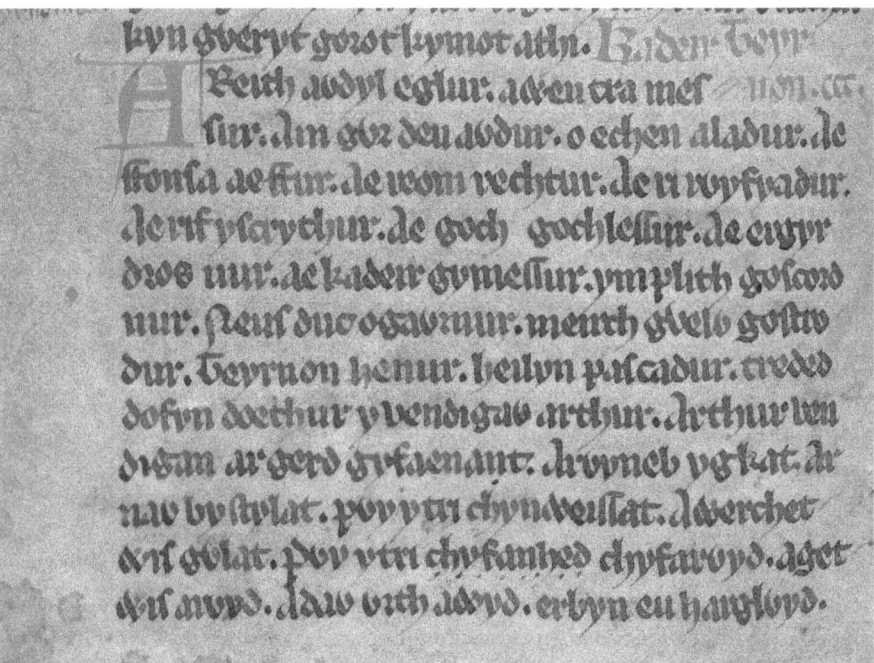

FIG. 4.2: NLW Peniarth MS 2, f. 16ᵛ.

Areith aɓdyl eglur. awen tra mes|sur. Am gǒr deu aɓdur. o echen aladur. Ae | ffonsa ae ffur. Ae reom rechtur. Ae ri rǒyfyadur. | Ae rif yscrythur. Ae goch gochlessur. Ae ergyr | dros uur. ae kadeir gymessur. ymplith goscord |nur. Neus duc ogaɓrnur. meirch gɓelɓ gostro|dur. teyrnon henur. heilyn pascadur. treded |

---

[23] On the evidence for Aladur and for references to further discussions, see *LPBT* 9.4n. On the significance of this reference if Arthur is, in fact, presented as a descendant of Aladur, see Thomas Green, 'A Note on *Aladur, Alator* and *Arthur*', *Studia Celtica*, 41 (2007), 237–41.
[24] NLW Peniarth MS 2, ff. 16ᵛ–17ʳ (pp. 34–35); *LPBT* 9.1–22.

dofyn doethur y vendigaw arthur. Arthur ven|digan ar gerd gyfaenawt. Arwyneb ygkat. Ar|naw bysytylat.

	Areith awdyl eglur,
	awen tra messur
	am gwr, *dewr awdur*
4	o echen Aladur.
	Ae *ffous* ae ffur,
	ae *Reon* rechtur?
	Ae ri rwyfyadur
8	a'e rif Yscrythur
	a'e goch gochlessur
	a'e ergyr dros uur,
	a'e kadeir gymessur
12	ymplith goscord nur?
	Neu's duc o Gawrnur
	meirch gwelw gostrodur.
	Teyrnon henur,
16	Heilyn pascadur
	treded dofyn doethur
	y vendigaw Arthur.
	Arthur *vendigat*
20	ar gerd gyfaenat —
	arwyneb yg kat,
	ar naw bystylat.

	[Here is] the declamation of a brilliant poem
	of immeasurable inspiration
	concerning a man, a brave authoritative one,
4	from the stock of Aladur.
	Is he a famous one, a wise one,
	or the ruler of Rheon?
	Or is he a royal ruler
8	With his reverence of Scripture
	And his red armour
	And his host [attacking] over the rampart,
	And his measured song
12	In the midst of a lordly warband?
	He bore off from Cawrnur,
	Pale harnessed horses.
	The venerable Teyrnon,
16	The fattener, Heilyn,
	[And] the third profound song of the sage
	[Was sung] in order to bless Arthur.
	Arthur has been blessed
20	In harmonious song —
	[As] a defence in battle,
	Trampling nine [at a time].

A number of unattested forms, some of which may be errors, make this text difficult to interpret.[25] It appears, however, that the qualities and achievements of the subject are firstly expressed by means of a series of rhetorical questions. He is called ruler of Rheon, which could be a place in the Old North or in Wales,[26] and pictures of him on the battlefield in blood-drenched armour alternate with those of him at his court performing or, more probably, receiving a song of praise with his warband around him. His feat of stealing Cawrnur's horses is not recorded elsewhere but Cawrnur's sons are named, possibly as opponents of Arthur's father, in the 'Elegy for Uthr Pendragon' which is discussed below. The form Cawrnur may be derived from a combination of *cawr*, 'giant', and the personal name *Nur*, which is thought to have developed into the common noun used in the previous line.[27] Sims-Williams has suggested that this may be an allusion to a lost tale, similar to the Wrnach Gawr episode in *Culhwch ac Olwen*, where Arthur and his men attack the giant Cawrnur and his sons, taking away their steeds as booty.[28] Arthur's name later appears as the third in a list of heroes, one of a number of triadic groupings in the poem. The form *heilyn*, like *teyrnon*, can be understood as a common noun, 'dispenser, provider', but is also found as a personal name in the poetic tradition.[29] Here, as in *Kat Godeu* above, Arthur is associated with a *doethur*, 'a wise man', who sings, not a prophecy this time, but a song of blessing. As the end rhyme changes, Arthur's name is repeated and confirmation is given that it is indeed the great champion who has been praised.

Word-list

a¹ *prep.* (causing spirant mutation) 'with' (*with infixed poss.pron. 3 sing.* 'e) 8
a² *conj.* (causing spirant mutation) 'and' (*with infixed poss.pron. 3 sing.* h'e) 9, 10, 11
ae *interrogative particle* 'is he?' (see *LPBT* 9.5n) 5(2), 6, 7
Aladur *personal name* (see *LPBT* 9.4n) 4
am *prep.* 'concerning' 3
ar *prep.* 'upon' 22; 'by means of' (*GPC* ar¹6) 20
areith *n.* 'speech, declamation' (*GPC* araith) 1

---

[25] Emendations are indicated with italic script in the edited text.
[26] For Pen or Penrhyn Rhionydd in the Old North, named as Arthur's seat of power in the Triads, see *TYP* nos 1 and 85, and p. 4. For this and other Reon place names in the Old North and in Wales, see *LPBT* 9.6n and *PBT*, 1. 49n.
[27] Lit. 'the warband of a lord'.
[28] See 'Arthurian Poems', p. 53.
[29] Heilyn is the subject of an elegy in the *Gododdin* collection and is the name of two twelfth-century noblemen praised by Cynddelw. Other examples of the form *heilyn* in the work of Cynddelw and Llywarch Brydydd y Moch may be interpreted as the name of a hero from the past: see *LPBT*, p. 9.16n, but cf. *GPC* heilyn, where some of these are understood as common nouns.

Arthur *personal name* 18, 19
ar{v}yneb *n.* 'defence' (*LPBT* 9.21n) 21
a{v}dur *n.* 'person in authority, authoritative one' (< Latin *auctor*, *GPC* awdur) 3
awdyl *n.* 'poem' (*GPC* awdl) 1
awen *n.* 'inspiration' 2

bendiga{v} *v.n.* 'to bless' (< Latin *benedīcō*, *GPC* bendigaf: bendigo) 18 ?*impers. pret.* **bendigat** (see *LPBT* 5.19n) 19
bystylat *v.n.* 'to stamp, trample' (*GPC* pystylad) 22
kadeir *n.* 'song' (*GPC* cadair) 11
kat *n.* 'battle' 21

Ca{v}rnur *personal name* (*LPBT* 5.13n) 13
kerd *n.* 'song' (*GPC* cerdd¹) 2
coch *adj.* 'red, bloody' 9
kyfaenat *adj.* 'harmonious' (*GPC* cyfaenad) 20
kymessur *adj.* 'measured' (*GPC* cymesur) 11

dewr *adj.* 'brave' (see *LPBT* 9.3n) 3
doethur *n.* 'wise man, poet' 17
dofyn *fem. form of adj.* **dwfyn**, 'deep, profound', *used nominally for a song or utterance* 17
dros *prep.* 'over' 10
duc *3 sing.pret. of* **dwyn**, 'to take away' 13

echen *n.* 'stock, lineage' 4
eglur *n.* 'manifest, clear, brilliant' 1
ergyr *n.* 'attack, vanguard, host' 10

ffous *adj.* 'famous' (< Latin *fāmōsus*, *GPC* fföus) 5
ffur *adj.* 'wise' *as n.* 'wise man' 5

gochlessur *n.* '?armour' (*GPC* gochlysur) 9
goscord *n.* 'warband' (*GPC* gosgordd) 12
gostrodur *adj.* 'under saddle, harnessed' (*LPBT* 9.14n) 14
g{v}el{v} *adj.* 'pale' (*GPC* gwelw) 14
gwr *n.* 'man' 3

Heilyn *personal name* (*LPBT* 9.16n) 16
henur *n.* '?venerable man' (*LPBT* 9.15n) 15

meirch *pl. of* **march** *n.* 'horse' 14

messur *n.* 'measure' (*GPC* mesur¹) 2
mur *n.* 'wall, rampart' 10

nav *numeral/n.* 'nine; nine warriors' 22
neu's *a combination of the preverbal particle* **neu** + *infixed obj. pron 3 pl.* 's 13
nur *n.* 'lord' 12

o *prep.* 'of, from' 4, 13

pascadur *n.* 'one who fattens, feeder' (*GPC* pasgadur) 16

rechtur *n.* '?ruler, chieftain' (< Latin *rector*, *GPC* rhechdyr, rhechdur) 6
Reon place name Rheon (see *LPBT* 5.6n) 6
ri *n.* 'king' (*GPC* rhi¹) 7
rif *n.* 'esteem, reverence' (*GPC* rhif¹ d) 8
rwyfyadur *n.* 'lord, ruler' (*GPC* rhwyfiadur) 7

Teyrnon *personal name* 15
tra *prep.* 'beyond' (*GMW*, p. 210) 2
treded *?fem. form of numeral* **trydyd**, 'third' (*LPBT* 9.17n) 17

y *prep.* 'to, in order to' 18
yg *form of prep.* **yn**, 'in' *before* **k-** 21
ymplith *prep.* 'among, in the midst of' (*GPC* ymhlith) 12
Yscrythur *n.* 'Scripture' (< Latin *scriptura*, *GPC* ysgrythur) 8

Song of the Steeds

Untitled, incomplete and in places unintelligible, this poem was first called 'Canu y Meirch' (Song of the Steeds) by the editor of the 'historical' Taliesin poems, Ifor Williams.[30] The second part of the text, like that of *Kadeir Teyrnon*, is spoken by Taliesin, starting with an account of his transformations. The first part also contains elements found in other poems featuring the legendary Taliesin, but at its core is a versified catalogue of famous horses and their owners. Marged Haycock suggests that, like that of *Kat Godeu*, this list may have had a dramatic setting. It may have corresponded to one of the episodes involving horses in *Ystoria Taliesin* ('the Story of Taliesin', preserved in a sixteenth-century chronicle), but the corrupt nature of the text makes this difficult to ascertain.[31]

Arthur is named along with twelve other great heroes, twelve famous horses and a pair of oxen, for whom the poet calls for heavenly protection in battle.[32]

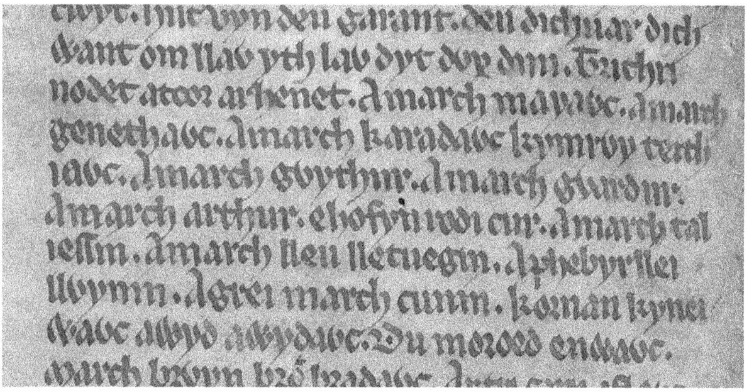

FIG. 4.3: NLW Peniarth MS 2, f. 23ᵛ.

Trithri | nodet actor ar henet. A march mayaẟc. A march | genethaẟc. A march karadaẟc kymrẟy teith|iaẟc. A march gẟythur. A march gẟardur. | A march arthur. ehofyn rodi cur. A march tal|iessin. A march lleu lletuegin.

        Trithri nodet
        atcor ar henet,
        a march Mayaẟc,
4   a march Genethaẟc,
        a march Karadaẟc —
        kymrẟy teithiaẟc —

---

[30] See *PT*, pp. xxiii–iv.
[31] See *LPBT*, p. 389. For a translation of 'Ystoria Taliesin' see Patrick K. Ford, *The Celtic Poets: Songs and Tales from Early Ireland and Wales* (Belmont, Massachusetts: Ford and Bailie, 1999).
[32] Only the first part of the list is presented here, based on Haycock's edition: see NLW Peniarth MS 2, 23ᵛ (p. 48); *LPBT* 15.25–36.

	a march G(v)ythur,
8	a march G(v)a[v]rdur,
	a march Arthur —
	ehofyn rodi cur —
	a march Taliessin,
12	a march Lleu, lletuegin …

	[May there be] the protection of the nine [Heavenly grades]
	for the ploughing-team beasts of yore,
	and [for] Maeog's horse,
4	and Genethog's horse,
	and Caradog's horse —
	a powerful one with the proper attributes-
	and Gwythur's horse
8	and Gwawrddur's horse
	and Arthur's horse —
	fearless in inflicting injury —
	and Taliesin's horse,
12	and Lleu's nurtured horse …

Rachel Bromwich argues for a close relationship between this part of the poem and *Trioedd y Meirch* (The Triads of the Horses), a set of triads listing the horses of traditional heroes, attributing the differences between them to the antiquity of the texts and a long process of written and oral transmission.[33] Neither Arthur or Llamrei, identified as his mare in *Culhwch ac Olwen* and listed later in this poem, appear in the triads, however, and as Haycock has shown, although there is some similarity between them, it is not likely that these triads were the poet's source.[34] The descriptions of the horses are reminiscent of those found in the court poetry of the twelfth and thirteenth centuries and the language of the poem also appears to belong to this period.[35]

Many of the owners named in the poem are obscure figures, but those known from other sources, such as Lleu, Rhydderch and Caradog Freichfras, are drawn from the native tradition. Gwythur and Gwawrddur may have been selected by the poet to appear along with Arthur on the basis of rhyme, but it is interesting to note that both are associated with him in other texts, Gwawrddur being the subject of the *awdl* in which Arthur is named in the *Gododdin*, and Gwythur found in the stanza on the grave of Arthur and in the 'Elegy of Uthr Pendragon'.[36] It is difficult to know the significance of their coupling, however,

---

[33] See *TYP*, pp. lxxx–lxxxvii, and Rachel Bromwich, 'The Triads of the Horses' in *HCC*, pp. 102–20.

[34] Haycock, *LPBT*, pp. 387–88. For Llamrei, see *LPBT* 15.51 and *CO*, l. 1016n, and Sioned Davies, 'Horses in the *Mabinogion*' in *HCC*, p. 129.

[35] See Nerys Ann Jones, 'Horses in Medieval Welsh Court Poetry' in *HCC*, pp. 82–101.

[36] On Gwawrddur, see Chapter 2 above. On Gwythur and the possibility that he is Gwythyr ap Greidawl, who appears in *Culhwch ac Olwen*, see Stanzas of the Graves, Chapter 1 above.

as so little is revealed about any of them. Arthur may be depicted as a great warrior, but it is possible that the epithet *ehofyn rodi cur*, 'fearless in inflicting injury', refers to his warhorse.[37]

Word-list

a *conj.* (causing spirant mutation) 'and' 3, 4, 5, 7, 8, 9, 10, 11, 12
ar *n.* 'arable land' (*GPC* âr) 2
Arthur *personal name* 9
atcor *n.* '?ploughing team' (*LPBT* 15.26n) 2
Karada6c *personal name* Caradog Freichfras (*TYP*, pp. 304–05) 5
cur *n.* 'injury' 10
kymr6y *adj.* 'lively, powerful' 6
ehofyn *adj.* 'fearless' (*GPC* eofn) 10
Genetha6c *personal name* Genethog (*LPBT* 15.28n)
G6a[6]rdur *personal name* Gwawrddur 8
G6ythur *personal name* Gwythur 7
henet *n.* '?antiquity, olden days' (*GPC* hened) 2
lletuegin *adj.* 'half-reared; hand-reared; well-fed' (*GPC* lledfegin) 12
Lleu *personal name* 12
march *n.* 'horse' 3, 4, 5, 7, 8, 9, 11, 12
Maya6c *personal name* Maeog (*LPBT* 15.27n) 3
nodet *n.* 'protection' (*GPC* nodded) 1
rodi *v.n.* 'to give, inflict' (*GPC* rhoddaf: rhoddi) 10
Taliessin *personal name* Taliesin 11
teithia6c *adj.* 'with proper attributes, thoroughbred' 6
trithri *numeral* 'three times three, i.e. nine' *?referring to the nine heavenly grades* (*LPBT* 15.25n) 1

'The Elegy for Uthr Pendragon'

In taking the abbreviated manuscript title of this poem, *Mar6nat Vthyr Pen.*, together with the incomplete guide title found in the margin, *Mar Vthyr ... dragon*, we can be fairly sure that it was thought at one time to be an elegy for Uthr Pendragon, the father of Arthur.[38] A close reading of the text, however, shows that it is neither a *marwnad* nor concerned with Uthr's death, but that it contains the boasting of a warrior-poet in a voice reminiscent of that of Taliesin.[39] Marged Haycock suggests that Taliesin may be the speaker of the

---

[37] For other allusions in the poetry to the ferocity of horses in battle, see Jenny Rowland, 'Warfare and Horses in the *Gododdin* and the Problem of Catraeth', *Cambridge Medieval Celtic Studies*, 30 (1995), 13–40 (p. 18).
[38] For the references to Uthr in medieval Welsh literature, see Chapter 1, *Pa gur*, 14n.
[39] The title, like many others in the Book of Taliesin, may derive from a phrase in the

whole poem but also puts forward the possibility that it is a composite piece.[40] Although most of it is composed using the same metre,[41] initial repetition of *neu vi*, 'it is I', gives the first twenty-four lines of the poem a discrete structure. In addition, the first line of the following section, which focusses on the speaker's qualities as a skilled poet, is similar to the openings of other poems spoken by Taliesin.[42] The meaning of some of its lines is far from clear but it can be argued that the opening section may be a monologue where an unnamed speaker looks back over his life and boasts of his extraordinary military accomplishments, which allow him, perhaps, to claim that he was nine times braver than Arthur.[43]

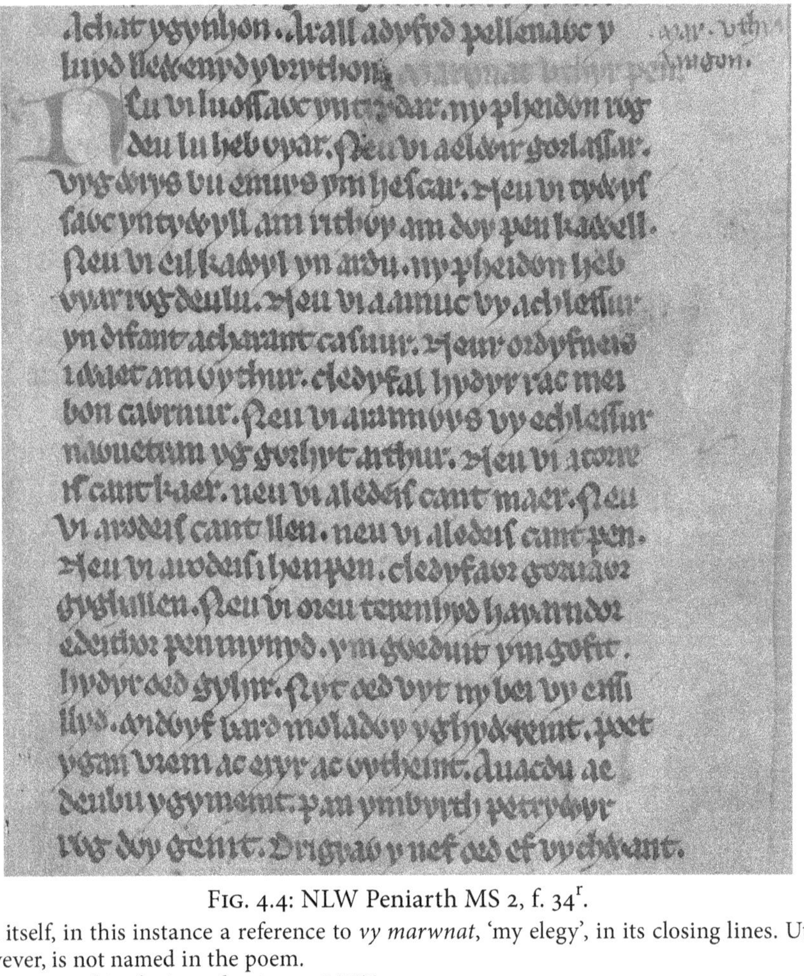

FIG. 4.4: NLW Peniarth MS 2, f. 34ʳ.

text itself, in this instance a reference to *vy marwnat*, 'my elegy', in its closing lines. Uthr, however, is not named in the poem.

[40] Discussed in the introduction to *LPBT* poem 24.
[41] The poem is mostly made up of eight- or nine-syllable tripartite lines. On this class of lines, see *LPBT*, p. 39. The second half of the poem is less regular than the first, containing some shorter, two-stress lines.
[42] See *LPBT* 24.25n for examples.
[43] NLW Peniarth MS 2, f. 34ʳ (p. 71); *LPBT* 24.1–24.

Neu vi luossaɤc yn trydar. ny pheidɤn rɤg | deu lu heb ɤyar. Neu vi aelwir gorlassar. | vyg wrys vu enuys ym hescar. Neu vi tywys|saɤc yn tywyll am rithwy am dɤy pen kawell. | Neu vi eil kawyl yn ardu. ny pheidɤn heb | vyar rɤg deulu. Neu vi a amuc vy achlessur. | yn difant acharant casnur. Neur ordyfneis | i waet am ɤythur. cledyfal hydyr rac mei|bon caɤrnur. Neu vi arannɤys vy echlessur | naɤuetran yg gɤrthyt arthur. Neu vi atorre|is cant kaer. neu vi aleddeis cant maer. Neu | vi arodeis cant llen. neu vi aledeis cant pen. | Neu vi arodeis i henpen. cledyfaɤr goruaɤr | gygallen. Neu vi oreu terenhyd hayarndor | edeithor pen mynyd. ym gɤeduit ym gofit. | hydyr oed gyhir. Nyt oed vyt ny bei vy eissi|llyd.

    Neu vi luossaɤc yn trydar:
    ny pheidɤn rɤg deulu heb ɤyar.
    Neu vi a elwir 'Gorlassar':
4   vy gwrys bu enuys y'm hescar.
    Neu vi tywyssaɤc yn tywyll:
    A'm rithwy am dɤy pen kawell.
    Neu vi eil *Sawyl* yn ardu:
8   Ny pheidwn heb wyar rwg deulu.
    Neu vi a amuc vy achlessur
    yn difant a charant Casnur.
    Neur ordyfneis-i waet am Uythur,
12 Cledyual hydyr rac meibon Caɤrnur.
    Neu vi a rannɤys vy echlessur:
    naɤuetran yg gɤrhyt Arthur.
    Neu vi a torreis cant kaer,
16 neu vi a ledeis cant maer,
    neu vi a rodeis cant llen,
    neu vi a ledeis cant pen,
    neu vi a rodeis *y* Henpen,
20 Cledyfaɤr goruaɤr gyghallen.
    Neu vi *a* oreu *cerenhyd,*
    hayarndor edeithor pen mynyd.
    Y'm gɤeduit, y'm gofit, hydyr *gyhyr,*
24 nyt oed vyt na bei vy eissillyd.

    It is I who has/had numerous hosts in battle:
    I would not give up [the fight] between two forces without bloodshed.
    It is I who is called 'Armed in Blue':
4   my ferocity snared my enemy.
    It is I [who is/was] a leader in darkness:
    may … transform me.
    It's I [who is/was] a second ?Sawyl in the gloom:
8   I would not give up without bloodshed [the fight] between two forces.
    It was I who defended my hiding-place
    in [the fight to] the death against ?Casnur's kin.
    I was used to blood[shed] around Gwythur,
12 with vigorous swordstroke against Cawrnur's sons.

	It was I who shared my stronghold:
	a [mere] ninth of my ?valour [has/had] Arthur.
	It was I who stormed a hundred citadels,
16	it was I who slew a hundred stewards,
	it was I who shared out a hundred mantles,
	it was I who cut off a hundred heads,
	it was I who gave Henben
20	swords of great protective power.
	It was I who forged friendship,
	an iron door, a fire break on the mountain top.
	In my bereft state, in my distress, [I was] strong of sinew,
24	there would not be life were it not for my progeny.

In the opening lines, the speaker presents himself as a great warleader known as *Gorlassar*[44] and likens himself, perhaps, to Sawyl Ben Uchel,[45] emphasising his tenacity and ferocity in battle. He reveals himself as the enemy of the descendants of an otherwise unknown figure, Casnur, and as a supporter of Gwythur in his opposition to the sons of Cawrnur, two characters who may have featured in lost stories about Arthur.[46] Arthur himself is named at the head of a series of statements enumerating the speaker's heroic activities, in a line whose meaning depends on the interpretation of the form *gwrhyt*.[47] Haycock's reading, taking *yg gwrhyt* to mean 'my manliness, valour', gives a line where the speaker boasts that he is nine times more courageous than Arthur.[48] This would not be surprising coming from the lips of Taliesin, who boasts of his martial qualities in poems like *Kat Godeu* and *Angar Kyfyndawt* and is associated with a military quest led by Arthur in *Preideu Annwn*. Taliesin is also associated with *Henben*, depicted here perhaps as an ally of the speaker. This figure may be Henin Henben, who has been tentatively identified with *Henin Vardd*, the chief poet at the court of Maelgwn Gwynedd who was defeated by Taliesin in a bardic debate, according to *Ystorya Taliesin*.[49]

It is interesting to note, however, that almost all the verbs in this section are

---

[44] For more on Haycock's suggestion that this form may contains *llasar*, 'azure', rather than *glasar* as noted in *GPC* gorlasar, see Jenny Day, 'Shields in Welsh Poetry up to c.1300: Decoration, Shape and Significance', *Studia Celtica*, 45 (2011), 38–40.
[45] On the name *Sawyl*, emended from MS *kawyl*, and references to traditional figures of that name, see *LPBT* 24.7n.
[46] On Gwythur and the possibility that he may be Gwythyr ap Greidyawl of *Culhwch ac Olwen*, see the Stanzas of the Graves above, p. 11–12, and on Cawrnur, see *Kadeir Teyrnon*.
[47] See *GPC* gwryd¹, where the main element is *hyd*, 'length', and gwryd², which derives from *gŵr*, 'man, warrior'. For the phrase *gwrhyt Arthur*, see also *Preideu Annwn*, l. 30.
[48] Lit. 'A ninth part of my manliness [is that of] Arthur'. See in Chapter 3 above the eulogies of Llywarch Brydydd y Moch for Rhodri ab Owain (*CBT* v 5.11–12) and for Gruffudd ap Cynan (*CBT* v 11.53–56), where the poet's patrons are praised for their superiority over Arthur. For other interpretations of the line which are possible but not as meaningful, see *LPBT* 24.14n.
[49] See *LPBT* 24.19n and *TYP*, p. 397.

in the past tense, like those in *Pa Gur* from the Black Book of Carmarthen.[50] If the reference to Uthr in the title has any substance in tradition, this may be the boasting of an old warrior who claims that he was in his day braver than his son.[51] In light of this, the difficult final couplet with its reference to his present state of distress and to his dependence on his *eisyllydd*, his offspring or descendants, could be significant.

Word-list

a *relative pron.* 'who' 3, 9, 15, 16, 17, 18, 19, 21
a *preverbal particle (with infixed obj.pron. 1 sing.)* **a'm** 6
a *prep. (causing spirant mutation)* 'with' 10
achlessur, echlessur *n.* 'hiding place' (*GPC* echlysur, see *LPBT* 24.13n) 9, 13
am *prep. (causing lenition)* 'around' 6 (see *LPBT* 24.6n), 11
amuc *3 sing. pret. of* **amwyn**, 'to defend' (*GPC* amygaf: amwyn¹) 9
ardu *n.* 'darkness, gloom' (*GPC* arddu) 7
Arthur *personal name* 14
bei *3 sing.imperf.subj. of* **bot**, 'to be' 24
bu *3 sing.pret. of* **bot**, 'to be' 4
byt *n.* 'world; life' (*GPC* byd¹) 24
kaer *n.* 'fort, stronghold, citadel' (*GPC* caer) 15
cant *numeral* 'a hundred' 15, 16, 17, 18
carant *pl. of* **car** *n.* 'relative, kinsman' (*GPC* câr) 10
Casnur *?personal name* (see *LPBT* 24.10n) 10
kawell 6 (see *LPBT* 24.6n)
Cawrnur *personal name* (see *LPBT* 9.13–14n) 12
cerenhyd *n.* 'friendship' (*GPC* carennydd) 21
cledyfawr *pl. of* **cledyf**, 'sword' (*GPC* cleddyf) 20
cledyual *n.* 'sword-stroke' (*GPC* cleddyfal) 12
kyghallen *n.* 'protective power' (*GPC* cynghallen, see *LPBT* 24.20n) 20
kyhyr *n.* 'muscle, sinew' (*GPC* cyhyr) 23
deulu *n.* 'two forces, opposing armies' 2, 8
difant *n.* 'total loss, fight to the death' 10
dwy 6 (see *LPBT* 24.6n)
echlessur see **achlessur**

---

[50] Out of the twenty-four translatable lines above, only one contains a verb in the present tense; thirteen have verbs in the past tense and the rest have no verb. Some of these, like the first and fifth lines, are interpreted by Haycock as using verbs in the present tense, but they could equally be referring to events in the past.

[51] This brings to mind the figure of the elderly father who compares his sons with himself at a similar age in some of the poems of the Llywarch Hen cycle, in particular 'Gwên and Llywarch' and 'Maen'; see *EWSP*, 17–19.

edeithor *n.* '?fire break' (see *LPBT* 24.22n for other possibilities) 22
eil *numeral / adj.* 'second, like, equal' (*GPC* ail¹c) 7
eissillyd *n.* 'offspring, progeny' (*GPC* eisillydd) 24
enuys *adj.* 'a ring, ?a snare' (*GPC* enfys, but see *LPBT* 24.4n for other possibilities) 4
escar *n.* 'enemy' (*GPC* esgar¹) 4
gelwir *impers.pres.indic. of* **galw**, 'to call, name' 3
gofit *n.* 'anxiety, distress' 23
gordyfneis *1 sing.pret. of* **gordyfneid**, 'to be used to' (*GPC* gorddyfnaf: gorddyfnaid) 11
goreu *3 sing.perf. of* **gwneuthur**, 'to make' (*GMW*, p. 147) 21
Gorlassar *?personal name/cognomen* Gorlasar *or* Gorllasar, one armed with blue-grey weapons or clad in blue-grey armour (see *LPBT* 24.3n) 3
goruawr *adj.* 'very great' (*GPC* gorfawr) 20
gwaet *n.* 'blood' (*GPC*, p. 11)
gweduit *n.* 'widowhood, a bereft state' (see *LPBT* 24.23n for other possibilities) 23
gwrhyt *n.* 'valour; measure' (*GPC* gwryd$^{1-2}$, see *LPBT* 24.14n) 14
gwrys *n.* 'ardour, ferocity' 4
gwyar *n.* 'blood' 2, 8
Gwythur *personal name* (see *LPBT* 15.31n) 11
hayarndor *n.* 'an iron door, defence' (*GPC* haearnddor) 22
heb *prep.* 'without' 2, 8
Henpen *personal name* Henben (*LPBT* 14.19n) 19
hydyr *adj.* 'brave, mighty, strong vigorous' (*GPC* hydr) 12, 23
-i *affixed pron 1 sing.* 11
lledeis *1 sing.pret. of* **llad**, 'to slay' (*GPC* lladdaf: lladd) 16, 18
llen *n.* 'mantle' 17
lluossawc *adj.* 'numerous, having a large following, having numerous hosts' (*GPC* lluosog) 1
maer *n.* 'steward' 16
meibon *pl. of* **mab** *n.* 'son' 12
mynyd *n.* 'mountain' 22
na *conj.* 'unless' (*GPC* na¹e) 24
nawuetran *n.* 'a ninth part' (< *nawfed + rhan*, see *LPBT* 24.14n) 14
neu *preverbal particle used as copula* 'it is' (see *LPBT* 24.1n) 1, 3, 5, 7, 9, 13, 15, 16, 17, 18, 19, 21 **neur** (*with preverbal particle ry*) 11
ny *neg.* 2, 8 **nyt** 24
oed *3 sing.imperf.indic. of* **bot**, 'to be' 24
peidwn *1 sing.imperf. indic. of* **peidiaw**, 'to stop, give up' 2, 8
pen *n.* 'head' 6 (see *LPBT* 24.6n), 18, summit, top 22

rac *prep.* 'against' (*GPC* rhag) 12
rannwys *3 sing.pret. of* **rannu**, 'to share' (*GPC* rhannaf¹: rhannu)13
rithwy *3 sing.pres.subj. of* **rithaw**, 'to transform' (*GPC* rhithiaf: rhithio; on *-wy* see *LPBT* 21–22) 6
rodeis *1 sing.pret. of* **rodi**, 'to give, share' (*GPC* rhoddaf: rhoddi) 17, 19
rwg *prep.* 'between' (*GPC* rhwng) 2, 8
Sawyl *?personal name* ?Sawyl (see *LPBT* 24.7n) 7
torreis *1 sing.pret. of* **torri**, 'to attack, storm' 15
trydar *n.* 'battle' 1
tywyll *n.* 'darkness, gloom' 5
tywyssawc *n.* 'leader' (*GPC* tywysog) 5
vi *independent personal pron.* 'I' 1, 3, 5, 7, 9, 13, 15, 16, 17, 18, 19, 21
vy *poss.pron. 1 sing.* (causing nasal mutation) 'my' 4, 9, 13, 24
y *prep.* (causing lenition) 'to' (*GPC* i²) 19 with **'m** *infixed poss.pron. 1 sing.* 4,
yn *prep.* (causing nasal mutation) 'in' 1, 5, 7, 10 **yg** (before *g-*) 14 with **'m** *infixed poss.pron. 1 sing.* 23(2)

Preideu Annwn

Our final text has often been presented as an Arthurian poem and a source of lost tales of Arthur's otherworldly adventures. Its evocative title, 'The Spoils of the Otherworld', is, however, an addition taken from the text itself by John Lewis of Llynwene in Radnorshire, who owned the manuscript in the late sixteenth and early seventeenth centuries.[52] Arthur's name appears five times in a repeated refrain as the leader of a disastrous expedition from whom only seven of his companions returned, but as its modern editor Marged Haycock has noted, the 'unifying personality' of the poem is the speaker, Taliesin, although he is not named.[53]

Preideu Annwn is one of eighteen poems in the Book of Taliesin collection where Taliesin boasts of his past exploits, his association with famous figures and his great learning, where he expresses his disdain for monks, clerics and other poets, and asks questions which imply that he has an unrivalled knowledge of the mysteries of Creation.[54] As Sims-Williams has proposed, it was probably intended as courtly entertainment, the poet using the persona of Taliesin to 'strike a playful blow for the secular poets or *cyfarwyddiaid* against

---

[52] For the title see l. 7 below. On John Lewis, who died *c.* 1616, see *LPBT*, p. 3.
[53] For the poem, see NLW Peniarth MS 2, ff. 25ᵛ–26ᵛ (pp. 54–56). It has been edited and translated by Haycock, '"Preiddeu Annwn" and the Figure of Taliesin', *Studia Celtica*, 18/19 (1983–1984), 52–78, and in *LPBT* no. 18.
[54] It is interesting to compare it with *LPBT* no. 8, *Golychaf-i Gulwyd ...*, which contains many of the same elements. See also Haycock, 'Taliesin's Questions'.

the vain pretensions of the Welsh clerical orders'.[55]

The main elements which make this poem unusual are the allusions in its first and second and perhaps its fourth sections to story episodes, characters and places concerning a raid on the Otherworld, which was led by Arthur in his ship Prydwen and which Taliesin survived and to which he attributes his superiority over his rivals, and the description of an Otherworld fort, referred to by a series of partly intelligible and partly cryptic names.[56] Some of these may be motifs from stories well known to the poet's intended audience. For example, a reference to the imprisonment of Gwair in the first section may have brought to mind a tale similar to that of the freeing of Mabon, who had been a prisoner since the beginning of time in *Culhwch ac Olwen*. It is presented, however, as an episode in *ebostol Pwyll a Phryderi*, 'The Tale of Pwyll and Pryderi', a rare example, perhaps, of Arthurian traditions mixed with those of the Four Branches of the *Mabinogi*.[57] In the second section, Taliesin's boasting takes him back to the Otherworld fortress, where song is heard, reminding him perhaps of the origin of his poetic gift, a magical cauldron lit by the breath of nine maidens which will not boil food for a coward. The audience might well have associated this with the famous cauldron of the giant Dyrnwch, listed as one of the Thirteen Treasures of the Island of Britain.[58] Lleog's sword in the following line recalls that of Llenlleog the Irishman in *Culhwch ac Olwen*, who slew Diwrnach the Irishman in order to take his cauldron on an expedition with Arthur to Ireland.[59] Since in *Culhwch* it is Arthur's sword, Caledfwlch, which is used to kill the owner of the cauldron, it is not impossible that Lleminog in the following line is to be identified with him.

It is not easy to date the poem as its language may be deliberately archaic or even pseudo-archaic.[60] Its tone is contradictory: its Latinate vocabulary and longer ornamented lines give it gravitas,[61] whilst Taliesin's light-hearted taunting of the *llawyr*, 'insignificant men', jars with the repeated expression of loss and grief in the poignant refrain which links six out of the eight *awdlau*.[62]

---

[55] Sims-Williams, 'Arthurian Poems', p. 54. For indications that Llywarch Brydydd y Moch might be the author of the poem, see *LPBT*, p. 31.

[56] Some of these descriptions may reflect learning which originated in written sources; see especially lines 25 and 30–32, discussed in the notes below.

[57] For discussion of the story of Brân's expedition to Ireland in the Second Branch as an analogue to Arthur's expedition, see Sims-Williams, 'Arthurian Poems', p. 55.

[58] See *TYP*, pp. 336–37.

[59] See *CO*, ll. 1036–56; *IIMWL*, pp. 160–62.

[60] On individual forms see the notes below.

[61] On the relatively high proportion of words derived from Latin, see *LPBT*, p. 434. On the very common metre, mostly consisting of nine- or ten-syllable lines divided into two sections with two beats in each section, see Haycock, 'Preiddeu Annwn', pp. 52–53.

[62] The incremental refrain is quite unusual in medieval Welsh poems but is also found in the Elegy of Cynddylan (Chapter 5) and in *Echrys Ynys* from the Book of Taliesin (see R. Geraint Gruffydd, 'A Welsh "Dark Age" Court Poem' in *Ildánach Ildírech: A Festschrift*

What is certain is that the primary focus of the poem as a whole is not on Arthur; he is, rather, one of many figures from the historical and legendary past with whom Taliesin is associated in this collection in order to give him status and authority.[63] The brief allusions, which can be partly elucidated by parallels in other texts, give us tantalising glimpses of legendary material concerning Arthur which was known to the poet and his audience but which in great part is lost to us.

The poem is presented here a section at a time, accompanied with detailed discussions of matters of dating and interpretation and a comprehensive word-list.[64]

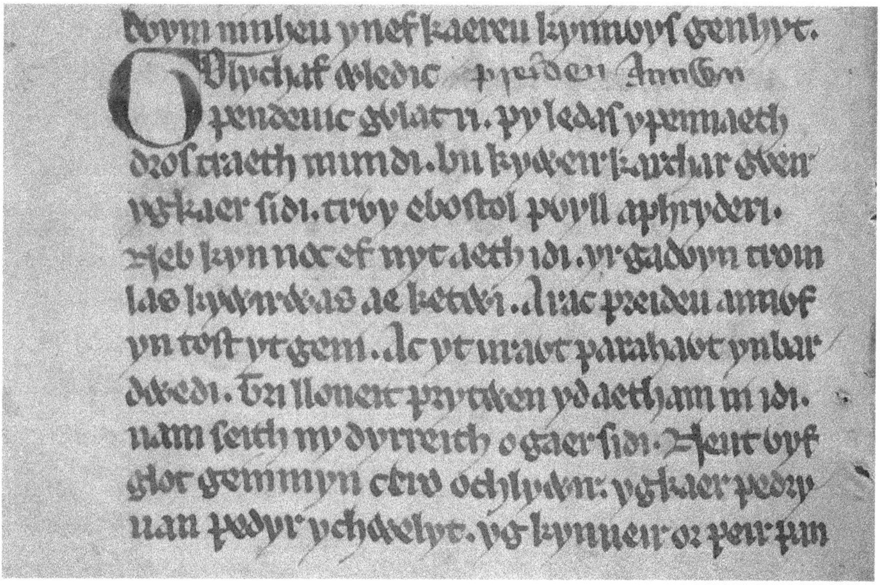

FIG. 4.5: NLW Peniarth MS 2, f. 25ᵛ.

Golychaf wledic | pendeuic gŏlat ri. py ledas y pennaeth | dros traeth mundi. bu kyweir karchar gŏeir | yg kaer sidi. trŏy ebostol pŏyll aphryderi. | Neb kyn noc ef nyt aeth idi. yr gadŏyn trom | las kywirwas ae ketwi. A rac preideu annŏf|yn tost yt geni. Ac yt uraŏt parahaŏt ynbar|dwedi. Tri lloneit prytwen yd aetham ni idi. | nam seith ny dyrreith o gaersidi.

---

for Proinsias Mac Cana, ed. by John Carey et al. (Andover and Aberystwyth: Celtic Studies Publications, 1999), pp. 39–48).
[63] See *Golychaf-i Gulwyd* (*LPBT* no. 8), where various figures, historical and legendary, are listed, and in particular Taliesin's boast that he had been with Brân in Ireland (l. 31).
[64] I am indebted to Oliver Padel, on whose working edition of the poem this study is based. Padel drew upon Marged Haycock's article 'Preiddeu Annwn', the precursor of her masterful edition of the poem in *LPBT*, pp. 433–51.

144   THE BOOK OF TALIESIN

          Golychaf Wledic, Pendeuic gwlat ri,
          ry ledas y pennaeth dros traeth Mundi.
          Bu kyweir karchar Gweir yg Kaer Sidi,
4   trwy ebostol Pwyll a Phryderi.
          Neb kyn noc ef nyt aeth idi,
          y'r gadwyn tromlas kywirwas (ae) ketwi.
          A rac preideu Annwfyn tost yt geni,
8   ac yt Urawt, parahawt yn bardwedi.
          Tri lloneit Prytwen yd aetham-ni idi:
          namyn seith ny dyrreith o Gaer Sidi.

          I praise the Lord, the ruler of the kingly realm [i.e. Heaven],
          who has extended his rule over the [whole] area of the world.
          [Well-]maintained was Gwair's prison in Caer Sidi
4   according to the tale of Pwyll and Pryderi.
          No-one before him went to it,
          into the heavy grey chain guarding the faithful youth.
          And before the spoils of Annwfn sadly he was singing,
8   and until Doom our poetic prayer will last.
          Three full [ship]loads of Prydwen we went into it:
          save seven [men], none came back from Caer Sidi.

A conventional opening, where the speaker's identity as a court poet is established with praise to God as ruler of the world, soon gives way to a reference to the imprisonment of Gwair in the Otherworld fortress, Caer Sidi, which is presented as an episode in 'The Tale of Pwyll and Pryderi'. This may be an allusion to a story similar to that of the freeing of Mabon in *Culhwch ac Olwen*. The memory of Gwair 'singing sadly' over the spoils of Annwfn prompts the speaker to boast that 'our' poetry will continue for ever. The first section concludes with a couplet, repeated with variations in sections 3 and 4, referring to an expedition to the Otherworld fort, again using the first plural 'we' but alluding this time to a band of warriors accompanied by their poet, in Arthur's ship, Prydwen, of which only seven return.

1   **Golychaf Wledic** It is customary in the formal poems of the Poets of the Princes to start with an invocation to God. It is less common in the Book of Taliesin collection, but very similar opening lines are found in three other poems, *LPBT* 8.1 *Golychaf-i Gulwyd* ..., 12.1 *Golychaf wledic* ..., 25.1 *Gvolychaf vyn Tat* ...; see *LPBT* 8.1n.

gwlat ri This phrase can be taken in two ways: either as a compound, with *gwlat* a preceding possessive ('land's king', i.e. 'king of the world', i.e. God) and the whole in apposition to *pendeuic* ('ruler, the king of the world'); or with *ri* as an ordinary possessive ('realm of a king', i.e. Heaven), in which case the whole phrase is itself a possessive depending upon *pendevic* ('ruler of the land of the king', i.e. 'ruler of Heaven').

2   **ry ledas** As MS *py*, 'what? why?' (*GPC* pa¹, py¹), is not suitable here, the form has been emended to the preverbal particle *ry*. One can easily see how the scribe might have made this error when so many lines start with the rhetorical question *Py* ...? For examples of the use of *ry* before a verb without *a* in relative clauses, see *GMW*, p. 62.

3   **Bu kyweir karchar G⟨v⟩eir yg Kaer Sidi** This line has a three-part structure, introduced perhaps to add variety to the poem, which consists mainly of two-part lines. For other examples see below, lines 8, 10, 13, 22 etc.

Gweir This could be an allusion to *Gwair ap Gweirioedd*, named as one of the Three Exalted Prisoners of the Island of Britain in *TYP* no. 52 (see pp. 373–74), or to *Gwair fab Gwestyl*, who is associated with grief in the work of some of the court poets (see above, Hendregadredd chapter), and whose father's name means 'hostage'. *Culhwch ac Olwen* contains two episodes relating the freeing of renowned prisoners by Arthur, but Gwair is not named as one of them; see *CO*, pp. lx–lxii.

Kaer Sidi A name for the Otherworld. Pronounced with /d/ according to the metre and orthography of a number of medieval sources. It was probably a learned borrowing from MIr *sídi* (genitive sing. or nominative/genitive plural of *síd*, 'fairy-mound', pronounced with δ), according to Sims-Williams; see *IIMWL*, pp. 66–78.

4   **ebostol** On the derivation and meanings of the word, see *GPC*. This is the only example of its use for a secular tale. It appears to refer to the story material of the Four Branches of the *Mabinogi*, which features Pwyll lord of Dyfed and his son Pryderi; see Sioned Davies, *The Mabinogion* [*Mab*] (Oxford: University Press, 2007), pp. 3–21. Gwair is not mentioned in these tales, but Pryderi is again associated with Caer Sidi in another poem in the Book of Taliesin; see *LPBT* 8.45–47.

6   **tromlas** This is the feminine form of an adj. derived from *trwm*, 'heavy' (*GMW*, pp. 36–37), and *glas*, 'grey', which is lenited as a second element in the compound. The lenition *tromlas > dromlas* following the feminine noun *kadwyn* is not shown.

kywirwas ketwi The last section of most of the other lines in this poem is four or five syllables long, but the MS reading of this line, *kywirwas ae ketwi*, has six syllables. It is possible that a scribe added the relative pronoun *ae*, having understood *kedwi* as the 3 sing.imperf. form of the verb *cadw* with an unusual -*i* ending (cf. *keni* l. 7, *seui* l. 31 and see *GMW*, p. 121). If *ketwi* is read as a rare form of the verb noun, however, *ae* can be omitted.

7   **a rac preideu Annwfyn** The meanings of both *rac* and *preideu* are ambiguous here; see word-list below. On the derivation, understanding and use of the term *Annwfyn*, see Sims-Williams, *IIMWL*, pp. 57–59.

tost yt geni Lit. '[it is] sadly that he was singing'. Cf. the account of Mabon ap Modron, who is heard lamenting from within the walls of Gloucester in *Culhwch ac Olwen* (*CO*, ll. 910–12).

8   **ac yt Uraŵt, parahaŵt yn bardwedi** For other examples of the verb *parhau* used with *Brawt* to refer to song or poetry continuing for ever, see *LPBT* 4.55n. The form *yt*, found again in *LPBT* 8.28n, may be an error for or a variant of the prepositions *hyd* or the rarer *bed*, *fed*, 'as far as, up to, until'. For a discussion of the form *parahaŵt*, which has an absolute ending, see Simon Rodway, 'Absolute Forms in the Poetry of the Gogynfeirdd: Functionally Obsolete Archaisms or Working System?', *Journal of Celtic Linguistics*, 7 (1998), 63–84. Many different interpretations of *yn* are possible, but the 1 plural poss. pronoun 'our' is the most likely here. There are no other examples of *bardwedi*, but similar compounds like *bardwawt* and *bardeir* are found in the work of the Poets of the Princes (see *GPC*).

9   **Tri lloneit Prytwen** His ship is not named by Arthur when he lists his prized possessions in *Culhwch ac Olwen* (ll. 159–62), but it is identified as Prydwen ('of white or fair appearance') more than once in other parts of the text; see l. 938n. The meaning of 'three full loads of Prydwen' is not clear, but it is interesting to note the place name *Messur Pritguenn* ('the measure of Prydwen') in a land grant in the Book of Llandaf.

yd aetham-ni idi Although this final section can be understood as having five syllables by assuming that the affixed pronoun *ni* is hypermetrical, the rhythm is different from that of most of the other lines in the poem. Haycock suggests that the influence of the beginnings of similar lines such as 21 and 41 may have caused an original *yd aeth idi* (with a 3 sing. form of the verb) to be changed.

10   **namyn seith** MS *nam* is emended to *namyn*, the form found in the final lines of the following five sections of the poem. For examples of the common motif of a small number of survivors from battle and for references to sevens in medieval Welsh poetry, see *LPBT* 18.10. Most significant in the context of this poem is the Second Branch of the *Mabinogi*, where Taliesin is named among the seven survivors who return from a disastrous expedition to Ireland; see *Mab*, p. 32.

ny dyrreith Note that, in this poem *ny* lenites initial *g*- (lines 29–30, 35–36 etc.), but not *b*- (*ny beirw*, line 17; see *GMW*, p. 62); *d*- was probably lenited, giving *ny ðyrreith* each time. On the orthography of the Book of Taliesin, see *LPBT*, p. 7.

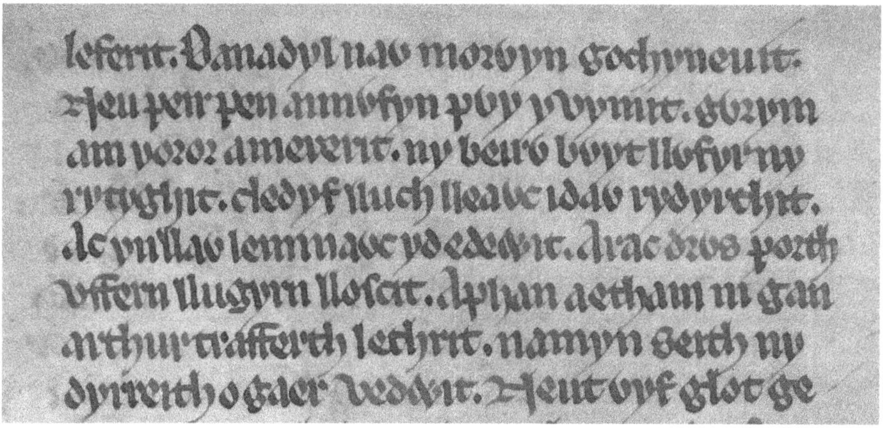

FIG. 4.6: NLW Peniarth MS 2, ff. 25ᵛ, 26ʳ.

Neut ỽyf | glot geinmyn cerd ochlywir. ygkaer pedry|uan pedyr ychwelyt. yg kynneir or peir pan ‖ leferit. O anadyl naỽ morỽyn gochyneuit. | Neu peir pen annỽfyn pỽy y vynut. gỽrym | am yoror a mererit. ny beirỽ bỽyt llỽfyr ny | rytyghit. cledyf lluch lleaỽc idaỽ rydyrchit. | Ac yn llaỽ leminaỽc yd edewit. Arac drỽs porth | vffern llugyrn lloscit. Aphan aetham ni gan | arthur trafferth lechrit. namyn seith ny | dyrreith o gaer vedwit.

	Neut ỽyf glot geinmyn: cerd ochlywi*t*
12	yg kaer pedryuan pedyrychwelyt.
	Yg kynneir, o'r peir pan leferit:
	o anadyl naỽ morỽyn gochyneuit.
	Neu peir Pen Annỽfyn, pỽy y vynut,
16	gỽrym am y oror a mererit?
	Ny beirỽ bỽyt llỽfyr, ny ry tyghit;
	cledyf lluch Lleaỽc idaỽ ry dyrchit,
	ac yn llaỽ Leminaỽc yd edewit.
20	A rac drỽs porth Vffern llugyrn lloscit.
	A phan aetham-ni gan Arthur, trafferth le*th*rit,
	namyn seith ny dyrreith o Gaer Vedwit.

	I am splendid [in bestowing] fame: song was/used to be/would be heard
12	in the four quarters of the perfectly revolving fort.
	My first utterance, [it was] from/about the cauldron that it was spoken:
	by the breath of nine maidens it was kindled.
	The cauldron of the chief of Annwn, what is its disposition
16	[with] dark-coloured material around its rim and pearls?
	It does not boil a coward's food, it has not been destined [to do so];

the flashing sword of Lleog was ?thrust into it,
and in the hand of Lleminog it was left behind.
20   And in front of the door of Hell's gate, lamps were burned.
And when we went with Arthur, famed in tribulation,
save seven [men], none returned from the Mead-Feast Fort.

This second section opens with the speaker boasting of his ability as a poet who bestows fame upon the subjects of his praise. We return to the Otherworld fortress, where once more song is heard. This reminds the speaker perhaps of the origin of his poetic gift, a magical cauldron lit by the breath of nine maidens. The first of the poem's many questions concerns the special qualities of the cauldron, which will not boil food for a coward.

11   **clot geinmyn** Lit. 'fame-splendid'. *Clot* is lenited as a predicate after *bot* (*GMW*, p. 20), and *ceinmyn* is lenited as the second part of the compound. Haycock (*LPBT*, p. 442) prefers to see the compound as meaning 'bestowing splendid fame' rather than simply 'famous'.

cerd ochlywit The MS form [*g*]*ochlywir* (impers.pres.) is emended for the sake of the rhyme. The omission of relative *a* is found elsewhere before compound verbs containing prefixes like *go-* (*GMW*, p. 61n), but the lenition is unexpected and one might, in fact, expect **goglywit* in a relative construction.

12   **yg kaer pedryuan pedrychwelyt** On the prefix *pedry-*, which derives from the numeral *pedwar*, 'four', and sometimes has the meaning 'complete, perfect', see *GPC* pedr(y)-. For a discussion of the other examples of *pedryuan* in medieval Welsh literature, see *LPBT*, p. 442. In this instance, *ban* could have the meaning 'top, pinnacle, turret', giving an adjective, 'four-turreted', to describe the fort. Another meaning of *ban* is 'corner, quarter, part', giving 'four-cornered, square'. Haycock favours understanding *pedryuan* as a noun, 'four ends or corners', with *kaer* as a genitive, 'in the four corners of the fort'. She also mentions that there may be play on *ban*, 'poem, song'; see *GPC* ban^1.

MS *pedyr ychwelyt* is understood as a compound *ped(y)rychwelyt*, a form found along with *pedryuan* in a gnomic poem in the Red Book of Hergest, where they describe the world; see *Early Welsh Gnomic and Nature Poetry* [*EWGNP*], ed. by Nicolas Jacobs (London: Modern Humanities Research Association, 2012), IX.41. It contains the element *chwel*, 'turn, course', with either a nominal or a verb noun ending (*GPC* -yd$^{1-2}$), 'turning in four directions, perfectly or completely revolving', or an impersonal imperfect or past form (*GPC* -id$^{1-2}$). For references to other revolving forts, see *LPBT*, pp. 442–43.

13   **o'r peir pan leferit** The prep. *o* can mean 'from', with the cauldron understood as the source of poetic speech; cf. Llywelyn Fardd *Cret 6e geir o'm peir*, 'believe my utterance from my cauldron' (*CBT* II 2.32), and Llywarch Brydydd y Moch, *Geir uy geir o'r peir*, 'my utterance is an utterance from the cauldron' (*CBT* v 19.9), and for further examples in the court poetry and in the

Taliesin collection, see *LPBT* 4.210n. Another possibility is that *o* means 'of, about, concerning', since a description of the cauldron follows.

14   **o anadyl naṽ morṽyn gochyneuit** The object of the verb may be either the cauldron or Taliesin's utterance. According to the sixteenth-century *Ystoria Taliesin*, Taliesin received poetic inspiration from the cauldron of Ceridwen; see *Ystoria Taliesin*, ed. by Patrick K. Ford (Cardiff: University of Wales Press, 1992). For earlier references to Ceridwen's cauldron, see *LPBT*, p. 14, and for groups of nine women with supernatural powers in medieval Arthurian literature, including the nine sisters of Avalon described by Telgesinus in Geoffrey of Monmouth's 'Life of Merlin', see *LPBT* 18.14n.

15   **neu peir** *neu* may be understood as the conjunction 'or', but it is more likely to be the preverbal particle *neu(t)* used as a copula here to introduce the subject of the sentence, which has been brought forward for emphasis, 'the cauldron it is ...'; cf. the 'Elegy for Uthr Pendragon' above, *neu vi* ..., and see J. E. Caerwyn Williams, 'MlW *Neu, Neut* as Copula', *Celtica*, 11 (1976), 278–85 (p. 282).

Pen Annwuyn 'Head of the Otherworld' is the title given to Pwyll in the First Branch of the *Mabinogi* after his stay in Arawn's kingdom, but this is not necessarily a reference to him.

15–16   **pwy y vynut ... mererit** These lines contain the only example in the poem of a form of partial rhyme called *proest*, where the consonants are identical but the vowel or diphthongs vary. The poem also contains a number of examples of generic consonantal rhyme (see Chapter 1 footnote 24, above), once thought to be found in *hengerdd* (early poetry) only. For a discussion of the form and content of the many questions posed by the figure of Taliesin, see Haycock, 'Taliesin's Questions'.

16   **gṽrym am y oror a mererit** This line may also be understood as the start of the answer to the question in line 15, giving a physical description of the cauldron first, then going on to its inherent nature.

17   **Ny beirṽ bṽyt llṽfyr, ny ry tyghit** This cauldron can be compared with that in the Life of Beuno which refuses to cook the food of St Beuno's evil visitors, and, more closely, with the cauldron of the giant Dyrnwch, one of the Thirteen Treasures of the Island of Britain, which would boil a brave man's food but not that of a coward: see *LPBT*, p. 443.

18   **cledyf lluch Lleaṽc** Usually assumed to be a personal name or nickname, *lleaṽc* may also be understood as an adjective containing the element *lle* found in the verb *dileaf: dilëu*, 'to destroy'. On the possibility that a misinterpretation of this line gave rise to the character *Llenllawc Vydel*, 'Llenlleog the Irishman', who in *Culhwch ac Olwen* went with Arthur in his ship Prydwen to Ireland to fetch the cauldron of Diwrnach Wyddel and slew him with Arthur's sword, see *CO*, ll. 1036–56; Sims-Williams, *IIMWL*, pp. 160–62.

idaṽ ry dyrchit Haycock suggests that the verb is a form of *tyrchu*, 'to burrow, to pierce', here perhaps with the meaning 'to thrust'. Sims-Williams draws attention to cauldrons in Irish texts into which each person would make a thrust and get what they deserved; see *IIMWL*, p. 161n. Another possibility is *dyrchu*, a short form of *dyrchafu*, 'to lift up, raise', although, according to *GPC*, there are no examples of *dyrchu* before the fifteenth century.

19   **Lleminaѡc** This name or nickname, derived from an adjective (see *GPC* llyminog), appears twice more in the Book of Taliesin and also in the Life of Gruffudd ap Cynan to refer to a deliverer of prophecy; see *PBT* 4.14n. It seems to be a term used for many different individuals, including perhaps Arthur in this case. For lenition after fem.sing. noun *llaѡ*, see *GMW*, p. 14.

20   **A rac drѡs porth Vffern llugyrn lloscit** Annwfn is here conflated with *Vffern* (< Latin *inferna*), the Christian Hell with its flaming entrance mentioned in biblical texts. *Llugyrn* may also be a borrowing from Latin (< *lucerna*). Emendation to its old singular form **llugern* would give full internal rhyme with *Vffern*. Note the word-order; standard prose would be *y lloscit llugyrn*; see *GMW*, p. 181n (e).

21   **trafferth lethrit** The mutation of *llethrit* suggests that it is in compound with *trafferth*, lit. 'the bright/famous one of/in tribulation'.

22   **Caer Vedwit** A second name for the Otherworld fort containing the hapax form *medwit*, thought to be a compound of *med*, 'mead', and *gwit*, 'feast, liquid, honey' (*GPC* gwid and cf. melwid). Haycock notes that, according to another Taliesin poem, *Kaer Sidi* contains a fountain of drink 'sweeter than white wine'; see *LPBT* 8.50–51n.

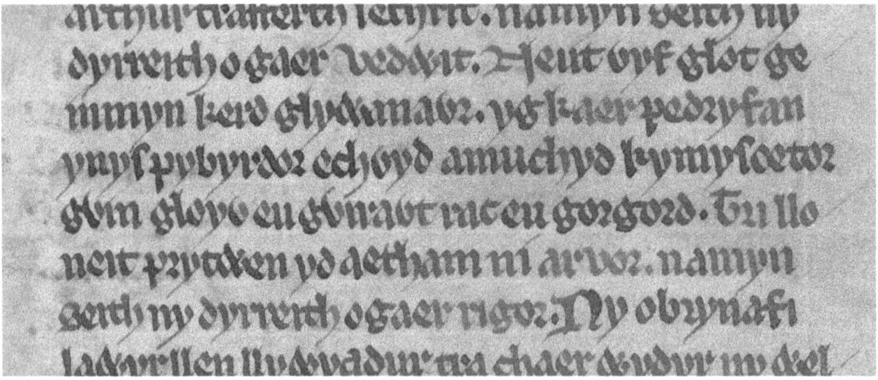

FIG. 4.7: NLW Peniarth MS 2, f. 26ʳ.

Neut ѡyf glot ge-|inmyn kerd glywanaѡr. yg kaer pedryfan | ynys pybyrdor echѡyd amuchyd kymyscetor | gѡin gloyѡ eu gѡiraѡt rac eu gorgord. Tri llo-|neit prytwen yd aetham ni ar vor. namyn | seith ny dyrreith o gaer rigor.

	Neut ỽyf glot geinmyn: kyrd glywan*n*or
24	yg kaer pedryfan, ynys pybyrdor.
	Echwyd a muchyd kymyscetor;
	gỽin gloyỽ eu gỽiraỽt rac eu gosgor.
	Tri lloneit Prytwen yd aetham-ni ar vor:
28	namyn seith, ny dyrreith o Gaer Rigor.

	I am splendid [in bestowing] fame: songs are heard
24	in the four quarters of the fort, stout defence of the island.
	Fresh water and jet are mixed together;
	sparkling wine [is] their drink, [set] in front of their retinue.
	Three full [ship]loads of Prydwen we went upon the sea:
28	save seven [men], none came back from the Petrification Fort.

The name *Caer Vedwit* in l. 22 may have prompted the concise but vivid description of feasting in the Otherworld fortress contained in this short section.

23   **kyrd glywannor** MS *glywanaỽr* appears to be a 3 plural form of *clybot*, 'to hear', with a passive or impersonal ending *-awr* (see *GMW*, p. 121, and for examples from the Book of Taliesin and twelfth-century court poetry, see *LPBT*, p. 23). It is corrected here to the unique form *clywannor* to provide an end-rhyme; cf. *CBT* II 5.3, *Gỽyrtheu goleu gỽelhattor*, 'clear wonders will be seen'. This may be a deponent verb (cf. l. 50 below, *gỽidanhor*) with *kerd* as its object, 'they hear a song', but in order to provide a parallel to the phrase *cerd ochlywit* in l. 11 above, the meaning 'is/will be heard' is required. Haycock (*LPBT* 18.23n) favours understanding the object, MS *kerd*, as an old spelling of the plural form *kyrd* that a scribe failed to modernise, giving the meaning 'songs are heard'.

24   **ynys pybyrdor** A description of the fort, 'strong door (i.e. defence) of the island'. The lenition of *pybyrdor* due to inversion is not shown.

25   **Echwyd a muchyd kymyscetor** Haycock suggests that this is a reference to a belief mentioned in Isidore's *Etymologiae* that jet, a shiny black form of coal used for ornament, is set alight by water. Was this, perhaps, the imagined method of lighting for feasts at the Otherworld fort? Note the unusual Object Verb word-order, lacking *a*, again without lenition, as in line 20, contrasting with lines 11 and 23.

26   **rac eu gosgor** MS *gorgord* is emended for rhyme and meaning to a variant of *gosgord*, 'retinue'.

28   **Caer Rigor** Understood by Haycock to be from Latin *rigor* with the meaning 'stiffness, hardness, numbness, rigidity', in either a physical or metaphorical sense, but for other possibilities see *LPBT* 18.28n.

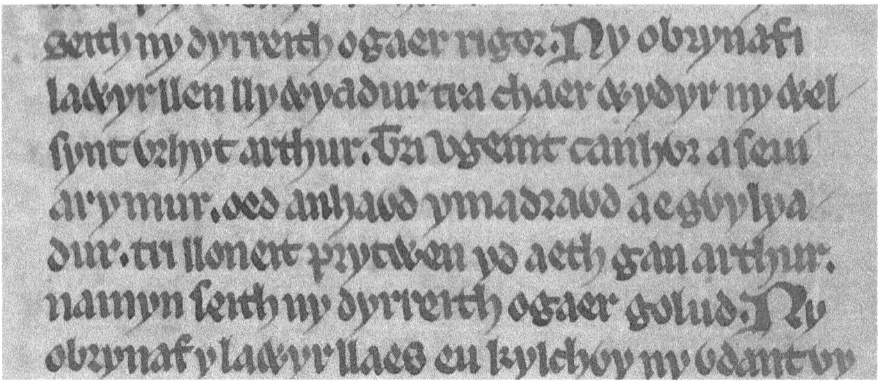

FIG. 4.8: NLW Peniarth MS 2, f. 26^r.

Ny obrynafi | lawyr llen llywyadur tra chaer wydyr ny wel-|synt ỽrhyt arthur. Tri vgeint canhỽr a seui | ar y mur. oed anhaỽd ymadraỽd ae gỽylya-|dur. tri lloneit prytwen yd aeth gan arthur. | namyn seith ny dyrreith o gaer golud.

        Ny obrynaf-i lawyr llen llywyadur,
        tra Chaer Wydyr ny welsynt ỽrhyt Arthur:
        tri vgeint canhỽr a seui ar y mur;
32   oed anhaỽd ymadraỽd a'e gỽylyadur.
        Tri lloneit Prytwen yd aeth gan Arthur:
        namyn seith ny dyrreith o Gaer Golud.

        I do not deserve [the company of] insignificant men of Godly
                                                                                       learning
        who had not seen the size/valour of Arthur beyond the Glass Fort:
        three score hundred men were standing on its wall;
32   it was difficult to speak with their watchman.
        Three full [ship]loads of Prydwen went with Arthur:
        save seven [men], none came back from the Fort of Impediment.

From this point, the speaker starts to voice his present concerns, using his arcane experience as one of the seven who returned from the Otherworld to pour scorn on those of lesser powers, particularly clerics whose learning is restricted to books. The description of the Otherworld fortress of glass and its inhabitants who do not speak echoes an episode recorded in *Historia Brittonum* that probably derives from a Hiberno-Latin text about the legendary origins of the peoples of Ireland. In that account, none of those who attacked the glass tower escaped with their lives, leaving just one ship-full to people the whole of Ireland.

29 **Ny obrynaf-i lawyr** The usual range of meanings given for *gobrynu*, 'to merit, deserve, be worthy of' (*GPC* gobrynaf: gobryn), needs to be stretched here: 'I do not deserve ...' may mean 'I deserve better than ...' (perhaps as audience, or as company). This line is interpreted in the light of *Ny charwyf*

llawyr 'ny llaȯr gythrut, 'I do not love paltry men with their pathetic fear', from Gwalchmai's Boasting Poem (*CBT* I 9.61). *Llawyr* is understood as a compound of *llaw*, 'small, low, mean' (*GPC* llaw²), and *gwyr* plural of *gwr*, 'man'. The form may alternatively be an error for *llewyr*, plural of *llawer*, 'many', or a unique plural of *llëwr*, 'reader' (see *GPC*).

llen Llywyadur Lit. 'the learning of the ruler', probably referring to God, i.e. 'Godly learning, Christian writing'.

30 **Caer Wydyr** For parallels for the glass fortress in the sea, see *LPBT*, p. 18 n. 30. The most important is an episode about the first settlers of Ireland in *Historia Brittonum*, chapter 13, who after a year 'saw a glass tower in the middle of the sea, and they could see men on the tower, and they sought to speak with them. They never replied …'

ny welsynt ȯrhyt Arthur This can be understood as a relative clause (qualifying *llawyr*) as in l. 36 below, or as another main clause (with *llawyr* understood as subject). *Gȯrhyt* is lenited as the object of a conjugated verb (*GMW*, p. 18).

34 **Caer Golud** Haycock prefers *golud*, 'impediment' (with lenition of *g-* after the fem. noun *kaer* not shown), to *colud*, 'bowels, intestines, entrails', used figuratively for a hidden interior (see *GPC* coludd and further *IIMWL*, p. 68 n. 122). Note the generic rhyme with *Arthur* (-δ with -r).

FIG. 4.9: NLW Peniarth MS 2, f. 26ʳ.

Ny | obrynaf y lawyr llaes eu kylchȯy ny ȯdant ȯy | py dyd peridyd pȯy. py aȯr ymeindyd y ganet | cȯy. pȯy gȯnaeth arnyt aeth doleu defȯy. ny | ȯdant ȯy yrych brych bras y penrȯy. seith | vgein kygȯng yny aerȯy. a phan aetham | ni gan arthur auyrdȯl gofȯy. namyn seith | ny dyrreith o gaer vandȯy.

36
Ny obrynaf-y lawyr llaes eu kylchȯy
ny ȯdant-ȯy py dyd peridyd pȯy,
py aȯr ymeindyd y ganet Dȯy,

p(v)y g(v)naeth ar nyt aeth Doleu Def(v)y;
ny (v)dant-(v)y yr Ych Brych, bras y penr(v)y,
40 seith vgein kyg(v)ng yn y aer(v)y.
A phan aetham-ni gan Arthur, auyrd(v)l gof(v)y,
namyn seith ny dyrreith o Gaer Vand(v)y.

I deserve better than [the company of] insignificant men with their trailing ?shields,
36 who don't know who is created on what day,
on what hour in the middle of the day was God born,
[nor] who made the one/those who did not go to the Meadows of Defwy;
those who do not know of the Brindled Ox, with its stout collar,
40 [and] seven score links in its chain.
And when we went with Arthur, wretched journey,
save seven [men], none returned from Mand[d]wy Fort.

In this section the narrative recollection takes second place to a catalogue of questions to which the speaker knows the answers but his rivals do not.

35 **llaes eu kylch(v)y** On the construction of this phrase, which qualifies *llawyr*, cf. below ll. 39 *bras y penr(v)y*, 46 *aryant y pen*, and see *GMW*, p. 37. The range of uses of *kylchwy* (from *cylch*, 'circle, ring') makes this phrase ambiguous, although its general intention as castigation of the *llawyr* is clear. If a round shield is intended, then *llaes* (< Latin *laxus*) may refer to shields becoming slack from misuse, or to the *llawyr* being too weak or cowardly to raise their shields in battle. If a loose girdle or garment is meant, then it could refer, contemptuously perhaps, to monks' habits. For similar ambiguity compare 'Claf Abercuawc', line 8b, *neur laesswys vyg kylchwy*, 'my *kylchwy* has become slack', and see *EWSP*, p. 619.

36 **ny (v)dant-(v)y py dyd peridyd p(v)y** Lit. 'who do not know on what day is/was created who'. It is unusual but not unknown to have a pronoun or preposition at the end of a line. For examples from the court poetry, see *LPBT* 18.36n. An emendation to *pl(v)y*, a form of the noun *plwyf*, 'parishioners, people' (*GPC*), perhaps referring here to the human race, is also possible. The form *peridyd* can be understood as an agent noun, 'creator' (see *GPC* peridydd), or a compound of *peri* + *dydd*, but a verbal form of *peri*, 'to cause, create', would make the most sense here and in l. 44 below. A passive meaning 'is/was created' could be given by the impers.pret. *perit* (*GMW*, p. 126) + 3 sg. relative suffix *-yð*, although this ending is otherwise found only with active, present-tense forms (*GMW*, p. 119); see *LPBT* 18.36n.

37 **py a(v)r ymeindyd y ganet D(v)y** The unknown MS form *c(v)y* is emended to a variant of *Duw*, 'God', cf. the parallel line 45 below. See *Kat Godeu* above for the tradition, also recorded by the twelfth-century Anglo-Norman writer Wace and others, that Taliesin had prophesied the birth of Christ, and see also *LPBT* 5.249n.

38 **Doleu Defẃy** The plural of *dôl*, 'meadow', is often used with river names (e.g. *Doleu Hafren*, 'the Vale of Severn', *LPBT* 8.7), but *Defwy* is unknown as a river name or otherwise. This makes the whole line obscure. *Defwy* could be 'black river' and if so, possibly to be compared with the River Styx, crossed to enter Hades in classical mythology; see *LPBT* 18.38n.

39 **ny ẃdant-ẃy yr Ych Brych, bras y penrẃy** A rare example of the verb *gwybot* used for 'to know of, to be acquainted with'; see *GPC* gwn²: gwybod¹ 2. *Yr Ych Brych* (note the rare use of the definite article) appears to be a well-known legendary creature. It is named in the Triads as one of the Three Principal Oxen of the Island of Britain (*TYP* no. 45), and as one of the two oxen specified to be won by Culhwch to plough a field for Ysbyddaden (*CO*, l. 593). *Penrẃy*, lit. 'head-ring' (*GPC* penrhwy and cf. *aerẃy* below), may refer to an ox-collar, yoke or halter. A similar phrase, *ych brych bras y beuren*, is found in the NLW Peniarth MS 47 version of the Triads (see *TYP*, pp. xxv-vi).

41 **auyrdẃl gofẃy** Note the word-order: either the lenition to the noun *gofẃy* caused by the preceding adjective has not been shown or this is not adj. + noun but a nominal sentence, 'wretched the journey'. The corresponding phrase in line 47 does show lenition, favouring the former option.

42 **Kaer Vandẃy** Also named in the Dialogue between Gwyddno Garanhir and Gwyn ap Nudd in the Black Book of Carmarthen as a place, in the Otherworld perhaps, before which a battle was fought; see *EWSP* 'Gwyn ap Nudd' 10c and 11a. In the orthographic systems of both manuscripts -d- is ambiguous.

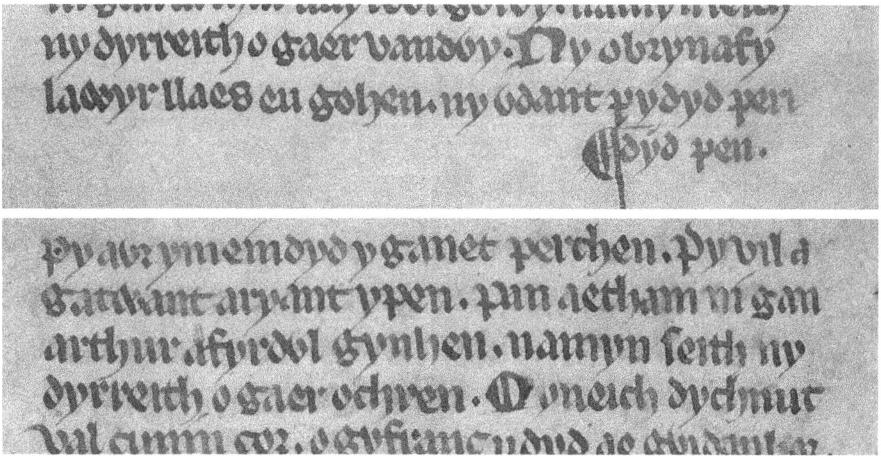

FIG. 4.10: NLW Peniarth MS 2, f. 26^{r-v}.

Ny obrynafy | lawyr llaes eu gohen. ny ẃdant pydyd peri | dyd pen. || Py aẃr ymeindyd y ganet perchen. Py vil a | gatwant aryant y pen. pan aetham ni gan | arthur afyrdẃl gynhen. namyn seith ny | dyrreith o gaer ochren.

	Ny obrynaf-y lawyr llaes eu gohen,
44	ny ʍdant py dyd peridyd Pen,
	py aʍr ymeindyd y ganet Perchen,
	py vil a gatwant, aryant y pen.
	Pan aetham-ni gan Arthur, afyrdʍl gynhen,
48	namyn seith ny dyrreith o Gaer Ochren.

	I deserve better than [the company of] insignificant men with their feeble resolve,
44	who do not know on what day the Ruler (i.e. God) is created,
	[nor] on what hour in the middle of the day the Lord was born,
	[nor] what animal is it they guard with its silver head.
	When we went with Arthur, wretched conflict,
48	save seven, none returned from the Angular Fort.

The speaker continues to taunt his opponents for their ignorance even in questions concerning their own field of religious learning.

43 llaes eu gohen For its construction, see l. 35, *llaes eu kylchʍy*. If *gohen* is taken literally as 'attack, course', the phrase may refer to the feebleness of the *llawyr* in battle. A more general criticism is suggested by the meanings 'aim, will, desire, inclination' (*GPC* gohen¹).

44 Pen is suspect, because it rhymes with the same word in line 46, which is metrically weak. It could be a corruption, introduced to create alliteration with *peridyd*. If allowed, it is 'ruler, chieftain, lord', possibly used here of God or Christ (for further examples, see *LPBT* 18.44n) or it could perhaps be emended to *nen*, 'roof', used figuratively for 'Lord' (*GPC*).

46 py vil a gatwant aryant y pen If *mil* is to be understood as 'animal' (see *GPC*), this may be the *Ych Brych* of line 39. It is unclear who is the subject of the verb, perhaps the *llawyr* of line 43 or the inhabitants of *Kaer Sidi*. The silver head of the creature has led Haycock to suggest that this may be a riddling question, referring to a silver-headed crozier; see 'Taliesin's Questions', p. 32.

48 Kaer Ochren Possibly from *ochr*, 'edge, side', for 'a fort with sides, an angular (as opposed to a round) fort', cf. l. 12, *kaer pedryuan*. For discussion of another reference to Caer Ochren by the fifteenth-century poet Hywel Swrdwal, see *LPBT* 18.48n. Cynddelw twice compares his patrons with a fearful figure called Ochren, perhaps a giant (*CBT* III 24.116 and IV 6.44).

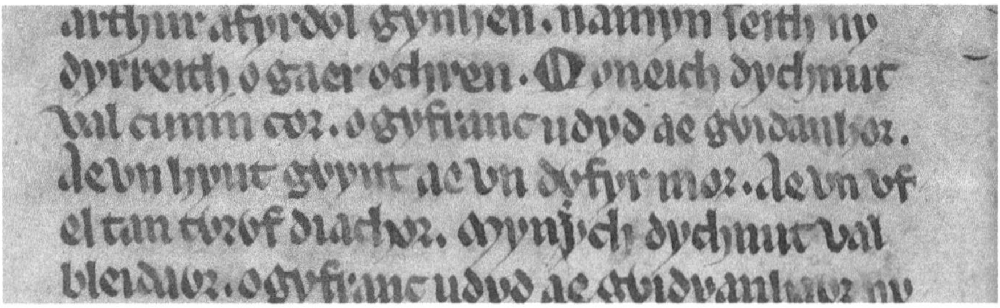

FIG. 4.11: NLW Peniarth MS 2, f. 26ᵛ

Myneich dychnut | val cunin cor. o gyfranc udyd ae gŵidanhor. | Ae vn hynt gŵynt ae vn dŵfyr mor. Ae vn vf|el tan tŵrŵf diachor.

	Myneich dychnut val cunin cor
	o gyfranc udyd ae gŵidanhor
	ae vn hynt gŵynt, ae vn dŵfyr mor,
52	ae vn vfel tan, tŵrŵf diachor.

	Monks gather like a pack of dogs
	because of a contest between masters who know
	whether the wind [follows] one course, whether the sea is one water,
52	whether fire — unstoppable tumult — is [?composed of] one spark.

The speaker's opponents are named as monks and possibly compared to a pack of hounds or wolves in the difficult opening couplet, which is repeated at the beginning of the next section. The closing refrain is absent in these final two sections and the first parts of their lines tend to be shorter than those of the first six *awdlau*. It is not likely that they are later additions, however, as there are strong thematic links between them and the rest of the poem, and also their two last lines (59–60), with their reference to God, echo the poem's opening.

49   **Myneich dychnut val cunin cor** Both *dychnut* and *cunin* are obscure. The first is understood as a verbal form with *myneich* as its subject; see *GMW*, p. 181n (c). The parallel line 53, which compares the monks with wolves, suggests that *dychnut* may contain the element *cnud*, 'pack (of wolves or dogs)', and that *cunin* is a collective form from *cun*, 'whelp, dog' (rather than *cun*, 'lord'), qualifying *cor*, 'host, company' (causing lenition which is not shown).

50   **O gyfranc udyd ae gŵidanhor** Another difficult line. *Udyd* is understood as a rare plural form of *ud*, 'lord', taken by Haycock to refer to 'masters of learning' [i.e. the native poets], rather than political lords. She suggests that the line may refer to a contest among the *udyd* themselves or between them and the monks, understanding *kyfranc* as 'clash, contest' rather than its secondary meaning 'story (of battle etc.), tale'. The form *gŵidanhor*, with a variant *gŵidyanhaŵr* for the sake of the rhyme in the parallel line 54, is obscure. They appear to be forms of the irregular verb *gwybot*, 'to know', but the spelling of *gwy-* with an *-i-* in both cases suggests that they have not been modernised, reflecting perhaps the scribes' uncertainty. They may be formed from the 3 plural pres. of *gwybod* (cf. *gwdant* used several times in the poem) + the old passive or impersonal ending *-aŵr* (*GMW*, p. 121), and a rare example of passive or impersonal *-or* as in l. 23, *kyrd glywanor*. This would give the meaning 'are known, will be known', with *udyd* as the object — another example of *gwybod* meaning 'to know of, to be acquainted with'; see above l. 39n. Another possibility, which gives better meaning in the first example, is that *gŵidanhor* is a 3 plural deponent, 'they know'; see *LPBT* 18.50n. The preceding form *ae* may be a combination of relative pronoun *a*, 'who', + infixed pronoun, or an older

form of the relative pronoun, a survival of Old Welsh *hai* which has escaped modernisation because of the occurrence of *ae?* in the following two lines.

    51–52 **ae vn hynt gṽynt** ... These phrases are nominal sentences in question form with the subject at the end: lit. 'whether the wind [is] a single course', etc. For parallels in the work of authors like Isidore and Aldhelm, see *LPBT*, pp. 51–52n.

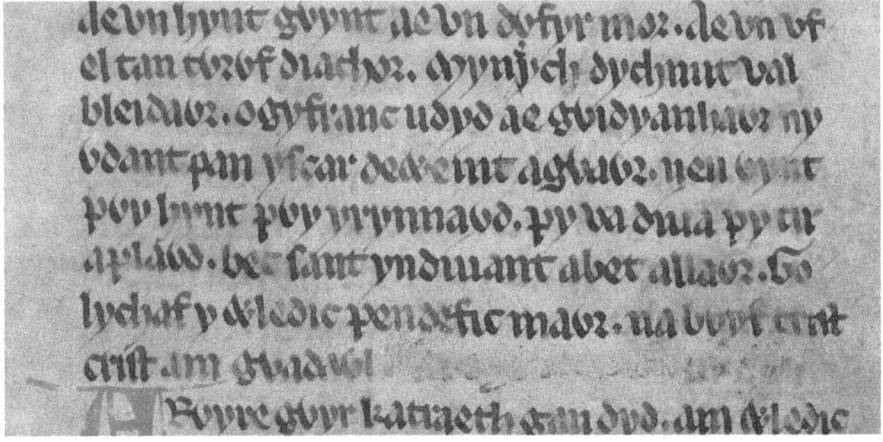

FIG. 4.12: NLW Peniarth MS 2, f. 26ᵛ.

mynᵉych dychnut val | bleidaṽr. o gyfranc udyd ae gṽidyanhaṽr ny | ṽdant pan yscar deweint a gṽaṽr. neu ṽynt | pṽy hynt pṽy yrynnaṽd. py va diua py tir | a plaṽd. bet sant yn diuant abet allaṽr. Go|lychaf y wledic pendefic maṽr. na bṽyf trist | crist am gṽadaṽl

	Myneych dychnut val bleidaṽr
	o gyfranc udyd a'e gṽidyanhaṽr,
	ny ṽdant pan yscar deweint a gṽaṽr,
56	neu ṽynt, pṽy [y] hynt, pṽy y rynnaṽd,
	py va [a] diua, py tir a plaṽd;
	*p*et sant yn diuant, a *ph*et allaṽr.
	Golychaf-y Wledic, Pendefic maṽr:
60	na bṽyf trist: Crist a'm gṽadaṽl!

	Monks congregate like wolves
	because of the clash between masters who know it [or them].
	They do not know how/why the darkness and light divide,
56	or the wind — what is its course, what its onrush,
	what place it devastates, what land it strikes;
	how many saints [are] in ?eternity, and how many altars.
	I praise the Lord, the great Ruler:
60	may I not be sad: Christ will reward me!

This catalogue of questions reaches a climax in the final stanza, which concludes with praise to God and an expression of assurance that the speaker will be rewarded by Christ.

55 pan yscar deweint a gẅaẅr For biblical references to the dividing of light from darkness at Creation, see *LPBT* 18.55n. *Pan* is understood as an interrogative particle, 'how?, why?'. Compare the series of questions to which Taliesin boasts of knowing the answers in *Angar Kyfyndawt* (*LPBT* poem 4), e.g. ll. 134–35, *llaeth pan yw gwyn, pan yw glas kelyn*, 'why milk is white, why holly is green', etc.

56–57 neu ẅynt, pẅy y hynt ... A syllable is added to each of these lines, which are linked to the rest of the section by generic rhyme.

58 *p*et sant yn diuant, a *p*het allaẅr On *pet*, 'how many', an interrogative form found only in the Book of Taliesin poems, see *LPBT* 4.116n. There are no other examples of a lenited form *bet*. It is assumed that *diuant*, the basic meaning of which is 'total loss, annihilation', refers here to eternity. If this is so, the intention may be to contrast the number of saints in heaven with those *a*[*r*] *llawr*, 'on earth'. Haycock, however, keeps the manuscript reading, *allaẅr*, 'altar', drawing attention to the connection made between saints and their altars in twelfth-century poems featuring St Cadfan and St David: *LPBT* 18.58n.

59 Golychaf-y Wledic, Pendefic maẅr This line closely echoes line 1, signalling the end of the poem.

60 na bẅyf trist: Crist a'm gẅadaẅl! For more regular line length, Haycock suggests emending to *mal na bóyf trist*, 'so that I may not be sad'. A very similar line is found in the refrain of the poem *Echrys Ynys* from the Book of Taliesin, dated to the ninth or tenth centuries: l. 16, *Am bwyf-i gan Grist, hyt na bwyf trist, ran ebostol*, 'May there be to me from Christ, so that I shall not be sorrowful, an apostle's lot', and ll. 29–30, *A'm bwyf-i gan Grist, hyt na bwyf trist, o drwc a da, | ran trugared y wlat ried, buched gyfa*, 'May there be to me from Christ, so that I shall not be sorrowful, from [my] evil and [my] good, | the lot of mercy in the land of majesty, life fulfilled' (see Gruffydd, 'Court Poem', pp. 44–45).

Word-list

a¹ *conj.* (causing spirant mutation, *GMW*, p. 21) 'and' 4, 7, 16, 20, 21, 25, 41, 55, 58
    ac (before a vowel) 8, 19
a² *preverbal particle* (causing lenition) 31, 46, 57(2)
ae¹ *relative pronoun* 50n, 54
ae² *interrogative particle* 'whether (it is)' (*GPC* ai¹) 51(2), 52
a'e *combination of prep.* a, 'with' + *infixed possessive pron. 3 pl.* 'their' 32
aerẅy *n.* 'chain' 40
aeth *3 sing.pret.* **myned**, 'to go' 5, 33, 38
aetham *1 pl.pret.* **myned**, 'to go' 9n, 21, 27, 41, 47

allawr *n.* 'altar' (*GPC* allor) 58
am *prep.* 'around' 16
a'm *combination of preverbal particle* **a** + *infixed 1 sing.pron.* '**m** 60
anadyl *n.* 'breath' (*GPC* anadl) 14
anhawd *adj.* 'not easy, difficult, hard' (*GPC* anodd) 32
Annwfyn (Annwuyn) *n.* 'otherworld, underworld' (*GPC* annwfn¹) 7n, 15n
ar¹ *prep.* 'on, upon' 27, 31
ar² *demonstrative pron.* 'the one who' (*GMW*, pp. 70–71) 38
Arthur *personal name* 21, 30, 33, 41, 47
aryant *adj.* 'silver, silvery' (*GPC* arian) 46
auyrdwl, afyrdwl *adj.* 'sad, wretched' (*GPC* afrddwl) 41, 47

bardwedi *n.* 'poetic prayer or invocation' (*GPC* gweddi) 8
beirw *3 sing.pres.indic. of* **berwi**, 'to boil' 17
bleidawr *pl. of n.* **bleid**, 'wolf' (*GPC* blaidd) 53
bras *adj.* 'thick, stout' 39
Brawt *n.* 'Judgement Day, the end of the world' (*GPC* brawd²) 8
brych *adj.* 'brindled, speckled' 39n
bu *3 sing.pret. of* **bot**, 'to be' 3
bwyf *1 sing.pres.subj. of* **bot**, 'to be' 60n
bwyt *n.* 'food' 17

kadwyn *n.* chain (*GPC* cadwyn) 6
kaer *n.* 'fort' 12, 22, 24, 28, 30, 34, 42, 48
Kaer Sidi *place name* Caer Sidi 3n, 10
canhwr *n.* 'a hundred men' (*GPC* cannwr) 31
karchar *n.* 'prison' 3
catwant *3 pl.pres.indic. of* **cadw**, 'to keep, guard' 46
ceinmyn *adj.* 'fine, splendid' 11n, 23
keni *3 sing.imperf.indic. of* **canu**, 'to sing' 7
cerd *n.* 'song, poem' 11; *pl.* **kyrd** 23n
ketwi *v.n.* 'to keep, to guard' (*GPC* cadwaf: cadw²) 6n
cledyf *n.* 'sword' 18
clot *n.* 'praise, fame' 11, 23
clywannor *3 pl. passive/impers. of* **clybot**, 'to hear' (*GPC* clywaf: clywed) 23n
cor *n.* 'host, company' (*GPC* côr¹) 49n
Crist *personal name* Christ 60
cunin *?collective n.* 'whelps, dogs' (*GPC* cunin²) 49n
kyfranc *n.* 'meeting, clash' (*GPC* cyfranc) 50n, 54
kygwng *n.* 'joint, knuckle, link in chain' (*GPC* cwgn, cygwng) 40
kylchwy *n.* 'round shield, belt, garment' 35n

kymyscetor *impers.pres.indic. of* **kymyscu**, 'to mix, blend' (*GMW*, pp. 120-21) 25n
kyn *conj.* 'before' (*GPC* cyn¹) 5
kynhen *n.* 'conflict, contention, battle' (*GPC* cynnen) 47
kynneir *n.* 'first utterance, song' (*GPC* cynnair) 13
kyweir *adj.* 'ordered, in good repair, maintained, prepared' (*GPC* cywair) 3
kywirwas *n.* 'loyal lad' 6

Defwy *river name?* 38n
deweint *n.* 'midnight, darkness' (*GPC* dewaint) 55n
diachor *adj.* 'irresistible, unstoppable' 52
diua *3 sing.pres.indic. of* **diua**, 'to destroy, devastate' (*GPC* difâf: difa) 57
diuant *n.* 'annihilation, void, death, ?eternity' (*GPC* difant¹) 58
doleu *pl. of n.* **dol**, 'meadow' (*GPC* dôl¹) 38
dros *prep.* 'over' (causing lenition) 2
drws *n.* 'door' 20
dwfyr *n.* 'water' (*GPC* dŵr, dwfr) 51
Dwy *n.* 'God' (*GPC* duw¹) 37n
dychnut *3 sing.pres.indic. of* ***dychnudaf**: **dychnudo**, 'to crowd together in a pack' 49, 53n
dyd *n.* 'day' (*GPC* dydd) 36, 44
dyrreith *3 sing.pret. of* **dyrein**, 'to run, hasten, return' (*GPC* dyreaf: dyrain) 10, 22, 28, 34, 42, 48

ebostol *n.* 'epistle, ?story' 4n
echwyd *n.* 'fresh water' (*GPC* echwydd²) 25
edewit *impers.imperf./pret. of* **adaw**, 'to leave (behind)' 19
ef *3 sing.masc. independent pron.* 'he' 5
eu *prefixed poss.pron. 3 pl.* 'their' 26(2), 35, 43

gan *prep.* 'with' 21, 33, 41, 47
ganet *impers.pret. of* **geni**, 'to be born' 37, 45
gloyw *adj.* 'bright, sparkling' 26
gobrynaf *1 sing.pres.indic. of* **gobrynu**, 'to set no value on' 29n, 35, 43
gochlywit *impers.imperf. of* **gochlywet**, 'to hear' 11n
gochyneuit *impers imperf. or pret. of* **gochynneu**, 'to kindle, light, heat' 14n
gofwy *n.* 'visit, journey' 41
gohen *n.* 'attack, course; aim, resolve' 43n
golud *n.* 'impediment' (*GPC* goludd) 34n
golychaf *1 sing.pres.indic. of* **golychu**, 'to praise' 1n, 69
goror *n.* 'border, side, rim' 16

gosgor *n.* 'retinue, company of soldiers' (*GPC* gosgordd) 26n
gwadawl *3 sing.pres./fut.indic. of* **gwadawl**, 'to endow, reward' (*GPC* gwaddolaf: gwaddoli) 60
gwawr *n.* 'dawn, brightness, light' 55n
gwdant *3 pl.pres.indic. of* **gwybot**, 'to know, ?to know of, be acquainted with' (see *GPC* gwn²: gwybod¹) 36, 39n, 44, 55
Gweir *personal name* Gwair 3n
gwelsynt *3 pl.pluperf. of* **gwelet**, 'to see' 30
gwidanhor, gwidyanhawr *3 pl. passive/impersonal of* **gwybot**, 'to know' (*possibly 3 pl. deponent here*) 50n, 54
gwin *n.* 'wine' 26
gwirawt *n.* 'drink' (*GPC* gwirod) 26
gwlat *n.* 'land, realm' 1
gwledic *n.* 'leader, lord' (lenited as object of conjugated verb, see *GMW*, p. 18) 1, 59
gwnaeth *3 sing.pret. of* **gwnaf: gwneuthur**, 'to do, make' 38
gwrhyt *n.* 'stature; manliness, bravery, might' (*GPC* gwryd$^{1-2}$) 30
gwrym *adj.* 'dark (-brown, -grey, -blue), dark-coloured' used here as a noun? (*GPC* gwrm) 16
gwydyr *n. or adj.* 'glass' (*GPC* gwydr) 30n
gwylyadur *n.* 'watcher, watchman' (*GPC* gwyliadur) 32
gwynt *n.* 'the wind' 51, 56

hynt *n.* 'path, course' 51, 56

i *1 sg. affixed pron.* 29, 59 **y** 35, 43
idaw *3 sing.masc. of conjugated prep.* **y**, 'to, into him, into it' (see *GMW*, p. 60) 18
idi *3 sing.fem. of conjugated prep.* **y**, 'to her, to it' (see *GMW*, p. 60), 5 (referring either to *Kaer Sidi* of l. 3 or to the *cadwyn dromlas* of l. 6), 9 (*referring to Kaer Sidi*)

llaes *adj.* 'loose, trailing, hanging' 35, 43
llaw *n.* 'hand' 19
llawyr *pl.n.* '?small or insignificant men' 29n, 35, 43
Lleawc *personal name or nickname* Lleog, 'destroyer or reader' 17n
lledas *3 sg.pret. of* **lledu**, 'to spread, extend' 2
lleferit *impers.pret. of* **llefaru**, 'to speak' 13
Lleminawc *personal name or nickname* Lleminog, '?the leaping or the keen one' (*GPC* llyminog) 19n
llen *n.* 'literature, learning, writings' (*GPC* llên) 29n
llethrit *adj.* 'bright, famous' (*GPC* llethrid¹) 21n

lloneit *n.* 'as much as something will hold, fullness', i.e. full load (*GPC* llond, llonaid) 9, 27, 33
lluch *adj.* 'brilliant, flashing' (*GPC* lluch¹) 18
llugyrn *sg./pl. n.* 'lamp(s), ?torch(es)' (*GPC* llugorn¹) 20
llvfyr *n.* 'a coward' (*GPC* llwfr) 17
llywyadur *n.* 'lord, ruler' (used of God) 29n

ma *n.* 'place' 57
Mandvy *place name* Mandwy/Manddwy 42n
mavr *adj.* 'great' 59
medwit *n.* 'mead-feast, honey-mead' 22n
meindyd *n. used adverbially* 'in the middle of the day' (*GPC* meinddydd, meinydd¹) 37, 45
mererit *n.* 'pearl(s)' 16
mil *n.* 'animal' 46
mor *n.* 'sea' (*GPC* môr¹) 27, 51
morvyn *n.* 'maiden' 14
muchyd *n.* 'jet' (*GPC* muchudd) 25
mundi *Latin, gen.sg. of* **mundus**, 'world' 2
myneich *pl. of n.* **mynach**, 'monk' 49, 53
mynut *n.* 'demeanour, manner' (*GPC* mynud²) 15
mur *n.* 'wall, rampart' 31

na *neg. particle* 'not' 60
namyn *prep.* 'except, save' (see *GMW*, p. 232) 10, 22, 28, 34, 42, 48
nav *num.* 'nine' 14
neb *pron.* 'someone' (with a following negative, see *GMW*, p. 173) 5
neu¹, neut *preverbal particle* (causing lenition, *GMW*, pp. 169–70) 11, 15n, 23
neu² *conj.* (causing lenition, *GPC* neu¹) 'or' 56
ni *1 pl. affixed pron.* 9n, 21, 27, 41, 47
noc *conj.* 'than' (see *GPC* no¹, nog¹) 5
ny *negative preverbal particle* (*GMW*, p. 173) 10, 17(2), 22, 28, 29, 30, 34, 35, 36, 39, 42, 43, 44, 48, 55 **nyt** 5, 38

o *prep.* 'from' 1, 22, 28, 34, 42, 48 'by, by means of' 14 'because of' 50, 54
Ochren *place name* 48n
oed *3 sing.imperf.indic. of* **bot**, 'to be' (used here as a copula) 32
o'r *a combination of prep.* **o**, 'from; of, about, concerning' (*GPC* o¹ 9c) + *definite article* '**r** 13n

pan¹ *conj.* 'that' (causing lenition; *GPC* pan⁴, *GMW*, pp. 79–80) 13

pan² *conj.* 'when' 21, 41, 47
pan³ *interrogative particle* 'how? why?' (*GPC* pan⁴ d) 55n
parahawt *3 sing.pres. of* **parhau**, 'to continue' 8n
pedyrychwelyt *adj.* '?revolving [to face] the four directions, perfectly or completely revolving' (*GPC* pedrychwelid) 12n
pedryuan, pedryfan *n. or adj.* 'four quarters, ends or corners, four pinnacles or turrets; four-cornered, four-turreted, square' (*GPC* pedryfan) 12n, 24
peir *n.* 'cauldron' (*GPC* pair¹) 13, 15
pen *n.* 'head, chief, ruler, lord' 15n, 44n, 46
pendeuic, pendefic *n.* 'ruler, sovereign' (*GPC* pendefig) 1, 59
pennaeth *n.* 'chieftainship, dominion, rule' (*GPC* pennaeth 2) 2
penrwy *n.* 'collar, yoke, halter' (*GPC* penrhwy) 39
perchen *n.* 'owner, lord' 45
peridyd *verbal form from* **paraf: peri**, 'to create' 36n, 44
pet *interrogative adv.* 'how many?' (*GPC* ped², *GMW*, pp. 78–79), 58(2)
plawd *3 sing.pres.indic. of a defective vb.* 'strikes, beats' (borrowing from Latin *?plaud(et)*, see *GPC* plawdd) 57n
porth *n.* 'gate' 20
preideu *pl. of n.* **preid**, 'flock; plunder, booty' (*GPC* praidd) 7n
Pryderi *personal name* Pryderi 4n
Prytwen *name of Arthur's ship* Prydwen 9n, 27, 33
pwy *interrogative pron.* 'who(m)' (*GPC* pwy¹ 1a) 36, 38; 'what?' (*GPC* pwy¹ 2) 15, 56(2)
Pwyll *personal name* Pwyll 4n
py *interrogative or relative adj.* (causing lenition, *GMW*, p. 21) 'which, what' (*GPC* pa¹, py¹, *GMW*, p. 75) 36, 44, 45, 46, 46, 57(2) **py awr** 'what hour, when' 37, 45
pybyrdor *n.* 'strong door, stout defence' 24n

'r *definite article* 'the' (a form used in combinations, *GMW*, p. 24) 6
rac *prep.* 'before, in front of; because of, on account of' (*GPC* rhag, *GMW*, pp. 206–07) 7n, 20, 26
ri *n.* 'king, lord' (*GPC* rhi¹) 1n
rigor *Latin* 'stiffness, rigidity' 28n
ry *preverbal perfective particle* (*GPC* rhy², causing lenition, see *GMW*, p. 62) 2, 17, 18
rynnawd *n.* 'rush, attack' (*GPC* rhynnawdd) 56

sant *n.* 'saint' 58
seith *num.* 'seven' 10n, 22, 28, 34, 40, 42, 48
seui *3 sing.imperf.indic. of* **seuyll**, 'to stand' (*GPC* safaf: sefyll) 31

tan *n.* 'fire' (*GPC* tân¹) 52
tir *n.* 'land' 57
tost *adj.* 'sad, troubled' (used adverbially without *yn*; *GPC* tost²) 7
tra *prep.* 'beyond' 30
traeth *n.* '? region, area, extent, tract' (see *GPC* traeth¹) 2
trafferth *n.* 'trouble, tribulation' 21
tri *num.* 'three' 9, 27, 31, 33
trist *adj.* 'sad, downhearted, anxious' 60n
tromlas *fem. form of adj.* **trymlas**, 'heavy and grey' (*GPC* glas 3c) 6n
trvy *prep.* 'through, according to' (see *GPC* trwy¹ f) 4
tvrvf *n.* 'tumult, commotion' (*GPC* twrf) 52
tyghit *impers.imperf. or pret. of* **tyghu**, 'to destine, preordain' (*GPC* tyngu) 17
tyrchit *impers.imperf. or pret. of* **tyrchu**, 'to dig, pierce, thrust into' 18

val *prep.* 'like' (*GPC* fel, fal) 49, 53
udyd *pl. of n.* **ud**, 'lord, master' (*GPC* udd) 50n, 54
vfel *n.* 'spark' (*GPC* ufel) 52
Vffern *n.* 'Hell' 20
ugein, vgeint *num.* 'twenty' (*GPC* ugain, ugaint) 21, 40
vn *num.* 'one' 51(2), 52

vy *3 pl. affixed pron.* 36, 39
vyf *1 sing.pres. of* **bot**, 'to be' 11, 23

y¹ *prefixed poss.pron. 3 sing.masc.* 'his, its' (causing lenition) 2, 15, 16, 39, 40, 46, 56(2)
y² *prefixed poss.pron. 3 sing.fem* 'her, its' 31
y³ *prep.* 'to, into' *combined with the article* y'r 6
y⁴ *see* **i**
ych *n.* 'ox' 39
yd, y *preverbal particle* (*GPC* ydd¹, y²) 9, 19, 27, 33, 37, 45
yg¹ *see* **yn¹**
yg² *prefixed poss.pron. 1 sing.* 'my' (before k-, g- causing nasal mutation, *GPC* fy¹) 13
ymadravd *v.n.* 'to speak, converse, communicate' (*GPC* ymadroddaf: ymadroddi) 32
ymeindyd *combination of* **yn¹** + **meindyd** (see above)
yn¹ *prep.* (*GPC* yn¹, causing nasal mutation, see *GMW*, p. 21) 'in' 19, 40, 58 **yg** (before k-) 3, 12, 24 **ym** (combined with m-) 37, 45
yn² *poss.pron. 1 pl.* (*GPC* ein, an, yn) 'our' 8
ynys *n.* 'island' 24

yr *definite article* 'the' 39
yscar *3 sing.pres.indic. of* **ysgaru**, 'to separate, divide' 55
yt¹ *preverbal particle* (causing lenition, *GPC* yd¹) 7
yt² *prep.* 'until' 8n

CHAPTER 5

Poems in Other Manuscripts

Most of the oldest texts of poetry composed in Welsh before 1282 are preserved in the five manuscripts termed by Daniel Huws the 'Five Ancient Books of Wales': the Black Book of Carmarthen, the Book of Taliesin, the Book of Aneirin, the Hendregadredd Manuscript and the Red Book of Hergest.[1] There are, however, many other medieval and early modern manuscripts which contain copies of this poetry, and a few which have poems which are not found in the main collections. Some of these are texts which have been lost from the five earlier manuscripts. Others may never have been collected by their compilers but have survived in copies made from other collections now lost.

Three such texts which feature Arthur and one which may contain a reference to him are presented in this chapter.

The Dialogue of Arthur and the Eagle

Of all the poems examined in this volume, this one has the most complicated textual history, testifying to its use over many generations as a work to be both performed and read. In a lengthy series of *englynion milwr*, a conversation between Arthur and his nephew, Eliwlad, is used as a framework for religious instruction. Didactic dialogues in verse, often set in a dramatic situation, appear to have been popular in early medieval Wales.[2] In this example, the deceased Eliwlad, in the form of an eagle perched at the top of an oak tree, gradually reveals his identity and then instructs his questioner in spiritual matters. Whilst there is a parallel in the scene featuring Gwydion and his nephew, Lleu, transformed into an eagle in the Fourth Branch of the *Mabinogi*,[3] it cannot be

---

[1] See Daniel Huws, 'Five Ancient Books of Wales' in *MWM*, pp. 65–83.
[2] For other examples of the genre and for the possibility that its source was the saga *englynion* dialogues, see Jenny Rowland, 'Genres' in *EWP*, pp. 197–200. For parallels, see Sims-Williams, 'Arthurian Poems', p. 58.
[3] See *Mab*, pp. 62–63, and on the *englynion* addressed by Math to the Eagle, see *Math* l. 520n.

assumed that this dialogue is based on a developed tale.[4] The characterisation of Arthur as 'a religiously uneducated, but sympathetic, pagan seeking enlightenment' is two-dimensional at best,[5] but the fact that he is portrayed as a warrior, rather than a king or an emperor, and associated with Cornwall, makes the poem of interest to literary historians and Arthurian scholars alike.

The earliest surviving copy of the text is found in Oxford Jesus College MS 20, kept at the Bodleian Library.[6] Most of the manuscript was written by an anonymous scribe in a style of handwriting which can be dated to the second half of the fourteenth century.[7] It opens with a collection of seven instructional poems in *englyn* metre, followed by a selection of narrative and religious prose texts and genealogical tracts. There are indications that a number of these texts were produced, or at least copied, in south Wales,[8] whilst some have been shown to descend from a source which was also used by the scribes of the White Book of Rhydderch and the Red Book of Hergest, the two great anthologies of medieval Welsh prose compiled in south Wales at about the same time as Jesus College MS 20.[9] There is no evidence to show, however, that the Dialogue is derived from that source, and it does not seem to have any particular geographical affiliation.

Its first editor, Ifor Williams, has shown that although its exemplar was no older than the thirteenth century, some of its linguistic forms like *dyw* and *nyw*, and imperfect forms in *-i*, suggest a manuscript tradition going back at least another hundred years.[10] The poem was written using medieval Welsh spelling but some errors indicate that the scribe was struggling with an orthography

---

[4] See Jenny Rowland, 'The Prose Setting of the Early Welsh Englynion Chwedlonol', *Eriu*, 36 (1985), 29–43.

[5] Sims-Williams, 'Arthurian Poems', p. 57, and for a comparison with the portrayal of Arthur in the Cambro-Latin Saints' Lives, where Arthur, unlike other secular figures who are portrayed as negative and hostile towards the saints, is used in the role of 'a slow-witted but well-intentioned questioner'; see *AMWL*, pp. 37–47, 123–24.

[6] A digital copy can be viewed on the 'Early Manuscripts at Oxford University' website at <http://image.ox.ac.uk/list?collection=jesus>.

[7] For information about the manuscript, see <www.rhyddiaithganoloesol.caerdydd.ac.uk>.

[8] The genealogies display a particular interest in figures from south Wales. For the genealogies see P. C. Bartrum, *Early Welsh Genealogical Tracts* (Cardiff: University of Wales Press, 1966), pp. 41–42. See also *Englynion y Clywaid*, a series of stanzas based on a collection of proverbs, many of which are assigned to heroes named in the southern tale *Culhwch ac Olwen*, and saints associated with the south.

[9] This includes the incomplete text of the Romance of Owein (see *Owein, or Chwedyl Iarlles y Ffynnawn [Owein]*, ed. by R. L. Thomson (Dublin: Institute for Advanced Studies, 1968), p. xvi), and five of the *englynion* series, described by modern scholars as gnomic and nature poems (see *EWGNP* II–V, VIII).

[10] Ifor Williams, 'Ymddiddan Arthur a'r Eryr', *Bulletin of the Board of Celtic Studies*, 2 (1923–1925), 269–86. For a more modern edition see *Blodeugerdd Barddas o Ganu Crefyddol Cynnar [BBGCC]*, ed. by Marged Haycock (Swansea: Barddas Publications, 1995), no. 30.

and also possibly a script that was alien to him. It opens the collection and is headed by a rubric added by the main scribe in red ink: *Llyma y mod y treythir o eglynnon yr eryr,* 'This is the way the Stanzas of the Eagle are declared'. At the end of forty-seven stanzas, the scribe has added, using the same ink as the poem itself, *Ac velly y teruyna eglynyon yr eryr,* 'And this is how the Stanzas of the Eagle terminate'.[11] The last five stanzas, however, belong to the beginning of another poem containing religious instruction which must have followed it in an earlier copy.[12]

Other versions of the poem survive in later manuscripts. Williams lists nine of these, but thirty have now been discovered, ranging in date from the late fifteenth century to the late eighteenth century.[13] In many of these, the language of the text has been modernised, unintelligible forms have been emended and lines have been reworked, but close comparison shows that they derive from a source or sources contemporary with that of Jesus College MS 20 but different from it. The earliest is NLW Peniarth MS 54, a collection of fourteenth- and fifteenth-century *cywyddau*, many of them autograph texts, compiled in south-east Wales c. 1475.[14] The poem is also listed in an index to the lost White Book of Hergest, another substantial collection of poetry compiled by Lewys Glyn Cothi in north-east Wales in the same period,[15] and survives in an early seventeenth-century copy probably made by Tudur Owen of Dugoed, an amanuensis of John Davies of Mallwyd.[16] At least eleven versions written by bards, antiquaries and humanist scholars date to the late sixteenth and early seventeenth centuries.[17]

---

[11] This suggests that the rubrics were present in the scribe's exemplar. It is the second rubric which probably caused the scribe to write in red ink *Eglynion yr eryr* instead of *Eglynion yr eiry* (Stanzas of the Snow) as a title for the following poem.

[12] It is one of a group of texts from various manuscripts including the Black Book of Carmarthen, known as *Kyssul Adaon* (The Advice of Addaon), introduced by a stanza asking *Pa beth orau rac eneit?* ('What is best for the soul?'); see *EWSP*, pp. 287–89.

[13] Many of these are listed in *Maldwyn, The Index to Welsh Poetry in Manuscript* <http://maldwyn.llgc.org.uk>. A new edition of the whole poem is yet to be compiled.

[14] NLW Peniarth MS 54A i, pp. 168–75. On the MS see *MWM*, pp. 95–96. A number of its scribes were poets themselves but the hand which copied the Dialogue has not been identified.

[15] On the White Book, which was destroyed by fire in 1810, see Huws, 'Transmission', p. 96.

[16] BL Add 14976, ff. 266^v–70^r. On the MS, see Huws, 'John Davies and his Manuscripts' in *Dr John Davies of Mallwyd: Welsh Renaissance Scholar*, ed. by Ceri Davies (Cardiff: University of Wales Press, 2004), pp. 88–120 (pp. 100, 110).

[17] These MSS are Cardiff 2.83 (unknown, c. 1550), pp. 89–92; NLW Peniarth 96 (Lewys Dwnn, 1565x1616), pp. 224–31; Peniarth 99 (William Salesbury, before 1576), pp. 557–64; Peniarth 77 (a copy of Peniarth 99 made by Thomas Wiliems, 1576), pp. 295–300; NLW Gwyneddon 3 (Jasper Gryffyth, 1590), ff. 191^v–93^v; Peniarth 65 (Owen John, late sixteenth century), pp. 121–27; Peniarth 111 (John Jones, Gellilyfdy, c. 1610), pp. 77–86; NLW Llanstephan 41 (Roger Williams, c. 1610–1630), pp. 202–06; Llanstephan 52 (unknown, post-1629), pp. 15–22; NLW 5268 (unknown, 1600–1650), pp. 461–63; Peniarth 206 (unknown, 1600–1650), pp. 209–16. On the compilers of these manuscripts, see Graham C. G. Thomas,

A close study of the order and variants of these versions suggests that they were copied from the same source or sources as those of the previous century, but almost all are independent of each other. The Dialogue seems to have been popular in the seventeenth and eighteenth centuries also, appearing in a wide range of manuscripts from all over Wales. These versions of the poem have a different ending from that of Jesus MS 20, finishing with six stanzas on the virtues of the Mass which seem to have been adapted for this dialogue from another series.[18] More significantly, after the tenth stanza there are in most of these manuscripts four *englynion* not found in Jesus MS 20 which appear to be crucial to the structural development of the poem. It is in these stanzas that Arthur's questioning shifts from his concern with the identity of the Eagle to the best way of finding salvation. He offers to use force to rescue his nephew from death.[19] This gives the poet an opportunity to contrast Arthur's military might with the power of God. The emphasis in most of the following thirty-two stanzas is on imparting basic Christian knowledge. The *englynion* fall into a very repetitive and mechanical pattern, with Arthur's questions alternating with the Eagle's answers.

Little is disclosed in the poem about Eliwlad apart from his full name, Eliwlad son of Madog ap Uthr, and his great eloquence, which is praised by Arthur.[20] The knowledgeable Eagle seems to bear no relation to the warrior figure referred to by the thirteenth-century poet Bleddyn Fardd (see Chapter 3 above). There is no evidence either of the influence of Geoffrey of Monmouth, who is thought to have been the first to connect Arthur and Uthr as father and son. The picture that emerges of Arthur himself, from the epithets and phrases used by the Eagle to describe him, is of an active, heroic figure accompanied by his men:[21]

'From Manuscript to Print I. Manuscript' in *A Guide to Welsh Literature c. 1530–1700*, ed. by R. Geraint Gruffydd (Cardiff: University of Wales Press, 1997), pp. 241–62.

[18] They belong to a body of floating verses also found in other series of instructional *englynion*, including a short dialogue involving St Tysul in the Book of the Anchorite (Jesus College MS 119), a manuscript dated to 1346: see *The Elucidarium and Other Tracts in Welsh from Llyvyr Ackyr Llandewivrevi AD 1346 (Jesus College M.S. 119)*, ed. by J. Morris Jones and John Rhŷs (Oxford: Clarendon Press, 1894), p. 151. They appear to have remained popular even after the Reformation when the word *offeren*, 'mass', was replaced by *gwasanaeth Sul*, 'Sunday service'.

[19] As Padel has suggested, this probably reflects traditions of Arthur and his men rescuing prisoners, as in *Culhwch ac Olwen* and *Preideu Annwn*; see *AMWL*, p. 66.

[20] It is interesting that he is named in the mid-fifteenth century list, the Twenty-four Knights of Arthur's Court, as one of the Three Golden-Tongued Knights: 'and there was neither king nor lord to whom those came who did to listen to them; and whatever quest they sought, they wished for and obtained it, either willingly or unwillingly'; see *TYP*, pp. 266–67.

[21] Although collocations are rare, these epithets are similar in style and syntax to those used in the court poetry, betraying, perhaps, the bardic origins of the poem.

> Arthur, bellglot ordiwes,
> arth llu, llewenyd achles ...
>
> Arthur, bellglot engyhynt,
> arth llu, llew[e]nyd dremynt ...
>
> Arthur, gl[edy]faw*t* aruthyr,
> ny seif dy alon rac dy ruthyr ...
>
> Arthur, penn kadoed Kernyw,
> arderchawc luydawc lyw ...
>
> Oh Arthur, one who gains far-flung fame,
> hero [lit. bear] of a host, protector of merriment ...
>
> Oh Arthur, one whose course [brings] far-flung fame,
> bear of a host, of joyful appearance ...
>
> Oh Arthur, ferocious one armed with a sword,
> your enemies do not withstand your attack ...
>
> Oh Arthur, chief of the hosts/battles of Cornwall,
> splendid leader with many armies ...

As Sims-Williams has shown, the phrase *penn kadoed Kernyw* in the thirty-fourth stanza recalls the *dux bellorum*, 'leader of battles', of *Historia Brittonum*, and the Cornish setting is reminiscent of *Culhwch ac Olwen*.[22] Arthur presents himself as a poet in the opening line of the series, but it is difficult to tell whether this bears any relationship to traditions represented in the Triads and *Culhwch ac Olwen*.[23] Unlike the authors of most of the other poems which have been outlined in this book, this poet does not aim to impress or entertain his listeners with his knowledge of traditional lore. It appears, rather, that Arthur has been recruited by him simply on the basis of his popularity as a vehicle for religious instruction.

The edition below consists of the first ten stanzas of the series from Jesus College MS 20, f. 1, where the identity of the Eagle is established, followed by the four stanzas which convey Arthur's reaction to his nephew's plight, which are found only in the later manuscripts.[24]

---

[22] 'Arthurian Poems', p. 58, and O. J. Padel, 'Geoffrey of Monmouth and Cornwall', *Cambridge Medieval Celtic Studies*, 8 (1984), 19–20. Stanza 34 is an exception in the second part of the poem, which otherwise reveals very little about Arthur.
[23] See further Bromwich, *TYP*, pp. 22–23.
[24] The first page of the text shows signs of wear, being the first page of the manuscript. Some letters have been overwritten by a later hand, others are illegible. This is indicated in the transcript with square brackets.

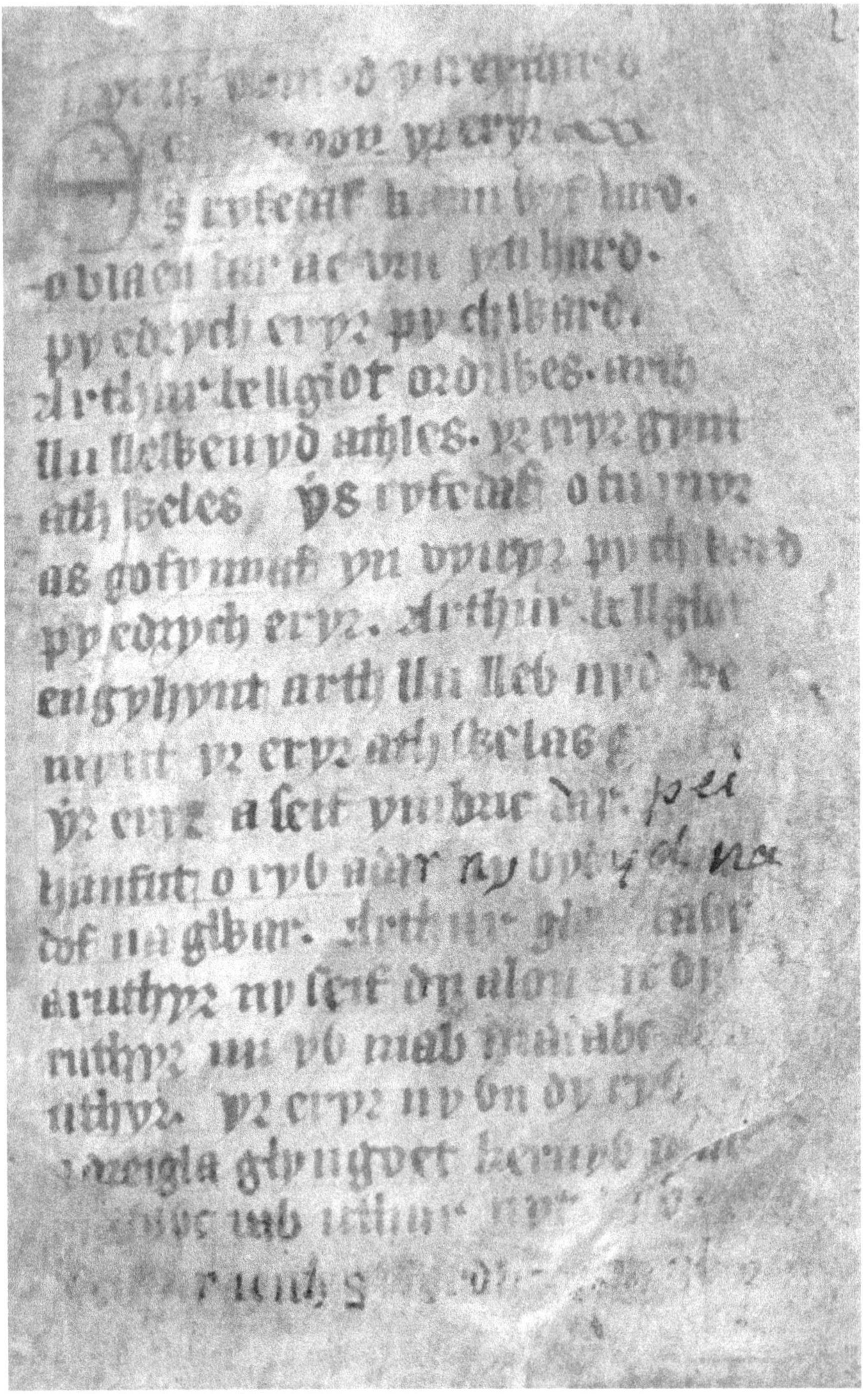

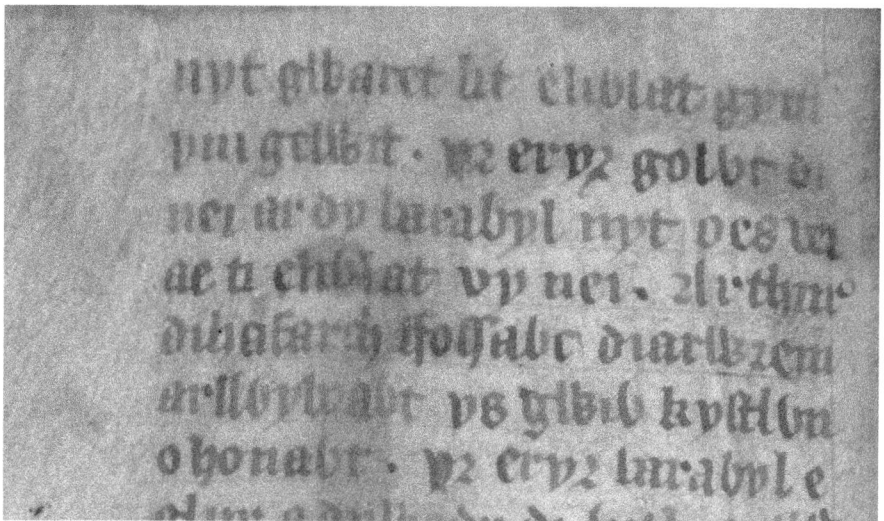

Fig. 5.1: Jesus College MS 20, f. 1ʳ⁻ᵛ.

Es ryfedaf kann wyf bard. | o vlaen dar ae vric yn hard. | py edrych eryr py chward. | Arthur bellglot ordiwes. arth | llu llewenyd achles. yr eryr gynt | ath weles Ys ryfedaf o tu myr | as gofynnaf yn vyvyr py chward | py edrych eryr. Arthur bellglot | engyhynt arth llu lleỽ[ ]nyd dre|mynt yr eryr ath welas gynt. | Yr eryr a seif ym bric dar. [pei] | hanfut o ryỽ ada[r ny] byd[yd na] | dof na gwar. Arthur, gl[ ]fawc | aruthyr ny seif dy alon [ ]c dy | ruthyr mi yw mab madawc [ ] | uthyr. Yr eryr ny ỽn dy ryỽ | a dreigla glyngoet kernyỽ [ ] |[ ]ỽc uab uthur, nyt [ ] ỽ [ ]r ieith g[ ]d[ ] || nyt gwaret lit eliwlat gynt | ym gelwit. Yr eryr golỽc di|uei ar dy barabyl nyt oes vei | ae ti eliỽlat vy nei. Arthur | dihafarch ffossawc diarwrein | arllỽybraỽt ys gwiỽ kystlỽn | ohonaỽt.

        Es ryfedaf, kan wyf bard
        o vlaen dar a'e *b*ric yn hard:
        py edrych Eryr, py chward?

4   Arthur, bellglot ordiwes,
        arth llu, lleỽenyd achles,
        Yr Eryr gynt a'th weles!

        Ys ryfedaf o tu myr,
8   as gofynnaf yn vyvyr:
        py chward, py edrych Eryr?

        Arthur, bellglot engyhynt,
        arth llu, llew[e]nyd dremynt,
12   Yr Eryr a'th welas gynt!

Yr Eryr a seif ym bric dar:
[pei] hanfut o ry(v ada[r,
ny] byd[ut na] dof na gwar!

16   Arthur, gl[edy]faw*t* aruthyr,
ny seif dy alon rac dy ruthyr:
mi yw mab Madawc [uab] Uthyr.

Yr Eryr (ny (vn dy ry(v),
20   a dreigla glyngoet Kerny(v:
[mab Mada](vc uab Uthur, nyt [by](v.

[Arthu]r, ieith g[yfyr]d[elit,
arth gwyr], nyt gwaret lit:
24   Eliwlat gynt y'm gelwit.

Yr Eryr golwc diuei,
ar dy barabyl nyt oes vei,
ae ti Eliwlat, vy nei?

28   Arthur dihafarch ffossaw*t*,
diarw[*y*]rein arllwybrawt:
ys gwiw kystlwn ohonawt.

I wonder at it, since I am a poet
[standing] before an oak tree whose top is beautiful:
why does the Eagle stare, why does [it] laugh?

4   Oh Arthur, one who gains far-flung fame,
bear of a host, protector of merriment,
The Eagle saw you previously!

I wonder at it beside the seas,
8   I ask it thoughtfully:
why does the Eagle laugh, why does [it] stare?

Oh Arthur, one whose course [brings] far-flung fame,
bear of a host, of merry appearance,
12   The Eagle saw you previously!

Oh Eagle who stands at the top of the oak tree:
if you were descended from a species/lineage of birds,
you would not be tame or gentle!

16   Oh Arthur of the ferocious sword-stroke,
your enemies do not withstand your attack;
I am the son of Madog son of Uthr.

Oh Eagle (I do not know your species/lineage)
20 who frequents the valley-wood of Cornwall:
the son of Madog son of Uthr is not alive.

Oh Arthur, ? one whose language is splendid,
bear of warriors, ??
24 Eliwlad was I called previously.

Oh Eagle of faultless vision,
with your power of speech there is no fault,
can *you* be Eliwlad my nephew?

28 Oh Arthur, courageous in battle,
leaving] a swathe of fallen [enemies]:
it is excellent to claim kinship by you.

1 **Es ryfedaf** Later MSS *ys*. *Es* is also found as an orthographical variant of *ys* at the beginning of a poem in the Hendregadredd Manuscript; see *CBT* II 21.1, and cf. III poem 18 *essym*, *esid*. Here it can be understood as a rare preverbal particle found mostly in early poetry; see *GMW*, p. 173. It may contain the infixed object pronoun 3 sing. -*s* (see *GPC* ys²), as *ryfedu* may have been a transitive as well as an intransitive verb in this period; see *GPC*. The pronoun probably refers to the Eagle named in line 3.
kann wyf The reading *kyd bwyf*, 'although I may be', found in some of the later MSS, along with the variant *kynn bwyf* (*GPC* cyd³, cyn³), is also possible.
2 **o vlaen dar** Later MSS *ar vlaen*. Both can be used idiomatically to mean 'before, in front of', which would make sense if the line refers to Arthur standing in front of the tree. *Ar vlaen* can also be understood as 'on the tip of', which gives a better meaning if the line refers to the Eagle; cf. *EWSP*, p. 203, *Ban ganhont cogev ar blaen guit guiw*, 'When cuckoos sing on the tips of fair trees'.
a'e bric yn hard J 20 and some of the later MSS have *a'e vric*. If the lenition to *bric* is correct, it shows that the infixed possessive pronoun 'e is masculine and must therefore refer to *blaen* (masc.), not *dar* (fem.).
3 **py edrych Eryr, py chward?** Later MSS *pa*. For another example of *py*, *pa* used substantivally, see above, *Pa gur*, 5n. 'What' is possible for *py* here, as *edrych* and *chwerthin* are both transitive and intransitive verbs in this period: 'at what does the Eagle look, at what does it laugh?'. 'Why' leads to a better meaning, however, in the light of the Eagle's response in the next verse; see *GMW*, p. 76 n. 2. This line is understood as reported speech; cf. l. 9 below.
4 **Arthur, bellglot ordiwes** The phrase *pellglot ordiwes*, lit. 'gaining far-fame', is used to describe Arthur. (For the lenition of a phrase in apposition to a personal name here and in ll. 10 and 16, see *GMW*, p. 15.) The compound noun consists of *pell*, 'far, distant (in place or time)' + *clot*, 'praise, fame', meaning 'fame from afar' or 'long-lasting fame' (for the only other example, see *CBT* III

3.168). *Pellglot* is in a genitival relationship to the verb noun *gordiwes*, a variant of *godiwes* (see *GPC* goddiweddaf), used here with the meaning 'to win, attain, obtain'. For similar combinations in the court poetry, see *CBT* V 5.55, *fra6t oddiwes clod*, 'keen to gain fame', VII 13.22, *clod dirper*, 'deserving praise', II 14.35, *clot obryn*, 'worthy of praise'.

5 **arth llu** For examples of the juxtaposition of *Arthur* and *arth* in the work of the Poets of the Princes, see Chapter 3 above.

llewenyd achles Another phrase to describe Arthur. The main element is *achles*, 'refuge, protection', cf. *CBT* III 21.88, *kerteu achles*, 'protector of poetry', and IV 5.41, *tud achles*, 'protector of [his] people'.

6 **Yr Eryr gynt a'th weles** The Eagle responds to Arthur's question but appears to be speaking about himself using the third person.

7 **o tu myr** Many of the later MSS have *o dy myr*, an error perhaps for the reading found in J 20 and some others, which can be understood as the prepositional phrase *o du*, '(from) beside'; cf. *CBT* II 1.165, *Kedwyr o du myr, o du morlann uchel*, 'Warriors beside the seas, beside the high shore'. Eagles are associated with the sea in the Welsh saga poetry and in the court poetry; cf. *EWSP* 'Canu Heledd' 38, *Eryr Eli echeidw myr*, 'The eagle of Eli watches over the seas'.

8 **as gofynnaf** The later MSS have a variety of forms prefixing the verb, including *ys, a'th, o'th*. As this stanza follows the same pattern as the first in the series, it is more likely that a 3 sing. pronoun would be used to refer to the Eagle rather than a 2 sing. pronoun. For the preverbal particle *as*, which is similar in form to *ys*, see *GPC* as¹.

10 **pellglot engyhynt** The word *engyhynt* appears to contain the element *hynt*, 'course, journey' (*GPC*). It is otherwise known only from a poem by Cynddelw: *CBT* III 29.13, *Ban wnaeth y angert engyhynt y'w glod*, 'when his ferocity caused a course for his fame [to spread]'. The form is clearly unknown to the scribes of the later MSS, who present a range of alternatives.

11 **llew[e]nyd dremynt** The first word contains one of the many gaps caused by wear to the parchment of J 20, which can be restored from the later manuscripts. The lenition of *tremynt* is caused by *llewenyd* as a preceding genitive, lit. 'appearance of joyfulness'.

13 **Yr Eryr a seif ym bric dar** Later MSS *ar vlaen dar*. It is interesting to note that the prepositional phrase used to describe the position of the eagle on the oak tree in the Fourth Branch of the *Mabinogi* is *ym mlaen*; see *Math*, ll. 516, 529. This line has eight syllables rather than the usual seven.

14–15 **[pei] hanfut ... [ny] byd[ut]** ... Some of the gaps in J 20's text have been filled by a later hand. This is the case with the verbal form *bydut*, but the scribe, like those of some of the later manuscripts, has modernised the 2 sing.imperf. subj. ending *-ud* to *-yd*.

Most of the disclosure of information in this section is led by the Eagle's voluntary revelations, but here Arthur spontaneously shows his suspicion that the Eagle is not what he seems.

16   **Arthur, gl[edy]faw*t* aruthyr** J 20 *gl[ ]fawc*, later MSS *gleddyfod, glyfyddod, gleddyddod*. (On the variant forms of *cleddyf*, caused by metathesis, see *GPC*.) It is possible that the scribe of J 20 struggled to differentiate between *-t* and *-c* in his exemplar; cf. l. 28 below. The noun *cleddyfod*, 'sword-stroke', gives a more straightforward meaning with *aruthr* than the adjective *cleddyfog*, 'armed with a sword'. Note the play here on *Arthur* and *aruthr*, itself derivative of *uthr*, 'terrible'; cf. the personal name with which it rhymes in line 18.

17   **ny seif dy alon rac dy ruthyr** The later MSS have the prepositions *dan* or *gan*, but *rac* gives a better meaning with *sefyll*, 'to stand one's ground (in battle)'; cf. *CBT* VII 24.117–18, *Seuis yn ryuel ... rac estra6n geneddyl*, 'He stood fast in battle ... against a foreign nation'. Even if *ruthyr* is read as a monosyllabic word (*GPC rhuthr*), this line is too long by a syllable unless the first *dy* is omitted.

18   **Madawc vab Uthyr** Apart from this poem, Madog son of Uthr (and thus Arthur's brother or half-brother) occurs in a fragment of a poem in the Book of Taliesin, *LPBT* no. 20, *Madawc Drut*. For another possible reference to him, see Chapter 3 above.

20   **a dreigla glyngoet Kernyw** The author probably did not have any specific Cornish place in mind, but if he did, then the wooded Glynn valley, near Bodmin, is the likeliest candidate. Its name contains one of the few instances of Cornish **glynn*, 'a large valley'; see Oliver Padel, *Cornish Place-Name Elements* (Nottingham: English Place-name Society, 1985), pp. 104–05.

22   **ieith g[yfyr]d[elit]** The second word is only partially legible in J 20 but the later MSS have variants such as *gyferddelid, gyfarddilid, gyfarddelid*. The adjective *cyfrdelid* (see *GPC*) used by the court poets seems a possible original reading, though this gives a short line of only six syllables. It can be read as an adjective, 'beautiful, dignified, splendid', mutated after a fem. noun, 'Arthur, one whose language is splendid', perhaps a reference to Arthur as a poet. It could also be an inversion as in previous phrases used in apposition to Arthur's name, 'Arthur, one who is splendid to his people', with *iaith* used in a more unusual sense for 'a community of people having the same language, nation, race, tribe' (*GPC*). A seven-syllable line is possible if *ieith* is emended to *cyfiaith*, 'language, people speaking the same language, fellow-countrymen' (*GPC*).

23   **[arth gwyr], nyt gwaret lit** The first part of the line has been reconstructed following the pattern of other stanzas. The second part is difficult to interpret as it stands and is short of a syllable. The readings provided by the scribes of the later MSS, *nid gwareddog dy lid*, 'not merciful is your wrath', and *nid gwaradwyddid*, 'it is not a disgrace' (*GPC gwaradwyddyd*), are not satisfactory and are probably attempts to interpret a corrupt text. There is no evident reason

for the lenition of *llit* after the *gwaret*, unless a preposition, pronoun or prefix has been omitted between the two words. One possibility is *Nyt gwaret [o'th] lit*, '[there is] no deliverance from your wrath'. Alternatively, if *gwaret*, which is a verb noun as well as a noun (see *GPC*), could be understood as a present participle, *nyt gwaret [dy] lit* could be understood as 'not sparing is your anger'. Another possibility is that the final word is *edlit*, 'regret, sorrow; extreme anger' (*GPC*), giving the meaning 'sorrow/anger gives no deliverance/relief'.

25   **golwc diuei** This probably refers to the Eagle's perfect eyesight, but 'perfect appearance' is also possible, cf. below Melwas l.18n.

26   **ar dy barabyl** The later MSS have a synonymous phrase, *ar d'ymadrodd*, the result of faulty memory perhaps, or the rewriting of a corrupt line. The final rhyme of lines 25–26 is weak.

27   **ae ti Eliwlat** For another example of an identifying question with the same emphatic word order, see *ae ti Yscolan* (*EWSP*, p. 465).

vy nei Arthur finally acknowledges what the Eagle already knew, that he is Eliwlad's uncle.

28   **fossawt** J 20 *fossawc*, with scribal confusion of *-c* and *-t*; but the rhyme shows the correct reading, cf. *gledyfawc* for *gledyfawt* in l. 16 above. The scribes of the later MSS have the lenited form of *gossod*, a synonym of *fossawt*, but which does not rhyme with *arllwybrawt* in the following line.

29   **diarw[y]rein arllwybrawt** Both are hapax forms. *Diarwyrein* is interpreted by Ifor Williams as an adjective consisting of the negative prefix *di-* and the verbal noun *arwyrein*, 'to rise, raise, praise', hence 'non-rising', i.e. 'fallen, prostrate' (*GPC* diarwyrain). *Arllwybrawt* is assumed to be the same as *arllwybr*, 'path, track, wake', with the noun-suffix *-awt*. It is difficult to be certain of the meaning of the phrase, but it may be an epithet, '[leaving] a swathe of fallen [enemies]'; Haycock (*BBGCC*, p. 310) suggests '[there is] prostration in [your] wake'. Another possibility is to emend *diarwyrein* to *dy arwyrain* and understand *arllwybrawt* as an impersonal present form of an otherwise unknown verb *arllwybraf*: *arllwybrau* (but see *GPC* llwybraf: llwybro), translating the line 'your praise is expedited'. The copiers of the later MSS struggled with this line because of the need for it to rhyme with *gossod*. A number have *Os mi ydyw Eliwlod*, 'If I am Eliwlod', which is probably a later rewriting of the line.

30   **ys gwiw kystlwn ohonawt** On the use of *ys* as copula, see *GMW*, p. 139 n. 3. It is common in early poetry: compare, for instance, *PT* III.23, *ys ehelaeth y braw*, 'its terror is extensive', and *EWSP*, p. 462 ('Gwyn ap Nudd' 13a), *ys tec vy ki ac is trun*, 'my dog is fair, and he is strong'. In this case the subject is the verbal noun *kystlwn*, followed by the preposition *o*, denoting its agent (*GMW*, p. 161). The later MSS do not have *ys*: some have *yw* following *gwiw* and others have the verbal form *ymgystlwn* (*GPC* ymgystlynaf: ymgystlynu).

The following four stanzas occur in all the later manuscripts except for NLW

Peniarth MS 54. They follow the tenth stanza and elaborate upon the situation between Arthur and the Eagle, before progressing naturally to Arthur's subsequent questions about good and evil. The text below is taken from the earliest manuscript, Cardiff MS 2.83, pp. 89-92, written by an unidentified hand *c.* 1550.

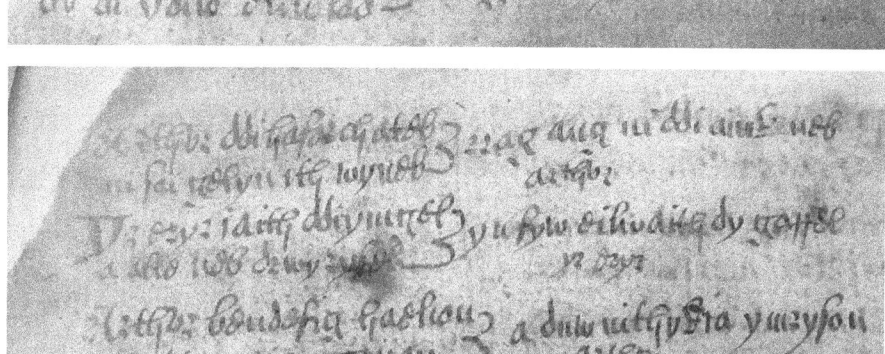

FIG. 5.2: Cardiff MS 2.83, pp. 89–90.

	Yr Eryr barabl difrad,
32	os di ydyw Eliwlad
	ai gwiw ymladd amdanat?

	Arthur ddihafarch ateb —
	ni sai' gelyn i'th wyneb —
36	rrag ang[au] ni ddianc neb.

	Yr Eryr iaith ddiymgel,
	a allo neb drwy ryfel
	yn fyw eilwaith dy gaffel?

40	Arthur, bendefig haelion:
	o chredir geirie'r Ganon,
	a Duw ni thykia ymryson.

	Oh Eagle of guileless speech,
32	if you are Eliwlad
	is it fitting to fight for you?

	Oh Arthur whose answer is courageous —
	No enemy stands fast against you —
36	from Death no one will escape.

>Oh Eagle of honest speech,
>could someone by means of warfare
>win you again alive?
>
>40   Arthur, leader of noble ones:
>if the words of the Canon are believed
>it is of no use to contend with God.

31 Yr Eryr barabl difrad The lenition of *parabl*, which occurs in all MSS, seems to indicate that *eryr* is treated as a personal name. It may therefore be that *golwc* in l. 25 should also be lenited.

33 ai gwiw ymladd amdanat? The adjective *gwiw* picks up the Eagle's previous reply; its various meanings include 'apt, fitting' ('is it appropriate …?') and 'useful, profitable' ('is it any use …?'), and both of these would suit the context. Arthur's first instinct is to use force to recover his kinsman. The original final consonant of the 2 sg. prep., *-d*, supplies the necessary rhyme (*amdanad*); see *GMW*, p. 59n1 (a).

35 ni sai' gelyn i'th wyneb Lit. 'an enemy does not stand fast against you'. Cf l. 17 above, *Ny seif dy alon rac dy ruthyr*. The 3 sing.pres.indic. of *sefyll* in MW is *seif* (*GMW*, p. 116) but in ModW the diphthong has become *ai* (cf. *ieith*, *iaith* in lines 22 and 37, and see *GMW*, p. 4 n. 3). For the loss of *-f*, common from the fourteenth century onwards, see *GMW*, p. 9. This remark of the Eagle's is not arbitrary, but a tactful observation that it is not any deficiency on Arthur's part that makes it inappropriate or useless to fight.

36 iaith ddiymgel The adjective is formed from the negative prefix *di-* and the root of the verb *ymgelaf*: *ymgel*(*u*), 'to hide oneself'. With *iaith*, 'speech', it can mean 'well-known, open, conspicuous, evident, clear', but here it may be a synonym of *difrad* in l. 31, 'not secretive, honest'.

38 a allo neb drwy ryfel In some MSS, *gallai*, the imperfect form of *gallu*, is used here as a conditional, 'could'. Despite the Eagle's tact, Arthur swiftly assumes that, even if *he* cannot, somebody else might be able to recover Eliwlad.

40 Arthur bendefig haelion Some of the MSS have *penadur*, another term for a ruler derived from *penn*, 'head, chief'. The plural of the adjective *hael*, 'generous', is commonly used as a noun, 'generous ones, noblemen', in the court poetry, cf. *CBT* III 3.216, *mechdeyrn haelon*, 'lord of noblemen'.

41 geirie'r Ganon For other examples of the ModW spoken plural ending *-e* (from MW *-eu*), see Melwas, 1.5n. The Latin borrowing *canon* is used in medieval Welsh poetry to mean 'rule, rule book', sometimes referring to the rules of poetry, but here it is undoubtedly a reference to the Bible.

Word-list

a¹ *rel.pron.* 'who' 13, 20
a² *preverbal particle (GPC* a¹*)* **a'th** *with infixed object pron. 2 sing.* **'th** 6, 12
a³ *interrogative pron. (GPC* a³*)* 38
a⁴ *prep.* 'with' 42 **a'e** *with. infixed possessive pron. 3 sg.masc.* **'e** 2
achles *n.* 'refuge, protection' 5n
adar *pl.n.* 'birds' 14
ae *interrogative particle (GPC* ai¹*)* 27n, 33
angau *n.* 'death' 36
ar *prep.* 'on' 26
arllwybrawt *n.* '?wake, track, swathe' 29n
arth *n.* 'bear' 5, 11, 23
Arthur *personal name* 4, 10, 16, 28, 34, 40
aruthyr *adj.* 'terrible, ferocious' *used as a noun (GPC* aruthr*)* 16
as *preverbal particle possibly containing infixed obj.pron. 3 sing. (GPC* as¹*)* 8n
ateb *n.* 'answer, response' 34

bard *n.* 'poet' *(GPC* bardd*)* 1
bei *n.* 'fault' *(GPC* bai*)* 26
blaen *see* **o vlaen**
bric *n.* 'top (of a tree)' *(GPC* brig*)* 2, 13
bydut *2 sing.imperf.subj. of* **bot**, 'to be' 15
byȽ (byw) *adj.* 'alive, living' 21, 39

caffel *v.n.* 'to have, gain, win, seize' *(GPC* caf: cael*)* 29
Canon *n.* 'rule, rule book, the Bible' 41n
KernyȽ *place name* Cernyw, Cornwall 20n
cledyfawt *n.* 'sword-stroke' *(GPC* cleddyfod*)* 16n
credir *impers.pres.indic. of* **credu**, 'to believe' 41
kann *conj.* 'since' *(GPC* gan¹*)* 1n
cyfyrdelid *adj.* 'beautiful, dignified, splendid' 22n
kystlwn *v.n.* 'to claim kinship' *(GPC* cystlynaf: cystlwn*)* 30n
chward *3 sing.pres.indic. of* **chwerthin**, 'to laugh' 3, 9

dar *n.* 'oak tree' *(GPC* dâr*)* 2, 13
di *independent pron. 2 sing.* 'you' 32
dianc *3 sing.pres.indic. of* **dianc** 36
diarwyrein *adj.* 'fallen, prostrate' 29n
difrad *adj.* 'without guile, without fault' 31
dihafarch *adj.* 'vigorous, brave, courageous' 28, 34
diuei *adj.* 'without fault, perfect' *(GPC* difai*)* 25

diymgel *adj.* 'clear, ?honest' 37n
dof *adj.* 'tame' 15
drwy *prep.* 'through, by means of' (causing lenition) 38
Duw 'God' 42
dy *poss.pron. 2 sing.* 'your' 17(2), 19, 26, 39

'e *infixed possessive pron. 3 sg.masc* 'his, its' 2 (with **a⁴**)
edrych *3 sing.pres.indic. of* **edrych**, 'to look' 3, 9
eilwaith *adv.* 'a second time, again' 39
Eliwlat *personal name* Eliwlad 24, 27, 32
engyhynt *n.* '?course, journey' 10n
eryr *n.* 'eagle' 3, 6, 9, 12, 19, 25, 31, 37
es see **ys**

ffossawt *n.* 'fight, battle, slaughter' (*GPC* ffosawd) 28n

galon *pl. of n.* **gal**, 'enemy, adversary' (*GPC* gâl¹) 17
gallo *3 sing.pres.subj. of* **gallu** 38
geirie *pl. of n.* **gair**, 'word' 41
gelwir *impers.pres.indic. of* **galw**, 'to call' 24
gelyn *n.* 'enemy, adversary' 35
glyngoet *n.* 'wooded glen' 20n
gofynnaf *1 sing.pres.indic. of* **gofyn**, 'to ask' 8
golwc *n.* 'eye-sight; appearance' (*GPC* golwg) 25
gordiwes *v.n.* 'to win, to gain' (*GPC* gorddiweddaf: gorddiwes) 4n
gwar *adj.* 'gentle' 15
gweles, gwelas *3 sing.pret. of* **gwelet**, 'to see' 6, 12
gwiw *adj.* 'apt, fitting, useful, profitable, excellent' 30, 33n
gẇn *1 sing.pres.indic. of* **gwybot**, 'to know' 19
gwyr *pl. of n.* **gwr**, 'man, warrior' 22
gynt *adv.* 'formerly, previously, in time past' (*GPC* cynt) 6, 12, 24

haelion *pl.n.* 'generous ones, noblemen' 40n
hanfut *2 sing.imperf.subj. of* **hanfot**, 'to be (from), to be descended (from)' (*GPC* hanwyf: hanfod) 14
hard *adj.* 'beautiful, fine' (*GPC* hardd) 2

ieith (iaith) *n.* 'language, people of the same language, nation' 22n, 37
i *form of preposition* **yn**, 'in', *used in combinations* (*GMW*, p. 199), **i'th** *with poss. pron. 2 sing.* 'th 35

llewenyd *n.* 'joy, merriment' (*GPC* llawenydd) 5, 11n
llu *n.* 'host, army' 5, 11
'm *infixed pron. 1 sing.* 24 (with y)
mab *n.* 'son' 18, 21
Madawc uab Uthyr (Uthur) *personal name* Madog son of Uthr 18n, 21
mi *1 sing. independent pron.* 'I' 18
myr *pl. of n.* **mor**, 'sea' (*GPC* môr) 7
myvyr *adj.* 'thoughtful' (*GPC* myfyr¹) 8

na *conj.* 'nor' 15(2)
neb *pron.* 'someone' 36, 38
nei *n.* 'nephew' 27
ny (ni) *neg.* 'not' 15, 16, 19, 35, 36, 42 **nyt** 21, 23, 26

o¹ *prep.* 'from' 14, **ohonawt** *conjugated prep. 2 sing.* 'with you' 30n and see **o tu**, **o vlaen**
o² *conj.* 'if' (causing spirant mutation, *GPC* o³) 41
o tu *compound prep.* '(from) beside, on the side of, near' (*GPC* o du) 7n
oes *3 sing.pres.indic. of* **bot**, 'to be' (causing lenition of the subject, see *GMW*, pp. 17–18) 26
ohonawt see **o¹**
os *conj.* 'if' 32
o vlaen *compound prep.* 'in front of, before' (*GPC* o¹) 1.2n

parabyl *n.* 'power of speech' (*GPC* parabl) 26n, 31n
pei *conj.* 'if' (*GPC* pe) 14
pellglot *n.* 'far-flung fame' 4n, 10
pendefig *n.* 'ruler, leader' 40n
py *interrogative pron. used as an adv.* 'why?' (*GPC* pa¹, py¹) 3(2)n, 9(2)

'r *definite article* 'the' (a form used in combinations, *GMW*, p. 24) 41
rac (rrag) *prep.* 'against, from' (*GPC* rhag) 17, 36
ruthyr *n.* 'rush, attack' (*GPC* rhuthr) 17
ryfedaf *1 sing.pres.indic. of* **ryfedu**, 'to wonder (at), marvel' (*GPC* rhyfeddaf: rhyfeddu) 1, 7
rhyfel *n.* 'warfare, battle' 38
ryw *n.* 'species' 14, 19

seif (sai') *3 sing.pres.indic. of* **sefyll**, 'to stand, stand fast, stand one's ground (in battle)' (*GPC* safaf: sefyll 2c) 13n, 17, 35

ti *independent pron.* 'you' 27
treigla *3 sing.pres.indic. of* **treiglo**, 'to roam, frequent' 20
tremynt *n.* 'appearance' 12
tykia *3 sing.pres.indic. of* **tycio**, 'to avail' 43
'th¹ *infixed object pron. 2 sing.* 6, 12 (with **a²**)
'th² *poss.pron. 2 sing.* 'your' 35 (with **i**)

vy *1 sing.possessive pron.* 'my' (*GPC* fy) 27

wyf *1 sing.pres.indic. of* **bot**, 'to be' 1
wyneb *n.* 'face' *in the prepositional phrase* **i'th wyneb**, 'in the face of, against' (*GPC* yn wyneb) 35

y *preverbal particle,* **y'm** *with infixed pron. 1 sing.* **'m** 24
ydyw *3 sing.pres.indic. of* **bot**, 'to be' 32
ym *preposition* **yn** (*combined with* **m-**) 'in' 13
ymryson *v.n.* 'to contend with, to strive against' 43
yn *predicative and adverbial particle* (*GPC* yn³, *GMW*, p. 139, causing lenition except in *ll-* and *-rh*) 2, 8, 39
yr *definite article* 'the' 6, 12, 13, 19, 25, 31, 37 (see also **'r**)
ys (**es**) *preverbal particle possibly containing infixed obj.pron. 3 sing.* (*GPC* ys²) 1n, 7,
ys *impers.pres. of* **bot** *used as a copula* 'it is' 30n
yw *3 sing.pres.indic. of* **bot**, 'to be' 18

Fragments of a Dialogue Between Melwas and Gwenhwyfar

Scholars believe that two short series of *englynion* preserved in sixteenth- and seventeenth-century manuscripts are fragments of a medieval dialogue poem between Arthur's wife, Gwenhwyfar, and Melwas, the character upon whom Chrétien de Troyes' Maheloas and Meleagant and Geoffrey of Monmouth's Modred are probably based. Both poems have some stanzas which appear to derive from a common source, but there are so many differences between them that it would be impossible to create a composite text.

The earlier of the two manuscript sources, NLW MS Wynnstay 1, is a miscellany of medieval poetry and short prose texts in the early hand of the sixteenth-century lexicographer Thomas Wiliems of Trefriw.[25] The pages on which the dialogue appears (pp. 212–13), are badly rubbed and difficult to read. The text contains examples of medieval orthography, suggesting that Wiliems was copying from an older written source. Its language has been very badly

---

[25] Daniel Huws has identified it as his earlier hand, dating it to *c.* 1580; see Huws, *A Repertory of Welsh Scribes* (forthcoming). On Thomas Wiliems, see J. E. Caerwyn Williams in the *Oxford Dictionary of National Biography* (Oxford, 1950–).

modernised, however, with little regard for the very simple three-line *englyn milwr* metre or even for rhyme in places. There are also signs that the poem has been redacted from faulty memory at some point. There are missing lines, lines which have clearly been reworked, verses that appear to be later additions and words which have been corrupted beyond recognition. The poem has no title but the superscription, *Melwas*, in an unidentified hand, provides a general indication of its subject. Melwas and Gwenhwyfar are named in the poem, along with Cai, who seems to be the subject of their debate.[26]

The second version is preserved in NLW Llanstephan MS 122, an anthology of *cywyddau* and *awdlau* compiled c. 1644–1648 by William Bodwrda, a cleric of noble descent who was a careful copier and a prolific collector of medieval Welsh poetry.[27] Written in Modern Welsh orthography, clumsily reworked in places and with extremely irregular line lengths and a number of missing words and phrases, the text is obscure but can be tentatively interpreted in the light of the earlier version. A title, *Ymddiddan rhwng Arthur a Gwenhwyfar* (Conversation between Arthur and Gwenhwyfar), followed by *q.* (*query*) was added by the eighteenth-century antiquary Lewis Morris, whilst his brother, Richard Morris, states in the contents list he created in 1746, *Ni wn pwy. Englynion i Wenhwyfar Impf.*, 'I don't know who. *Englynion* for Gwenhwyfar. Imperfect'. It is only Gwenhwyfar and Cai who are named in the poem itself.[28]

As their first editor, E. D. Jones, has shown, some of the stanzas clearly derive from the same source, but there are also major differences between the two versions, possibly due to a long period of oral and written transmission.[29] Late rhymes, modern endings and expressions appear along with medieval forms and meanings, and four-line stanzas are mixed with *englynion milwr*, making dating very difficult.[30] In style and metre, many of the stanzas are similar to the opening verses of the Dialogue of Arthur and the Eagle and other medieval dialogue poems and, as in these series, it may be that one of these characters is unknown to the other, his identity revealed during the course of the poem. [31]

Because of the corrupt and incomplete nature of both texts, it is difficult to establish the nature of their background story. The fact that it is set in south-west Britain rather than Wales, and that there are no obvious signs of the influence of Geoffrey of Monmouth, suggest that it may be early. Some scholars argue that it is an episode derived from a native tale about the abduction of Gwenhwyfar

---

[26] Note that the stanza divisions of the edited text are those of Thomas Wiliems.
[27] It was R. Geraint Gruffydd who identified the hand of Bodwrda in this manuscript. On Wiliam Bodwrda, see Dafydd Ifans in the *Oxford Dictionary of National Biography*, <www.oxforddnb.com>.
[28] NLW Llanstephan MS 122, pp. 426–67.
[29] 'Melwas, Gwenhwyfar, a Chai', *Bulletin of the Board of Celtic Studies*, 8 (1935–1937), 203–08.
[30] *EWSP*, p. 330.
[31] For example, the dialogues between Gwyn ap Nudd and Gwyddno, Taliesin and Ugnach, and Gwalchmai and Drystan: see *EWSP*, pp. 243–49.

by Melwas and her rescue by Arthur from the Otherworld Island of Glass.[32] It is thought that this lost legend was adapted for the monks of Glastonbury Abbey (identified as the idyllic Isle of Glass) by Caradog of Llancarfan in the early twelfth-century *Vita Gildae*, 'The Life of St. Gildas', and that it may also have inspired various accounts of the queen's abduction in the romances of Chrétien de Troyes and in *Historia Regum Britanniae*.[33] If this is so, these stanzas would represent the only substantial evidence for traditions about Gwenhwyfar before Geoffrey of Monmouth.[34]

The light mocking tone of the dialogue, however, may point to a different context. Jenny Rowland sees in the diminutive size of Melwas and his horse 'of the colour of leaves' evidence of the magical powers attributed to him in a love poem by the fifteenth-century poet Dafydd ab Edmwnd, where the poet wishes he could 'through magic and enchantment' take a woman to the ends of the earth like Melwas did.[35] A century earlier, in a *cywydd* by Dafydd ap Gwilym, Melwas is depicted as Gwenhwyfar's lover, who ventures to her room through a window.[36] He is also mentioned favourably as a youthful warrior in fourteenth- and fifteenth-century praise poems.[37] In light of these references, Ian Hughes has argued that the background to the series is similar to that of *Ystorya Trystan*, a love story influenced by foreign *fabliaux*, where the stock characters have been replaced by well-known figures from the native storytelling tradition.[38] Ceridwen Lloyd-Morgan, on the other hand, suggests that in this dialogue, as in Dafydd ap Gwilym's poem, the native tale of the abduction of Gwenhwyfar by Melwas has been influenced by French romances concerning Lancelot's relationship with Arthur's queen.[39]

A great deal of uncertainty surrounds these two *englyn* series, not least because of the deficient way in which the texts have been transmitted. There is no doubt that they derive from a medieval dialogue poem between Gwenhwyfar

---

[32] See *EWSP*, pp. 527–58, and *AMWL* pp. 68–69.

[33] See Sims-Williams, 'Arthurian Poems', pp. 58–61; *TYP*, pp. 378–80. It is thought that the story behind these stanzas is especially similar to Chrétien de Troyes' *Chevalier de la Charette*, in which Meleagant abducts Guenièvre from Arthur's court and takes her to the otherworldly kingdom of Goirre ('glass'). In *Historia Regum Britanniae*, it is thought that Modredus has taken the place of Melwas as Guinevere's abductor.

[34] See *TYP*, pp. 377: 'In the absence of any references by the *Gogynfeirdd* or in earlier sources, the evidence for an authentic pre-Geoffrey tradition of *Gwenhwyfar* in Wales is highly doubtful'; but cf. Chapter 3 above.

[35] *EWSP*, p. 257.

[36] *TYP*, p. 378.

[37] These poets may have understood his name as a combination of *mêl*, 'honey' (used figuratively) + *gwas*, 'young lad'; see below.

[38] Ian Hughes, 'Camlan, Medrawd a Melwas', *Dwned*, 13 (2007), 11–46 (pp. 33–46). On the Trystan *englynion* see *EWSP*, pp. 252–55, and Jenny Rowland, 'Trystan and Esyllt' in *ACL*, 51–63.

[39] Ceridwen Lloyd-Morgan and Nerys Ann Jones, 'Ymryson Melwas a Gwenhwyfar' (forthcoming).

and Melwas. The exact nature of the relationship of the protagonists and the precise date of composition is, however, extremely difficult to establish. The two texts are treated independently below. A transliteration of each MS is followed by a tentative edition of each stanza in turn. Because of their corrupt nature, a translation has not been attempted, but comprehensive notes are provided suggesting possible emendations and interpretations along with a comprehensive word-list.
Fragment 1

NLW Wynnstay MS 1, pp. 212–13

FIG. 5.3: NLW Wynnstay MS 1, p. 212.

Pa eistedd gwr yn gyffredinrwydd gwledd
eb eiddaw nai dechreû nai diwedd
eiste obry islawr cyntedd

y Melwas o ynys wydrin
di aûr vlyche goreûrin
ni lewais i ddim oth win

Aro ychydic snevin
ni wallaf vi vyngwin
ar wr ni ado ag ni safai mewn trin
ni ddaliai Gai yn i vin

ni arveisiwn ryd
ag a vo gemyn a gwryd
a llûric drom drai
mi ywr gwr a ddaliai Gai

Taw was taw a'th salwet
onit well nath welet
ni ddalut Gai ar d'wythvet

Gwenhwyvar olwg hyddgan
na'm dirmic cyd bwy bychan
mi ddaliwn Gai vyhunan

Tydi was ar ben maint
ai ben coch val ysgyvaint
anhebic i Gai wyt o vaint

Gnawd i veddw gwecry
Iawn a gadwn velly
mi ywr Melwas gadwn ar hyny

canys dechreûasoch
ymddiddenwch rhagoch
ef a edwyn mab ai lloch
ymhle gynt yr ymdelsa6ch

mewn llys vrddasol i braint
yn yvet gwin o Geraint
lle dwir gwir ar dir dyfnaint

cas gennyf wên gwrllwyd hen
ai gledde n waell dan i en
a chwenych eb allel amgen

casach genyf ine
gwr balch llwrf ond geirie
ni thaw ni thyn i gledde
hwde di hwde dithe

Stanza 1

    Pa eistedd gwr yn gyffredinrwydd gwledd,
    eb eiddaw na'i dechreû na'i diwedd,
    eiste obry islaw'r cyntedd?

1   **Pa eistedd gwr yn gyffredinrwydd gwledd** The word-order is very unusual if *pa* is to be understood as complementing *gwr*, 'what man?', but it may have the meaning 'why?' (*GPC* pa¹ adv.). Another possibility is that it is a rare example of substantival use of *pa*, *py*, 'who?', with *gwr* a later addition (*GPC* pa¹d and above, *Pa gur*, 5n). The abstract noun *cyffredinrwydd* is mostly found in religious texts with the meaning 'communion, community' (*GPC*), but it can be understood in the light of line 3 below to mean 'the commonality', referring to the part of the hall where the common people sat at a feast. (The combination of the prep. *yn* causing nasal mutation and the noun, probably written as one word in the original, has been mis-modernised with separation of the two words.) The line may be translated as 'why does a warrior sit in the common part of the feast?' or, without *gwr*, 'who sits in the common part of the feast?' It is possible however, that *cyffredinrwydd* is a scribal correction of the rare early form *cyffred*, 'course; habitation, society' (*GPC*). This would give a regular seven-syllable line.

2   **eb eiddaw na'i dechreû na'i diwedd** Lit. 'without his neither its beginning nor its end', i.e. without having the right to do so. The earliest example of *eb* as a variant of the preposition *heb*, 'without', listed in *GPC* eb¹ is in the work of fifteenth-century poet Dafydd Nanmor. The *û* is typical of the orthography of Thomas Wiliems.

The line has nine syllables but could be read as part of an Englyn Penfyr and rendered into Modern Welsh thus:

> Pa eistedd yng nghyffred gwledd — heb eiddaw
> na'i dechrau na'i diwedd ...

> 'Who sits in the ?community of the feast without his [having] |
> neither its beginning nor its end?'

3   **eiste obry islaw'r cyntedd** 'Sitting down below, below the upper end of the hall.' On *cyntedd*, the upper, more honourable part of the hall where the king sat in medieval times, see the First Branch of the *Mabinogi* (*Pwyll Pendeuic Dyuet*, ed. by R. L. Thomson (Dublin: Institute of Advanced Studies, 1986), l. 312), and the Welsh Laws of Court (*The Law of Hywel Dda* [*LHDd*], ed. by Dafydd Jenkins (Llandysul: Gomer Press, 1986), pp. 223–24). The line has eight syllables; its first part, where the verb is repeated, may have been reworked. There are examples of *eistedd* without its final -ð in thirteenth-century texts (see *GPC* eisteddaf: eistedd, eiste) and its use in the first line of the stanza would avoid rhyme with *gwledd*.

This opening stanza, questioning the identity of a guest at a feast, brings to mind other conversations between two characters where one is unknown to the other and identification is established during the course of dialogue, such as that of Arthur and the Eagle above and the beginning of *Pa gur* in Chapter 1. The identities of the questioner, the subject of the question and the person addressed are all unknown at this point.

Stanza 2
>Y Melwas o Ynys Wydrin;
>di aûr vlyche goreûrin,
>ni lewais-i ddim o'th win.

4   **Y Melwas** This may be a greeting, 'Oh, Melwas', as suggested by E. D. Jones, 'Melwas', p. 206 (cf. Dialogue of Arthur and the Eagle above and see *GMW*, p. 25, for further examples of the definite article used with a vocative common noun), but the definite article appears with the name again in line 26 below, giving rise to the possibility that it is an answer to the question of the previous stanza. A false etymology, *mel*, 'honey', used figuratively (cf. *TYP*, p. 248, *Y Fêl Ynys*) + *gwas*, 'lad', may have given rise to the use of the definite article before the name. The poets of the fourteenth and fifteenth centuries may well have understood it thus, but among the forty-five references to him in their work there are no examples of *Y Melwas*. The definite article may be a later addition as the line is too long by a syllable.

Ynys Wydrin William of Malmesbury, Caradog of Llancarfan and Gerald of Wales, all writing in the twelfth century, claim that this was the original name for Glastonbury in Somerset: see *The Early History of Glastonbury: An Edition, Translation and Study of William of Malmesbury's De Antiquitate Glastonie Ecclesie*, ed. by John Scott (Woodbridge: The Boydell Press, 1981), pp. 44–45, 52–53, 88–89; *Two Lives of Gildas by a Monk of Ruys and Caradoc of Llancarfan*, trans. by Hugh Williams (1889, reprinted Felin-fach: Llanerch Press, 1990), p. 99; Gerald of Wales, *Speculum ecclesie*.

The name is a borrowing from Latin *vitrum*, which is used for glass and for woad and the blue dye (of the colour of glass) produced from it. It is thought that Ynys Wydrin originally meant 'woad-growing island', but in Welsh, *gwydrin* also means 'made of glass, shining' (see *GPC* gwydrin^{1,2}). The name was probably connected in popular imagination with the idea of an Otherworld fort of glass; cf. *Kaer Wydyr* in *Preiddiau Annwn*, l. 30. It corresponds to *Urbs Vitrea* (the Fortress of Glass) where Gwenhwyfar is imprisoned by Melwas in Caradog of Llancarfan's Life of Gildas, and *Isle de Voirre* (the Island of Glass), the kingdom of Melwas in *Erec et Enide*, both twelfth-century texts.

E. D. Jones ('Melwas', p. 205) is of the opinion that Ynys Wydrin is the original Welsh name for Glastonbury, but examples in the Welsh literary tradition are extremely scarce and late. It is found in a late fourteenth-century adaptation of Gerald's text known as 'Claddedigaeth Arthur', and in a poem by Guto'r Glyn from the fifteenth century; see Ceridwen Lloyd-Morgan, 'From Ynys Wydryn to Glastynbri: Glastonbury in Welsh Vernacular Tradition' in *Glastonbury Abbey and the Arthurian Tradition*, ed. by James P. Carley (Rochester, New York: D. S. Brewer, 2001), pp. 161–78 (167–68). *Ynys Afallach* and *Glastynburi* are much more common in texts reflecting popular traditions about Glastonbury and Arthur. It is likely therefore that the Welsh name was derived from the English.

 5 **di aûr vlyche goreûrin** Although written as two words, *aûr vlyche* is probably the plural of *eurflwch*, 'golden vessel', a compound of *aur*, 'gold, golden', + *blwch*, 'box, receptacle', also found in a poem by Llywarch Brydydd y Moch (*CBT* v 1.104) and cf. also Cynddelw Brydydd Mawr *gorflwch eurin* (III 17.26). For other examples of the Modern Welsh spoken plural form *-e* (from MW *-eu*), see the final two verses of this series. On references to gold in connection with drinking vessels in the court poetry, see Gruffydd Aled Williams, 'The Feasting Aspects of *Hirlas Owein*' in *Ildánach Ildírech: A Festschrift for Proinsias Mac Cana*, ed. by John Carey et al. (Andover and Aberystwyth: Celtic Studies Publications, 1999), pp. 289–302 (p. 299). The phrase *aûr vlyche goreurin* may be dependent upon the independent pronoun *di*, which may be vocative, 'you of the golden, gilded vessels'. Although the line is reminiscent of the intricate syntax of formal court poetry, no parallel has been found, and although *eur-* is extremely common in compounds in this poetry, it is not usual for these compounds to be followed by an adjective containing the same element. It is likely, therefore, that the line is corrupt.

 6 **ni lewais-i ddim o'th win** Lit. 'I did not consume any of your wine'. The indefinite pronoun *dim*, 'anything', is lenited as the object of a conjugated verb (*GMW*, p. 18). Because the following noun is definite, *o*, 'of', is required; see *GMW*, p. 107. If the affixed pronoun *-i* is not included in the syllable count, as is common in medieval poetry, then the line is short.

 The first line of this stanza can be interpreted as an answer to the question in the opening stanza, followed by an address to the questioner, who is the host at the feast, and a claim that he (or she) did not drink his (or her) wine. It may be spoken by Melwas, identifying himself as the unknown guest, or by another. This early disclosure of the identity of the guest is unexpected. If *Y Melwas* is understood as vocative, then the stanza may be addressed to Melwas by the unknown guest or by another, and Melwas is the owner of the court.

Stanza 3
  Aro ychydic ?snevin:
  ni wall[of]af-vi vyngwin
  ar wr (ni ado ag) ni safai mewn trin,
  ni ddaliai Gai yn i vin.

 7 **Aro ychydic snevin** The verbal form *aro* is medieval. In the modern period the verb noun ending *-s* was understood as part of the stem *arho-*, so 1 sing. pres. *arhoaf* became *arhosaf* and 2 sing.imper. *ar(h)o* was replaced by *ar(h)os*. The obscure form *snevin* is likely to be a personal name or perhaps a derogatory

term for the speaker of the previous stanza. There may be a link with the name *Sefin* connected to Cai in the other version; see below 2.8n. If Melwas is greeting Cai here, then he may be the host and Cai has come to his court in disguise.

 8-9 ni wall[of]af-vi vyngwin | ar wr The MS form *gwallaf* betrays ignorance of the conjugation of the medieval verb *gwallaw* and causes the line to be a syllable short. The combination *gwallaw ar* is unusual but is found in the section on the chamberlain's duties in the Laws of Court, *Ef a dele gwallav ar e brenhyn en wastat*, 'It is right for him to pour drink for the king at all times' (see *LHDd*, p. 9).

 9 ar wr (ni ado ag) ni safai mewn trin The closest verbal form to (*g*)*ado* is *gato*, 3 sing.pres.subj. of *gadaf*: *gadu*. It is likely that the imperf.indic. form of the verb *sefyll* is used here as a conditional (for other examples, see *GMW*, pp. 110-11). The meaning with *mewn trin*, perhaps a modernisation of *yn nhrin*, commonly found in the court poetry, is probably 'to stand one's ground, to resist'; see Arthur and the Eagle above, l. 17n. The usual meanings of *gadu*, 'to permit, allow; to leave, leave behind, abandon', seem to be the opposite of what is required in this line, which has eleven syllables. Without the words *ni ado ag*, the line has seven syllables.

 10 ni ddaliai Gai yn i vin Forms of the verb *daliaf*: *dal* with Cai as their object occur in the last line of this and the following three stanzas. The most suitable meanings are 'to capture, seize, hold fast, restrain' and the imperfect forms probably have a conditional meaning as in the previous line. (On the lenition of *Cai* as the object of a conjugated verb, see *GMW*, p. 18.) Mary Williams ('An Early Ritual Poem in Welsh', *Speculum*, 13 (1938), 38-51 (p. 42)) suggests that *yn i vin* is an error for *yn i win*, 'in his wine, in his cups, drunk'. This gives a suitable meaning, 'who would not seize/restrain Cai, even when he was drunk' — cf. l. 17 below — but there are no other examples of *yn ei win* or *yn ei gwrw* and the equivalent, *yn ei ddiod*, is found in modern texts only according to *GPC*. Another possibility is an otherwise unknown idiom involving *min*, 'sharpness, keenness', used figuratively perhaps for 'enthusiasm for the fight'.

 This four-line stanza has the same end-rhyme as the previous verse, with the word *gwin* used as a rhyme in lines 6, 8 and possibly 10. The syllable length is so irregular that it can be argued that, as with the first stanza, they have been clumsily forced into the shape of an *englyn*. The first three lines of this stanza appear to be a riposte to the claim in l. 6 that he (or she) had not drunk any of the host's wine. The host retaliates by claiming that he (or she) doesn't serve wine to a coward. The final line is the first of a sequence of five final lines in which Cai is named. E. D. Jones ('Melwas', p. 206) has suggested that it may have originally belonged to a different stanza. If this is so, the verb may have originally been 2 sing., giving a closer parallel to l. 17 below.

Stanza 4
>*Mi* arveisiwn ryd
>ag a vo gemyn a gwryd
>a llûric drom, drai:
>mi yw'r gwr a ddaliai Gai.

11   *Mi* **arveisiwn ryd** Williams ('Ritual Poem', p. 41) suggests emending the MS form *ni* to *mi*, the 1 sing. pronoun used as a preverbal particle. See *GPC* mi¹ for medieval examples of *mi* immediately before a verb in the first-person singular. and cf. l. 20 below. The verb is interpreted as a compound formed from the noun *bais*, which is used for a ford or the act of wading. The only other literary example is found in a *cywydd* by Tudur Aled (*c.* 1465–1525). A seven-syllable line is possible by reading *myfi a arveisiwn ryd*; cf. the use of *tydi* below.

12   **ag a vo gemyn a gwryd** No examples of *ac a*, a form of the relative pronoun, have been found in medieval poetry, but for examples in the prose texts, see *GMW*, p. 63 n. 3. Emending *ag a vo* to *a vai* gives a seven-syllable line and explains the mutation which is common after the ending *-ai*. *Cemyn* may be understood as a variant of the equative adj. *cymaint*. There are early examples of forms such as *cymyn*, *cymin*, *cimin* and *cimyn*; see *GPC*. The *e* in the first syllable may be an error in modernising, made by a scribe who did not understand the word. For *gwryd* as a measurement of depth, see *GPC* gwryd¹, gwrhyd. There may be play here on the place name *Gwryd Cai* in Snowdonia.

13   **a llûric drom drai** This line has five syllables only. It has an acceptable meaning if *trai* is understood as a noun, 'ebb-tide', used adverbially, or if the preposition *ar* is added (see *GPC* trai¹): 'I would wade across a ford | which would be as much as a fathom [deep] | with a heavy coat of mail, [even] at ebb-tide'. This line, however, does not rhyme with the previous lines, and it is likely that we have fragments of two stanzas. If so, it is better to take this line with the following one and to interpret *trai* as an adjective commonly used with words for a shield in the court poetry, with the meaning 'full of holes, shattered' (see *GPC* trai²), as a sign of great heroism in battle: ' … with a heavy, shattered coat of mail, I am the man to seize/restrain Cai'.

These stanzas form a dialogue between two speakers who are arguing, the one boasting that he has the ability to seize or restrain Cai, and the other refuting his claims and praising Cai. This suggests that Cai himself is not part of the dialogue. Could he be the unknown guest at the feast, who has come in disguise to the court of Melwas to rescue Gwenhwyfar? It can be argued that the references to Cai's superiority as a warrior here and in the following stanza may echo early native traditions about him, reflected in *Culhwch ac Olwen*, rather than the later French texts where he is usually depicted as a disagreeable character and sometimes as a coward.

Stanza 5
>Tydi, was, taw a'th salwet!
>onit well na'th welet,
>ni ddalut Gai ar d'wythvet.

15   **Tydi, was, taw a'th salwet** Williams ('Ritual Poem', p. 42) suggests reading *tydi*, 2 sing. independent pronoun, as in l. 21, instead of the MS reading *taw*, to give the line seven syllables. The abstract noun *salwet* (ModW *salwedd*) from *salw*, which has a wide range of meanings including 'poor, mean, vile, ugly, foolish', is also found in poetry from the fourteenth century onwards. The spelling of this stanza, however, is different from the previous one, with *-t* rather than *-d* for /d/. In order to preserve the rhyme, therefore, it would be better to read *salwet* as ModW *salwed*, understanding it as the equative form of the adjective *salw* used as a noun (see *GMW*, p. 42). The structure of *taw a'th salwet* may be compared with that of *tewi â sôn*, 'to be quiet' (see *GPC* tawaf: tewi), and the line may be translated: 'You, lad, be quiet with your vileness!'

16   **onit well na'th welet** Williams ('Ritual Poem', p. 42) suggests adding *wyt* to give a seven-syllable line, which corresponds to 2.13 below. The verb noun *gwelet*, 'to see', used as a noun with the meaning 'appearance' is appropriate here, but according to *GPC* there is no other medieval example with this meaning. *Na*, 'than', is not recorded before the sixteenth century (*GPC* na³) and is probably a modernised form of *no* (see below 2.13). The line can be restored to *onid wyd well no'th weled*, 'unless you are better than your appearance'.

17   **ni ddalut Gai ar d'wythvet** 'You would not seize/restrain Cai [even] as one of eight [men]'. The 2 sing.imperf. ending *-ut* is medieval: see *GMW*, p. 121, and cf. 2.14 *dalid*. For other examples of the preposition *ar* used before ordinals with the meaning 'as one of, with', see *GMW*, pp. 48–49, and *GPC* ar¹ 3d. The 2 sing.poss. pronoun *dy* is sometimes abbreviated before a vowel. This is extremely unusual in the court poetry of the twelfth and thirteenth centuries. Here it is necessary to give the line seven syllables.

The opening pronoun *tydi* contrasts with *mi* or perhaps *myfi* of the previous stanza. Although it is difficult to ascertain the tone of the vocative *gwas* here (as in l. 21 below, see *GPC* gwas¹), the stanza appears to be a robust rebuttal of the previous speaker's claim that he is the one to overcome Cai. There is no indication of the identity of either of the two speakers unless there is, in the use of *gwas*, play on the name Melwas (< *mael*, 'prince, lord' + *gwas*).

Stanza 6
>Gwenhwyvar olwg hyddgan,
>na'm dirmic, cyd bwy' bychan:
>mi ddaliwn Gai vy hunan.

18   **Gwenhwyvar olwg hyddgan** It is interesting to compare this with similar lines in two *englynion* series, the Dialogue of Arthur and the Eagle above,

l. 25, *Yr Eryr golwc diuei*, 'Oh Eagle of perfect vision', and *Englynion y Clywaid* (*BBGCC* 31.46b), *Dremynwr golwc unyawn*, 'a watchman of accurate vision'. The phrase may refer to Gwenhwyfar's perspicacity as the one who noticed the visitor to the court, but for the possibility that *golwg* might mean 'appearance' here, see below 2.15n. *Hyddgan* is in origin a collective noun, 'herd of deer', derived from *hydd*, 'stag', and *cant*, 'throng, troop', but it appears to be used as a singular as early as the thirteenth century (see *CBT* VII 8.12). The line may be translated as 'Oh Gwenhwyfar who has the [keen] eye-sight/appearance of a stag'.

19 **na'm dirmic, cyd bwy' bychan** 'Do not disparage me, although I am *bychan*'. *Bychan* has a range of suitable meanings: 'young, inexperienced' is consistent with the fact that the speaker is earlier addressed as *gwas*; 'inconspicuous, unimportant' is also possible in the light of l. 16, but it has also been argued that l. 23 suggests 'little, small in stature', especially as Cai is often referred to as *Cai Hir* (Cai the Tall); see 2.8 below. The loss of *-f* in *bwyf* is a modern development but the spelling of *dirmic* (*GPC* dirmyg) suggests a medieval written source which has been inconsistently modernised (cf. the spelling of *golwg* in the previous line and *anhebic* in l. 23).

20 **mi ddaliwn Gai vy hunan** There is a clear connection between this line and lines 14 and 17 above. The identity of one of the speakers is revealed. It is Gwenhwyfar, Arthur's wife and queen, who has been taunting her unnamed adversary about his appearance and his inferiority to Cai. She may also be the hostess at the feast.

Stanza 7
    Tydi, was, ar ben maint,
    a'i ben coch val ysgyvaint:
    anhebic i Gai wyt o vaint.

21 **Tydi, was, ar ben maint** This line is short, at only six syllables, and *maint*, 'size, stature', is used again at the end of the third line of the stanza. Here it could be an error for *mainc*, 'bench'. This would provide generic rhyme, which is quite unusual but not unknown in *englynion* series; see 2.2n below and *EWSP*, pp. 333–34. In the Laws of Court the seat of the Court Smith at a feast is *em pen y ueyng*, 'at the end of the bench'; see *LHDd*, p. 8. The line may be emended to *Tydi, was, ar ben y fainc*, referring to the lad's seat at the feast.

22 **a'i ben coch val ysgyvaint** *Coch* is used in Welsh for ginger hair, cf. *pengoch*, 'redheaded', and many personal names. The comparison with *ysgyvaint*, 'lungs', which have a pink hue, is a curious one and is probably the result of a scribe grappling with a form that was obscure to him.

23 **anhebic i Gai wyt o vaint** On Cai's legendary stature, see above, *Pa gur*, 67n.

Stanza 8
>   Gnawd i veddw [air] gwecry,
>   iawn a gadwn [y]velly.
>   mi yw'r Melwas: gadwn ar hyny.

24   **Gnawd i veddw [air] gwecry** 'Usual for a drunkard [is] a fickle word'. This line forms a nominal sentence with the verb 'to be' omitted. This construction is common in medieval Welsh gnomic poetry: see in particular the series *Gnawt gwynt* (*EWGNP* II). Although there are examples of *gwecry* as a noun (cf. *CBT* VI 12.41, *O dywedais-i air ar wecry*, 'if I said a word in fickleness', and see *GPC*), adding *gair*, 'word', before it gives a seven-syllable line (if *meddw* is monosyllabic, *GMW*, p. 10), and an appropriate meaning, especially if the speaker is referring to Cai (cf. l. 10).

25   **iawn a gadwn [y]velly** For *cadw iawn*, lit. 'to keep justice', i.e. 'treat fairly, act justly', see *YG*, l. 1238n. This is perhaps another example of the imperfect used as a conditional, which leads to a better meaning than 1 plural pres./fut. indic. The older form of the adverb *velly* gives the line seven syllables (see *GPC* felly).

26   **mi yw'r Melwas: gadwn ar hyny** This line is too long and the form *cadwn* of the previous line is repeated. It has probably been reworked, but it is interesting to note the parallel with l. 14 above. It may be emended to *Mi Felwas: gadwn ar hynny*, 'I am Melwas: let us separate at that *or* let us leave it at that', a request, perhaps, that the conversation be brought to an end.

This stanza confirms that Melwas is the *gwas* derided by Gwenhwyfar. He insists that he is the one to defeat Cai.

Stanza 9
>   Canys dechreûasoch,
>   ymddiddenwch rhagoch:
>   ef a edwyn mab a'i lloch.

27–28   **Canys dechreûasoch, | ymddiddenwch rhagoch** Second plural endings occur in this stanza, introducing perhaps another voice which is addressing both the previous speakers. (This is more likely than the polite 2 sing. although this may indicate a change in attitude towards her adversary on the part of Gwenhwyfar.) Note that the 2 plural pret. verbal ending -*awch*, which weakened to -*och* during the medieval period, is not usually found rhyming with -*och* endings (as in *rhagoch*) in the court poetry or in the saga *englynion*. Both lines are a syllable short.

29   **ef a edwyn mab a'i lloch** *Mab* is the subject of the main verb, which is preceded by *ef*, a meaningless preverbal particle. *Edwyn* is a reformation of *adwaen*, 3 sing.pres.indic. of *adnabod*, 'to know, to recognise'. Another example of this unusual form is found in '*Englynion*' *y Misoedd* (*EWGNP* XII 3f), dated to the early to mid-fifteenth century. The vowel of the 3 sing.pres.indic. form of

llochi has been weakened (for the medieval form, *llawch*, see, for example, *CBT* II 3.64). The verb *llochi* has a wide range of meanings, from the intimate 'stroke, caress' to a more general 'nurture, protect, patronise', and also a more negative 'appease, coax, flatter' (see *GPC*). Here the relative clause *a'i lloch* can be translated as 'the one who succours him', as the relative pronoun incorporates its own antecedent. The line appears as part of a proverb in the Red Book of Hergest, *Atwen mab ae llocha ac nyt atwen ae kar*, 'A lad knows the one who pets him; he knows not the one who loves him' (*Diarhebion Llyfr Coch Hergest*, ed. by Richard Glyn Roberts (Aberystwyth: CMCS, 2013), B38 and A15n). It is difficult to be sure of the thrust of this saying in the context of the dialogue.

Stanza 10
> Ymhle gynt yr *ym*welsawch?
> Mewn llys urddasol i braint,
> yn yvet gwin o [g]eraint,
> lle dwir gwir ar dir Dyfnaint.

30 **Ymhle gynt yr *ym*welsa(v)ch?** MS *Ymhle gynt yr ymdelsa6ch* is corrupt, as *ymdelsa6ch* is not from a known verb, and the fact that the ending is spelt in medieval orthography with 6 for /u/ suggests that its copiers did not feel able to modernise it. Williams ('Ritual Poem', p. 42) proposes *y'm gwelsa6ch*, guided by 2.23 below. A simpler solution is to understand the verb as a reflexive (see *GPC* ymwelaf: ymweled) and the line spoken, like the previous stanza, by someone who is addressing both Melwas and Gwenhwyfar: 'where did you see each other before?'. This line may be the final line of the previous stanza, with which it shares an end-rhyme, or the last line of a missing stanza, cf. 2.21–23. The remaining lines form an *englyn milwr* which provides an answer to the question it contains.

31 **Mewn llys urddasol i braint** 'In a court whose privilege is dignified'. Note that the lack of lenition after *i* (3 sg. poss. pronoun referring to *llys*) shows that *llys* is here treated as a feminine noun, though it is normally masculine (see *GMW*, p. 34). It is difficult to know whose court is referred to here. The stanza may well refer to a visit by Melwas to Arthur's court.

On the native legal concept of *braint*, which means the right of enjoying full legal status or privilege, see *LHDd*, p. 319, and Huw Pryce, *Native Law and the Church in Medieval Wales* (Oxford: Clarendon Press, 1993), pp. 237–39. According to the Welsh law texts, the royal *llys* had *braint* whether the king was present or not; see *WKC*, p. 562 (Glossary), and cf. Cynddelw's *englynion* of praise for the court of Madog ap Maredudd, *bre uchel, breint ardangos, | lle trydar, Llech Ysgar llys*, 'a high hill, displaying privilege, | a place of commotion, the court of Llech Ysgar' (*CBT* III 2).

32 **yn yvet gwin o geraint** The MS reading, *Geraint*, with capital G-, implies that this is the Dumnonian king, subject of the Black Book *englynion* series

above; but the common noun *ceraint*, plural of *câr*, 'kinsman, companion, friend', makes more sense here (see also 2.26).

33 **lle dwir gwir ar dir Dyfnaint** The first part of the line is obscure and appears to be corrupt. Internal rhyme and alliteration are unusual in the poem. A two-syllable adjective probably followed *lle*.

The following metrically irregular and linguistically late stanzas seem to contrast an old man and a garrulous coward, and imply that combat between them is to follow. They may be a later addition to the series.

Stanza 11
> Cas gennyf wên gwrllwyd hen,
> a'i gledde 'n waell dan i en,
> a chwenych eb allel amgen.

34 **Cas gennyf wên gwrllwyd hen** 'Hateful to me is the smile of an old grey-haired man'. Note that the lenition to *gwên* is due to *sangiad* (dislocated word-order): the conjugated prep. has been brought forward from its 'natural' position in the nominal sentence, and the postponed subject is lenited (cf. l. 24). *Gwrllwyd* is an improper compound (cf. *gwrda*). It is used by Dafydd ap Gwilym of himself in 'The Magpie's Advice', 25.37–38. *Hen* usually precedes its noun (*GMW*, p. 37), and often implies some deliberate contrast when following it instead. Note the internal rhyme between *gwên* and *hen*, which is unusual in an *englyn milwr*.

35–36 **ai gledde'n waell dan i en | a chwenych eb allel amgen** Note that these two lines have eight syllables each. *Cledde* is a modern spoken form of *cleddau*, a variant of *cleddyf*, 'sword'; see *GPC* cleddyf. It may be used figuratively here to express the sexual inability of the hunchbacked old man; cf. the use of *clöyn* in 'Cân yr Henwr' (*EWSP*, p. 544). *Gwaell* is used for a spear in the Dream of Rhonabwy and by Dafydd ap Gwilym, but is more commonly used for smaller objects like a skewer, knitting needle or pin. If this is so, bearing in mind Dafydd ap Gwilym's depiction of Melwas, could this, perhaps, be a derogatory reference to the cuckolded husband, Arthur, by Gwenhwyfar's young lover, the *gwas* of l. 21 above, with Cai responding in the following stanza by challenging Melwas to a fight?

Stanza 12
> Casach genyf ine
> gwr balch llwrf ond geirie,
> ni thaw, ni thyn i gledde:
> hwde di! hwde dithe!

37 **Casach genyf ine** This conjunctive affixed pronoun generally has a contrastive implication ('I for my part, I on the other hand'), suggesting that stanzas 11 and 12 are to be attributed to different speakers ('I hate ...' 'Well, *I* hate even more ...'). There are medieval examples of conjunctive affixed pronouns where final *-eu* has been reduced to *-e* (see *GMW*, p. 49 n. 3), but it is

not usual to find reduced forms of the plural -*eu* ending of nouns (as in lines 38 and 39) in medieval Welsh texts.

38 **gwr balch llwrf ond geirie** 'A proud man [who is] cowardly except for [his] words'. *Onid*, 'except for' (*GPC*), may be substituted for *ond*, its contracted form, to make a seven-syllable line. *Llwrf* is the metathesized form of *llwfr*.

39 **ni thaw, ni thyn i gledde** The negative particle *ni* twice here causes spirant mutation of *t-*, but elsewhere in this poem it causes lenition (of *ll-*, *gw-* and *d-*), whether in a main or relative clause; see *GMW*, p. 62.

40 **hwde di! hwde dithe!** *Hwde* normally means 'take' in the conventional sense (e.g. *Hwde di y votrwy honn a dot am dy vys*, 'Take this ring and put it on your finger', *Owein*, ll. 300–01); but here it appears to have the same combative sense as English 'Take (that)!'. The contrastive sense of the conjunctive pronoun *dithe* suggests that two different speakers are to be envisaged for this line ('Take that! *You* take *that*!'). This fourth line may be a later addition to the *englyn*.

Fragment 2
NLW Llanstephan MS 122, pp. 426–27

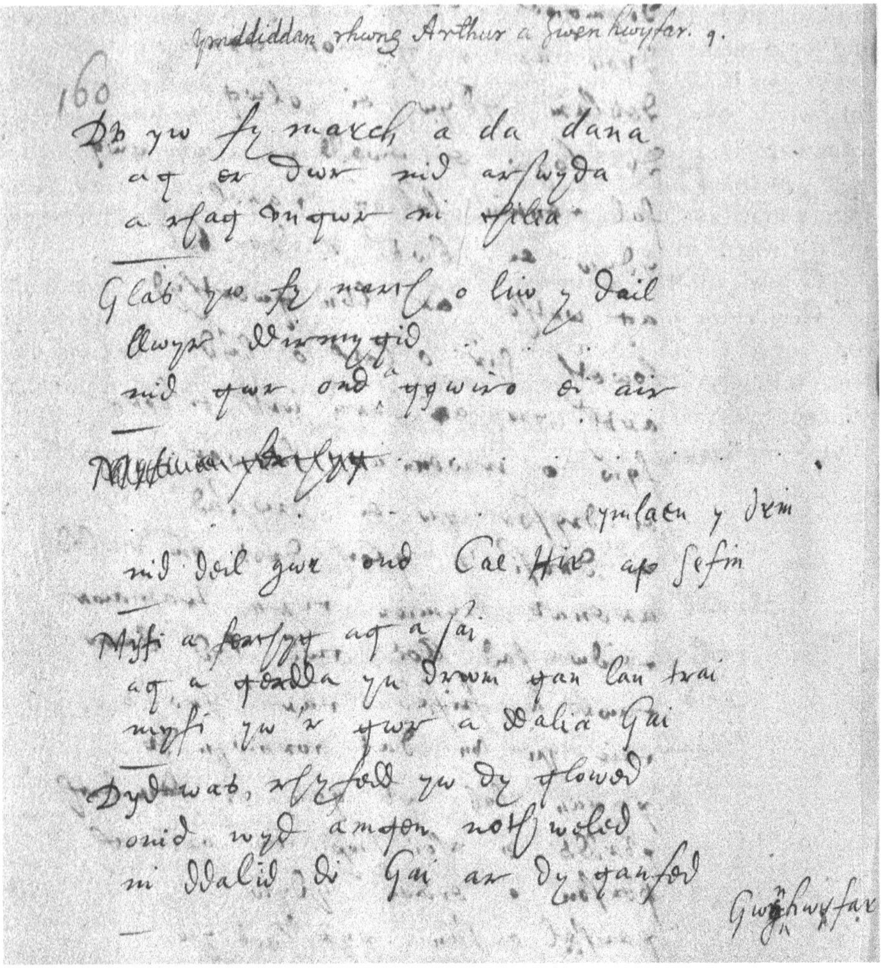

FIG. 5.4: NLW Llanstephan MS 122, pp. 426–27.

Dv yw fy march a da dana
ag er dwr nid arswyda
a rhag vngwr ni chilia

Glas yw fy march o liw y dail
llwyr ddirmygid
nid gwr ond a gywiro ei air

~~Myfi a ferchyg~~ …
… … ymlaen y drin
nid deil gwr ond Cae Hir ap Sefin

Myfi a ferchyg ag a sai
ag a gerdda yn drwm gan lan trai
myfi yw'r gwr a ddalia Gai

Dyd was, rhyfedd yw dy glowed
onid wyd amgen noth weled
ni ddalid di Gai ar dy ganfed

Gwenhwyfar olwg Eirian
na ddifrawd fi cyd bwy bychan
mi a ddaliwn gant fy hunan

Dyd was, o ddv a melyn
wrth hir edrych dy dremyn
tybiais dy weled cyn hyn.

Gwenhwyfar olwg wrthroch
doedwch i mi os gwyddoch
ymha le cyn hyn im gwelsoch.

Mi a welais wr graddol o faint
ar fwrdd hir ... dyfnaint
yn rhannu gwin iw geraint.

Gwenhwyfar barabl digri
cnawd o ben gwraig air gwegi
yno y gwelaist di fi

Stanza 1

  Dv yw fy march, a da dana';
  ag er dwr nid arswyda;
  a rhag vngwr ni chilia.

1 **Dv yw fy march, a da dana'** The line is a syllable too long unless *yw* is omitted (cf. l. 4 below) and ends with a spoken form of the 1 sing. conjugated prep. *dan*. The second half of the line may have been reworked.

2 **ag er dwr nid arswyda** For another figure riding a black horse and associated with water, see Ysgolan, the subject of a dialogue poem in *englyn* metre preserved in the Black Book of Carmarthen (*EWSP*, pp. 202–01).

3 **a rhag vngwr ni chilia** The compound derived from *un* + *gwr* can mean 'any man' or 'a special man, a champion, lone-fighter'. Both would be appropriate here. On initial mutation after *ni* see above, 1.39n.

Stanza 2

  Glas yw fy march, o liw y dail
  llwyr ddirmygid ...
  nid gwr ond a gywiro ei air.

4 **Glas yw fy march, o liw y dail** The reference to horses of different hues is reminiscent of the final section in the Geraint series (see Chapter 1). There may be play here on the meanings of *glas*, the term commonly used for a grey horse, which can also mean 'untamed, not broken in'; see *GPC* glas¹. The second half of the line, however, suggests that *glas* here is used for 'green', the colour of leaves. This has led scholars to suggest that it is a magical beast conjured up from

vegetation; cf. the steeds and hounds created from mushrooms by Gwydion in the Fourth Branch of the *Mabinogi*, and the cattle made from bracken in the Life of Cadog; see *EWSP*, p. 257. Melwas wears a cloak of the colour of leaves, *unlliw a'r dail*, in a fragment preserved in a late sixteenth-century manuscript; see Hughes, 'Camlan', p. 42. It is possible that the original form was *addail*, a term used for vegetation by Dafydd ap Gwilym and his contemporaries. Note, however, that it is generic rhyme which links this line with l. 6; see above, 1.21n.

5 **llwyr ddirmygid ...** A loose compound, 'utterly despised'. The line is only four syllables long, and does not rhyme with the other lines in the *englyn*, so has presumably lost its ending. Wiliam Bodwrda has left a gap which is filled by the words *mefl mowrair* in the manuscripts of the Morris brothers.

6 **nid gwr ond a gywiro ei air** Lit. 'no warrior except the one who fulfils his word', i.e. 'he is no warrior who does not fulfil his word.' The syntax is unusual, but see *GPC* ond^1 c.

This text has a different opening from the previous one, with no obvious connection to the dialogue between Melwas and Gwenhwyfar. This pair of *englynion*, however, contains echoes of ideas in the other series which suggest that the speaker may have been Melwas. Compare, for example, the first stanza with the boastful reference in 1.11–13 to fording a deep river, and in the second stanza the verb *dirmygu* used by Melwas in 1.19. The final line may be a proverbial saying with the same emphasis as 1.25 on the importance for a warrior of keeping his word.

Stanza 3

... ...
... ... ymlaen y drin
ni ddeil gwr ond Cai Hir ap Sefin.

7 ... ... **ymlaen y drin** It is clear from the manuscript that the whole of the first line and the first part of the second were not available to Wiliam Bodwrda. The Morris brothers added the words *pwy a ferchyg ag a ...* | *ag a gerdda*, 'Who rides and ... and travels'; cf. ll. 9–10 below.

8 **ni ddeil gwr ond Cai Hir ap Sefin** MS *nid deil* appears to be a misdivision in copying. For initial mutation after *ni*, see 1.39n. Out of the eight instances of *daliaf: dal* in the two fragments, this is the only example of its use as an intransitive verb: 'No man holds out'. For *gwr* in negative sentences with the meaning '(any) man, anyone', see *GMW*, p. 105 n. 3. The MS form *Cae* is likely to be an error for *Cai*; cf. ll. 11 and 14 below. On Cai's epithet, see *Pa gur*, 67n. Cai is said to be the son of *Kynyr Keinuaruawc* in *Culhwch ac Olwen* (*CO*, ll. 264–65) and in Triad 21 (from the earliest version of the Triads, *TYP*, pp. 308–12). The phrase *ap Sefin* may be a corruption, or may be the name of Cai's mother, as proposed by P. C. Bartrum (*A Welsh Classical Dictionary: People in History and Legend up to About A.D. 1000* (Aberystwyth: National Library of Wales, 1993), p. 582). Sefin appears in a number of Welsh place names,

Glansefin, Abersefin, Cwm Sefin and Dysefin, and may be a Welsh form of the names of Roman martyrs Savinus or Sabina (see Egerton Phillimore's note in George Owen, *Description of Pembrokshire*, Part IV (London: Chas Clark, 1936), p. 377).

Stanza 4
> Myfi a ferchyg, ag a sai',
> ag a gerdda'n drwm gan lan trai:
> myfi yw'r gwr a ddalia Gai.

9   **Myfi a ferchyg ag a sai'** Cf 1.9 where Melwas is described by Gwenhwyfar as *gwr ... ni safai mewn trin*. The line is too long by a syllable unless *myfi* is emended to *mi*; cf. l. 12 below and 1.11. On the ModW form *sai'*, see above, Arthur and the Eagle, 35n.

10   **ag a gerdda'n drwm gan lan trai** The line as it appears in the MS has nine syllables. The 3 sing.pres.indic form *cerdda* is used alongside the older form *cerdd* in MW texts. The adverbial particle following a vowel can be reduced to '*n* and *ag* can be omitted. The meaning of *yn drwm* is obscure here, but the line corresponds partially to 1.13, *a llûric drom drai*, so it may mean 'heavily-laden'. Another possibility is that this instance of *trwm* was originally a noun, 'battle', as in some of the court poetry (*GPC* trwm¹); cf. *AyG*, l. 374, *Nid engis yn nhrwm*, 'there did not escape in battle', and l. 407, *Disgynid yn nhrwm*, 'he attacked in battle' (MS *en trwm*). It may have been misinterpreted by a moderniser of the text as an adjective preceded by an adverbial particle and lenited. The prep. *gan* can mean 'alongside, beside' (*GPC* gan¹ 1c); cf. *gan lann y weilgi*, 'along the sea shore' (*Math*, l. 283). Williams ('Ritual Poem', p. 42), however, suggests accepting the reading of later copies, *gaulan*, understanding it as *ceulan*, '(hollow) bank of a river' (*GPC*), but this does not give an acceptable meaning with *trai*.

11   **myfi yw'r gwr a ddalia Gai** Cf. 1.14, *Mi yw'r gwr a ddaliai Gai*. Both the present and imperfect tenses are possible, but *dalia* may be an error for *daliai* under the influence of the present tense forms in the previous two lines. Note that it is the older 3 sing.pres. form *deil* which is used in the previous stanza.

This *englyn*, in which the un-named speaker, probably Melwas, asserts that he is equal to Cai, appears to be closely related to the third and fourth lines of the fourth *englyn* in the first series.

The following pair of *englynion* are clearly variants of the fifth and sixth stanzas of the first series with more inconsistent line lengths. Comparing them gives an insight into the way the text changed as it was transmitted orally and in writing.

Stanza 5
> Dyd[i], was, rhyfedd yw dy glowed!
> Onid wyd amgen no'th weled,
> ni ddalid-di Gai ar dy ganfed.

12 **Dyd[i], was, rhyfedd yw dy glowed!** The MS form *dyd*, here and in l. 18, can be interpreted as an exclamation, 'aha!, hey!, stop!', a late form possibly borrowed from English *tut!* (*GPC* dỳd²). It is more likely, however, that it is an error for a lenited form of the 2 sing. reduplicated pronoun *tydi*, contrasting with *myfi*; cf. l.15, 21, and see *GPC* tydi, dydi. Although an elided form, *tyd'*, *dyd'*, is possible, as the stress in MW poetic texts is sometimes on the penultimate syllable of the reduplicated pronouns rather than on the final, no other examples have been found: see John Morris Jones, *A Welsh Grammar Historical and Comparative* (Oxford: Clarendon Press, 1913), pp. 271–72. The emended line has, therefore, nine syllables, unless *yw* is omitted. *Clowed* is probably an orthographical variant or an error for the verb noun *clywed*, lit. 'strange is your hearing'.

Stanza 6
>Gwenhwyfar olwg *eirian*,
>na ddifrawd fi, cyd bwy' bychan:
>mi a ddaliwn gant fy hunan.

15 **Gwenhwyfar olwg *eirian*** 'Gwenhwyfar of fair appearance', cf. 1.18, *Gwenhwyvar olwg hyddgan*, where *golwg* may have a different meaning (see *GPC*). This more conventional utterance is probably the result of the reworking of the line. A scribe, probably Wiliam Bodwrda, seems to have understood the adjective *eirian* as a personal name, but there is no evidence of such use in medieval sources.

16 **na ddifrawd fi, cyd bwy' bychan** Cf. 1.19, *Na'm dirmic, cyd bwy' bychan*, noting the use of the affixed object pronoun *fi*, with the negative imperative here (which gives the line eight syllables), rather than the older construction with the infixed pronoun *'m*. The main meaning of *difrodi*, 'to devastate, ravage, squander', is possible, but 'to deny' or 'misjudge, undervalue', found in later sources, are more appropriate here; see *GPC*.

17 **mi a ddaliwn gant fy hunan** Comparison with 1.20, *Mi ddaliwn Gai vy hunan*, suggests that *cant* might be emended to *Cai*.

Stanza 7
>Dyd[i], was o ddv a melyn:
>wrth hir edrych dy dremyn,
>tybiais dy weled cyn hyn.

18 **Dyd[i], was o ddv a melyn** The colours probably refer to the cloak Melwas was wearing; cf. the descriptions of colourful clothing in the Dream of Rhonabwy.

Stanza 8
>Gwenhwyfar olwg wrthroch,
>doedwch *imi*, os gwyddoch:
>ym [m]ha le cyn hyn *y*'m gwelsoch?

21   **Gwenhwyfar olwg wrthroch** The adj. *gwrthroch* may be the only example of a combination of prefix *gwor-*, *gor-* + *troch* (fem. form of adj. *trwch*, 'unfortunate, sad, wretched, bad, evil'), as suggested by *GPC*, or a variant or a miscopied form of *gwrthgroch*, 'gruff, sullen, angry, fierce' (< *gwrth-* + *croch*, 'loud, strident, fierce'), which is attested in the Romance of Owain and in fourteenth-century poetry.

22   **doedwch imi, os gwyddoch** For *doedyd*, a variant form of *dywedyd*, attested in fourteenth-century poetry, see *GPC*. The speaker now addresses Gwenhwyfar using the polite 2 plural form, though he returns to the 2 sg. by the end of the poem. The ModW forms in *-och* (MW *-awch*) in this stanza are confirmed by the rhyme with *gwrthroch*; see 1.27–28n.

23   **ym [m]ha le cyn hyn y'm gwelsoch?** This line may be emended to *ymhle cyn hyn ymwelsoch?* in the light of 1.30, which may be the last line of a missing stanza, in which a third speaker enquires where Melwas and Gwenhwyfar first met. The following stanza, which contains the answer to the question in both versions, clearly derives from a common source.

Stanza 9
>Mi a welais wr graddol o faint,
>ar fwrdd hir ... Dyfnaint,
>yn rhannu gwin i'w geraint.

24   **Mi a welais wr graddol o faint** The preverbal particle *a* may be omitted as in 1.11 and 20. The adj. *graddol*, 'noble, dignified', along with *gradd*, 'dignity', are not found in poetry before the fourteenth century; see *GPC*. Gwenhwyfar may be contrasting her memory of Melwas as 'a man of dignified stature' at a previous encounter and his present diminutive appearance. Jenny Rowland (*EWSP*, p. 257) has suggested that this stanza indicates that Melwas was a shape-shifter, drawing attention to a *cywydd* by the fifteenth-century poet Dafydd ab Edmwnd, where he is referred to as *y lleidr, drwy hud a lledryd, | aeth â bun i eitha' byd*, 'the thief, who through magic and enchantment took a woman to the ends of the earth'.

25   **ar fwrdd hir ... Dyfnaint** The scribe has indicated that words are missing in the middle of this line. This gap is filled by *Celliwig*, the name of Arthur's court, in the later manuscripts. A phrase such as *ar dir*, 'in the land', as in the corresponding line in the first series (1.33), would fit, though the repetition of *ar* would be weak. It is possible that in both versions of the stanza scribes were grappling with forms that were obscure to them.

Stanza 10
>Gwenhwyfar barabl digri,
>cnawd o ben gwraig air gwegi:
>yno y gwelaist di fi.

27 Gwenhwyfar barabl digri Cf. Arthur and the Eagle, l. 31, *Yr Eryr barabl difrad*, 'Oh Eagle of guileless speech'. *Digrif* has a wide range of meanings, including 'delightful, pleasant; entertaining, facetious, amusing'. The rhyme between *digri*, *gwegi* and *fi* is late. For the form *digri*, another example of the loss of *-f* common from the fourteenth century onwards, see *GMW*, p. 9, and above, 9n.

28 cnawd o ben gwraig air gwegi 'usual from the mouth of a woman is a frivolous word'; cf. 1.24, *Gnawd i veddw [air] gwecry*. For *cnawd* as a late variant of the adj. *gnawd*, 'usual', which arose through an imagined connection with *cnawd*, 'flesh', see *GPC* gnawd.

29 yno y gwelaist-di fi The object pronoun *fi* is used in this phrase where the infixed pronoun (*y'm gweleist*) would be normal in MW; cf. l. 23 above.

In this last stanza, the speaker, who is anonymous in this series but named as Melwas in the first series, finishes by confirming to Gwenhwyfar that it was in Devon that he saw her previously. Space has been left at the bottom of the page and the following page is also empty. Was Wiliam Bodwrda perhaps hoping to find more stanzas?

Word-list

a¹ *preverbal particle* (causing lenition) 1.25, 29, 2.9(2), 10, 17, 24

a² *rel.pron.* (causing lenition) 'who' 1.14, 36, 2.6, 11 (*with infixed object pron. 3 sg.* 'i'), 1.29n; **ag a** 1.12n

a³ *conj.* (causing spirant mutation, *GMW*, p. 21) 'and' 2.1, 3, 18, **ag** 2.2, 9, 10 (before a vowel), 1.9 (before *ni*), for **ag a** see **a²**

a⁴ *prep.* (causing spirant mutation) 'as' (*GPC* â¹ 4a) 1.12, 'with' (*GPC* â¹ 2a) 1.13, 15 (*with infixed poss.pron. 2 sg.* 'th'), 1.22, 35 (*with infixed poss.pron. 3 sg.masc.* 'i')

ado see 1.9n

ag see **a²**, **a³**

amgen *adj.* 'different, better' 2.13, *with nominal force* (see *GPC*) 'something different, something better' 1.36

anhebic *adj.* 'unlike, dissimilar' (*GPC* annhebyg) 1.22

ap see **Cai**

ar *prep.* 'upon, at, beside, to' 1.9n, 21n, 26, 33, 2.25, 'as one of, with' (before ordinals, *GPC* ar¹ 3d) 1.17n, 2.14

aro *2 sg.imper. of* **aros**, 'wait, stay' 1.7

arswyda *3 sg.pres.indic. of* **arswydo**, 'to dread, fear greatly' 2.2

arveisiwn *1 sg.imperf.indic. of* **arveisio**, 'to cross, to wade across' (*GPC* arfeisiaf: arfeisio) 1.11n

aûr *adj.* 'gold, golden' 1.5n

balch *adj.* 'proud, arrogant, insolent' 1.38
blyche *pl. of* **blwch**, 'box, receptacle' 1.5n
bod *vb.* 'to be' *2 sg.pres.indic.* **wyt** 1.16n, 23, **wyd** 2.13; *3 sg.pres.indic.* **yw** 1.14, 2.1, 4n, 12n (combined with '**r**), 1.26, 2.11; *1 sg.pres.subj.* **bwy'** 1.19n, 2.16; *3 sg.pres.subj.* **bo** 1.12
braint *n.* 'status, privilege, prestige' 1.31n
bwrdd *n.* 'table' 2.25
bwy' see **bod**
bychan *adj.* 'little, small in stature; inconspicuous; young, inexperienced' 1.19n, 2.16

cadwn *1 sing.imperf.indic. of* **cadw**, 'to keep, uphold' 1.25n
Cai *personal name* 1.10, 14, 17, 20, 23, 2.11, 14 **Cai Hir ap Sefin** 2.8n
canfed *ordinal numeral* 'hundredth' 2.14
cant *numeral* 'a hundred, a hundred people' 2.17n
canys *conj.* 'since' (*GPC* canys¹) 1.27
cas *adj.* 'hateful, hated, disagreeable' 1.34; *comparative* **casach** 1.37
cemyn *equative adj.* (variant form of *cymaint*) 'as great, as much' 1.12n
ceraint *pl. of n.* **câr**, 'kinsman, friend, companion' 1.33n, 2.26
cerdda *3 sg.pres.indic. of* **cerdded**, 'to walk' 2.10
cilia *3 sg.pres.indic. of* **cilio**, 'to retreat, recede' 2.3
cledde *n.* 'sword' (*GPC* cleddau, cleddyf) 1.35n, 39
clywed *v.n.* 'to hear' 2.12
cnawd see **gnawd**
coch *adj.* 'red, ginger (of hair)' 1.22n
cyd *conj.* 'although' (*GPC* cyd³) 1.19, 2.16
cyffredinrwydd *n.* 'commonness, the commonality, the common part' 1.1n
cyn *prep.* 'before' 2.20, 23
cyntedd *n.* 'the upper part of the hall in which the king sat' 1.3n
cywiro *3 sg.pres.subj. of* **cywiro**, 'to rectify, make good, fulfil (promise)' 2.6
chwenych *3 sg.pres.indic. of* **chwenychu**, 'to desire, lust, long for' (*GPC* chwennychaf: chwennych) 1.36

d' see **dy**
da *adj.* 'good' 2.1
dail *collective n.* 'leaves' 2.4
dal *vb.* 'to capture, seize, hold fast, restrain; endure, remain' *3 sg.pres.indic.* **deil** 2.8n, **dalia** 2.11n; *1 sg.imperf.indic.* **daliwn** 1.20, 2.17; *2 sg.imperf.indic.* **dalut** 1.17n, **dalid** 2.14; *3 sg.imperf.indic.* **daliai** 1.10n, 14
dan *prep.* 'under' 1.35, *conjugated form 1 sg.* **dana'** (*GPC* tan¹, dan) 2.1n
dechreû *n.* 'beginning' (*GPC* dechrau) 1.2

dechreûasoch *2 pl.pret. of* **dechreu**, 'to begin' 1.27n
deil see **dal**
di[1] *independent pron. 2 sing.* 'you' (*GPC* ti[1], di[3] a) 1.5n
di[2] *affixed pron. 2 sing.* (*GPC* ti[1], di[3] b) 1.40, 2.14, 29
difrawd *2 sg.imper. of vb.* **difrodi**, 'to devastate, ravage, squander, deny, misjudge, undervalue' 2.16n
digri *adj.* 'delightful, pleasing, amusing, comical' (*GPC* digrif) 2.27n
dim *pron.* 'anything' 1.6n
dirmygu *vb.* 'to despise, disdain, disparage' *2 sg.imper.* **dirmic** 1.19, *impers.impf.* **dirmygid** 2.5
dithe *conjunctive affixed pron. 2 sg.* 'you for your part, you too' (*GPC* tithau) 1.40n
diwedd *n.* 'end' 1.2
doedwch *2 pl.imper. of vb.* **doedyd** (*GPC* dywedyd), 'to say, tell' 2.22n
dv *adj. and n.* 'black' 2.1, 18
dwir see 1.33n
dwr *n.* 'water, river' (*GPC* dŵr) 2.2
dy *2 sg. poss.pron.* 'your' (causing lenition) 2.12, 14, 19, 20, **d'** 1.17n
dydi see **tydi**
Dyfnaint *place name* Dyfnaint, Dumnonia, Devon and Cornwall 1.32n, 2.25

eb *prep.* 'without' (causing lenition, *GPC* heb[1], eb[1]) 1.2n, 36
edrych *v.n.* 'to look at' 2.19
edwyn *3 sg.pres.indic. of* **adwaen: adnabot**, 'to know, recognise' 1.29
ef *preverbal particle* (with **a**[1], *GPC* ef 2b) 1.29
ei see **i**[1]
eiddaw *stressed poss.pron.* 'his' 1.2n
eirian *adj.* 'beautiful, fair, bright' 2.15n
eiste *v.n.* 'to sit' 1.3; *3 sg.pres.indic.* **eistedd** 1.1
er *prep.* 'because of, on account of' 2.2n

val *prep.* 'like' 1.22
fi *affixed object pron.* 'me' 2.16n, 29n
-vi see **-i**
vin see 1.10n
vy, fy *1 sg.poss.pron.* 'my' (causing nasal mutation) 1.8 (combined with *gwin*), 1.20, 2.1, 3, 17
vyngwin see **vy**

gadwn *1 pl.impv. of* **gadael**, 'to leave, part, separate, to leave off, desist' 1.26
gair *n.* 'word, promise' 1.24, 2.6, 28, *pl.* **geirie** 1.38

gallel *v.n.* 'to be able (to accomplish a thing)' 1.36
gan *prep.* 'with; along, beside' 2.10n, *conjugated form 1 sg.* **gennyf** (-n-) 1.34n, 37 (with **cas**, see *GPC*)
geirie see **gair**
gen *n.* 'jaw, chin' (*GPC* gên) 1.35
gen(n)yf see **gan**
glan *n.* 'shore' 2.10n
glas *adj.* 'grey, untamed, not broken in, green' 2.4n
gnawd, cnawd *adj.* 'usual, customary' 1.24n, 2.28n
golwg *n.* 'sense of sight, vision' 1.18n, 'appearance' 2.15n, 21
goreûrin *adj.* 'gilt, gold-covered' 1.5
graddol *adj.* 'noble, dignified' 2.24n
gwaell *n.* 'knitting-needle, skewer, pin' (*GPC* gwäell) 1.35n
gwallofaf *1 sg.pres.* of **gwallaw**, 'to pour out, serve' 1.8n
gwas *n.* 'lad' 1.15, 21, 2.12, 18
gwecry *adj.* 'fickle' 1.24n
gwegi *n.* 'levity, frivolousness' 2.28
gweled (-t) *v.n.* 'to see' 2.20; *as a n.* 'appearance' 1.16n, 2.13; *1 sg.pret.* **gwelais** 2.24; *2 sg.pret.* **gwelaist** 2.29; *2 pl.pret.* **gwelsoch** 2.23
gwell *comparative adj.* 'better' 1.16
gwên *n.* 'a smile, smirk, happy face' 1.34
Gwenhwyvar (-far) *personal name* Gwenhwyfar 1.18, 2.15, 21, 27
gwin *n.* 'wine' 1.6, 8, 32, 2.26
gwir *adj. and n.* 'true, right; truth' 1.33n
gwledd *n.* 'a feast' 1.1
gwr *n.* 'man, warrior' 1.1, 9, 14, 38, 2.6, 8, 11, 24
gwraig *n.* 'woman' 2.28
gwrllwyd *n.* 'grey, pallid man, grey-haired man' 1.34n
gwrthroch *adj.* 'wretched, surly, fierce' 2.21n
gwryd *n.* 'a fathom' (*GPC* gwryd¹) 1.12n
gwyddoch *2 pl.pres.indic.* of **gwybod**, 'to know' 2.22n
gynt *adv.* 'formerly, before' (*GPC* cynt, gynt) 1.30

hen *adj.* 'old, ancient' 1.34n
hir *adj.* 'long, tall, lengthy' 2.19, 25, see also **Cai Hir**
hunan *a reflexive pron. used in apposition to a poss.pron.*, **vy hunan**, 'myself, on my own, alone' (see *GMW*, pp. 89–90) 1.20, 2.17
hwde *2 sg.impv.* of defective vb. 'take!' (see *GPC*) 1.40(2)n
hyddgan *collective or singular n.* 'a herd of deer, a stag' 1.18n
hyn *demonstrative pron.* 'this' 2.20, 23
hyny *demonstrative pron.* 'that, that thing' (*GPC* hynny) 1.26

'i¹ *infixed poss.pron. 3 sg.masc.* (causing lenition) 1.29 (with **a¹**), 1.22, 35 (with **a³**), see also **'w**

'i² *infixed poss.pron. 3 sing.fem.* 1.2(2) (with **na**)

i¹, ei *prefixed poss.pron. 3 sing.masc.* 'his' (causing lenition, *GPC* ei¹) 1.10, 35, 39, ei 2.6

i² *prefixed poss.pron. 3 sing.fem.* 'her' (causing spirant mutation) 1.31n

i³, -vi *affixed pron. 1 sg.* 1.6, 8

i⁴ *prep.* 'to' 1.22, 24, *conjugated form 1 sg.* **imi**, 'to me', 2.22, *with infixed poss. pron. 3 sg.masc.* **i'w** (*GMW*, p. 53 n. 2) 2.26

iawn *n.* 'what's right, justice, truth, fairness' 1.25n

imi see i⁴

ine *conjunctive affixed pron. 1 sg.* 'I for my part, I on the other hand' (*GPC* innau) 1.37n

islaw *prep.* 'below, lower or further down than' (see *GPC*) 1.3

lle *n.* 'place' 1.33n, see also **ymhle, ymha le**

llewais *1 sg.pret. of vb.* **llewaf**: **llewa**, 'to drink' 1.6

lliw *n.* 'colour' 2.4

lloch *3 sg.pres.indic. of* **llochi**, 'to caress, fondle, protect, foster, coax' 1.29

llûric *n.* 'coat of mail, breastplate, armour' (*GPC* llurig) 1.13

llwrf *adj.* 'cowardly, timid, mean' (*GPC* llwrf¹, llwfr) 1.38

llwyr *adj. used as adv.* 'completely, utterly' 2.5n

llys *n.* 'court' 1.31n

'm *1 sg.infixed object pron.* 1.19 (with **na³**), 2.23 (with **y²**)

mab *n.* 'son, boy' 1.29

maint *n.* 'size, stature' 1.21n, 23, 2.24

march *n.* 'horse' 2.1, 4

meddw *n.* 'drunken person, drunkard' 1.24n

Melwas, Y *personal name* 1.4n, 26

melyn *adj. and n.* 'yellow' 2.18

merchyg *3 sg.pres.indic. of* **marchogaeth**, 'to ride (a horse)' 2.9

mewn *prep.* 'in' 1.9n, 31

mi *independent pron. 1 sg.* 'I' 11n, 14, 20, 26, 2.17, 24

myfi *reduplicated independent pron. 1 sg.* 'I, it is I' 2.9n, 11

'n see yn³

na¹ *conj.* 'or, and' (causing spirant mutation, *GPC* na⁴) **na** ... **na** '(n)either ... (n)or' *with infixed poss.pron. 3 sg.fem.* **na'i** 1.2(2)

na² see **no**

na³ *negative preverbal particle* (before an imper.vb., *GPC* na²) 2.16, *with infixed obj.pron. 1 sg.* **na'm** 1.19

ni *neg. preverbal particle* (*GPC* ni²) 6, 8, 9(2), 10, 17, 2.8, 14 (causing lenition), 1.39(2)n, 2.3 (causing spirant mutation), **nid** 2.2 (before a vowel)
nid *negative of copula* 'it is not, he is not' (*GPC* nid² and *GMW*, p. 141) 2.6n
no, na² *conj.* 'than' (*GPC* no¹, na³) *with infixed poss.pron. 2 sg.* **na'th** 1.16n, **no'th** 2.13

o *prep.* 'from, of' 1.4, 2.4, 28, 'from, given by' 1.32, 'as regards' 1.23, 2.24, 'wearing' (*GPC* o¹19) 2.18n *with infixed poss. 2 sg.* **o'th** 'of your' 1.6
obry *adv.* 'down below, down there' (*GPC*) 1.3
ond *prep.* 'except for, except, but' (*GPC* ond¹) 1.38, 2.6, 8
onit (-d) *conj.* 'if ... not, unless' 1.16, 2.13
os *conj.* 'if' 2.22

pa *interrogative pron.* 'what? what kind? why? who?' (*GMW*, p. 75, *GPC* pa¹, py¹) 1.1n
parabl *n.* 'speech, utterance' 2.27
pen *n.* 'head, end' 1.21n, 'hair' 1.22n, 'mouth' 2.28

'r see **y¹**
rhag *prep.* 'before, in front of, in the presence of, in the face of' 2.3; *2 pl.* **rhagoch**, 'further, more' (*GMW*, p. 207, with verbs of motion) 1.28n
rhannu *v.n.* 'to distribute, share out' 2.26
rhyd *n.* 'a ford' 11
rhyfedd *adj.* 'strange, astonishing, wonderful' 2.12

safai *3 sing.imperf.indic. of* **sefyll**, 'to stand, to stand one's ground (in battle), to withstand' 1.9n, *3 sg.pres.indic.* **sai'** 2.9n
salwet *n.* 'vileness, meanness' 1.15n
Sefin see **Cai**
snevin see 1.7n

tewi *vb.* 'to be quiet, to shut up' *3 sg.pres.indic.* **taw** 1.39, *2 sing.imper.* **taw** 1.15n
tir *n.* 'land' 1.33
trai¹ *n.* 'an ebb-tide, low tide' 1.13n, 2.10
trai² *adj.* 'full of holes, shattered' 1.13n
tremyn *n.* 'sight, appearance' (*GPC* tremynt¹) 2.19
trin *n.* 'battle, fighting' 1.9, 2.7
trom see **trwm**
trwm *adj.* 'heavy, weighty, substantial' 2.10; *fem.* **trom** 1.13
tybiais *1 sg.pret. of* **tybio**, 'to suppose, believe, imagine' 2.20
tydi *reduplicated independent pron. 2 sg.* 'you' 1.15n, 21 **dydi** 2.12n, 18

tyn *3 sg.pres.indic. of* **tynnu**, 'to pull, draw (sword, etc.)' 1.39
'th *infixed poss.pron. 2 sg.* (causing lenition) 'your' 1.6, 15, 16, 2.13

ungwr *n.* 'any man; special man, champion' 2.3n
urddasol *adj.* 'dignified, honoured' 1.31n

v see **f**

'w *infixed poss.pron. 3 sg.masc.* 2.26 (with **i⁴**)
wrth *prep.* 'as a result of' 2.19
wyt see **bod**
wythvet *ordinal numeral* 'eighth' 1.17n

y¹ *definite article* 'the' 1.4n, 2.4, 7, **'r** 1.3, 14, 26, 2.11 (after vowels)
y² *preverbal particle* 2.29, with infixed pron. object 1 sg. **y'm** 2.23
ychydic *n. with adverbial force* 'a little, a short while' (*GMW*, p. 103) 1.7
ymddiddenwch *2 pl.impv. of* **ymddiddan**, 'to converse' 1.28n
ymhle, ym mha le *interrogative pron.* 'where? in what place?' 1.30, 2.23
ymlaen *prep.* 'in the front of, before' (*GPC*) 2.7
ymwelsawch *2 pl.pret. of* **ymweled**, 'to see each other' 1.30n
yn¹ *prep.* (*GPC* yn¹, causing nasal mutation, see *GMW*, p. 21) 'in' 1.1n, 10, see also
    ymhle, ym mha le
yn² *particle with v.n.* (*GPC* yn², *GMW*, p. 215, causing no mutation) 1.32, 2.26
yn³ *predicative and adverbial particle* (*GPC* yn³, *GMW*, p. 139, causing lenition
    except in *ll-* and *-rh*) **'n** 1.35, 2.10n (after vowels)
yno *adv.* 'there' 2.29
Ynys Wydrin *place name* Glastonbury 1.4n
yr *preverbal particle* (*GPC* yr⁴) 1.30
ysgyvaint *n.* 'lungs' (*GPC* ysgyfaint) 1.22n
yvet *v.n.* 'to drink' (*GPC* yfaf: yfed) 1.32
yw see **bod**

The Elegy for Cynddylan

This poem, generally assumed to have been composed in the seventh century, contains a line which may describe its subject and his fellow warriors as 'whelps of great Arthur'. This reference to Arthur is uncertain, however, as it is based on a textual emendation, and another reading of the line which does not involve Arthur is possible. The uncertainty surrounding the reference is compounded by the fact that the earliest surviving copy of the poem was made during the early years of the seventeenth century.

NLW MS 4973B is one of three collections of medieval Welsh poetry compiled by John Davies, Rector of Mallwyd in Meirionnydd and a Welsh Renaissance scholar.[40] The other two are copies of the Hendregadredd Manuscript and the Black Book of Carmarthen. MS 4973B, known as Liber B, is a more varied compilation containing court poems from now lost pages of the Hendregadredd Manuscript,[41] a copy of the Book of Taliesin, miscellaneous poems taken from various copies of the Red Book of Hergest and from the Red Book itself, as well as some historical and religious prose texts.[42]

The unattributed poem entitled *Marwnad Cynddylan*, 'The Elegy for Cynddylan', was copied from an unknown source.[43] The text, written in modern spelling, contains a number of words and phrases which are obviously corrupt. Some of these errors reveal traces of an older orthographic system, similar to that of the Black Book of Carmarthen, which was clearly unfamiliar to the moderniser of the text.[44] This is not likely to have been John Davies, as his modernisations of other medieval texts show that he was an intelligent and accurate copier.[45] It may have been Thomas Gruffudd, a sixteenth-century nobleman of Lampeter in Ceredigion, from whose 'book' the prophetic poem which follows the elegy in John Davies' manuscript is said to be taken.[46] This prophetic poem is also found in a copy by the early seventeenth-century

---

[40] For John Davies, see *Dr John Davies*, ed. by Davies, and for the collections he made of medieval Welsh poetry, see in particular Chapter 4, Daniel Huws, 'John Davies and his Manuscripts', and Chapter 7, Nerys Ann Jones and Morfydd E. Owen, 'John Davies and the Poets of the Princes: *Cognoscere, Intellegere, Scire*'.

[41] These include poems by Seisyll Bryffwrch and Llywarch Brydydd y Moch discussed in Chapter 3 above.

[42] A digital copy can be viewed on the National Library of Wales website at <http://www.llgc.org.uk/index.php?id=4057>.

[43] It appears on ff. 108–09ʳ following a transcript of the Book of Taliesin. Its first editor, Ifor Williams, in 'Marwnad Cynddylan', *Bulletin of the Board of Celtic Studies*, 6 (1932), 134–41, based his text on later copies. John Davies' text has been edited by R. Geraint Gruffydd in 'Marwnad Cynddylan', *Bardos: Penodau ar y traddodiad barddol Cymreig a Cheltaidd*, ed. by R. Geraint Gruffydd (Cardiff: University of Wales Press, 1982), pp. 10–28, by Jenny Rowland, *EWSP*, pp. 174–89, and by John T. Koch, *Cunedda, Cynan, Cadwallon, Cynddylan: Four Welsh Poems and Britain 383–655* [CCCC] (Aberystwyth: University of Wales Centre for Advanced Welsh and Celtic Studies, 2013), pp. 231–92. The latter discusses the possibility that the poem was composed by Meigant, named as its author in the *Myvyrian Archaiology* (London, 1801); CCCC, pp. 260–63.

[44] See *EWSP*, p. 180.

[45] Jenny Rowland notes that John Davies' tendency, when unsure of a reading, was to copy his original faithfully; see *EWSP*, p. 180.

[46] Thomas Gruffydd of Mynydd Hywel is described as *Lord of Llanbedr-pont-Estevan* by the poet and genealogist Lewys Dwnn, who visited the area in 1591: see S. R. Meyrrick, *The History and Antiquities of the County of Cardigan* (London: Davies and Co., 1907, reprint, Rhaeadr, 2000), pp. 219, 223. There are also poems attributed to him and, according to Daniel Huws (personal correspondence), he is probably the relative of John Dee, who gave him a manuscript of Welsh poetry to be translated by Maurice Kyffin in 1578 and who visited him in 1590.

scholar John Jones of Gellilyfdy, of a similarly garbled modernisation by a sixteenth-century antiquarian of a medieval original said to be written on a *dalen o femrwn* (a leaf of parchment).[47] It contains indications of a similar orthographic system and even the same letter formations as those underlying the text of the prophetic poem copied by Thomas Gruffudd, and is followed by another prophetic poem also found in the Book of Taliesin.[48] It is tempting to speculate that the page once belonged to the lost thirteenth-century manuscript containing the Elegy for Cynddylan, which was copied by Thomas Gruffudd, but as yet there is no way of testing this hypothesis.

John Koch has suggested that an even older system of spelling may be discerned in places, but the extent of antiquarian interference with the text makes it very difficult to be certain.[49] The poem's metre is so common that it provides no aid to dating,[50] but it is similar in style and structure to two poems from the Book of Taliesin, *Preideu Annwn* (see Chapter 4 above) and *Echrys Ynys*, a mid-eleventh-century elegy for Aeddon, a lord in Anglesey.[51] The repetition of the opening phrase and much of the concluding couplet in most stanzas is a striking feature that they have in common.[52] Williams claimed that the poem's language is full of echoes of early poetry, but a detailed comparison does not yield a great number of similarities in vocabulary or syntax. Neither does it contain many of the stock phrases or motifs found in the eulogies and elegies of later centuries.

Cynddylan is named in the final line of each *awdl* except for the last. He is praised for his heroic qualities, but there is also an emphasis on the tragedy of his death in battle and the loss suffered by his people and by the poet himself who, now in exile in Anglesey, longs for the life he once enjoyed in the courts of the kingdom of Powys. References to raiding beyond the river Tern, which formed part of the old border of Powys (l. 22), and to 'the sons of Cyndrwynyn' (see below), suggest that he is Cynddylan son of Cyndrwyn, the early seventh-century ruler in Powys who features as brother to the speaker of the ninth-

---

[47] For the text, see Ifor Williams, 'Dalen o femrwn', *Bulletin of the Board of Celtic Studies*, 4 (1927–1929), 41–48, poem 1. An English edition by Marged Haycock is forthcoming.
[48] See *PBT* poem 6.
[49] See *CCCC*, p. 275.
[50] It is a series of nine short *awdlau* of varying length, consisting of fourteen eleven-syllable lines, twenty-two ten-syllable lines, thirty-two nine-syllable lines and three eight-syllable lines. It is difficult to determine to what extent this variation in syllable length is due to the corruption of the text, but similar variation is found in poems by the twelfth-century court poets Gwalchmai and Gwynfardd Brycheiniog, and cf. two poems from the Book of Taliesin, 'The Praise of Tenby' and *Armes Prydein*, where the lines are mostly of nine syllables with some of ten syllables.
[51] For the dating of the poem, see Thomas Charles-Edwards, *Wales and the Britons 350–1064* (Oxford: Oxford University Press, 2013), pp. 665–68.
[52] See Chapter 4 above and Gruffydd, 'Court Poem', pp. 39–48.

century cycle of saga poems *Canu Heledd*.⁵³ Very little is known of him from other early sources and little is known of the history of Powys in this period,⁵⁴ but R. Geraint Gruffydd has suggested that *mab pyd* in l. 28 of the elegy may be a reference to Penda, a ruler of Mercia (fl. 626–55), and that Cynddylan was an ally of his against the kings of Northumbria.⁵⁵ The reference to fighting before Lichfield at the heart of the Mercian kingdom (ll. 47, 53) has been interpreted by Jenny Rowland as further evidence of a Powys-Mercia alliance.⁵⁶ There is no firm evidence as to the circumstances of Cynddylan's death.⁵⁷ The extant elegy, which appears not to contain any historical anachronisms, is thought by Rowland to be a reworking of an elegy for him which was composed soon after his death, intended as an appeal to an unnamed ruler of Gwynedd (addressed as 'the prince of Dogfeiling' in lines 9 and 15) on behalf of the descendants of Cyndrwyn.⁵⁸ Sims-Williams has suggested that the elegy, along with *Canu Heledd*, was preserved by a church of the cult of St Beuno in the territory of the Cyndrwynin in southern Powys, perhaps St Beuno's church of Berriw.⁵⁹ The question of whether it was composed by Cynddylan's court poet or by another using the *persona* of that sorrowful exiled poet has not been addressed by scholars; neither has the possibility that the speaker is depicted as a relative of Cynddylan, like Llywarch Hen, who is presented as a cousin of Urien in *Canu Urien*.⁶⁰

It is in connection with warriors referred to as the poet's brothers that a possible reference to Arthur appears in the poem. The section in which this occurs, the seventh *awdl*, is presented and discussed in detail below.⁶¹ Because of the corruption of the text, it is difficult to produce a definitive translation. An edited text with detailed notes and a comprehensive word-list follows.

---

⁵³ It has been suggested that this poem may have been the inspiration for *Canu Heledd*. Unlike the *englynion*, however, there are no signs that it was well known to the court poets of the twelfth and thirteenth centuries.
⁵⁴ Assuming that he is a historical figure, the fact that he does not appear in the genealogies of the family of Cyndrwyn may be due to the fact that he died young, as is indicated in l. 29 of the elegy. For a summary and discussion of the information that can be gleaned from historical and literary sources, see *EWSP*, pp. 120–41.
⁵⁵ See Gruffydd, 'Court Poem', p. 14, and *EWSP*, p. 184.
⁵⁶ *EWSP*, p. 133.
⁵⁷ For a discussion of various possibilities, see Patrick Sims-Williams, 'Powys and Early Welsh Poetry', *Cambrian Medieval Celtic Studies*, 67 (2014), 41–43.
⁵⁸ See *EWSP*, p. 135.
⁵⁹ 'Powys and Early Welsh Poetry', pp. 50–52.
⁶⁰ The 'brothers' the poet lost in the fighting at Lichfield (ll. 4–6 below) are described as 'the sons of the family of Cyndrwyn' (l. 8) and are likely to be the warriors with alliterating names in the previous section, one of whom is listed as a son of Cyndrwyn in a genealogy: see *EWSP*, p. 186. Rowland, however, interprets *brodyr* as 'brothers (in arms)'.
⁶¹ A digital copy of the manuscript can be viewed on the National Library of Wales website at <http://www.llgc.org.uk/drychdigidol>.

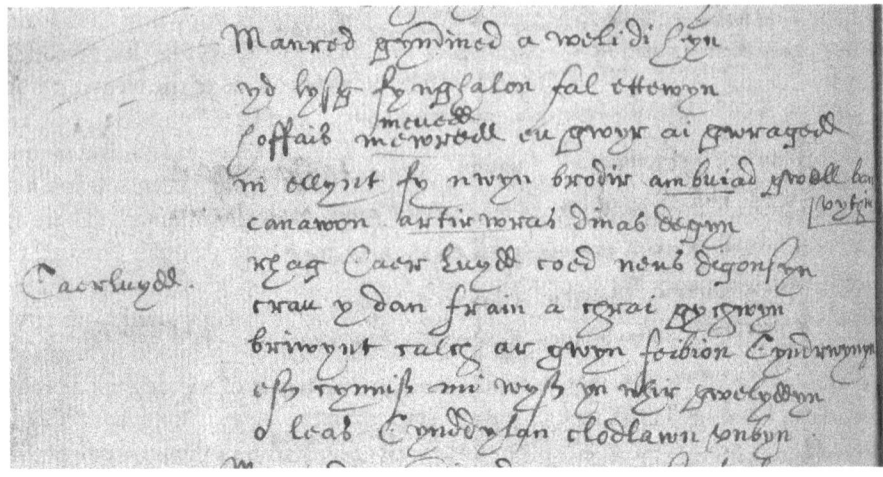

FIG. 5.5: NLW MS 4973B, f. 108ᵛ.

Manred gymined a weli di hyn | yd lysg fy nghalon fal ettewyn | hoffais mewredd[62] eu gwyr ai gwragedd | ni ellynt fy nwyn brodir am buiad gwell ban vythin | canawon artir wras dinas degyn | rhag Caer Luydd coed neus digonsyn | crau y dan frain a chrai gychwyn | briwynt calch ar gwyn feibion Cyndrwynyn | ef cynnif mi wyf yn nhir gwelyddyn | o leas Cynddylan clodlawn vnbyn

        Ma*u*red gymined — a weli-di hyn?
        Yd lysg fy nghalon fal ettewyn.
        Hoffais *ueuuedd* eu gwyr a'*u* gwragedd. Ni ellynt fy nwyn.
        Brodir a'm buiad, gwell ban vythin.
5   Canawon artir wras, dinas degyn,
        rhag *Caer Luytcoed* neu's digonsyn:
        crau y dan frain a chrai gychwyn.
        Briwynt calch ar gwyn feibion Cyndrwynyn.
        Ef *cuynif ini wuyf* yn nhir gwelyddyn
10   o leas Cynddylan clodlawn vnbyn.

1 **Maured gymined** This phrase is repeated at the beginning of each *awdl* apart from the first, which may be acephalous. The erroneous form *manred* may be due to a scribe's unfamiliarity with the use of *u* for /u/ in the thirteenth-century orthography of his exemplar (cf. *buiad*, l. 4). The final *-ð* (represented by *-t* in earlier spelling) is confirmed by the end-rhyme of the first stanza. If the mutation of *cymined* is correct (initial mutation would probably not have been indicated in older orthography), it would suggest that *maured* is a genitive, perhaps giving the meaning 'a battle of greatness'. The unusual form of the *-m-*

---

[62] With *meuedd* written above *mewredd* by the same hand.

in *gymined*, which looks like *-nd-* here, is repeated in the other stanzas.

a weli-di hyn? Koch (*CCCC*, p. 298) suggests that the second half of the line has been altered in transmission as there is no rhyme or repetition to connect it to the opening phrase.

   2   **Yd lysg fy nghalon fal ettewyn** Two twelfth-century court poets use the same image to express their grief: Gwalchmai (*CBT* I 10.30), *callonn klywaf yn llosgi*, 'I feel my heart burning', and Daniel ap Llosgwrn Mew (II 18.22–23), *yd lysc uy ghallonn yg cof meith | mal yd llysc gwynna6n gan oteith*, 'my heart burns in a long memory just as dry twigs burn in a bonfire'.

   3   **meuuedd** It was probably John Davies himself who provided the better reading, *meuedd*, 'wealth', above the corrupt form *mewredd* in the text. The original word may well have been *meuvedd*, a variant of *meuedd* (see *GPC* meufedd, meuedd), with *w* used for /v/ as in the Black Book of Carmarthen (cf. *wras* in l. 5 below). Lenition to the object of the verb is not shown here.

Hoffais ueuuedd eu gwyr a'u gwragedd. Ni ellynt fy nwyn. The metre of this line is different from the rest of the poem and it is difficult to find an appropriate meaning for *ni ellynt fy nwyn* (see *GPC* dygaf: dwyn). Williams suggests emending the beginning of line 4 to *Fy ngomedd ni ellyn*, 'they could not refuse me' (see *GPC* gomeddaf: gomedd and for *gellyn(t)* see l. 4, *bythin*). This would provide an internal rhyme and an end-rhyme, giving a regular *Traeanog*, with the addition of an affixed pronoun to *hoffais* to give the right number of syllables (see *WCP*, pp. xlii–iii):

>   Hoffais [i] ueuu*edd* * eu gwyr a'u gwrag*edd*.
>   fy ngom*edd* ni ellyn.

Gruffydd offers another emendation of the final section which keeps closer to the manuscript text but has no internal rhyme or alliteration, linking it to the previous two sections as is usual in a *Traeanog*:

>   Hoffais [i] ueuu*edd* * eu gwyr a'u gwrag*edd*.
>   fy niwyn ni ellyn.

Gruffydd interprets the manuscript form *dwyn* as an error for *diwyn* (*GPC* diwygiaf: diwyn), giving the meaning 'they could not recompense me [enough]'. Koch accepts the manuscript reading but takes *gellyn(t)* to be the final word of a twelve-syllable line, causing an unusual enjambement:

>   Hoffais ueuuedd eu gwyr a'u gwragedd. Ni ellyn
>   fy nwyn. Brodir a'm buiad, gwell ban vythin.

He posits, however, that *dwyn* is a cognate of Old Irish *dúan*, 'song, poem', otherwise unknown in Welsh; see *CCCC*, p. 289.

None of the interpretations of this line are satisfactory. Whilst *Toddaid* or *Cyhydedd Hir* is commonly found with lines of *Cyhydedd Naw Ban*, a combination of *Cyhydedd Naw Ban* and *Toddaid Byr* or *Traeanog* is extremely rare. (For an example, see the closing lines of *Kadeir Kerrituen, LPBT* 10.40–42).

  4 **Brodir a'm buiad, gwell ban vythin** An unusual form of the verb 'to be' preceded by an infixed dative pronoun is used here to denote possession, 'brothers there were to me' (*GMW*, p. 57). Cf. three very similar lines in *Canu Heledd* (*EWSP* 'Canu Heledd', stanzas 85, 86 and 99) which may be echoes of this line, and also *Gueisson a'm buyint, | oet guell ban uitint* (*Pa gur*, l. 62–63). Williams (*CLlH*, p. 52) adds *oedd* as a copula to the second half of the line, but this is not necessary. *Bythin* could be an error for the 3 plural consuetudinal past form of *bot* (*GMW*, p. 137), '[it was] better when they used to be [alive]', but the fact that its medial consonant is -th- suggests that it might be a variant of the 3 plural imperf.subj. (*GMW*, p. 138), '[it was] better at such a time as they might be [alive]'. 3 plural verbal forms in rhyme position with *-n* rather than *-nt* are found in many genres of Welsh poetry throughout the medieval period. (For examples, see *PBT* 4.1n, and for discussion, see *DMWL*, pp. 58–60.) The use of *-in* rather than *-yn* is a feature of earlier orthography (cf. *uitint* above from the Black Book).

  5 **Canawon artir wras** The form *artir* is a puzzle. It could be Old Welsh spelling for *arðyr* or *arthyr*, but both words are unknown. Williams suggested emending it to *Arthur* and understanding *wras* as older spelling of *uras*, the lenited form of the adj. *bras* (*GPC* bras¹). This was adopted by Gruffydd, who understands the phrase as 'the lion cubs of Great Arthur'. Rowland, however, suggests a different emendation, *artirnuras*, which gives a compound adjective containing a form of *arddwrn*, 'wrist, fist, hand', and *bras*, 'strong, sturdy' (*GPC* arddyrnfras). This form is found in a poem praising Llywelyn the Great by Llywarch Brydydd y Moch, *wyt prifwyr eryr arddyrnuras*, 'you are the strong-fisted leader (lit. eagle) of great men' (*CBT* v 18.32). Koch dismisses this emendation, arguing that 'the name or epithet of a founder figure is expected after *canawon*' (*CCCC*, p. 290). An examination of the sixteen instances of *canawon* used figuratively for sons or descendants and for young warriors in medieval Welsh poetry (*GPC* cenau) shows, however, that this is the case in only a small minority of examples. It is more common for the term to be qualified by an adjective or a genitive noun, as in the following instances: Stanzas of the Graves (Jones, 'The Black Book'), Stanza 47, *kanavon cylchuy drei*, 'whelps with broken shields'; *CBT* II 14.20, *kanawon hydwyth*, 'mighty warriors'; IV 5.25, *canaon keidryon*, 'powerful warriors'. Another consideration that mitigates against the emendation to *Arthur* is that *bras* is not used as an epithet in the Welsh genealogies or in the poetry except in a line in the Gododdin which is itself based on an emendation (see *AyG*, l. 187). It is also used in the derogatory name *Hu Vras*, 'Hugh the Fat', given to Hugh Earl of Chester in the Chronicle

of the Princes (Thomas Jones, *Brut y Tywysogyon or the Chronicle of the Princes: Red Book of Hergest Version* (Cardiff: University of Wales Press, 1955), pp. 40–41).

dinas degyn This combination of noun + adjective is also used in *Oianau Myrddin* from the Black Book of Carmarthen to describe Degannwy, 'a mighty fortress' (*Llyfr Du Caerfyrddin*, ed. by A. O. H. Jarman (Cardiff: University of Wales Press, 1982), 17.66). Here it may be employed in a similar way to describe *Caer Luytcoed* of the following line, but it is more likely that it is used to complement the opening words of this line. If these are, in fact, *canawon Arthur Wras*, then *dinas dengyn* could be a metaphor for Arthur 'the mighty fortress'. If *canawon artirnuras* is read, the phrase could be in a genitival relationship to it, with *dinas* used figuratively to allude to their leader, 'the strong-fisted young warriors of the mighty protector'. Note that *dinas* is a masculine noun in Middle Welsh (see *GMW*, p. 34).

6 **rhag Caer Luytcoed neu's digonsyn** The MS form *Caer Luydd coed* is a mis-modernisation of the place name *Caerlwytgoed*, the Welsh name for Lichfield. The central element, *llwyd*, 'silver, grey', spelt in the orthography of the mid-thirteenth century, would have been *luyt*, here read as *lluydd*, 'a host, a hosting'. In order to give the line nine syllables, Williams (*CLlH*, p. 52) prefixes *rhag* with *y* to make it a compound preposition (*GPC* i⁴). Gruffydd and Rowland understand the preposition *rhag*, 'before', but Koch translates it as 'for the sake of', taking Caerlwytgoed to represent the rulers of Mercia. The latter meaning is, however, not listed in *GPC* or *GMW* (p. 206). The *-s* attached to the preverbal particle *neu* is probably a proleptic infixed pronoun (*GMW*, pp. 56–57) referring to the object of the verb, found in the following line: 'before Lichfield they had caused it'. For discussions of the conflict at Lichfield, see Sims-Williams, 'Powys and Early Welsh Poetry', n. 42.

7 **Crau y dan frain a chrai gychwyn** The scene of carnage caused by the young warriors is conveyed in a concise and allusive manner. For the idea of bloody corpses 'under' scavenging ravens, cf. *Canu Aneirin*, ed. by Ifor Williams (Cardiff: University of Wales Press, 1938), ll. 18–19, *Ku kyueillt Ewein,* | *Kwl y uot a dan vrein*, 'A beloved friend was Owain, | It is wrong that he is beneath ravens' (but see *AyG*, l. 29, where *vrein* is emended to *vein*, 'stones'). The collocation of *crau* and *crai* may suggest that play on the meanings of the latter is intended; see *GPC* and cf. *CBT* IV 4.189, *Brwysc lafneu yg kreu, yg krei — calanet*, 'vigorous blades in blood, in the raw flesh of corpses'. With the verb noun *cychwyn*, 'to start, to arise [to battle]', however, it probably has its more usual meaning as an adjective, 'rough, severe'. Williams (*CLlH*, p. 52) adds *oedd* as a copula to the beginning of the line in order to give it a regular nine syllables.

8 **briwynt calch** *Calch*, 'limewashed shield', could be the subject or the object of *briwaw*: 'shields used to shatter' or 'they used to shatter shields',

although the latter is more likely. (On the lenition (not shown in the text) of both subject and object in this position, see *GMW*, pp. 18–19.) For other examples of *briwaw* with *calch*, see *LPBT* 24.35n and the compound *briwgalch* used by the court poets (*CBT* VI 4.25, VII 37.2).

ar gwyn feibion Cyndrwynyn This has been interpreted in different ways by scholars. Koch, keeping close to the MS reading, has suggested the preposition *ar* followed by *gwyn(n)*, 'white, fair, blessed' (with lenition not shown), translating 'Lime-washed shields used to break in front of the fair sons of Cyndrwynyn'. Another possibility, which avoids the necessity of giving *ar* a very unusual meaning, is to read *arwyn(n)*, 'fair, fine, splendid' (*GPC*). This could qualify both *calch* or *meibion Cyndrwynyn*, but the fact that there is no other example of it used to describe a person, combined with its situation in the metrical line, might suggest that the former is most likely. It is unusual, however, for a word in the middle of a line of *Cyhydedd Naw Ban* to rhyme with the final syllable. Gruffydd has interpreted *gwyn* as a lenited form of *cwyn*, stretching its usual meaning of 'complaint, grievance' (*GPC* cwyn¹) to 'dispute, conflict'. Rowland suggests emending *ar gwyn* to *angwyr*, 'warriors', translating 'they broke the shields of warriors, the sons of Cyndrwynin', but this is a form only otherwise found in *Canu Llywarch* (*EWSP*, p. 517).

Cyndrwynyn This is a combination of the name of Cynddylan's father and the ending *-yn*, *-in*, a variant of the *-ing* which is added to personal names to give the name of a family (*GPC* -ing). With *meibion Cyndrwynyn*, 'the sons or warriors of the family of Cyndrwyn', compare the references in *Canu Heledd* to *plant Kyndrwynyn*, 'the children of the family of Cyndrwyn' and *etiued Kyndrwynyn*, 'the heir of the family of Cyndrwyn' (both emended by Williams for metrical reasons; see *EWSP*, p. 587).

9 Ef cuynif ini wuyf The MS reading, *ef cynnif mi wyf*, found in each stanza, is restored by Ifor Williams to give a similar meaning to a couplet in the Book of Aneirin, *ys meu e gwynaw | ene vwyf y dyd taw*, 'It is mine to mourn him | until I am in my silent day' (*AyG*, ll. 1091–92). A very similar line in the Black Book of Carmarthen gives an indication of the likely spelling of this text's exemplar: *Ew kuynhiw iny wuiw* (Trystan Fragments, l. 9, see Rachel Bromwich, 'The "Tristan" Poem in the Black Book of Carmarthen', *Studia Celtica*, 14/15 (1979–1980), 54–65 (pp. 59–60)). This was mis-modernised by a scribe, rendering *cwynif*, 'I will lament', as *cynnif*, 'to labour, to fight' (see *GPC*, and on the archaic *-if* ending see *DMWL*, pp. 44–47).

It is interesting to compare this couplet with the coda which appears at the end of some of the 'historical' Taliesin poems: *Ac yny vallwyf-y hen | y'm dygyn agheu aghen, | ny bydif yn dirwen | na molwyf-i Vryen* (*PT* II 33–36), 'Until I perish in old age, | in my dire destined death, | I will not be in my delight [i.e. cheerful] | unless I praise Urien'.

10 **clodlawn vnbyn** This epithet contains the only example in the corpus of the compound adj. *clodlawn*, 'full of praise, famous', used substantively and qualified by *vnbyn*, 'famous one of lords' (i.e. famous hero of lords).

Word-list

a¹ *interrogative particle* (*GPC* a³) 1
a² *preverbal particle* (causing lenition, *GMW*, pp. 172–73) *with infixed dative pron. 1 sing.* **a'm** 4n
a³ *conj.* 'and' 7; **a'u** *with 3 pl. infixed poss.pron.* 'their' 3
ar *see* 8n
artir *see* 5n

ban *conj.* 'when' (*GPC* pan¹) 4
brain *pl. of n.* **bran**, 'raven, crow' 7
bras *see* 5n
brodir *pl. of n.* **brawd**, 'brother, ?brother in arms' 4
briwynt *3 pl.imperf.indic. of* **briwaw**, 'to break, smash, shatter' 8n
buiad *3 sing.imperf. of* **bod**, 'to be' (*GMW*, p. 122) 4n
buyf *1 sing.pres.subj. of* **bod**, 'to be' 9
bythin *see* 4n

Caer Lwytcoed *place name* Caerlwytgoed, Lichfield 6n
calch *n.* 'lime-washed or decorated shield' 8n
calon *n.* 'heart' 2
canawon *pl. of n.* **cenau**, 'cub, whelp, fig. son, descendant, young warrior' 5n
clodlawn *adj.* 'full of praise, famous, renowned' 10n
crai *adj.* 'raw, crude, severe' 7n
crau *n.* 'blood, gore' 7
cuynif *1 sing.pres./fut.indic. of* **cwynaw**, 'to complain, lament, mourn' 9n
cychwyn *v.n.* 'to set off, arise, ?attack' 7
cymined *n.* 'combat with swords, sword-play, battle' (*GPC* cyminedd) 1
Cynddylan *personal name* 10
Cyndrwynyn *adj.* 'of the family of Cyndrwyn' 8n

degyn *adj.* 'steadfast, strong, resolute, brave' 5n
-di *affixed pron. 2 sing.* (*GPC* ti¹ b) 1
digonsyn *3 pl.pluperf. of* **digoni** (*GPC* digonaf: digoni) 'to do, make, cause' 6n
dinas *n.* 'fortress, *fig.* protection, defence' 5n
dwyn *v.n.* 'to take away' 3n

ef *preverbal particle* 9

ettewyn *n.* 'firebrand, torch' 2
eu *poss.pron. 3 pl.* 'their' 3

fal *prep.* 'like' (*GPC* fel, fal) 2
fy *poss.pron. 1 sing.* 'my' (*GMW*, p. 53, causing nasal mutation, *GMW*, p. 22) 2, 3

gellynt *3 pl.imperf.indic. of* **gallu**, 'to be able to' 3
gweli *2 sing.pres.indic. of* **gweled**, 'to see' 1
gwelyddyn *n.* 'resting place, grave, ?graveyard' (see *GPC*) 9
gwell *comparative form of adj.* **da**, 'good' 4
gwragedd *pl. of n.* **gwraig**, 'wife' 3
gwyn see 8n
gwyr *pl. of n.* **gwr**, 'men' (*GPC* gŵr) 3

hoffais *1 sing.pret. of* **hoffi**, 'to like, delight in, enjoy' 3
hyn *demonstrative pron.* 'this' 1

ini *conj.* 'until' (*GPC* yny¹) 9

lleas *n.* 'death, slaughter' 10
llysg *3 sing.pres.indic. of* **llosgi**, 'to burn' 2

maured *n.* 'greatness, splendour, nobility, excellence, ?enormity' (*GPC* mawredd) 1n
meibion *pl. of n.* **mab**, 'son, youth, descendant' 8
meuuedd *n.* 'wealth, riches' (*GPC* meufedd) 3n

neu's *a combination of the preverbal particle* **neu** (*GMW*, pp. 169–70) + *infixed obj.pron. 3 sing.* 's 6
ni *neg.* 3

o *prep.* 'because of' 10

rhag *prep.* 'before, in the presence of' 6

tir *n.* 'land, ground, soil' 9

vnbyn *pl. of n.* **vnben**, 'chief(tain), nobleman, prince, lord' (*GPC* unben) 10

yd *preverbal particle* (causing lenition, *GPC* yd¹) 2
y dan *compound prep.* 'under, below, beneath' (*GPC* i⁴) 7
yn *prep.* 'in' (causing nasal mutation, *GMW*, p. 21) 9

AN INDEX OF THE DISCUSSIONS OF THE NAMES OF CHARACTERS, PLACES AND OBJECTS ASSOCIATED WITH ARTHUR

Characters

Afarnach 42
Aladur 128
Anwas Edeinawg 38
Arthur 91, 177
Bedwyr (Bedrydant) 44, 46
Benlli 82
Brydlaw 46
Cai (Wyn, Hir) 32, 49, 202
?Casnur 138
Cath Palug 52
Cawrnur 130, 138
Cibddar 93 n.81
Cynon 10, 81–82
Cynyr 76, 202
?Cysgaint mab Banon 34
?Disethach 42
Drystan 108
Dullus ab Efrai 76
Dyfneual 76
Eiddol 91, 95
Elifri 94
Eliwlad 170
Emrais 49
Garwlwyd 44
Garwy Hir 96
Geraint 18
Glewlwyd Gafaelfawr 32
Godiar 95
Gogrfan 95
Gorlasar 138
Greidwyr 76
Greiddur 98–99
Gwair 145
Gwalchmai 10, 75

Gwalhafed 107
Gwawrddur, Gworddur 64, 68, 134
Gwenhwyfar 96
Gwgawn Gleddyfrudd 12
Gwrfan 75–76
Gwyn Goddyfrion 34
Gwythur, Gwythyr 11, 75–76, 134–35, 138
Henben 138
Llachau 15–16, 17, 50, 94
Lleog 142, 149
Lleminog 150
Llwch Llaw-wynnog 38
Mabon (am Melld, am Mydron) 34, 37
Madog (ap Uthr) 99, 170, 177
Manawyd(an) 35
March 11
Medrawd 39, 80, 190
Melwas 184, 186, 194
Odiar 95
Ogrfan 95, 96
Osfran 11
Penpalach 42
Peredur 108, 113–14
Pryderi 145
Pwyll 107, 145
?Sawyl 138
?Sefin 192, 202–203
Trwyd 76
Uthr (Pendragon) 16 n.40, 34, 96, 106

Places

Annwfn 145, 149
Badon 77
Caer Fand(d)wy 155
Caer Fenlli 109
Caer Llion 108
Caer Ochren 156
Caer Sidi 145
Camlan 11, 77–78
Celli 40, 77, 205
Cernyw 177

?Defwy 155
Dyfnaint 198
Eidyn 38, 42
Elái 33
Llanbadarn 10
Llongborth 19
Môn 52
Mynydd Eidin 42
Peryddon 10
Tryfan 11
Tryfrwyd 36, 44
Ynys Wydrin 190–191
Ystafnwn 51

Objects

Prydwen 146
Rhôn Ofyniad 114

www.ingramcontent.com/pod-product-compliance
Lightning Source LLC
Chambersburg PA
CBHW071432150426
43191CB00008B/1102